Rebuilding War-Torn States

Rebuilding War-Torn States

The Challenge of Post-Conflict Economic Reconstruction

Graciana del Castillo

Columbia University

Foreword by Edmund S. Phelps

Columbia University. Winner of the 2006 Nobel Prize in Economics

OXFORD
UNIVERSITY PRESS

OXFORD
UNIVERSITY PRESS

Great Clarendon Street, Oxford OX2 6DP

Oxford University Press is a department of the University of Oxford.
It furthers the University's objective of excellence in research, scholarship,
and education by publishing worldwide in

Oxford New York

Auckland Cape Town Dar es Salaam Hong Kong Karachi
Kuala Lumpur Madrid Melbourne Mexico City Nairobi
New Delhi Shanghai Taipei Toronto

With offices in

Argentina Austria Brazil Chile Czech Republic France Greece
Guatemala Hungary Italy Japan Poland Portugal Singapore
South Korea Switzerland Thailand Turkey Ukraine Vietnam

Oxford is a registered trade mark of Oxford University Press
in the UK and in certain other countries

Published in the United States
by Oxford University Press Inc., New York

British Library Cataloguing in Publication Data

Data available

Library of Congress Cataloging in Publication Data

Castillo, Graciana del.
   Rebuilding war-torn states : the challenge of post-conflict economic
reconstruction / Graciana del Castillo.
       p. cm.
   ISBN 978–0–19–923773–9
1. Postwar reconstruction—Case studies.   2. Peace—Economic
aspects—Case studies.   I. Title.
HV639.C37   2008
338.9–dc22   2008022388

Typeset by SPI Publisher Services, Pondicherry, India
Printed in Great Britain
on acid-free paper by
CPI Antony Rowe, Chippenham, Wiltshire

ISBN 978–0–19–923773–9

10 9 8 7 6 5 4 3 2 1

To Nico,
for his unflappable support over 40 years

☐ FOREWORD

by Edmund S. Phelps*

A wave of civil war and cross-border conflict has swept over numerous countries in the past two decades: Afghanistan, Kosovo, El Salvador, Iraq, and others in Africa and Asia. It could have been expected that, when the conflict stopped, these countries would have found their footing again and set about to make up the lost ground. In fact, economic development has still not restarted in most of these war-torn countries. Many of them have regressed to a lower stage of development than they had attained before their conflicts. This state of affairs presents dangers to the rest of the world but it must be understood before it can be addressed with any prospect of success.

That the post-conflict countries, generally speaking, have not yet returned to visible development might be seen by some as an indication that these countries are permanently resistant to development—or have become so as a result of their conflicts. We know, however, that development has proved widely possible in spite of difficulties: on every continent we find countries that had overcome enough hurdles for development to have begun. Indeed, some of the war-torn countries had shown some development prior to their conflicts. Rather than jump to the conclusion that most war-torn countries are barren of development possibilities, we might better look to see whether development has not resumed because some key preconditions for development have not been satisfied.

It could well be that governmental efforts at "reconstruction" in the war-torn countries have failed to address and even to identify some preconditions that have been missing in the aftermath of the conflicts. It is inevitable that governments will not get right all the conditions that a resumption of development would require. Reconstruction aid might be shaped by a conceptual framework for thinking about development and that framework is inadequate to the task—in all less-developed countries and particularly in the war-torn countries.

The classical theory of development has undoubtedly been influential in shaping reconstruction aid, in part because of its outstanding simplicity. In this theory, development will self-start in a country once it undertakes the task of establishing property rights and the more difficult task of establishing

* McVickar Professor of Political Economy and Director of the Center on Capitalism and Society, Columbia University. Winner of the 2006 Nobel Prize in Economics.

the rule of law, which the economy's participants can depend on. Then private interests can safely form enterprises and invest in the kinds of business for which they are best suited. By doing so, they will earn a living according to their human capital and the amount of land and other resources available to them.

Unfortunately, the classical perspective on development does not fully comprehend the richness of what development is—or could be. In the classical theory, leisure is better than work. Passive consuming is the final purpose of economic life. In any adequate view of what a rich development means, there is far more to development than that.

To set up a well-aimed reconstruction program it is necessary to have in mind a clear idea of what a rich development is and what it requires. The central elements in any such conception of development include mental stimulation, work to become engaged in, personal growth from meeting opportunities and challenges, the excitement of the new and the tingle of uncertainty. In my terminology, this means an economic dynamism—an economy of innovativeness in directions believed to be profitable. Of course, economic justice requires ample inclusion in this sort of economy. Obviously, these elements are fundamentally foreign to the classical conception of development.

Such development, it may be argued, requires what the Scottish Enlightenment called a "commercial society." Thus, real development requires a country to create market institutions and a market culture in which business firms may safely function as well as a supply of conventional infrastructure and public services. As a result, the classical perspective, to the extent it is influential, focuses reconstruction efforts on a woefully narrow subset of the preconditions needed for development to start or restart. The baleful influence of classical thinking could be a large part of the explanation why economic assistance has not been directed toward the reactivation of legitimate business enterprise, with its attendant investment projects, job creation, and increases in productivity—and why little progress toward these goals has been seen.

Carrying out an effective reconstruction program to hasten the restart of such a rich development is a challenge, of course. There is no cookbook with recipes for all the institutions and cultures that serve to build an enterprising economy. In deciding on institutions and mores it will not do to look at other economies to infer what would work well or badly in a given country: copying institutions and cultures from countries at very different levels of development or different contexts is particularly risky. The idea of Rational Institutions—that a country can be depended on to choose the right institutions simply by virtue of its rationality and careful observation of other countries—is seriously mistaken. As the Enlightenment's David Hume would have said, choosing the right institutions requires "imagination."

Besides its shortcomings, the classical doctrine is pernicious. It proscribes some kinds of programs that may be sorely needed. The idea promoted by some multilateral and bilateral donors that the war-torn countries can afford to follow laissez-faire policies—that in these countries unfettered markets work best and only the advanced countries need the paraphernalia of subsidies, licenses, regulations, corrective taxes, and so forth—is a costly ideology.

In a war-torn country where the economy has been devastated and may not bear the fruits of centuries of experimentation and diversification, there may be a need for judicious and well-designed departures from laissez-faire—just as the United States in the early years of the republic adopted some of the infant industry ideas of Alexander Hamilton. Prohibitions against any and all interventions in the market place in a country whose institutions and culture have been destabilized seems dogmatic and injudicious.

In her insightful and timely book *Rebuilding War-Torn States*, Graciana del Castillo understands that reconstruction in the war-torn countries must aim toward a commercial society. She points to the failures of most of these countries, ranging from Afghanistan to Iraq and Kosovo, to create adequate job opportunities for the population, particularly for the younger population, which constitutes a large part of the labor force in these countries. Inclusion, integration, jobs, and the dynamism that helps to realize these qualities: these ought to be the quest of the war-torn countries, del Castillo implies, just as they ought to be the quest of the economically advanced countries.

A vicious circle has followed in the war-torn countries. Lack of productive alternatives has driven farmers in post-conflict countries to grow illicit crops and has led others in these countries to engage in all kinds of illegal activities. The resulting lack of adequate jobs has contributed to public insecurity; it has also been a major factor in the tendency of these countries to revert to war. These results have in turn weakened the already slender incentives to restart normal business activities in farms and towns.

The author understands also that the nature of economic aid from the advanced economies of the West has much to do with the plight of the war-torn nations. She notes that there is no lack of Western aid and assistance going to these countries. There has been humanitarian aid, which serves to support life and provide minimum levels of consumption. But it does nothing to promote the survivors' development. There has also been much "reconstruction aid" channeled with the aim of creating conditions for subsequent redevelopment. But there are evidently deficiencies of understanding—and misunderstandings—of what reconstruction must do in these war-torn countries. Reconstruction aid has not been directed toward the reactivation of legitimate business enterprise and thus creation of jobs and increases in productivity.

The author understands too that some departures from laissez-faire are acutely needed in the war-torn nations. On the evidence of these countries, del Castillo argues that effective reconstruction, besides establishing the usual preconditions for development, needs to carry out a number of activities to reintegrate into the productive activities of the business sector an array of former combatants, returnees, displaced persons, and other groups dislocated by the conflict. The economic, financial, and operational challenges of carrying out those activities are particularly difficult amid the democratization and the institution of the rule of law that must take place simultaneously and that impose a variety of constraints on reconstruction.

The book recognizes that one of the challenges of reconstruction is the difficulty of reactivating investment in the presence of uncertainty about property rights. Such uncertainty is always present in countries coming out of war where governments may lack legitimacy to solve long-standing conflicts with regard to property rights, or to establish property rights going forward, since investors will fear that these may change as a legitimate government takes over. At the same time, establishing law and order is particularly difficult in these countries where "spoilers," who benefited from illicit activities during the war, make every possible effort to restore unlawfulness.

On the basis of case studies and other relevant experiences, the author presents the basic premises, lessons, best practices, and policy guidelines which she posits are necessary to design an effective strategy for post-conflict economic reconstruction. In her view, unless jobs are created and the political and security objectives are assured, rebuilding war-torn states will not succeed and peace will be ephemeral.

New York
April 2008

☐ ACKNOWLEDGMENTS

When I started working on *Rebuilding War-Torn States*, I did not realize that I would be addressing issues on which I have worked at different times in my professional career spanning a quarter of a century. Policymaking in countries coming out of war in the post-Cold War period is not unlike policymaking in developing countries coming out of other crises, as for example, financial crises in Latin American and elsewhere, where I have done much work. From my privileged position in the Office of the Secretary-General at the UN in the early 1990s, and later at the IMF and at Standard & Poor's, I have met with Presidents, Prime and Foreign Ministers, Ministers of Finance, and Presidents or Governors of Central Banks. With the Secretary-General, I also had the opportunity to meet with his Special Representatives in many countries coming out of war. I am grateful to all of them for meetings in which their frankness and the thoroughness with which they discussed their views allowed me to better understand and think of solutions to the many problems and challenges of countries in and out of crises.

As a trained economist, I am deeply indebted to Nobel Laureates Robert A. Mundell and Edmund S. Phelps for getting me involved in international economics and macroeconomics when I was a Ph.D. student at Columbia University. I was fortunate not only to have them as teachers and advisers but also for the opportunity to work with them on several projects over the years. I am particularly grateful for the privilege of their long-standing friendship, as I am for that of Viviana Phelps.

As an aspiring political scientist, my first exposure to the political world was in Boutros-Ghali's office as the first economist in the Cabinet. I am grateful to him, as I am to his deputies, particularly Alvaro de Soto and Marrack Goulding, for all I learned from them. I am also indebted to Enrique ter Horst, who recruited me to the Director-General's office, where I was fortunate to work with him and the Director-General Antoine Blanca in interesting issues including Iraq in the aftermath of the Gulf War and the Commonwealth of Independent States after the fall of the Berlin Wall. Although I was always aware of the political constraints on economic policymaking, my years at the Secretary-General's office and previously at the office of the Director-General were an eye-opening experience on how ignoring such constraints often meant going back to war or chaos. I also learnt about the economic consequences of peace and how costly failure at post-conflict economic reconstruction was—not only in terms of human lives but also in terms of huge military and peacekeeping expenses if the countries reverted to war.

My experiences at both the UN and the IMF were invaluable in writing this book and William McDonough was instrumental in my move from one to the other. I am grateful to him for an old friendship (dating back to the period before he became President of the New York Fed), for most interesting discussions, and for his support over the years.

There is nothing in my professional work of the last decades that I have not discussed with two of the most talented people I know: Mario Blejer and Alvaro de Soto. As a former President of the Central Bank of Argentina and Director of the Centre for Central Banking Studies of the Bank of England, and with broad experience at the IMF and in academia, Mario's views on economic matters are always important to me. As a main political adviser to three secretary-generals at the UN, more recently with rank of Under-Secretary-General, Alvaro was the one who introduced me to work in post-conflict countries, for which I am eternally grateful. I have cherished co-authoring important work with both of them and being Mario's partner at Macroeconomic Advisory Group. Alvaro and Mario have been, and continue to be, not only an inspiration but a source of unreserved friendship.

Other colleagues, students, and friends with whom I have had fruitful discussions over the years have influenced my views in *Rebuilding War-Torn States* in many and different ways and I have learned enormously from their work and writings. These include (alphabetically) Margaret Joan Anstee, Blanca Antonini, Katherine Baer, Ana Mercedes Botero, Camilla Bustani, Lisa Buttenheim, Lakhdar Brahimi, Luis Carranza, Warren Coats, Enzo Croce, Mercedes da Costa, Juan Carlos Di Tata, Jolly Dixon, Michael Doyle, Sebastian Edwards, Charles Frank, José Gil Díaj, Javier Guzmán, Peter Hansen, Barry Herman, Richard Jolly, Eliot Kalter, Angela Kane, Mohsin Khan, Bernard Kouchner, Nina Lahoud, Alfonso López, Alejandro López-Mejía, Claudio Loser, Pedro Malan, Roger Manring, Marcilio Marques Moreira, Bernard Miyet, Diana Negroponte, José-Antonio Ocampo, Cristián Ossa, Augusto Ramírez-Ocampo, Carmen Reinhart, Gert Rosenthal, Silvia Sagari, Karl Sauvant, Andrés Solimano, Jim Sutterlin, Steven Symansky, Vito Tanzi, Cecilia Todesca-Bocca, Luis Valdivieso, Andrés Velasco, Francesc Vendrell, Tom Weiss.

It is impossible for me to acknowledge all the important influences on my work from my experience in El Salvador—which remains the most successful experience with post-conflict economic reconstruction—but I want to thank in particular, President Cristiani and his successor President Calderón, Ricardo Castaneda, Roberto Orellana, Nidia Diaz, David Escobar Galindo, Ana Maria Guadalupe, Mirna de Liévano, Salvador Samayoa, Oscar Santa-maría, Mauricio Vargas, and Rubén Zamora.

I am also indebted to the late Sidney Dell and Goran Ohlin, who influenced my earlier work at the UN, and to Sergio Vieira de Mello and Nadia Younes who taught me so much about Kosovo and who tragically died in the attack on the UN in Baghdad in 2003.

A number of conferences I have attended in the last two years have allowed me to discuss different parts of the volume with different audiences and I am grateful to them for their views and feedback. It has also allowed me to discuss recent work that they have produced and that is relevant to my own. Although a complete list of acknowledgements would be too long, I want to mention my good fortune in being able to discuss the findings of the *Independent Inquiry Committee* on the UN's oil-for-food program with Paul Volcker and the currency exchange in Afghanistan and Iraq described in *Global Financial Warriors* with John Taylor in Siena. I also enjoyed the opportunity to discuss post-conflict economic reconstruction with Tony Addison in Bellagio and with a number of experts and policymakers from countries in the transition to peace in the U.S., Canada, and Europe to learn from their inside perspectives. I also want to mention my gratitude to Roman Frydman and Andrzej Rapaczynski, the Directors of Project Syndicate, through which my work on post-conflict economic reconstruction (one with Edmund Phelps) was published in over fifty top newspapers across the world.

I used an earlier draft of the book to teach a course at Columbia University, School of International and Public Affairs (SIPA) in the Fall of 2007. I am grateful to my students for questioning every aspect of my arguments and for interesting suggestions based on their own experiences.

I am always grateful to Jacob Frenkel, a former chief economist of the IMF and President of the Central Bank of Israel and now Vice-Chairman of AIG, and Onno Wijnholds, formerly at the Board of the IMF and now the Representative of the European Bank in Washington, for frequent discussions on economic and financial issues and for their encouragement and support throughout the writing process. I have also greatly benefited from detailed comments by Barnett Rubin, Antonio Donini, Gerard Fischer, Susan Woodward, Frank Randall, Felipe Paolillo, and Kristen Boon. My profuse thanks go to Professor Laura Randall, who introduced me to economics and who generously went through an earlier version of the book, making not only substantive comments but editorial suggestions which have greatly improved the final product.

Anyone reading this book will realize that I have an intellectual debt to Nobel Laureate Joseph Stiglitz, whom I met at the UN when he co-chaired a group of experts that Boutros-Ghali had appointed. Much of Joe's work, although not specifically addressing the context of post-conflict situations, is extremely relevant to them. This is because, in addition to political constraints, information is asymmetric in countries coming out of war and there are all kinds of other distortions inhibiting the proper use of markets which require government intervention.

I am forever grateful to Anya Schiffrin, a journalist at SIPA and my former economics student there, for her advice and for putting me in contact with Sarah Caro, the Publisher for Economics and Finance at Oxford University

Press. Sarah was a strong supporter from the very beginning. She has not only steered the project unflinchingly through inside and outside reviewers, but has made very useful comments and suggestions on substance and organization of the book. I am also grateful to the reviewers who made constructive criticisms and suggestions that have improved the volume and to Jack Sinden, the Copy Editor, for his indefatigable search for elegance, consistency, and coherence in the text. At OUP, I am also indebted to Jennifer Wilkinson, Assistant Commissioning Editor, to Production Editors Carol Bestley and Jenni Crosskey for their effective role in seeing the volume through production, and to Andrea Nagel, Assistant Marketing Manager, for marketing and publicizing it.

I was fortunate to have over the long gestation of this book the editorial support of Jonathan Stein. Also, this book would not have seen the light of day without the research, data, technical support, and advice provided by Bruce Culmer, Rosie San Inocencio, and Melani Redondo.

Last but not least, long-term involvement in writing a book deprives the family of precious time together, and I am grateful for their understanding, and that of my close friends whom I have neglected for quite some time. My children, Gaspar and Matias, have been involved in this project in different ways. Gaspar, a Junior at Rochester University, worked hard on the Bibliography and Matias, who is joining Columbia College in the Fall, has consistently provided articulate and assertive comments on world events, which often forces me to look at things from a different angle.

☐ CONTENTS

☐ ABBREVIATIONS

AAK	Alliance for the Future of Kosovo (ex-KLA)
ADB	Asian Development Bank
ANDS	Afghanistan National Development Strategy
ARENA	Alianza Republicana Nacionalista (El Salvador)
ARTF	Afghan Reconstruction Trust Fund
BCPR	UNDP Bureau for Crisis Prevention and Recovery
BPK	Banking and Payments Authority of Kosovo
CACM	Central American Common Market
CAS	country assistance strategy
CEEC	Committee of European Economic Cooperation
CEPAL	Economic Commission for Latin America and the Caribbean (Spanish acronym)
CFA	Central Fiscal Authority of Kosovo
CIA	US Central Intelligence Agency
CIDA	Canadian International Development Agency
CMEA	Council of Mutual Economic Assistance
COPAZ	National Commission for the Consolidation of Peace (Spanish acronym)
CPA	Coalition Provisional Authority (Iraq)
CPO	Cash Payment Office of Kosovo
CPRU	World Bank Conflict Prevention and Reconstruction Unit
CIS	Commonwealth of Independent States
CSIS	Center for Strategic and International Studies
DDR	disarming, demobilization, and reintegration
DESA	UN Department for Economic and Social Affairs
DESIPA	UN Department of Economic and Social Information and Policy Analysis
DFID	UK's Department for International Development
DHA	UN Department of Humanitarian Affairs
DM	Deutsche Mark
DNO	DNO Norwegian oil company
DPA	UN Department for Political Affairs
DPI	UN Department of Public Information
DPKO	UN Department of Peacekeeping Operations

DRC	Democratic Republic of Congo
DSRSG	Deputy Special Representative of the (UN) Secretary-General
EBRD	European Bank for Reconstruction and Development
ECLAC	Economic Commission for Latin America and the Caribbean
ECOSOC	UN Economic and Social Council
ECPS	UN Executive Committee on Peace and Security
EFF	IMF Extended Fund Facility
EIB	European Investment Bank
EITI	UK's Extractive Industries Transparency Initiative
EPCA	IMF Emergency Post-Conflict Assistance
ERP	European Recovery Program
ERSG	Executive Representative of the (UN) Secretary-General
ESAF	IMF Enhanced Structural Adjustment Facility
ESCAP	UN Economic Commission for Asia and the Pacific
ESPIG	Economic Strategy and Project Identification Group (Kosovo)
EU	European Union
FAO	Food and Agriculture Organization
FDI	foreign direct investment
FIS	Social Investment Fund (Spanish acronym)
FMLN	Frente Farabundo Martí para la Liberación Nacional (El Salvador)
FRY	Former Republic of Yugoslavia
FYROM	Former Yugoslav Republic of Macedonia
G-7	Group of Seven (Canada, France, Germany, Italy, Japan, UK, US)
G-8	Group of Eight (G-7 plus Russia)
GA	UN General Assembly
GDP	gross domestic product
GNDI	gross national disposable income
GNI	gross national income
GNP	gross national product
HDI	human development index
HIPC	IMF/World Bank highly indebted poor countries
HIV/AIDS	human immunodeficiency virus/acquired immunodeficiency syndrome
HPC	Housing and Property Directorate of Kosovo
IADB	Inter-American Development Bank
I-ANDS	Interim Afghanistan National Development Strategy
ICG	International Crisis Group
ICRC	International Committee of the Red Cross

IDA	International Development Assistance
IFAD	International Fund for Agricultural Development
IFIs	international financial institutions
ILO	International Labour Organization
IMF	International Monetary Fund
IPA	International Peace Academy (Starting 2008: International Peace Institute)
IRFFI	International Reconstruction Fund Facility for Iraq
ISAF	International Security Assistance Force
IsDB	Islamic Development Bank
ISTA	Instituto Salvadoreño de Transformación Agraria (Land Institute)
JIAS	Joint Interim Administrative Structure (Kosovo)
KEK	Kosovo Electricity Company
KFOR	(NATO-Led) Kosovo Force
KLA	Kosovo Liberation Army
KPC	Kosovo Protection Corps
KPS	Kosovo Police Service
KTA	Kosovo Trust Agency
LDK	Democratic League of Kosovo
LICUS	World Bank low-income countries under stress
MDG	UN Millennium Development Goals
MEF	Ministry of Economy and Finance
MINUGUA	UN Verification Mission in Guatemala
MINUSAL	UN Mission in El Salvador
MSE	mini- and small enterprises
MTI	Ministry of Trade and Industry (Kosovo)
NATO	North Atlantic Treaty Organization
NDF	National Development Framework (Afghanistan)
NDS	National Development Strategy (Afghanistan)
NFPS	non-financial public sector
NGO	non-governmental organization
NRC	National Reconstruction Coordinator
NRCO	National Reconstruction Coordinator Office
NRP	National Reconstruction Plan
OAS	Organization of American States
OCHA	UN Office for the Coordination of Humanitarian Affairs
ODA	official development assistance

OECD	Organization for Economic Cooperation and Development
OED	World Bank Operations Evaluation Department
ONUSAL	UN Observer Mission in El Salvador
OSCE	Organization for Security and Cooperation in Europe
OSRSG	Office of the Special Representative of the (UN) Secretary-General
PCF	World Bank Post-Conflict Fund
PCNA	post-conflict needs assessment
PCRC	Post-Conflict Reconstruction Coordinators
PCRU	Post-Conflict Reconstruction Unit
PER	post-conflict economic reconstruction
PDK	Democratic Party of Kosovo (ex-KLA)
PISG	Provisional Institutions of Self Government in Kosovo
PNC	National Civil Police (Spanish acronym)
POEs	publicly owned enterprises (Kosovo)
PPP	public–private partnership
PRGF	Poverty Reduction and Growth Facility
PRSP	World Bank/IMF Poverty Reduction Strategy Paper
PRSTF	World Bank Poverty Reduction Strategies Trust Fund
PRT	Provincial Reconstruction Team
PSBR	public sector borrowing requirements
PSO	UN Peacebuilding Support Office
PTK	Post and Telecommunications Company of Kosovo
RIINVEST	Institute for Development Research (Kosovo)
SAF	Securing Afghanistan Future
SAL	World Bank structural adjustment loans
SBA	IMF stand-by arrangement
SCR	UN Security Council Resolution
SFRY	Socialist Federal Republic of Yugoslavia
SIDA	Swedish International Development Cooperation Agency
SMG	UN Senior Management Group
SOEs	socially owned enterprises
SRSG	Special Representative of the (UN) Secretary General
TSS	World Bank Transitional Support Strategy
UNAMA	UN Assistance Mission in Afghanistan
UNAMI	UN Assistance Mission for Iraq
UNAMSIL	UN Mission in Sierra Leone
UNCTAD	United Nations Conference on Trade and Development

UNDG	United Nations Development Group
UNDP	United Nations Development Programme
UNFPA	United Nations Population Fund
UNHCR	United Nations High Commissioner for Refugees
UNICEF	United Nations Children's Fund
UNIOSIL	UN Integrated Office in Sierra Leone
UNITA	National Union for the Total Independence of Angola
UNMIK	UN Interim Administration Mission in Kosovo
UNSC	United Nations Security Council
UNODC	United Nations Office on Drugs and Crime
UNOPS	United Nations Office for Project Services
UNTAC	UN Transitional Authority in Cambodia
UNTAET	UN Transitional Administration in East Timor
URNG	Unidad Revolucionaria Nacional Guatemalteca
USAID	US Agency for International Development
VAT	Value Added Tax
WFP	United Nations World Food Program
WHO	United Nations World Health Organization
WTO	World Trade Organization

Introduction: Reconstruction off track

Iraq may not have started as a global problem, but it has become one. It reshaped relations between the United States and the rest of the world, and in some cases led to violent opposition to US policies. Just as worrisome, the war created a split among the permanent members of the United Nations Security Council as well as among other UN member states. This, in conjunction with the findings of the Independent Inquiry Committee on the UN's oil-for-food program, chaired by Paul Volcker, greatly diminished the UN's potential role in efforts aimed at peace, security, and reconstruction. The Committee reported on widespread incompetence in the UN Secretariat and a pervasive culture resistant to accountability and responsibility. This, together with evidence of sexual exploitation and abuse by peacekeepers in the Democratic Republic of Congo (DRC) and elsewhere, shattered the organization's reputation at a critical time. The UN's malaise is putting the world at greater risk, since failed states provide a fertile culture for terrorist and criminal networks.

The situation might have been quite different had an international force to remove Saddam Hussein gained the Security Council's approval, or even if, immediately after starting the occupation of Iraq, the US had been prepared to collaborate closely with the UN in order to deal effectively with the political economy of peacetime. Instead, not only was there little overall planning for the war-to-peace transition, but the policies and operational strategies that were promoted early on—while perhaps adequate for countries undergoing the normal process of economic development—were clearly ill-suited to the prevailing political and security conditions in the country. At the same time, the UN was marginalized from post-conflict reconstruction in favor of programs designed and administered by the US Agency for International Development (USAID) and the US Treasury. Furthermore, the implementation of many of these programs was given to US contractors rather than to organizations that could create employment for the Iraqi people.

The result has been an unnecessarily high cost in human lives, empowerment of radical sectarian and nationalist groups, and deep polarization of the Iraqi society and the international community. Despite the election of a national government in 2006, sectarian violence, most vividly represented by Sunni–Shiite clashes in Baghdad, plunged the country into what many analysts considered civil war, and frustrated efforts at reconstruction, despite a massive commitment of resources. The surge in military forces in 2007 made some improvement in the security situation. This will not be long lasting, however, unless serious efforts are made at political reconciliation, economic reconstruction, and the improvement in living conditions of the population at large.

Similarly, the transition to peace in Afghanistan is on the wrong track. Lack of productive alternatives has driven farmers to turn to growing poppies and to the production of heroin. The UN Office on Drugs and Crime estimates that over 90 percent of the world's total poppy production takes place in Afghanistan and that the country converts about 90 percent of the 8,000 tonnes of raw opium it produces into heroin within the country. In December 2007, four of the G-7 countries met at the highest level with President Karzai in Kabul to pledge an increase in troops and equipment. This, on its own, will not suffice to stop the resurgence of the Taliban. The strategy for the transition to peace also requires an urgent revision in Afghanistan.

Iraq and Afghanistan are hardly the only countries to face failure in their transition to peace. In fact, the UN reckons that countries in post-conflict transition have roughly a fifty percent chance of reverting to war or chaos. Since the end of the Cold War, a large and diverse group of countries in the developing world—ranging from Haiti to Timor-Leste,[1] to many countries in Africa and a few in the Balkans—have emerged from civil conflict or other form of chaos to establish a fragile peace. Others, one hopes, will begin such a transition soon. In these cases, early planning and a well-formulated and realistic strategy are crucial to ensuring that the transition is long lasting and that conflict does not resume, as has occurred in Angola, Haiti, Liberia, Timor-Leste, Lebanon, Sri Lanka, and many other countries at various points in time.

Indeed, Timor-Leste was filed away as a success story after the UN oversaw the post-conflict transition to sovereignty, only to see organized violence return in mid-2006. After painstakingly carrying out economic reconstruction for more than a decade, Lebanon sank once more into war when Israel attacked Hezbollah in the summer of 2006 following the capture of three Israeli soldiers patrolling along the Blue Line. Rather than disarming, demobilizing, and reintegrating into productive activities after Israel's withdrawal south of the Blue Line, Hezbollah avoided it by claiming that Israel remained in occupation of Lebanese territory in the form of the Sheba'a farms (which the UN considers to be Syrian). Thus, despite its transformation into a political party, Hezbollah remained fully armed and carrying out provocative actions across the Blue Line. At the same time, the political deadlock in Lebanon, with delays in electing a new president, created a situation of instability having important regional implications. It is critical that the Lebanon crisis be resolved and that the move under way toward peace between Israel and the Palestinians be well planned in an integrated and coherent manner. Otherwise, chances of peace in the Middle East will remain slim. The same applies to Africa, unless there is a new approach to reconstruction in the DRC.

The war-to-peace transition is often multi-faceted, entailing a move from violence to peace and improved security; from political exclusion to a participatory system based on democratic principles and respect for the rule of law and human rights; from ethnic, religious, class, or ideological confrontation to national reconciliation of the different groups involved in conflict; and from an economy based on illegal transactions, stagnation, large imbalances, and damaged infrastructure to the economic reconstruction of the country. In addition to the rehabilitation of basic services and infrastructure, reconstruction involves stabilization and structural reform and the creation of an adequate macro- and microeconomic framework for the reactivation of licit investment and sustainable and equitable growth. Thus, war-to-peace transitions place a heavy burden not only on the countries undergoing reconstruction, but also on the UN and its programs and agencies, the international financial institutions (IFIs),[2] other international and regional organizations, bilateral donors, and non-governmental organizations (NGOs), all of which must play a critical role in ensuring the success of these transitions.

In many ways, the challenges of post-Cold War economic reconstruction are no different from those faced by world leaders at the Versailles Conference of 1919 or the Paris Conference in 1947, when the economic reconstruction of Europe following World Wars I and II was being planned. In other respects, however, the challenges are quite different—and more overwhelming—owing to the low levels of development of many of the countries involved. Indeed, post-conflict economic reconstruction nowadays frequently takes place in a context of failed states and non-sovereign provinces or territories, defined by inadequate human resources, weak institutions, lack of technology and industrialization, and low administrative and managerial capacity to use aid effectively.[3]

Regardless of the peculiarities of particular war-to-peace transitions, policymakers must deal early on with serious macroeconomic imbalances and fiscal, monetary, and exchange-rate management issues that are critical for stabilization and for the resumption of employment-creating growth. They also must oversee the development of strong microeconomic foundations, including an appropriate legal and institutional framework, a functioning financial sector and an effective public sector to create an adequate business climate, and promote policies to alleviate poverty and support human development. This is particularly challenging in the midst of the political, social, and institutional uncertainties that are the legacy of conflict.

Because post-Cold War economic reconstruction has taken place in countries and provinces at low levels of development, it has been treated as "development as usual." But countries in post-conflict economic reconstruction confront a two-pronged challenge: alongside normal socio-economic development, they must consolidate peace and restore basic services and physical and human infrastructure. To consolidate peace it is imperative to reintegrate former combatants and other groups affected by the conflict effectively and permanently into the productive life of the respective countries. Other groups affected by conflict include returnees, internally displaced persons, and the resident population in former conflict zones.

Productive reintegration is a *sine qua non* for national reconciliation, and for the prevention of a recurrence to hostilities. Countries that fail to address post-conflict economic reconstruction effectively face an even chance of reverting to war. Moreover, because economic policymaking is constrained by political considerations and the need for reconciliation, "optimal economic policies" are often not possible or even desirable in the short run. Indeed, pursuing policies that are optimal from an economic viewpoint—particularly in terms of financing—can have tragic consequences for the political, security, and social transitions.

At the same time, putting economies on a path of stabilization and growth is imperative during post-conflict economic reconstruction. Reintegration and reconciliation will not be possible in stagnant economies. The financial implications of these parallel challenges always clash, and the way countries and the international community deal with them will determine the success or failure of the war-to-peace transitions. Although countries in post-conflict economic reconstruction must rely to a large extent on external financing (mostly on concessional terms), it is important that they have fiscal and growth policies that allow them to create employment and pay decent wages so as to create an effective civil service. Such policies are all the more important in view of donors' reluctance to finance expenditures of a recurring nature, including wages and salaries, except in the very short run.

The purpose of the book is to integrate theoretical and practical issues related to post-conflict economic reconstruction in a methodical, comprehensive, consistent, and rigorous way. It is based on personal experiences as well as a comprehensive review of the literature on post-conflict reconstruction. It is thus aimed at policymakers, academics, students, and practitioners of peace-building and state-building, as well as for others interested in the political economy of peacetime.

Like war, peace has important economic and financial consequences. Contrary to the debate generated on economic reconstruction following the two world wars, such debate has been absent in relation to the transitions to peace following the Cold War. In fact, economic reconstruction during this period has followed a "development as usual" approach without much previous debate. Given the disturbing record with economic reconstruction and the large number of countries in, or with possibilities of starting, the transition to peace, it is never too late to change course and put reconstruction on track.

Thus, the purpose of this book is also to stimulate a policy debate about post-conflict economic reconstruction within the UN, the IFIs, other development and regional organizations, bilateral development agencies, other donors, NGOs, and the academic community. The debate should involve the national authorities of countries in the process of economic reconstruction. Their participation is critical if policies and aid flows are to contribute to effective reconstruction and peace consolidation in the future, rather than be a factor in creating aid dependencies and in failing to consolidate peace.

Part I

War-to-Peace Transitions

"It is not enough to end the war; we must build the peace.
It is not enough to reject the dark past; we must build
a bright future."

President Clinton at Sarajevo, Bosnia and Herzegovina,
July 30, 1999

Part I

War-to-Peace Transitions

1 Features of recent transitions

Common and distinct features

Although war-to-peace transitions share some common features, each is distinct, owing to the specific interplay of the many factors that influence them.[1] These factors include the circumstances in which conflict or chaos began—for example, internal strife, regional conflict, ethnic rivalries, or control of natural resources—and whether they reached peace through negotiation versus military intervention. Another factor that will clearly affect these transitions is the extent of international financial and technical assistance, as well as international troops and police, that the country can expect to obtain; this in turn may depend on the country's strategic or regional importance vis-à-vis donors and troop-contributors.

The wars addressed here were in general characterized by internal conflict, although some involved several countries in the region, as was the case in the Democratic Republic of Congo (DRC), Bosnia and Herzegovina, and Croatia. In other cases, conflict was the legacy of Cold-War confrontation, with examples including wars in Central America (El Salvador, Guatemala, and Nicaragua) and Africa (Namibia, Mozambique, Angola, and Somalia). Moreover, in some cases, although Cold-War confrontations clearly fueled the conflict, a social class dimension was also evident. This was clearly true in El Salvador and Guatemala, where a large part of the population lived in poverty as a result of income disparities that were among the widest in the world. In still other cases, ethnic rivalries, as in the Balkans (Bosnia and Herzegovina, Croatia, Kosovo), Rwanda, and Burundi, or sectarian and religious rivalries, as in Lebanon and Iraq, underpinned conflict.

Countries where control of natural resources has been the root cause of war—and a serious impediment to peace—include Angola, the DRC, and Sierra Leone where diamonds were the main source of conflict, and Sudan, where oil was the disputed commodity. The plunder of natural resources has also increased regional conflict in the area of the Great Lakes in Africa. Although efforts to gain political power may lead "spoilers" to reject transitions to peace—often through violent means—access to natural resources is a main target for such actors. Peace agreements that do not contemplate fair use of natural resources will make the transition particularly difficult, as the collapse of the Bicesse Peace Agreement in Angola in 1993 attests.

Some countries enter the transition to peace more than once, owing to a relapse into conflict following the failure of past agreements. Relapses have been serious and often more bloody than previous conflicts. The genocide in Rwanda that followed the collapse of the Arusha Peace Agreement in 1994 (with close to 1 million people dead) and the collapse of the agreements in Angola in 1993 and 2001 (with about 350,000 dead) made national reconciliation even more difficult. On the other hand, such countries may benefit in their renewed transitions to peace from recent experience of what is at stake if the process fails. This may be the case in Iraq, where the violence that broke out in 2006 is diminishing, providing a new opportunity for economic reconstruction. Moreover, whereas in some cases, ceasefires extend to the whole country, elsewhere conflict may persist in isolated and unreachable areas—as in Afghanistan and the DRC—for example, while the rest of the country is actively involved in economic reconstruction.

Even the more recent war-to-peace transitions are also quite distinct because of different levels of development, which imply differences in human capital and absorptive capacities. In this respect, the situation of Kosovo was quite distinct from that of Afghanistan and Timor-Leste, two of the poorest and most undeveloped countries at the time of the transition. Looking forward, one would expect that reconstruction of the Palestinian territories (the West Bank and the Gaza Strip) would also be quite distinct from that of, say, Colombia, given their relative levels of development.

The relative development of countries undergoing peace transitions highlights the importance of initial conditions more generally. The transition in a country devastated by war and/or sanctions, such as Timor-Leste, Kosovo, or Iraq, will require major emergency programs and large investment in physical and human infrastructure. This was not the case in El Salvador and Guatemala, where conflict was less severe and more localized. Initial conditions with respect to the level of debt and other economic and social factors will also be important determinants of the transition. In some cases, debt arrears with the international financial institutions (IFIs) will have to be resolved before these institutions can provide financial assistance. Other countries may require debt forgiveness by donors if they are to have any chance to reactivate their economies in a sustained way.[2]

Political support for the transition to peace is key to a successful transition. The UN Security Council provides the strongest support. Thus, peacekeeping and peacebuilding operations, such as those in El Salvador, Mozambique, Kosovo, and Timor-Leste, were under the magnifying glass of the Council, which followed the operations and provided support in the transition from war to peace. In El Salvador, for example, the Security Council's mandate for

ONUSAL (UN Observer Mission) was not terminated until the UN could certify full implementation of the agreements. In Guatemala, on the other hand, MINUGUA (the UN Verification Mission) had a mandate from the General Assembly rather than the Security Council, which clearly diminished its leverage vis-à-vis those involved in the implementation of the peace agreements. This was partly because the military fate of the guerrilla movement was largely sealed before the peace agreement, making military issues—the ambit of the Security Council—less important. Likewise, the peace agreements contemplated wide-ranging development goals that the Security Council considered beyond its mandate.[3]

External financing and technical assistance are also crucial to peace transitions. In particular, a country's geopolitical interest to the main donor countries may make foreign assistance markedly uneven across cases. For example, the level of support of European donors to Kosovo, and Bosnia and Herzegovina, or of Japan to Cambodia was quite different from the support offered to Guatemala and Rwanda—countries that were in no large donor's "backyard." Foreign assistance to small and poor countries will also be different from that offered to large and potentially rich countries with abundant natural resources. Resource-rich countries such as Angola, Iraq, and the DRC are expected to foot more of the reconstruction bill than countries like Haiti, Guatemala, Rwanda, Mozambique, and Afghanistan.

Moreover, aid per capita is expected to be less in countries with large populations, like Afghanistan, than in countries with small populations, like Timor-Leste. The presence of a large diaspora in rich countries may also make a difference in terms of financing, as the country receiving aid may have access to large private remittances. This was certainly the case in El Salvador, where remittances were often larger than export earnings, and in Kosovo, where remittances represented roughly one-third of GDP.

The potential for "aid dependency" in the transition to peace will also be strikingly higher in poor countries, where aid may account for as much as 50 percent of GDP, as was the case in Kosovo, and even reach 95 percent of GDP, as happened in Rwanda in 2004. By contrast, during the European Recovery Program (ERP), better known as the Marshall Plan, aid amounting to $12.6 billion[4] represented only slightly more than 2 percent of the GDP of the recipient countries.[5] In terms of money spent for each European, this represented a third of what was approved for each Iraqi in the reconstruction package approved by US Congress amounting to $18.6 billion (Stiglitz and Bilmes 2008: xvi).

Finally yet importantly, not all countries have achieved peace in the same manner. The transition in general and economic reconstruction in particular, will be remarkably different when it follows peace negotiations rather than military intervention. Some countries, such as El Salvador and Guatemala, have reached peace through negotiations—often under UN sponsorship—between the warring groups. Others have relied on countries that were not involved in the conflict to bring an end to it, as occurred in Cambodia, Angola, Haiti, and Bosnia and Herzegovina. Still others achieved a tenuous peace after military intervention, led by the North Atlantic Treaty Organization (NATO), Australia, the United States, or another country, as occurred in Kosovo, East Timor, Afghanistan, Iraq, and Burundi.

In cases where member states give the UN a mandate to monitor and enforce peace agreements, the character of the transition will partly depend on whether the UN or a group of countries was behind the negotiations. Thus, the war-to-peace transition in El Salvador was quite different from that in Angola, where the US, Russia, and Portugal brokered the 1991 Bicesse agreement, and the demise of Jonas Savimbi led to the collapse of UNITA (National Union for the Total Independence), without any UN involvement, but the UN had to facilitate its implementation. Likewise, the consequences of military intervention for the transition partly depend on whether the UN authorized the intervention, as in the case of Afghanistan, or it takes place without the Security Council's consent, as in Iraq. In particular, reconstruction will play out differently in cases where a political mandate is given to the UN (and/or other international or regional organization) rather than remaining with the country (or countries) that carried out the military intervention, as the legitimacy conferred by an international mandate will determine distinct policy.

Peace transitions following UN-led peace negotiations

One of the criticisms of the Marshall Plan was that it excluded the UN, through which many in the late 1940s believed that all great international projects should be channeled (Dulles 1993: 106). The UN, however, could not have carried out the Plan at the time since Russia and its satellites would have vetoed it. The same would have happened with similar projects throughout the Cold War.

Thus, with the winding-down of Cold War-related confrontations in the late 1980s, the UN was briefly back in fashion.[6] Following UN-led peace negotiations, numerous complex operations—encompassing both military and civilian responsibilities—were established to facilitate war-to-peace transitions. In this capacity, peacebuilding missions in countries such as Namibia, Cambodia, El Salvador, Mozambique, Guatemala, and Haiti engaged a wide range of agencies within the UN system.

In many of these operations, the UN had participated in the "peacemaking" phase, as either facilitator or mediator, which was often documented in complex peace agreements.[7] It also participated in the "peacekeeping" phase, which involved overseeing ceasefire and disarmament arrangements through the deployment of blue-helmet forces, whose role was to help keep former belligerents apart.[8]

In the early 1990s, the UN became increasingly involved in the "peacebuilding" phase, playing a critical role in preventing the recurrence of violence by ensuring that political, social, economic, and institutional reforms agreed to during the negotiations were implemented. This entailed myriad functions, including disarmament and demobilization of former combatants, controlling small arms, establishing and training civilian police forces, monitoring and promoting human rights, overseeing judicial and other institutional reforms, electoral assistance and monitoring, and socio-economic activities such as emergency humanitarian assistance, landmine removal, rehabilitation, and reconstruction.

The UN's activities related to peace and security had rapidly become multidisciplinary in character and quite burdensome for an organization unprepared for such demands on its resources. Soon after he took office, at the Security Council's request, UN Secretary-General Boutros Boutros-Ghali presented to the membership *An Agenda for Peace* (1992), a set of recommendations on how to strengthen the ability of the UN to cope with the unfolding post-Cold War challenges, in which he argued that the political and economic realities of the time required "an integrated approach to human security." Boutros-Ghali's approach called for humanitarian, political, military, and socio-economic problems to be addressed jointly by the various UN institutions, in order to avoid potential clashes of competence and waste of resources. In his view, while an integrated approach to human security was important as a rule, it was imperative in peace transitions as a means to avoid the recurrence of major crises or violence.

In a 1994 *Foreign Policy* article entitled "Obstacles to Peacebuilding," Alvaro de Soto and I posited that, as a general rule, it was the role of sovereign governments to harmonize policies and set priorities.[9] We argued that "an arbitrary model of nation building" should not be imposed on reluctant, sometimes faraway countries. Thus, we envisaged war-to-peace transitions in which the sovereign government would be in the front seat designing and implementing policies, with the UN system and the IFIs in the back seat, facilitating, coordinating, and monitoring the international community's technical and financial support. This was the pattern of the 1990s in countries as diverse as Namibia, Cambodia, El Salvador, Mozambique, and Guatemala. But operationally, transitions to peace were soon to change in a radical and unpredictable way.

Peace transitions following military intervention

The nature of conflict immediately following the fall of the Berlin Wall took a turn for the worse, which changed the operational nature of peace transitions. By the mid-1990s, conflicts were often interrupted through military intervention rather than negotiation. After the human tragedies in Rwanda and Srebrenica, Boutros-Ghali's *Supplement to An Agenda for Peace* (1995) noted that a new breed of intra-state conflicts presented the UN with operational challenges not encountered since the Congo operation in the early 1960s. A key feature of these conflicts was the collapse of state institutions, especially the police and judiciary; as a result, international intervention had to extend beyond military and humanitarian tasks to include the promotion of national reconciliation and the reestablishment of effective government. This was the case in Rwanda and Burundi, where France led military interventions in the mid-1990s, and by the turn of the century in Kosovo and East Timor, where NATO and Australia, respectively, led interventions.

Transitions to peace confronted another twist after the terrorist attacks of September 11, 2001 (hereafter referred to as 9/11), which gave rise to the US government's "war on terror" and to US-led military interventions in Afghanistan in October 2001, and Iraq in March 2003. At the time of our *Foreign Policy* article, de Soto and I did not envisage the more recent types of operation, in which the UN assumed "corner positions" in peace transitions— that is, either a very intrusive role (transitional UN administrations in Kosovo and Timor-Leste)[10] or a marginal one (transitional US administration in Iraq).[11]

In the first case, Kosovo and East Timor were not independent countries when they embarked on the transition to peace with the Security Council having put the UN transitionally in charge. In fact, in both cases, the Security Council mandated the Special Representative of the Secretary-General (SRSG) to exercise all executive and legislative power through the issuance of regulations. As a result, the UN, supported by other bilateral and multilateral organizations, performed, for the first time, macroeconomic management, civil administration, and economic reconstruction functions that had been previously the sole prerogative of sovereign governments.

In the second case, in the aftermath of the US-led occupation of Iraq and Afghanistan, the UN was left to play a marginal role in supporting economic reconstruction. This was particularly true in Iraq, where the Security Council did not approve the military intervention and where the UN presence, which the Security Council had mandated following the intervention, was discontinued after an attack in August 2003 that killed 22 people, including Special Representative Sergio Viera de Mello. The UN also played a marginal role in Afghanistan, where it opted for a "light" operational approach. With an interim government installed in Kabul soon after the military intervention, and with the UN and the US both involved, Afghanistan has been allowed to make sovereign decisions concerning the transition—although clearly constrained by lack of resources, as I will discuss in Chapter 9. Kosovo and Iraq, on the other hand, became protectorates, although they differed from each other in terms of their legitimacy. Iraq formed a government only in mid-2006 and Kosovo is still negotiating its "final status," eight years after NATO intervened.

According to Malone (IPA 2003a), transitional administrations represent the most complex operations attempted by the United Nations. In his view, the missions in Kosovo (1999–) and East Timor (1999–2002) are commonly regarded as unique in the history of the UN. But they may also be viewed as the latest in a series of operations that have involved the UN in peacebuilding activities, in which it has attempted to develop government institutions by assuming some or all sovereign powers on a temporary basis. Chesterman (IPA 2003a) has questioned whether it is possible to establish the conditions for legitimate and sustainable governance through a period of benevolent foreign autocracy under UN (or US) auspices. In his view, this contradiction between means and ends has plagued recent efforts to govern post-conflict territories in the Balkans, East Timor, Afghanistan, and Iraq. The case studies that I have selected will illustrate the challenges of economic reconstruction for the respective countries and for the international community amid efforts to establish conditions for legitimate and sustainable governance in the transition to peace.

The multi-pronged transition to peace

The key challenge of the war-to-peace transition is to prevent the recurrence of hostilities, that is, to make the transition irreversible. This entails the complex political task of addressing the root causes of the conflict. Despite the peculiarities of each particular case, when wars end, countries confront a multi-pronged transition. All aspects of this transition are closely interrelated and reinforce each other: Violence must give way to public security. Lawlessness, political exclusion, and violations of human rights must give way to the rule of law, inclusive and participatory government, and respect for basic human rights. Polarization among different groups must give way to national reconciliation. In addition, ruined, mismanaged, and illicit war economies must transform into functioning market economies that enable ordinary people to work and earn a decent living.

Failure in any one of these areas will put the others at risk. Planning, management, coordination, and financing of this multi-pronged transition are highly burdensome. Given the state of countries coming out of protracted conflicts, the international community will need to provide financial aid, technical assistance, and capacity building at every stage of the transition. Issues related to the mandates, legitimacy, and competencies of the different organizations involved in providing assistance have been critical to the peace transitions in general, and to economic reconstruction in particular. Inadequate mandates, insufficient expertise, poor governance and lack of legitimacy have been present to different degrees in all recent experiences with post-conflict reconstruction.

THE SECURITY TRANSITION[12]

The transition from war and violence to public security is a necessary condition for embarking in the transition to peace. As the High-Level Panel (UN 2004a: 70) notes,

Unlike inter-states war, making peace in civil war requires overcoming daunting security dilemmas. Spoilers, factions who see a peace agreement as inimical to their interest, power, or ideology, use violence to undermine or overthrow settlements. Peacekeeping fails when resources and strategies are not commensurate to meeting the challenge they posed—as occurred repeatedly in the 1990s, for example, in Rwanda and Sierra Leone.

More recently, we have seen in Timor-Leste how security problems can derail post-conflict economic reconstruction, even where the international community is under the illusion that reconstruction is proceeding rather well.

Rubin et al. (2003: 1) recommend putting security first, since all recovery will prove futile in a chronically insecure environment. In their view, resources will be squandered at best; at worst, they will be hijacked by violent power-seekers. Addison and McGillivray (2004: 363) posit that efforts of donors and national actors (governments, the private sector, and communities) will not succeed in the absence of security since insecurity lowers the return on donors' projects and distorts domestic actors' incentives.

As Feil (2004: 40) notes, security is the foundation on which progress in other areas rests. Often, it is the UN or occupying forces that must provide basic support to enforce ceasefires, disarmament, and demobilization of former combatants, as well as other confidence-building measures that are necessary to improve security in the short run. But, as Feil also points out, for it to be lasting, indigenous actors must ultimately bear the responsibility for providing security.

To establish minimum public security will require tough legislation, an active and well-trained civil police force, and an effective judiciary. Without these, addressing the twin problems of impunity and human rights violations will not be possible, and it will be difficult for the international community to remain actively and effectively involved in the transition to peace. This does not mean that security conditions will be optimal at all times. In fact, many peace transitions have taken place, or are currently taking place, under security conditions that are far from ideal, often with large parts of the territory outside the control of the authorities, as is true of the ongoing transitions in Afghanistan and the DRC. Nevertheless, efforts to improve security should always be at the top of the post-conflict policy strategy, both for the countries involved, and to ensure the viability of the international community's support.

In addition to causing human suffering, a lack of adequate security may have serious economic consequences. Despite the presence of roughly 140,000 American troops in Iraq in 2006, supplemented by over 20,000 troops from other countries, security conditions deteriorated severely in Baghdad and other cities in mid-2006. As Glanz (2006d) graphically describes it, bank activities have been badly impaired, with bankers drawn into business practices rarely seen elsewhere. As cash goes out, it risks being lost in the wash of robbery, kidnapping, and intrigue that plagues the country. Bank insurance covers burglary and damage, but not acts of war or terrorism. With an average of one major robbery a month in 2006, money is often unavailable to depositors and banks' interest-rate spreads are high. Acts of sabotage and terrorism also have had a serious negative impact on oil production, which accounts for more than 80 percent of the country's exports.

Although security is a precondition for the success of the overall transition to peace, the political, social, and economic transitions will in turn affect the security conditions in the country.[13] In Iraq, Afghanistan, and other countries undergoing peace transitions, delays and other problems in carrying out the political transition, and, most importantly, inefficiencies and lack of progress with respect to national reconciliation and economic reconstruction, have led to unsustainable security situations. Perhaps in no case is this clearer than in Iraq, where many argue the country is in civil war. The chances of success of economic reconstruction under such conditions are indeed slim.

However, it is not true that no economic policy or economic reconstruction project can succeed in the absence of peace. Many employment-creating, service-providing, or other welfare-improving reconstruction projects have succeeded in conflict areas, and in fact have contributed to resolving the conflict. I would argue that an effort to implement projects with wide economic and social impact in the Palestinian territories and even in southern Lebanon may well be the best path to peace in the region. Welfare-improving projects between unfriendly nations have often served as confidence-building measures and have contributed to better security and improved relations.

Countries in which post-conflict policies are not effective or sustainable are often characterized by high interpersonal violence and public insecurity. This is certainly the case in El Salvador and Guatemala, even many years after the conclusion of the implementation of the respective peace agreements. It is rarely the case that security in a post-conflict situation is good. Kigali, the capital of Rwanda, seems to be an exception. After the genocide that took about a million lives, Kigali has become one of the safest, most functional cities in Africa (Whitelaw 2007).

THE POLITICAL TRANSITION

The political transition involves the passage from autocracy and political exclusion towards a more inclusive, multiparty system based on the rule of law, respect for human rights, and a free press.[14] It often also involves the transformation of a militarized society into a civilian one. Weak political systems and dictatorial governments have often been the main cause of conflict, and have at times resulted in total state collapse. Failed states and breakaway provinces present special challenges to war-to-peace transitions.[15]

Often, the social and economic transitions lag as a result of slippages in the political transition, which are frequently accompanied by worsening security conditions. This has clearly been the case in Haiti. Despite the international community's large investments in time and money to bring President Jean-Bertrand Aristide back to power in 1994, the political situation never improved enough to allow for any meaningful reconstruction and reconciliation. In February 2004, an armed uprising drove Aristide into exile once again. In May 2006, President René Preval was inaugurated, and his government faced several critical challenges, not unlike those prevailing a decade earlier, which included the need for political and judicial reform, institution building, and fighting crime, violence, and corruption.

In transitions from conflict or chaos to peace and stability, the new national authorities need to consolidate their legitimacy. In some cases, legitimacy may require power-sharing government coalitions, a scenario for which the international community often presses. In other cases, interim or transitional authorities need to be established. Whatever political solution is reached, new governments need to provide effective security, justice, human rights protection, and basic services to the population. To achieve these goals, and thus ensure a successful political transition, they must establish functioning relationships with legislative and judicial bodies, as well as with external actors such as the UN, the IFIs, and other major supporters and donors.[16]

THE SOCIAL TRANSITION

The social transition implies the passage to national reconciliation in countries divided by ideological, ethnic, religious, sectarian, political, and/or economic cleavages. Even after experiences of ethnic cleansing, such as in Rwanda for example, former adversaries must live with each other, and, to succeed, they must overcome the sharp polarization and confrontation that often fueled the conflict and are the legacy of war. Only through the establishment of an adequate institutional framework to create trust and respect for human rights, to facilitate the resolution of disputes, and to foster national reconciliation will they be able to address their grievances through peaceful means in the future. A lack of reconciliation may doom reconstruction efforts to failure, as has been the case so far in Kosovo and Iraq.

The institutional framework to ensure that future grievances can be addressed through peaceful means often includes the creation of civil society organizations, a national ombudsman, and a human rights prosecutor. In many cases, including in El Salvador and Rwanda, "truth commissions" were established to examine the most notorious human rights violations, not only as a catharsis, but also to make recommendations aimed at preventing the recurrence of such abuses. In 2002, during the celebration of the tenth anniversary of Mozambique's peace agreement, the Minister of Foreign Affairs and Cooperation noted that when the conflict ended, profound traumas suffered by the people had to be addressed. Through a successful process of confidence-building and reconciliation, disarmed and demobilized former rebels were forgiven and reintegrated into society. That process also had positive effect for de-mining, since former rebels played a vital role in identifying the devices, which in turn was essential to rebuilding basic infrastructure. This process of reconciliation, healing, reintegration, and collaboration is essential in every post-conflict transition.[17]

THE ECONOMIC TRANSITION

The economic transition—or post-conflict economic reconstruction—is a fundamental component of the transition to peace and the main focus of this book.[18] Economic recovery needs to begin as soon as possible, not only because this is essential to maintaining political and social stability, but also because donors will not be willing to support peace transitions unless countries do their part to create an environment conducive to ensuring their sustainability. This is most challenging in the midst of the political, social, and institutional vulnerabilities and the damage to human and physical infrastructure that are the legacy of conflict.

Post-conflict economic reconstruction has been a much-neglected aspect of the extensive and fast-growing literature on war-to-peace transitions. Most studies and reports by academics, practitioners, and the many organizations involved, focus primarily on issues related to "peacebuilding" or "nation-building," such as enforcing security, human rights, and the rule of law, training civilian police forces, supporting the judicial system, and preparing elections. In these studies, issues related to post-conflict economic reconstruction are addressed only tangentially or as an afterthought, and with little economic rigor, specificity, or comprehensiveness. These studies are nonetheless often highly critical of economic reforms supported by the IFIs.[19] Other studies, mostly conducted by the IFIs and other development institutions, are also inadequate, because they generally treat post-conflict economic reconstruction as "development as usual" and recommend "optimal economic policies," largely ignoring the political and security constraints that often threaten the consolidation of peace.[20]

2 Debate on the economic consequences of peacetime

Peace is not only difficult to build, but, like war, it also has important economic and financial consequences. However, contrary to the periods following the two world wars, post-Cold War reconstruction has not generated a rigorous theoretical and practical debate about the implications of such consequences, how to address them, and the trade-offs involved. Given the reversal of the peace process in Lebanon and the failing transitions to peace in Iraq, Afghanistan, and many other conflict areas, it is not too late to initiate such a debate.

The starting point should be recognition that the political economy of peacetime was historically quite different in the periods following the two world wars, which involved a number of countries in different continents, mostly in the industrialized world, with educated and rather homogeneous populations and viable political and economic institutions. By contrast, wars in the post-Cold War period have generally involved intra-state conflicts in countries or territories at low levels of development, despite their often large resource endowments, and often aggravated by ethnic divisions and weak institutions.

Post-World War I: The transfer problem

The economic consequences of peace following World War I were extensively discussed in policymaking circles as well as in the economic literature, particularly with respect to the issue of reparations to the Allies for the human and economic destruction caused by Germany.[1] After the Versailles Treaty in 1919, the Allies faced the problem of how to enforce compensation without inflicting such pain on Germany that the arrangement would become unsustainable. This gave rise to a vast economic literature on the "transfer problem," that is, the relationship between international payments, the terms of trade, and the real exchange rate. In his renowned 1919 book *The Economic Consequences of the Peace,* John Maynard Keynes argued against the excessive reparations charged to Germany. To pay reparations, he argued, Germany would have to run a current account surplus, partly through a massive real devaluation of its currency and partly through recession, both of which would severely compress imports.[2]

As Nobel Laureate Robert A. Mundell (1968a: 91) noted,

inflation is not confined to wartime. In the aftermath of the First World War the defeated Central Powers had huge reconstruction expenses, and the Treaty of Versailles had saddled them with heavy reparation debts. With a greatly reduced tax base the governments could not finance all their expenditures through taxes and resorted to the printing press. In the course of a year and a half the price level in Germany and many other countries doubled, then tripled, then quadrupled, until by 1923 prices were trillions of times what they had been before the process started.

Indeed, historians have often noted that the unpopularity of reparation policies in Germany, and the hyperinflation that followed, gave rise to the extremist nationalism that opened the way to World War II.

Post-World War II: The Marshall Plan (1948–52)[3]

The economic consequences of peace were quite different after the Paris Treaty of 1945. The issue of reparations was still at the top of the agenda, but two years after the treaty was signed the debate had fully focused on the need for a post-conflict economic reconstruction strategy financed and supported by the US, but in which countries undergoing reconstruction would have a major say. Although America had considerable experience in relief operations, a program of reconstruction and rehabilitation on the scale of the Marshall Plan was novel, not only for the US, but worldwide (Dulles 1993). Nevertheless, the Marshall Plan was to become the most successful such program of all time, not only in terms of the reconstruction of Europe, but also in setting the stage for world peace. It thus holds far-reaching lessons for the debate on economic reconstruction and the design of such strategies in the post-Cold War context.

The Marshall Plan provides conclusive evidence of the importance of building broad support for reconstruction. In 1947, the US had political, strategic, and economic interests in helping the countries of Western Europe to stabilize democratic institutions through the provision of aid and the promotion of close cooperation among the Western European nations. The region's desperate economic situation had disrupted the system of international trade, and dwindling international reserves in Europe made it difficult to pay for imports, with a significant negative impact on US exports.

Policymakers in the United States had to promote the Marshall Plan, which they considered critical for their own foreign policy and trade objectives, amid the reluctance of taxpayers to finance activities in faraway countries. The US Department of State faced major difficulties in promoting reconstruction as envisioned in the Marshall Plan. Arthur H. Vanderberg, the Chairperson of the Senate Committee on Foreign Affairs, argued at the time that the American public was not ready for such burdens. With this in mind, the government created a Committee for the Marshall Plan to sell the proposal to a reluctant public and a skeptical Congress.

It was as part of this effort that Allen W. Dulles, a former director of the US Central Intelligence Agency (CIA), a diplomat and foreign affairs expert, and a Committee member, published *The Marshall Plan* in January 1948 (Dulles 1993). In this book, Dulles provided a fascinating account of the challenges faced by the European countries as well as the United States. Dulles pointed out how the Plan—which was still merely an expression of attitude and intent—was worthless unless Congress backed it, and strongly argued that Congress would not back it unless the public understood and approved it (p. 4).

In the Introduction to Dulles's book, Michael Walla argued that the Committee for the Marshall Plan represented the most explicit attempt to shape public opinion during the beginning of the Cold War. He described how Dulles and the other Committee members accomplished their goal and induced Congress to believe that the American people overwhelmingly supported Marshall's initiative.[4] They achieved this by using lobbying, advertisements, and business skills energetically, persuasively, and intelligently (Dulles 1993: xi).

Walla (p. xxi) also argued that whereas Marshall had been rather subdued in addressing the target of the proposed aid program, Dulles was quite outspoken. At Brown University, where Marshall and Dulles had been invited to receive honorary degrees, Dulles argued that, "it is by restoring the economic life of a county, and by this alone, that we can meet the threat of dictatorship from a Fascist Right or a Communist Left." Dulles was quite emphatic that by concentrating aid "on those countries with free institutions," the "common cause of democracy and peace" would be promoted. Dulles promoted the idea that the United States had to "confront Communism, not with arms or atomic bombs, but with a restored economic life for the men and women of Western Europe."

Another issue of debate at the time the Marshall Plan was planned concerned domestic ownership of policies supported by the Plan. Perhaps the main reason why the Plan was, by any account, the most successful experience in reconstruction of all time was that those in favor of domestic ownership had the upper hand. Indeed, it was clear from the very beginning that the countries would be in charge of their own reconstruction. The invitation to twenty-two countries on July 12, 1947, to join the Paris Conference (officially known as the Committee of European Economic Cooperation, or CEEC) posited that Europe must begin by helping itself and by developing its own basic production. In addition to US assistance, which would play a decisive part, this would be the best way to insure economic recovery. The CEEC established six committees to deal with issues related to food supplies and agriculture, power, transport, raw materials, equipment, and iron and steel. This did not mean that the United Nations, or the United States as the main bilateral donor, would not take an active role. On the contrary, the invitation also stated that there would be consultation with the UN and various other technical organizations. The strategy, however, was to be clearly in the hands of the countries undergoing reconstruction.

With the Soviet withdrawal, sixteen countries participated at the CEEC in Paris. The CEEC report clearly acknowledged that these countries' recovery depended primarily upon themselves. Furthermore, aid would represent only a small percentage of their total output. Originally estimated at about $20 billion over a four-year period it would account for only 3–5 percent of their combined GDP.[5] The report was not only a request for aid, but also set forth economic reforms that the countries would implement to ensure that the aid would be used effectively. Since countries voluntarily participated in the strategy and agreed to the aid, it is hard to think of the Marshall Plan as interference in the internal affairs of the countries involved.

Another important issue debated at the time of the Marshall Plan concerned the distinction between "humanitarian" and "reconstruction" aid. In his book, Dulles argued that it would be a waste of money merely to provide humanitarian aid to feed the Europeans for a year or two. He argued that reconstruction aid was necessary to give them the tools without which they would have little chance of righting their own (post-war) economies. He stressed that policies adopted in the first year of the Plan would be decisive in determining how reconstruction proceeded.

At the time the Marshall Plan was debated in 1947, Dulles argued that the free enterprise system was the best, most efficient, and productive system in the world. Henry Hazlitt, a renowned journalist and advocate of free enterprise, made the case that aid would be of little value unless Europe "discontinues policies which unbalance its trade and discourage or prevent production. . . . Unsound fiscal and economic policies can make any outside help futile." (Dulles 1993: 101–2).

Likewise, De Long and Eichengreen (1993: 190–1) argued that the Marshall Plan significantly sped Western European growth by altering the environment in which economic policy was made.

In the immediate aftermath of World War II, politicians who recalled the disasters of the Great Depression were ill-disposed to "trust the market," and eager to embrace regulation and government control. . . . Yet in fact the Marshall Plan era saw a rapid dismantling of controls over product and factor markets in Western Europe. To some degree this came about because underlying political-economic conditions were favorable (and no one in Europe wanted a repeat of inter-war experience).

As Dulles also argued, a stable exchange rate was important to bring out hoards of dollars and other hard currencies that people had stashed away during the war. In his view, the chaotic currency situation in Europe was one of the great obstacles to recovery before the US government adopted the Marshall Plan.

In the CEEC report, most of the sixteen countries that would benefit from the Plan recognized that there was a surplus of purchasing power and too little to buy, thus creating an enormous inflationary pressure. As a result, they recognized that the success of their efforts to put Europe on its feet depended "in no small measure on the restoration of internal economic and monetary stability." In many of these countries, reserves were depleted and governments recognized that to restore confidence in their currencies, it was necessary to strengthen international reserves (Dulles 1993: 44).

Post-Cold War: Development as usual?

The economic consequences of peace nowadays are quite different from those that followed the two world wars, owing to fundamental changes in the nature of conflict since the end of the Cold War, the principal one being the proliferation of internal strife, albeit with regional or international ramifications. As a result, the issue of reparations is no longer of prime concern for economic reconstruction.

Equally importantly, the two world wars involved conflict among industrial economies with well-educated labor forces and developed socio-economic and political institutions that could easily be adapted to economic reconstruction. By contrast, many of the civil wars and other forms of internal conflicts of recent decades resulted from economic and political underdevelopment, were often triggered by ethnic, religious, or ideological factors, and involved failed states or breakaway provinces or territories.[6] Economic reconstruction thus takes place within a context of low levels of development, inadequate human capacity and institutional arrangements for project implementation, and a lack of resources that makes large levels of aid imperative, but, at the same time, difficult to administer and channel effectively and without corruption.

At the same time, the triumph of liberal democracy and market-oriented economic policies since the fall of the Berlin Wall has clearly affected the search for solutions—both theoretical and practical—in the large number of countries that have emerged from these conflicts. Thus, there has been pressure to couple the transition to peace and the move towards democratization with fundamental changes in these countries' macro- and microeconomic frameworks.

Unfortunately, however, contrary to what happened following the two world wars, no serious debate among policymakers, scholars, and practitioners has taken place since the end of the Cold War concerning post-conflict economic reconstruction. As a result, efforts to prepare these countries to become more competitive in a globalized world economy have followed a misplaced "development as usual" approach, as if economic development were not constrained by the consequences of war.[7]

The development as usual approach is unfortunate, because post-conflict economic reconstruction is a fundamentally different process. Reconstruction requires an alternative set of policies and practices that should be debated as vigorously as at the time of the Marshall Plan in order to build support, both in countries undergoing reconstruction and within the donor community. It is essential for people in post-conflict countries to perceive a peace dividend in the immediate transition to peace in terms of better services and living conditions. In addition, they need to understand the benefits that they can eventually expect from a successful reconstruction strategy, even if it carries short-term costs. Likewise, unless taxpayers in donor countries support international assistance to countries in the post-conflict transition, and can appreciate the impact that the reconstruction strategy may have in the region or internationally, their political leaders will not allocate the necessary resources. Without proper financing, technical assistance, and strengthening of national governments' capacities, the chances of effective reconstruction are indeed slim.

Nor has there been much debate on the respective roles of national governments and of the international community in post-conflict economic reconstruction. I will argue that, just as at the time of the Marshall Plan, sovereign countries in the post-Cold War context need to take the lead in reconstruction, with the UN, the IFIs, and other relevant organizations and donors playing a supporting role. Neither the UN nor an occupying force should impose the reconstruction strategy, as has frequently occurred.[8] Lack of ownership in Kosovo, Iraq, Timor-Leste, and to some extent in Afghanistan has been—and will continue to be—a major impediment to economic reconstruction in these countries. Moreover, and more worrisome, it has greatly contributed to increased violence and discontent in these countries.

Given the overall failure of recent war-to-peace transitions in so many countries, it is time to promote precisely such a debate. Policies for economic reconstruction have not worked. New and innovative options should be debated. Staying the present course is not a promising option.

Part II

Post-Conflict Economic Reconstruction

"Peace and development are intrinsically linked: one cannot be achieved if the other fails."

Jan Pronk, Former Dutch Minister for Development
Cooperation (UNHCR 1996)

3 Definitions and characteristics

Reconstruction's meaning and significance

The term reconstruction often represents different things to different people. After the two world wars, the term was used for the rebuilding of infrastructure and services. The term has also been used for political and security reconstruction, where the economic dimension is relegated to a minor role. By contrast to these narrow definitions, I use the term "post-conflict economic reconstruction" in a broad sense.[1] Thus, it includes not only rehabilitation of basic services and rebuilding of physical and human infrastructure, but also the stabilization and structural reform policies, as well as the microeconomic foundations required to create a market economy and reactivate investment and broad-based economic growth. These foundations include an appropriate business climate, adequate financing and infrastructure for the private sector, an effective bureaucracy, and an appropriate legal, regulatory, and institutional framework.

The peculiarities of countries in the midst of post-conflict economic reconstruction, particularly the weakness of political and legal institutions, the inadequacy of the labor force, and the shortage of qualified civil servants, make the formulation of economic policy difficult. Although conditions vary widely from country to country, the common requirement for the implementation of effective and sustainable reconstruction policies is the return of peace, the rule of law, and acceptance by the population of the new government and the legislative bodies that are tasked with managing the economy. Thus, economic reconstruction takes place within the context of the multi-pronged transition to peace—not independently from it—even though political conditions are often far from optimal and reconstruction often takes place only in certain regions, while other parts of the country may lack security or still be in conflict.

Consolidation of peace following violent conflict has very little chance of success unless jobs are created and the economy is quickly stabilized and brought onto a path of investment and growth with low inflation. Creating opportunities for employment in the short run is critical, as this will facilitate the long, complex, and expensive process of reintegrating former combatants, returnees, and displaced persons into society and into productive activities.

This often requires policies which are not optimal from a pure economics point of view.

While employment creation should have a short-term focus in post-conflict reconstruction, development objectives such as sustainable growth, poverty alleviation, and environmental protection are long-term objectives, particularly in countries that start from very low levels of development.[2] In addition to good policies, such objectives require time and significant resources. It would be naive to think that these objectives could be fully realized—as many analysts of war-to-peace transitions seem to expect—during post-conflict economic reconstruction. Effective reconstruction, however, should set the stage for an eventual move towards "normal development," at which point optimal economic policies and long-term objectives should clearly prevail.

One of the most serious challenges in economic reconstruction is to design and implement an economic program—usually sponsored by the IMF and supported by the other multilateral organizations—within the constraints and financial requirements of national reconciliation efforts resulting from the peace agreement. If the political agreement and economic program are not integrated, the country will most likely plunge back into conflict. In fact, the UN reckons that roughly 50 percent of countries in the war-to-peace transition revert to conflict, and it is at the early stages of peace implementation that societies are most vulnerable.[3] As a result, the *Report of the High-Level Panel on Threats, Challenges and Change* (UN 2004a: 70) concluded that the resources spent on implementation of peace agreements and peacebuilding are one of the best investments that can be made for conflict prevention.

If early planning, a good strategy for economic reconstruction, and donor support are lacking, the transition from war to peace will not succeed or be long-lasting. The challenges of this transition—as the current situation in Iraq, Afghanistan, and the DRC well illustrate—certainly do not end with military intervention, the signing of a peace accord, or national elections. On the contrary, that is just the beginning.

Characteristics and peculiarities of countries undergoing reconstruction

COMMON FEATURES WITH COUNTRIES IN NORMAL DEVELOPMENT

Countries in post-conflict economic reconstruction do indeed share a number of characteristics with countries in the normal process of development (del Castillo 2001a: 1969–70). First, post-conflict countries have, as a general rule, devastated or at least severely distorted economies. Both human capital and physical infrastructure are often in a shambles. Statist and populist policies of the past may have led to major macroeconomic imbalances that often require tough stabilization policies and structural reform.

Second, post-conflict countries are often characterized by a lack of transparency, poor governance, corrupt legal, judicial, and police systems, inadequate protection of property rights, incompetent central banks, weak tax and customs administrations, and non-credible public expenditure management. Furthermore, the rule of law frequently remains tenuous, with continued violations of human rights.

Third, post-conflict countries are highly dependent on official aid flows, mostly in the form of grants. This dependency is particularly strong immediately after the resolution of the conflict and at the early stages of what often proves to be a long and difficult transition.

Fourth, post-conflict countries often have protracted arrears on payments of foreign debt. Thus, the provision of financial aid is constrained by the need to normalize relations with creditors, particularly with the IFIs, which have restrictions on assisting countries that are in arrears. In addition, post-conflict countries usually require relief on unsustainable external-debt burdens.

Finally, several generic principles apply in equal measure to most development activities and to those that occur within the context of post-conflict reconstruction. For example, an overriding principle of development is the need to develop national capabilities in a number of areas as soon as possible, in order to reduce external dependence and create employment. Similarly, in post-conflict economic reconstruction, training, capacity and institution building, and employment-generating activities should take priority, so that former combatants, returnees, and other groups marginalized during the conflict can quickly and successfully be reintegrated into the productive life of the country.

RECONSTRUCTING COUNTRIES ARE DIFFERENT AND HAVE SPECIAL NEEDS

The similarities between post-conflict reconstruction and countries in the normal process of development, while real, should not lead to their conflation, as has unfortunately often been the case.[4] As I argued in the mid-1990s (del Castillo 1995a: 29–30), countries coming out of conflict face a double challenge:

On the one hand, they have to confront the normal challenge of socio-economic development which often comprises tough choices in terms of stabilization and structural reform. This is particularly difficult because most countries in (post conflict) are at a low level of development and have become even more impoverished by the conflict. On the other hand, they have to settle for less than optimal policies in their economic reform efforts so as to accommodate the additional financial burden of reconstruction and peace consolidation. The latter includes the reintegration of former combatants and other estranged groups into productive activities and the development of an adequate institutional framework to foster national reconciliation. The imperative of peace consolidation competes with the conventional imperative of development, putting tremendous pressure on policy decisions, especially budgetary allocations.

In May 1999, I made a presentation on "Economic Reconstruction in Post-Conflict Transitions" at a conference in Prague, organized by the Institute of International Relations with the support of the Czech Republic and NATO. After noting that I had been "arguing for a long time that these transitions are not 'development as usual,'" I mentioned, however, that this was not something everyone was willing to accept. I referred to the United Nations Development Programme (UNDP) in particular that "would like to see these transitions as special cases of normal development. But I see these transitions as different, and I think they should be treated very differently from normal development." (del Castillo 2000: 227–30).

It may not be possible to consolidate peace unless all involved acknowledge that post-conflict countries are in a unique situation relative not only to countries in the normal process of development, but also to countries recovering from natural disasters or financial chaos. In particular, the very high risk of relapse into conflict makes short-term reconstruction necessary, demanding, and promising if it succeeds.

The fact that post-conflict countries are different and have special needs has important policy implications. When Alvaro de Soto and I drafted the Introduction to *An Inventory of Post-Conflict Peacebuilding Activities* (UN 1996a), we argued that[5]

Post-conflict activities should be incorporated as soon as feasible into the development strategy of the country. However, during the immediate, fragile post-conflict phase, which is by nature transitory, such activities are quite distinct from normal development.

This was because the political objective should prevail during this phase, an issue that de Soto and I had addressed in our *Foreign Policy* article in 1994 and raised at the International Colloquium on Post-Conflict Reconstruction Strategies in Stadtschlaining, Austria, in June 1995. At the time, the UNDP and some of the other UN agencies vehemently objected, arguing for a "continuum from humanitarian relief to development"—an operational concept that UNDP later acknowledged was not useful (UNDP 2000). Because of the political nature of post-conflict peacebuilding activities, including economic reconstruction, de Soto and I emphasized the leading role that the UN—through the political department—had to play vis-à-vis the agencies of the UN system and the IFIs. Dame Margaret Anstee, the Chairperson of the Colloquium, came to share our position fully, which was reflected in her letter of July 15, 1995, to the Secretary-General to report on the Colloquium, as well as in *The Chairman's Synopsis and Conclusions* of the Colloquium (UN 1995a).[6] Only in 2003, the World Bank (2003a: 14) acknowledged that

The main objective over the short to medium term must be to consolidate peace— poverty strategies and policies cannot succeed without it. PRSPs [Poverty Reduction Strategy Papers] in conflict-affected countries therefore should look and feel very different from other countries. For example, it will be important to focus on the factors that affect the risk of conflict.

The same year, the World Bank (2003b: 6) also acknowledged that

Economic development is central to reducing the global incidence of conflict; however, this does not mean that the standard elements of development strategy—market access, policy reform, and aid—are sufficient, or even appropriate, to address the problem. At the most basic level, development has to reach countries that it has so far missed. Beyond this, development strategies should look different in countries facing a high risk of conflict, where the problems and priorities are distinctive.[7]

According to Pronk (1996), a practitioner and one of the most lucid analysts of post-conflict economic reconstruction, countries in this fragile condition require sensitive and multi-sectoral assistance in dealing with the unresolved problems of refugees, combatants, lack of reconciliation, failing civil society, weak governance, and fading economic opportunity. In his view, the inter-dependency of the solutions to all of these problems implies that peace and development are intrinsically linked: one cannot be achieved if the other fails.

Countries in post-conflict situations share some characteristics with other countries coming out of crises such as natural disasters or financial collapses. Because of such characteristics, policymaking in post-crisis situations is different from policymaking under normal development. The differences arise with respect to the horizon over which economic policies are planned, equity considerations, the nature and extent of the international community's involvement, and the amount and stability of technical and financial assistance flows.

POLICYMAKING UNDER NORMAL DEVELOPMENT

Countries in the normal process of development have a government in place that makes all executive decisions. They often also have a legislative body and a functioning judiciary, however weak they may be. Institutions may be corrupted and inefficient but they exist. These countries are not coming out of a crisis that has made short-term policies and emergency programs necessary, even when these may be inefficient and/or distortionary in the medium and long-term.

Indeed, policymaking under "normal development" is marked by five characteristics that distinguish it from policymaking in post-crisis countries:

- Development policies aimed at addressing economic stagnation, backwardness, weak institutions, poor human resources, poverty, and other pathologies of underdevelopment can be established with a medium and long-term perspective in mind.

- The "equity principle," or the "ethics of development" according to which people in need are treated equally, guides all development policies and activities, with any violation seen as an aberration.

- The flow of foreign assistance and the involvement of the international community in normal development activities are rather stable. A range of multilateral, regional, and bilateral development institutions, as well as non-governmental organizations (NGOs), are involved in providing technical assistance and financing to the country on an established and regular basis.

- Security conditions are not of special concern. Of course, this does not mean that countries undergoing normal development do not have to allocate resources and efforts towards reducing crime and other security problems. But they do not generally require external assistance to establish basic public order.

- The political involvement of the international community is practically non-existent, and would be regarded by most as illegitimate interference in the country's domestic affairs.

POLICYMAKING IN POST-CRISIS CONTEXTS

Countries that are recovering from crises such as devastating natural disasters, financial chaos, or wars differ in fundamental ways from normal developing countries, with important implications for policymaking:

- Short-term emergency programs are needed to deal with homeless populations, hunger, disease, demobilizing soldiers, and other short-term needs in post-conflict situations. Similarly, short-term emergency programs are often needed following financial chaos or natural disasters. These programs may serve a short-term humanitarian purpose but will probably distort long-term plans to create employment, construct housing, or stimulate food production.[8]

- Emergency programs following serious crises frequently attract media attention, with images of destitute and starving children, raped women, physical destruction, and other tragedies facilitating large inflows of international financial and technical assistance. Important emerging countries at the edge of financial default, like Mexico in 1995, the Asian countries in 1997, or Russia in 1998, also attract media attention and large flows of assistance because of the potential impact on international markets. But media frenzies are short-lived, and foreign assistance, which is stable during normal development, often exhibits sharp spikes.[9] In many cases, absorptive capacity is too low to use the aid bonanza productively, and the opportunities for corruption are much larger, owing to the large amount of funds, the improvised way in which they are channeled, and the lack of solid institutions and good procurement policies.

- The "equity principle" that prevails in normal development activities is often overshadowed by the "ethics of reconstruction." In the post-crisis period, the latter often justifies giving preferential treatment to those groups most affected by the crisis, even if other groups in the country have comparable needs.

- The large need for international financial and technical assistance in the immediate post-crisis period implies intensive and often intrusive political involvement by the international community in countries' internal affairs. Indeed, in some cases such aid specifically includes military and police assistance, since an improvement of the security situation is often imperative before starting reconstruction and the reactivation of economic growth.

Table 1 summarizes the reasons why policymaking under normal development is so different from policymaking in countries coming out of crisis or chaos.

Table 1. Differences between policymaking in normal development and in crisis situations

Policymaking under normal development	Policymaking in crisis situations
Medium- and long-term framework	Requires (distortionary) emergency programs
Application of the "equity principle"	Application of the "ethics of reconstruction"
Low and stable foreign assistance	Sharp spikes in foreign assistance
Government establishes rule of law	Foreign troops and police support rule of law
Political involvement of international community considered interference	Intensive and often intrusive political involvement

NATURAL DISASTERS

Although natural disasters—including floods, droughts, earthquakes, and hurricanes—hit rich and poor countries alike, such events can have far more dire economic consequences in countries at low levels of development. For example, while the series of hurricanes in the United States in 2005, which devastated New Orleans and the Gulf Coast, exacted a heavy toll on public finances, there was no serious disruption to the national economy. Moreover, whereas Hurricane Katrina, in particular, clearly showed that low-income groups in a country are typically the worst affected by natural disasters, the suffering is far more widespread in poor countries, where housing and other buildings and infrastructure are less resistant and hence are easily destroyed. Furthermore, the financial costs of reconstruction leave poor countries' economies particularly vulnerable. Indeed, natural disasters themselves are often an important determinant of underdevelopment. Short-term emergency programs generally help palliate the short-run humanitarian crises, but they may not contribute much to the longer-term development of the country.

In the face of a major natural disaster, decisions concerning aid and other assistance to the affected countries are often delayed by political considerations and inefficient local bureaucracies. This was certainly the case with the 2004 tsunami, which devastated many parts of Asia, despite an unprecedented amount of aid and goodwill. Natural disasters often hit a country in rapid succession—frequently while it is still recovering from a previous disaster. This was the case in Indonesia in 2006, where an earthquake hit Java on May 27, killing close to 6,000 people and leaving a million more homeless. As relief groups were still busy with reconstruction, a tsunami hit West Java on July 18. Similarly, two earthquakes struck in close succession in El Salvador in early 2003. Moreover, natural disasters and conflict often go hand in hand. In Aceh, for example, where the Indonesian government was trying to suppress a separatist rebellion, the 2004 tsunami exacerbated the existing conflict, and reconstruction was highly politicized.

Natural disasters in poor countries often impede ongoing economic reforms. As a result, in addition to humanitarian assistance, aid is often also necessary to ensure that such reforms are not derailed or even reversed. For example, in October 2005, after an earthquake killed more than 55,000 people, Pakistan needed assistance for survivors and reconstruction of devastated areas. The World Bank and the Asian Development Bank (ADB) assessed these costs at over $5 billion (ADB 2006). The international community pledged more than $6 billion for earthquake relief and reconstruction.[10] Although not all the funds were disbursed, such assistance helped in mitigating the earthquake's adverse impact on the economy. The quake hit Pakistan at the time it was making progress in moving towards market-oriented structural programs, conducting sound fiscal policy, and experiencing healthy economic growth. While the economic reforms had improved business confidence and enhanced competitiveness, the earthquake created major budgetary challenges, requiring, as in other post-crisis situations, concessional assistance from the donor community.

FINANCIAL CHAOS

Middle- and higher-income countries have more developed financial sectors than lower-income countries and are thus more vulnerable to financial chaos. Inconsistent policies in many countries, in conjunction with external shocks and contagion effects, have led to financial-sector collapse, large contraction in output, high rates of unemployment and social distress, and overwhelming levels of debt.[11]

In the 1990s, several middle- and higher-income countries went through this type of crisis, while Argentina and Uruguay experienced similar crises in the early 2000s. The magnitude of the assistance required to avoid default in Uruguay in 2002 was so large that decisions for external assistance were made at the highest political level.[12] Large rescue packages to other countries following financial crises such as those in Mexico in 1995, Argentina in 1995 and 2001, Korea and Russia in 1998, Brazil in 1999, and Turkey in 2002 were also largely determined by political considerations, rather than by the imperatives of normal development in those countries.

The deterioration in the social fabric is often large and long-lasting after such colossal crises, making emergency programs a necessity.[13] The challenge after such crises is to ensure that employment created by the emergency program does not become recurrent government expenditure, as earmarked international financing for the program dries up. Beneficiaries of these emergency programs—the groups most affected by the crisis—will eventually have to find employment in the private sector, which makes reactivation of the economy imperative.

However, economic recovery is particularly difficult after financial crises. While external shocks played an important role in the financial crises of the last decade, to a large extent they were the result of inconsistent domestic policies. The most common problem was that countries fixed their exchange rates without allowing for wage flexibility, when it is clear that if prices cannot adjust, wages should. Fixed exchange-rate regimes were also frequently inconsistent with fiscal deficits that had to be monetized.[14]

Since many of the countries that went through these crises were in the midst of structural reform, policymakers and others who did not understand the impact of inconsistent policies often came out against further reform.

"Neo-liberalism" and the "Washington Consensus" were often blamed for what really were blatantly inconsistent domestic policies, often with external or internal shocks as detonators.[15] Critics often failed to understand that these countries may have adopted many of the policies associated with the Washington Consensus, but not others that were critical.[16] This confusion has made further reform, necessary to reactivate growth after the crisis, particularly difficult.

Following financial crises—just as following wars or natural disasters—people do not want charity. They want jobs, and under weak fiscal conditions, it is only the private sector which can create them. But it is often quite difficult for private investment to reactivate itself after financial crises, since mistrust and resentment of government economic policies tend to be widespread. In general, people find it difficult to understand the combination of inconsistent, badly conceived, or incomplete policies, the different types of shocks, both external and internal, and the contagion factors that resulted in the crisis and that must be overcome to recover from it.

WAR AND CONFLICT

As in other post-crisis situations, post-conflict countries are the focus of media attention, and must forgive distortions, make concessions to particular groups, and deal with spikes of foreign assistance and political interference. As a result, post-conflict countries usually start with emergency programs, with strong political and financial support from the international community, and under the magnifying glass of the Security Council and the foreign press. Eventually, they have to move to policies and programs that are sustainable as international support and aid wither.

The international community is often more indulgent of post-conflict countries than it is of those coming out of financial crises. Although it is true that the latter have a high probability of relapsing into financial difficulties, the international community is less willing to run the risk of allowing countries to return to conflict. For this reason, countries undergoing post-conflict reconstruction are more likely than other countries in crises to be granted at least partial condonation of their foreign debt, or at least be permitted to negotiate better terms for their debt restructuring packages.[17]

Post-conflict reconstruction versus preventive action

Before establishing the premises under which post-conflict reconstruction should take place and elaborating the strategy needed to carry it out, it is important to emphasize the distinction between post-conflict peacebuilding and preventive diplomacy. According to Secretary-General Boutros-Ghali (1992: 33), preventive diplomacy aims at avoiding a crisis, while post-conflict peacebuilding aims at preventing its recurrence.

From an economic point of view it is true that many of the policies and much of the expertise needed for preventive diplomacy and post-conflict peacebuilding are indeed the same. Therefore, it would make sense for the same organizations and group of experts to address both jointly, with the same resources and the same set of tools. It is reasonable to assume that humanitarian disasters, failed states, and different types of conflict could often be prevented by large and rapid improvements in the welfare of the population. But, this is a long-term proposition that would require huge financial resources that are clearly not available.

For this reason, I argue that it is neither politically nor operationally wise to treat preventive action and post-conflict action together. Furthermore, diverting resources and attention from countries that face a high risk of reverting to conflict would be a mistake. In choosing between preventive action and post-conflict reconstruction, focusing on the latter represents a better investment of scarce international resources, yielding an expected higher rate of return in terms of social welfare. Obviously, the development institutions should continue to support countries that are not in conflict in their development efforts, and they should strive to improve the effectiveness with which they provide assistance.

There is another reason why resources may be used more effectively in post-conflict reconstruction than in preventive action. Before conflict breaks out, the different parties are normally unwilling to compromise, often because they expect to get their way eventually, even by force. Armed intervention by NATO, the UN, or another country can be a strong signal that warring parties cannot find a military solution and/or that the conflict is no longer acceptable to the international community. A peace negotiation—that often follows a military stalemate—may be an indication that there is no clear winner. Under either condition, the parties to the conflict are more likely to be willing to receive support of the international community after the conflict than before it. As we will see in the case studies, efforts at conflict prevention failed in El Salvador before the strong military FMLN offensive on San Salvador in December 1989, and failed in Kosovo before NATO's military intervention in 1999.[18]

Economic reconstruction policies and strategies, on the other hand, could be used effectively in some cases to strengthen peacemaking. Efforts at reconstruction of the Palestinian Territories with an immediate impact on the wellbeing of the population, as well as programs for disarming, demobilizing, and reintegrating FARC guerrillas and paramilitaries in Colombia are possible examples.

4 Basic premises for policymaking

A strategy for post-conflict economic reconstruction should rest on six basic premises. Although closely interrelated, these premises may have different implications for policymaking. Failure to follow them will endanger "peace-building" and "state-building" efforts, as it did in Angola, Sierra Leone, and Liberia in the past and as it is doing now in Afghanistan, Iraq, Kosovo, and Timor-Leste.[1] Indeed, as the case studies that I analyze demonstrate, the transition to peace in these countries would have been greatly facilitated by adherence to these premises.

Premise 1: The transition to peace is a development-plus challenge

Countries in the war-to-peace transition face a development-plus challenge. That is, in addition to the normal challenge of socio-economic development, they must accommodate the extra burden of economic rehabilitation and national reconciliation. Critical activities in this regard include the delivery of emergency aid to former conflict zones (many of which may not yet be under government control); the disarmament, demobilization, and reintegration (DDR) of former combatants; the return of refugees and internally displaced groups; the reform of the armed forces and the creation of a national civilian police. It also includes the rehabilitation and reconstruction of economic assets destroyed because of the conflict and the clearance of mines. The effective DDR of former combatants into society is a *sine qua non* for a successful transition to peace. It requires advance planning, bold and innovative solutions, large financial resources, and "staying the course" with the right policies, frequently for many years.[2]

Post-conflict reconstruction is a development-plus challenge for two additional reasons. First, the political, ideological, and/or ethnic polarization of the country during the years of war makes building consensus for reconstruction policies in the transition to peace particularly difficult compared to policymaking in countries undergoing normal development. Moreover, in the fiscal and financial area, policymaking is necessarily constrained by the need to include extra expenditure directly related to the peace process to the normal expenditure needs of developing economies. Thus, policymaking will need to be more pragmatic and ad hoc. Furthermore, fiscal and monetary targets in post-conflict countries—particularly those under IMF-sponsored programs—may have to be more flexible to ensure financing of critical programs.

Second, the actors involved in post-conflict reconstruction are more diverse than in countries undergoing normal development. Reconstruction actors include Security Council or General Assembly mandated peacekeeping operations as well as the UN programs and agencies, the international financial institutions (IFIs), the development organizations, bilateral and regional donors, and often a large number of non-governmental organizations (NGOs).[3] This inevitably creates larger distortions, demands special efforts at coordination, and requires broad-based expertise, including in the political and security areas, that is not normally available at development institutions.

In designing peace agreements, as well as in designing the strategy for post-conflict economic reconstruction, it is necessary that these extra activities be explicitly identified and their financial implications estimated to ensure sufficient funding to carry them out. Because these countries have to carry out normal socio-economic development, while at the same time settling for less than optimal policies to accommodate the financial burden of reconstruction and peace consolidation, I refer to it as a "development-plus" challenge.

Premise 2: The political objective should prevail at all times

The overarching goal after a war is stability and the avoidance of a return to conflict. It follows that, should a conflict arise between peace (political) and development (economic) objectives, the first one should be paramount at all times. Because peace is a precondition for sustainable development, all actors should recognize and accept that political priorities will often constrain economic policymaking. This often means that optimal and best-practice economic policies are not attainable—or, indeed, even desirable. It also means that peace-related programs should receive priority in budget allocations.

Thus, in designing the strategy for post-conflict economic reconstruction, or in implementing it, one should not condition the demobilization, disarmament, and reintegration of former combatants on economic or financial considerations, as has often been the case in the past. Although economists will find this principle highly controversial if not simply aberrant, it obviously does not mean that financial constraints and efficiency issues should not be taken into consideration. It simply means that, in allocating resources, priority should be given to these peacebuilding activities.

The first such clear conflict arose in the case of El Salvador. Financial constraints imposed by the IMF-sponsored stabilization program brought the demobilization of the FMLN to a standstill, paralyzing the unfolding of the balanced calendar of implementation and putting peace at risk early on in the transition to peace. Later financial efforts at completing the demobilization and reintegration paid off. Likewise, failure to demobilize was an important factor in the collapse of UN efforts at peacebuilding in Angola and was responsible for serious setbacks in Cambodia and Nicaragua. In other, less extreme cases, such as Guatemala, the ceasefire was broadly respected, but public insecurity and human rights violations continued because of the failure to disarm and reintegrate former combatants productively into society. In Kosovo, the inability fully to demobilize and disarm former combatants of the Kosovo Liberation Army (KLA), while enlisting many of them as part of an improvised civilian peace force under the same command structure, not only spread the conflict into neighboring countries, but has been a constant source of instability.[4]

Successful experiences with demobilization, disarmament, and reintegration of former combatants demonstrate the importance of dedicating enough financial and technical resources to this task to ensure the political objective of peace consolidation. Doing so is worth the cost, even if the financial implications delay the overall process of stabilizing the economy and putting it on a sustainable growth path with low inflation.

Likewise, when the economic potential of certain projects is being analyzed, the political implications should always be taken into consideration. For example, when the costs and benefits of restarting the Trepca mining complex in the ethnically divided city of Mitrovica in the north of Kosovo were being assessed, the decision could not be made on simple profit-maximizing criteria, as many argued. Political considerations had to predominate: the complex was controlled by the few remaining Serbs in Kosovo and was very much a political target of Kosovar Albanians, particularly those who had been fired from the complex a decade earlier, when Kosovo lost its autonomy from Serbia. These political factors eventually weighed in favor of reopening the complex, even if it did not make much sense on economic and environmental grounds alone, given the appalling state of the mines, the low price of their minerals at the time, and the pollution they created. The UN's indecisiveness unnecessarily delayed the process of putting the two groups working together, as part of a political strategy for national reconciliation.

Premise 3: Lack of leadership legitimacy will limit policymaking choices

If post-conflict economic reconstruction is carried out by an interim or transitional national government—or in more extreme cases by the UN or an occupying country—policymakers will probably lack the legitimacy needed to adopt key economic measures, such as privatization, market deregulation, opening critical sectors to foreign investment, and other major legal, institutional, or regulatory changes. Even the proposal of such policies by policymakers lacking legitimacy may lead to political resistance, a backlash against the sponsors, and a setback for reconstruction efforts. Witness the failure of efforts by the US Agency for International Development (USAID) in Iraq to privatize the country's oil industry and by the UN to privatize the Trepca mines in Kosovo.

Moreover, investors are clearly not attracted to assets for which property rights might change once a legitimate government takes over. Indeed, uncertainty about the stability of property rights played a significant role in the failure of early efforts at privatization in Iraq and Kosovo. Such policies aimed at increasing foreign investment also have made reconciliation more difficult. USAID's decision to present a bidding contract for international consulting firms to advise and carry out economic governance projects, including the privatization of Iraq's oil assets as well as of other state-owned property, was one of the factors directly related to increased violence in the country. Although USAID eventually abandoned its effort to privatize the oil industry, it continued to push for privatization of other assets, despite the uncertainty regarding property rights and its own lack of legitimacy.

Policies of interim national governments or other transitory authorities such as the Coalition Provisional Authority (CPA) in Iraq or the UN in Kosovo and East Timor may not be sustainable. Freely elected governments are likely to question many such policies, and even change them, as the experience of Iraq well attests.

Premise 4: A different yardstick is necessary to measure success

Given the primacy of the political objective in post-conflict economic reconstruction, a different yardstick should be used to measure success than is the case under conditions of normal development. The overall success of policymaking should not be measured in terms of poverty alleviation, economic growth, and low inflation. It should be measured according to whether, and to what extent, it contributes to national reconciliation and the consolidation of peace, thereby allowing the country eventually to enter the normal development path. In this sense, El Salvador is a success story, whereas Kosovo, Iraq, and Afghanistan may never be.

The same criteria should apply at the micro level, both in considering particular projects for inclusion in the reconstruction strategy and in evaluating them after the fact. For example, after 12 years of war in El Salvador, the main objective of the arms-for-land program was to ensure that former combatants had a productive activity and would not return to fighting. While this program was part of the UN-brokered peace agreement, development institutions—most notably the World Bank, but also the UNDP—had problems accepting it. Following the "equity principle" of normal development, rather than the "ethics of reconstruction", World Bank officials responsible for El Salvador argued in 1993 that there were 300,000 peasants without land in El Salvador, and that preference should not be given to a few.[5]

If judged with conventional yardsticks, the arms-for-land program in El Salvador may not get high marks. But the success of the program should not be measured by the purely economic or financial criteria that are used in normal land reform programs (e.g. production per acre, debt repayment, etc.). It should be judged by whether it contributed to maintenance of the ceasefire and national reconciliation, and whether it allowed beneficiaries to find productive employment that would permit them to make a decent living without resorting to arms. By the "reconstruction yardstick," this program was a resounding success. On the other hand, efforts to privatize the Trepca mines in Kosovo were unsuccessful from an economic point of view, and they also affected negatively prospects for national reconciliation. Thus, both the design and subsequent evaluation of alternative economic policies and peace-related projects should use the reconstruction yardstick.

An additional problem in measuring success relates to the scarcity of and distortions in the post-conflict data. Some countries did not have data during the war. For example, in Iraq, there were no data from international organizations because of sanctions. In Kosovo, data on output and other variables were lacking because it was treated in national data as a province, just as there were data problems in Yugoslavia's successor states. This makes comparisons of economic performance before and after the conflict difficult.

Large movements of people and capital also hinder such comparisons. For example, the food situation and other indicators may worsen after the war if there are large numbers of returnees who were refugees in neighboring countries. Moreover, the behavior of certain variables can become highly anomalous during the conflict, further complicating economic analysis. For example, in the early 1990s, Somalia, a country that had no government, no monetary authority, and a failed economy, saw its domestic currency appreciate. This puzzled many observers, who failed to realize that it reflected the inability to print domestic currency amid plentiful inflows of international aid. Despite the collapse in government, Somalis had a preference for their national currency, which resulted in significant appreciation.

Premise 5: Development institutions should not lead reconstruction

Given that political factors are of decisive importance, that former rebel groups are often equal partners to peace agreements, and that the relationship with groups that challenge peace is critical if peace is going to be long-lasting, development institutions are not well positioned to lead post-conflict economic reconstruction.

Many development institutions, including the UNDP, other UN agencies, the World Bank, the regional development banks, and the bilateral development agencies, can play a "best supporting actor" role in post-conflict economic reconstruction.[6] These organizations play a key role as catalysts and coordinators of reconstruction aid. The World Bank and the UNDP also organize donors' meetings, including consultative group meetings and round tables, where donors pledge funds for reconstruction. They also establish Trust Funds for budgetary support or project financing. Furthermore, as I have argued elsewhere, these organizations are unquestionably better positioned to deal with strictly development issues, at both the theoretical and operational levels, than the UN.[7] However, only the UN—that is the Secretariat under the leadership of the Secretary-General[8]—has the mandate, the impartiality, the ability, and the political imperative to include the opposition on the equal footing that is necessary to integrate the many political, humanitarian, military, and socio-economic activities which are critical to the war-to-peace transition.[9]

UN impartiality goes beyond the Secretary-General's unique ability to negotiate with rebel and other opposition groups and incorporate them into the political, economic, and peace framework. It also relates to the Secretary-General's ability to use his "good offices" to incorporate the concerns of former rebel groups into the national reconstruction plan of the country as well as to verify their compliance with peace agreements.[10] Furthermore, only the UN can justifiably violate the "equity principle" that prevails in normal development activities, in favor of the "ethics of reconstruction." This ability is particularly important in reconstruction activities relating to DDR programs, where special treatment is given to former combatants and their supporters, often to the detriment of other groups in society which are otherwise at similar levels of need.

On the other hand, even the UNDP does not have the impartiality required in post-conflict reconstruction. This is because, like other development organizations, the UNDP has a clear mandate to collaborate with governments.[11] Because the UNDP often had a presence in the country during the war, collaborating with previous and often unpopular governments, former rebel groups often view the organization with suspicion.[12] The same is often true of other development organizations, including the World Bank. Moreover, development organizations have become increasingly concerned about consulting with national authorities to ensure government ownership of policies they support.[13] Although this is a welcome policy change in development-as-usual situations, in the transition to peace, the UN must often consult equally with national governments and other groups involved in or affected by the conflict, since policies frequently must be designed according to peace agreements or national consensus.

In addition to impartiality, the time framework is no less critical. As discussed earlier, development policies can be established with a medium- and long-term perspective in mind. Hence, development institutions do not have the "sense of urgency" that is frequently required for policymaking during post-conflict reconstruction.[14] Indeed, many programs must be established on an emergency basis under suboptimal conditions. Moreover, because the World Bank, the regional development banks, and the UNDP typically execute through the government, this normally results in slow disbursements. Furthermore, given lingering post-conflict distrust, former rebel groups may oppose government execution of peace-related programs.

Finally, funding for peace-related projects, including politically sensitive projects that donors are reluctant to finance since they fall outside traditional development aid—the creation of new police forces, support for political parties, and arms-for-land programs to reintegrate former combatants—is largely decided at consultative group meetings. The UN, with the authority of the Security Council behind it, is best placed to play a catalytic role in convincing donors of the critical importance of these programs for the peace process. It is precisely at these meetings where the interests of the UN and those of the development institutions often clash, with the latter seeking to channel financing into purely development projects, rather than peacebuilding activities.

Given all these factors, the UN (or on special occasions some other political organization—say, the Arab League, the Organization of African Unity, or the Organization of American States) must play the leading role in post-conflict reconstruction, with the UNDP, the World Bank, and other development organizations playing a supporting role. However, the UN's lack of the qualified expertise required for economic reconstruction implies that it must find a modus operandi with other organizations—not only the UN agencies, but also the IFIs, bilateral development organizations, and others that will have to take the lead on technical matters. As I argue in Chapter 5, the UN must improve its institutional arrangements and in-house expertise, both in the field and at headquarters, in order to establish an effective working relationship with these other organizations. The situation as it stands today is a clear impediment to the leading role that the UN should play.

While the UN peacebuilding mission should take the lead in "post-conflict economic reconstruction", the UNDP and other UN agencies that have operations in the field can play the leading role in "preventive diplomacy". Since these institutions are in the field, they are ideally positioned to provide information to the UN political and humanitarian departments and even to be a source of assistance and support in cases where the political situation deteriorates quickly. On political issues, however, they should always be directed by the UN Department for Political Affairs (DPA), to avoid the danger of working at cross-purposes, and thus aggravating the situation.[15]

Premise 6: Keep it simple and flexible

As discussed earlier, most countries coming out of war in the post-Cold War period are at a low level of development. Moreover, years of conflict and war have depleted their scarce human resources, technical capabilities, and physical infrastructure, leaving them all the more vulnerable.

Despite these conditions, countries in post-conflict transitions must establish as soon as possible a framework for macroeconomic policymaking, as well as for regulation of microeconomic policies that can create an appropriate environment for investment, production, and trade. In such circumstances, it is unrealistic and certainly counterproductive to create a framework that is too sophisticated for the country and requires resources that it does not have and that may not exist for a long time.

The credo in post-conflict situations—both for policymaking as well as for the establishment of new institutions—should therefore be "keep it simple and flexible." As I will discuss in the case of Kosovo, this principle was applied to the design of the customs office and commercial policy, with very good results. By contrast, in the case of Afghanistan, the macroeconomic framework in general was much too complex for the available human resources. More worrisome, the central bank law was not only too sophisticated but also extremely restrictive, more so than in many higher-income and even industrial countries, eliminating any flexibility for domestic financing of peace-related programs.

Part III

International Assistance

"Better the Arabs do it tolerably than that you do it perfectly. It is their war, and you are to help them, not to win it for them."

T.E. Lawrence (Lawrence of Arabia) in "Twenty-Seven Articles,"
Arab Bulletin, August 20th, 1917

5 The multilateral framework for international assistance

> "After more than fifty years [of UN existence] …, I've had plenty of opportunity to observe first-hand the frustration of good intentions—seemingly endless debate among UN member states, too much narrow self-interest, missed opportunities, corruption, and grand vision lost amid political impasse and administrative ineptitude."
>
> Paul A. Volcker in the Introduction of *Good Intentions Corrupted: The Oil-for-Food Scandal and the Threat to the UN*

> "Indeed, one of my main criticisms of the international economic institutions is that, regardless of the circumstances, they have supported one particular economic perspective—one which I think, in many ways, is misguided."
>
> Joseph E. Stiglitz in *Making Globalization Work*

Operationally, post-conflict economic reconstruction involves a wide variety of international actors, ranging from the UN system as a whole, to the international financial institutions (IFIs), the development organizations, bilateral and regional donors, and often a large number of non-governmental organizations (NGOs). The role that these actors should play in reconstruction is a matter of great debate, as is the relationship they should have with local actors in developing strategies and establishing priorities. External support is necessary to countries in post-conflict situations, but creating aid dependencies is not good and discourages sustainability.[1]

Irrespective of the role international actors play, and whatever their relationship with national actors, the participation of so many reconstruction actors creates serious operational and logistical challenges. Furthermore, the large involvement of the international community in countries undergoing reconstruction normally causes numerous distortions and coordination problems.

The purpose of this chapter is to discuss the impact (both positive and negative) of the main actors—the UN system and the IFIs—on post-conflict economic reconstruction, past and current reforms to improve their capacity in this field, and to make specific recommendations for strengthening their performance further. This chapter will also examine the implications of globalization and other changes in international relations for the role of the IFIs in post-conflict assistance. The role of other actors will be incorporated as necessary into the discussion of the political and economic framework set up by these institutions. Empirical evidence for many of the issues will be discussed in more detail in the case studies.

The readiness and resources of the different organizations to deal with peacebuilding in general, and post-conflict reconstruction in particular, has been questioned in most recent post-conflict experiences. Tschirgi (2004: 1), for example, wonders why, after more than ten years of practice, the international peacebuilding project is still experimental, amorphous, and tenuous in nature.

But questioning the ability of the organizations involved in post-conflict reconstruction is nothing new: similar questions were raised after World War II. In promoting the Marshall Plan in 1947, Dulles (1993: 63) argued that the Bretton Woods institutions were slow in getting under way and had great difficulties in securing adequate financial resources. In his view, this justified the Marshall Plan, despite the fact that these institutions had been created for financing and supporting longer-range reconstruction projects (the World Bank), and promoting financial stability in post-war Europe (the IMF).

The lack of readiness and sufficient resources has been true of the UN system and the IFIs in the post-Cold War period as well. Despite reforms aimed at improving these institutions' capacity for post-conflict reconstruction, their bureaucratic procedures, financial and legal constraints, or professional staff limitations still make a quick and effective response to countries at the early stage of the war-to-peace transition almost impossible. Yet as discussed in the case studies, such a response may well be essential to a successful move towards global human security.

The United Nations and the political framework

As discussed earlier, the UN Secretariat led by the Secretary-General (hereinafter referred to as the "UN", as opposed to the "UN system" which also includes UN programs and agencies) is uniquely positioned—in theory and by its mandate—to help countries in the transition from war, where it is critical to reconcile the objectives of peace and development. In this transition, the UN has often played the role of "honest broker," verifying peace agreements and facilitating and promoting their operational implementation, mostly under mandates of the Security Council, although in a few cases of the General Assembly. In this capacity, the UN has addressed mainly political and security, but also legal, institutional, and judicial issues. It has also played a role in disarming, demobilization, and reintegration (DDR) programs. More recently, in Kosovo and East Timor, the UN has played an intrusive role by performing civil administration functions that are normally the sole prerogative of sovereign governments. By contrast, the UN's role in economic reconstruction has been minor in Afghanistan, reflecting what Brahimi referred to as a "light footprint," and in Iraq, owing to the US-led occupation following US-led military intervention, as well as the exceptionally poor security conditions prevailing in the country.

Although, in theory, the UN is best placed to lead post-conflict reconstruction, in practice, its potential to lead an integrated approach in matters of human security has not yet been fully developed, either internally in the Secretariat's relevant departments or in conjunction with its programs and agencies (the "rest of the UN system"), as well as with other actors. Mismanagement, corruption, and influence peddling (most clearly associated with the "oil-for-food" program and overall procurement practices), sexual abuse and exploitation of women and children by peacekeeping forces, and visible cases of incompetent and unaccountable staff members at the highest levels have led many observers to question the ability of the UN to provide such an approach.[2] Furthermore, the strong resentment—particularly in the Muslim world—of comprehensive sanctions imposed by the Security Council and maintained for a dozen years in Iraq has undermined the organization's credibility and led to its increased marginalization in the new millennium.[3]

At the same time, the work and resources of the UN in post-conflict economic reconstruction have been constrained by a tendency, particularly among some members of the Security Council, to regard reconstruction as simply "development in disguise." This has led to the Council's reluctance to undertake commitments that go beyond peacekeeping *strictu sensu*, with the notable exceptions of Kosovo and East Timor. Even in the latter, despite the UN's intense involvement, its early exit was most unfortunate, as security conditions rapidly deteriorated because of unfinished reconstruction business.

Understandably, the permanent members of the Security Council do not want to finance non-military activities under the peacekeeping assessment scale, in which they share a larger burden than in the regular UN budget.[4] Over time, they have also invoked strong institutional constraints against involving the Council in affairs that they do not regard as directly related to the maintenance of international peace and security—often ignoring the clear empirical evidence that post-conflict economic reconstruction is critical in avoiding recurrence of hostilities.

THE UN'S OPERATIONAL CAPACITY

The UN Secretariat has faced, and continues to face, several operational short-comings that prevent it from playing a leading role in reconstruction. Member states have failed to strengthen the Secretariat's analytical and operational capacity and to provide peacekeeping and peacebuilding operations in the field with adequate resources for economic reconstruction. Because of this, the UN has been unable to help countries formulate reconstruction policies that are well conceived, transparent, and credible, and that can be implemented from both a political and socio-economic viewpoint. These shortcomings have also affected negatively the organization's capacity to design and carry out policies for the reintegration of former combatants and other estranged groups into civilian life and productive activities.

UN involvement in post-conflict economic reconstruction has thus lagged, largely as a result of lack of leadership at the top (including the Secretary-General and his deputies) and inadequate human and financial resources. Furthermore, reform proposals to strengthen the UN in the specific area of post-conflict economic reconstruction, including my own, have gone largely unnoticed. In 1995, when I was senior officer in charge of this area in the Office of the Secretary-General, I argued that the need for the UN to become more immersed in the multidisciplinary aspects of peacebuilding clearly required a major rethinking and an analytical and operational redefinition of relationships and comparative advantages. The dramatically enlarged scope of what was expected from the international community was putting tremendous pressure on the human and financial resources of the UN system as a whole. Unfortunately, many of the flaws I discussed in an article in *CEPAL Review* a dozen years ago seem to persist.[5] The most notorious is the lack of integration of the work of the Department for Political Affairs (DPA) and the Department for Peacekeeping Operations (DPKO) on one side, and the Department for Economic and Social Affairs (DESA) on the other in matters of economic reconstruction.[6]

At the time, I offered three recommendations to make the integrated approach operational. The first was to assign a high-level adviser (or team, depending on the case) on economic reconstruction in all peace negotiations, since stipulations in peace agreements are likely to have an important effect—either positive or negative—on their implementation. This was missing from the Salvadoran negotiations and the UN—including the peace mediator—had come to regret it. While such counsel has become common practice in more recent negotiations, for example, in Cyprus, the right kind of expertise has not always been available.

The second recommendation was that peacebuilding missions should include a unit headed by a high-level official to deal solely with economic reconstruction. Although missions such as that in Kosovo have had an economic pillar, this was led by a different organization (the EU) and has not been well integrated into the overall mission headed by the UN. In fact, this pillar operated rather independently from UNMIK, and thus, the economic transition followed basically an EU agenda, which was not always fully in synchronization with or supportive of the political, security, and social transitions.

In some UN missions, the Deputy Special Representative of the Secretary-General (DSRSG) has been appointed from the UNDP to lead economic reconstruction and carry out simultaneously the task of humanitarian coordinator, resident coordinator of the UN system, and resident representative of the UNDP. This is the case in Haiti and Liberia, for example. Although such arrangements have often been hailed as an example of increased integration, they are, in my view, a recipe for a "development as usual" approach. Because the UNDP's mandate is to collaborate with governments, such an arrangement is likely to alienate former rebel groups, which were often equal partners in peace agreements, but which, having given up their arms, are in a weaker position during reconstruction than the government. Furthermore, in its search for development financing, the UNDP often competes with the financing needs for political and security programs of peacekeeping operations, which are critical to the war-to-peace transition. Similarly, there are conflicts between the financing of humanitarian and reconstruction activities, at a time when the latter are critical in avoiding aid dependency. In the case study on El Salvador, I will argue, however, that the UNDP should have the leading role in the transition from post-conflict economic reconstruction to normal development, but certainly not during the immediate transition from war to peace where reconstruction should take priority and the UNDP development activities should take the back seat.

The third recommendation was that responsibility for post-conflict economic reconstruction at UN headquarters be clearly assigned. A Post-Conflict Economic Reconstruction Unit (PCRU), located within DPA could assist the department, given the essentially political nature of reconstruction, to give guidance to the mission in the field on reconstruction activities (see Figures 2–4 below). A PCRU would be responsible for taking decisions and coordinating support for economic reconstruction, as well as ensuring its integration into other peacebuilding activities at UN headquarters. Unfortunately, more than a decade after I made my proposal in the *CEPAL Review*, not only is there no such unit, but also responsibilities for reconstruction continue to be shared between the DPA and the DPKO in a confusing and ineffective way. Thus, the political and economic objectives of post-conflict transitions continue to be as poorly integrated at UN headquarters as they have been in the field.[7]

Former Secretary-General Boutros Boutros-Ghali did attempt to increase the links between the political and the economic departments. His first move was to ask the head of the DESA to convene and chair an interdepartmental task force for the purpose of drawing up *An Inventory of Post-Conflict Peace-building Activities*, that I mentioned in Chapter 3. The purpose of the Inventory was to identify actions and techniques relevant to post-conflict situations and the UN agencies that could provide support (UN 1996a). But there was no follow-up, partly because of the lack of qualified staff and a recruitment freeze at the time which prevented the UN from bringing in people with the right skills and experience from outside. Even more significant was the attitude of the respective heads of the DESA and DPA.[8] The latter gave low priority to economic issues, and the former thought that reconstruction issues were not rigorous enough for serious economists. Thus, political work was regarded with suspicion in the economics department, while the political department had little understanding of the importance of economic factors involved in creating and preserving peace. Boutros-Ghali failed to assign responsibility for the UN role in post-conflict reconstruction.

Boutros-Ghali's successor, Kofi Annan, was no more successful. In fact, it is not even clear how much he tried. Although the Secretary-General appointed a Deputy Secretary-General,[9] supposedly so that he could delegate to her (or, subsequently, him) the responsibility for many economic and social issues, the lack of a link between economic and political issues remained. Moreover, the Secretary-General made no specific effort to get the DESA seriously involved in post-conflict economic reconstruction, although—with good leadership and appropriate resources—it could have strengthened the UN's capacity to play its impartial role.[10] The Secretary-General did not make any effort to bring the issue of post-conflict economic reconstruction to the Senior Management Group (SMG), which had acted since 1997 as his cabinet and the central policy planning body. Nor did he bring the issue to the Policy Committee established in 2004 as the highest decision-making body within the UN Secretariat.[11]

More worrisome, the continuing lack of communication between diplomats and other political officials at the UN and economic officials at the IFIs is clear from the *Report of the Panel on UN Peace Operations* (UN 2000c), known as the *Brahimi Report*. This report appeared in August 2000 and has since been a guiding force for the UN's work in this area. The report essentially ignored the economic reconstruction issues associated with peacebuilding, allocating responsibility for the formulation of peacebuilding strategies—including both preventive and post-conflict activities—to a committee in which neither the DESA nor the IMF participated (although the World Bank did). Such exclusion seems to be an indication that members of the group that wrote the report do not consider the work of the DESA and the IMF to be relevant to peacebuilding activities.[12]

Moreover, the *Brahimi Report* emphasized the need to distinguish between strategy formulation and its implementation. With regard to implementation, the report concluded that the UNDP has "untapped potential in this area," and that, in cooperation with other UN agencies, funds, and programs and the World Bank, it is best placed to "lead peacebuilding activities" (a recommendation that runs counter to my Premise 5 for effective post-conflict reconstruction). As Tschirgi (2004: 5) recognized, peacebuilding found temporary and tenuous shelter under the roof of the development agencies. In my view, the *Brahimi Report* clearly proposed continuation of the failed "development as usual" approach to post-conflict reconstruction that has proved so ineffective in consolidating peace. In fact, Brahimi felt himself victim of his own advice when he was Special Representative (SRSG) in Afghanistan in 2001, and was undermined by the agencies from the very beginning. The UNDP's Administrator got himself appointed coordinator for recovery for the first six months, in direct contradiction to the concept of an integrated mission under the leadership of the SRSG. When Brahimi's office circulated a paper proposing that the funds and agencies should not have separate offices, but should all operate out of an integrated office under the SRSG and a single UN flag, he was ignored.

An important contribution of Brahimi's report was to point out the shortcomings of the UN that impeded early deployment, and how key this phase was for a successful transition to peace. As the report makes clear,

The first six to 12 weeks following a ceasefire or peace accord is often the most critical period for establishing both a stable peace and the credibility of the peacekeepers. Credibility and political momentum lost during this period can often be difficult to regain. Deployment timelines should thus be tailored accordingly. However, the speedy deployment of military, civilian police and civilian expertise will not help to solidify a fragile peace and establish the credibility of an operation if these personnel are not equipped to do their job.

In December 2004, *A More Secure World: Our Shared Responsibility*, the Report of the High-Level Panel on Threats, Challenges and Change (UN 2004a), again focused UN reform on peace and security issues.[13] The Panel was convened because of what the International Peace Academy (March 2005: 1) described as a genuine and broad awareness that collective responses to global challenges were "in dire need of repair and upgrade: in concepts, in procedures, in institutions and in commitments." The report argued in favor of a single intergovernmental organ dedicated to peacebuilding, empowered to monitor and pay close attention to countries at risk, to ensure concerted action by donors, agencies, programs, and financing institutions, and to mobilize financial resources for sustainable peace and development (UN 2004: 71, 83–4).

In response to this report, Secretary-General Annan wrote yet another report in March 2005, entitled *In Larger Freedom*. Acknowledging that, at the time he was head of peacekeeping, the UN's record had been blemished by some devastating failures (notably in Angola and Rwanda), and that "roughly half of all countries that emerged from war relapsed into violence within five years", Annan argued for the need to ensure that peace agreements are implemented in a substantial and sustainable manner. In this light, his report proposed that member states establish an inter-governmental Peacebuilding Commission, as well as a Peacebuilding Support Office (PSO) within the UN Secretariat to make the transition from war to peace lasting (UN 2004a: 31).

Given the expense that Annan was willing to incur with groups of experts and endless reports, as well as his bleak view of the UN's record in the early 1990s and the high probability of the recurrence of conflict, it took him surprisingly long to recommend changes to strengthen the peacebuilding capacity of the organization. Indeed, the obvious need for improvement had been clearly established more than a decade earlier. Be that as it may, the issue now is whether his recommendation would strengthen the capacity of the organization, or be just another layer of bureaucracy, duplication, expense, and delays in the support the UN should provide to countries coming out of war.

The new peacebuilding infrastructure

The newly created Peacebuilding Commission is unlike any other UN body. It is an inter-governmental "advisory" subsidiary organ of both the General Assembly and the Security Council, with 31 members selected by the Security Council, the General Assembly, the Economic and Social Council (ECOSOC), and contributors of troops and aid. As per a General Assembly Resolution 60/180 adopted on December 30th, 2005, the Assembly will have overall responsibility for reviewing the Commission's work by debating its annual report, although the report would be available to other bodies, including the IFIs.

The main purposes of the Peacebuilding Commission are

- To bring together all relevant actors to marshall resources and to advise on and propose integrated strategies for post-conflict peacebuilding and recovery;

- To focus attention on the reconstruction and institution-building efforts necessary for recovery from conflict and to support the development of integrated strategies in order to lay the foundations for sustainable development;

- To provide recommendations and information to improve the coordination of all relevant actors within and outside the UN, to develop best practices, to help to ensure predictable financing for early recovery activities and to extend the period of attention given by the international community to post-conflict recovery.

The resolution states that, given the primary responsibility of the Security Council for the maintenance of international peace and security, in countries in which there is a UN-mandated peacekeeping mission on the ground or under way, the main purpose of the Commission will be to provide advice to the Council at its request. The resolution also underlines that the Commission's advice will be of particular relevance to the ECOSOC, given its role as a principal UN body for coordination, policy review, policy dialogue, and recommendations on issues of economic and social development. The relationship with the General Assembly and the ECOSOC has the purpose of ensuring that the international community and donors maintain interest in post-conflict countries, even after they have vanished from the headlines.

Neither the Peacebuilding Commission nor the Peacebuilding Support Office that the same resolution creates, however, has any "operational" capacity, which is indeed a problem since that is where the UN has largely failed. Finally, the Peacebuilding Fund, also created by the same resolution and launched by the Secretary-General in October 2006, has the purpose of supporting countries in the early transition to peace, when other financing mechanisms are not yet available.[14]

Despite the fact that it may be too early to make a definite judgment on the new peacebuilding infrastructure, there are many reasons to be skeptical. First, the fact that the Peacebuilding Commission's 31 members must take decisions "by consensus" seems like a recipe for paralysis. Second, the fact that the General Assembly rather than the Security Council has main responsibility over its work suggests that post-conflict reconstruction will remain "development as usual." Although the General Assembly may address any matter within the scope of the UN Charter, in accordance with Article 12, it is excluded from any matter in which the Security Council is seized, which are those that matter the most for international peace and security. By member states having each one vote, a bias in favor of development issues is guaranteed at the General Assembly. Third, it is not clear how the Commission will integrate its work or what leverage it will have to coordinate the UN system, given the problems discussed earlier regarding different mandates and accountability to different governing bodies of the UN agencies. Indeed, given its characteristics, the Commission seems like a perfect candidate to contribute further to the large bureaucracy, inefficiency, mismanagement, and waste at the UN.

THE PEACEBUILDING COMMISSION: FIRST ANNUAL REPORT

During its first year, the Peacebuilding Commission focused on two countries, Burundi and Sierra Leone. The presentation of its first report to the

General Assembly took place on October 10, 2007 and to the Security Council on October 17 (UN 2007a, 2007b). The Chairman of the Organizational Committee of the Peacebuilding Commission noted that the Commission had been established "to bring together all relevant actors, to marshal resources and to advise on and propose integrated strategies for post-conflict peace-building and recovery." If this were the objective, perhaps the Commission should have started with a country like Nepal, which is in the transition from war after the Comprehensive Peace Agreement of 2006 and needs to establish a strategy for reconstruction as soon as possible, whereas the two countries selected had made this move long time ago.

Furthermore, in the case of Sierra Leone, for example, the country already had a UN structure to support the government in the transition to peace. There had been two peacekeeping operations. UNOMSIL (UN Observer Mission in Sierra Leone), in place from July 1998 to October 1999, had a military mandate and a civilian one, which included advice and training of the new civilian police and reporting on violations of international law and human rights. In October 1999, after the signature of the Lomé Peace Agreement, UNAMSIL (the UN Mission in Sierra Leone) was created to support the government with the implementation of the agreement, including with the disarmament, demobilization, and reintegration of former combatants.

Despite little progress in the reintegration of former combatants and other war-affected groups, the Security Council decided that UNAMSIL had successfully completed its mandate in December 2005. In January 2006, the Security Council established UNIOSIL (UN Integrated Office), a political mission under the leadership of DPA rather than DPKO. The mandate of UNIOSIL included support to the government to address the root causes of conflict, to improve governance, the rule of law and respect for human rights, transparency and accountability of public institutions, and to coordinate with other bodies on the smuggling and illegal trade in natural resources. An Executive Representative of the Secretary-General (ERSG) was appointed to head the Mission and to head, at the same time, the UN Country Team and be Resident Coordinator of the UN system in Sierra Leone. In 2006, UNIOSIL had about 300 staff (82 international and 192 local staff plus over 20 UN Volunteers). The cost of the mission was over $23 million.[15]

One would have thought that with a UN Integrated Office in place (Figure 1), the UN was prepared to support the transition to peace in Sierra Leone. Although UNIOSIL does not have an ideal structure to deal with economic reconstruction and is likely to follow a "development as usual" approach, it should nevertheless have the capacity to identify the critical problems of the transition—such as lack of productive employment in general and youth unemployment in particular—and be able to assist the government in addressing them. An indication of the Commission's failure to find its place in the system and set its priorities is that, with an integrated mission in place,

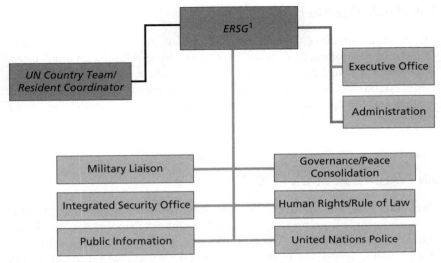

Figure 1. UNIOSIL (UN Integrated Office in Sierra Leone) organizational chart

Note: 1. Executive Representative of the SG.

Source: UNIOSIL web site.

it nevertheless had to send a team of nine members to Sierra Leone—with the cost that this implies—to obtain "first-hand information about the situation on the ground, in particular, the challenges to peace consolidation." This not only points out the inadequacy of institutional arrangements at the UN to deal with post-conflict countries but also the waste of money and resources that these inadequate arrangements lead to.

THE PEACEBUILDING SUPPORT OFFICE

The second piece of the peacebuilding infrastructure is the Peacebuilding Support Office. The Secretary-General specified that the Peacebuilding Support Office "will not replace or duplicate the capacities of existing operational actors." However, by establishing the PSO "within existing resources," the latest reform might have contributed to depriving the operational departments (DPA, DPKO, and others) and, more importantly, the UN peacekeeping operations, of critical staff. Nor is it clear what capacity the PSO has to "coordinate" the UN agencies or aid flows, particularly given its skeleton staff. Other specified PSO functions, such as the dissemination of information, analysis of lessons learned, lobbying for larger aid flows, and ensuring that all relevant actors participate in country meetings, are useful, but should not come at the expense of the UN's "operational" capacity.

THE PEACEBUILDING FUND

The potential impact of this fund, with pledges of only $250 million at the end of 2007, seems limited. Donors will have to provide this fund with much larger resources if it is to have any significant impact. As a comparison, the Holst Fund, established in the mid-1990s for budgetary and employment support in Gaza and the West Bank, had a comparable level of resources (World Bank 1998a: 38).

AN EVALUATION OF UN REFORM

Over the years, reform at the UN has often involved the shifting of mandates and people from one office to another without bringing any new blood into the system. The PSO, for example, was created by drawing staff from peacekeeping operations in the field. The DESA was also reformed several times, breaking it up and putting it back together on several occasions.[16] The UN's leadership does not seem to understand that, in the absence of new expertise and talent to address the pressing issues that the UN is facing, the same problems will reappear, regardless of where the existing human resources are located. Most recently, on February 5, 2007, Ban Ki-moon, the new Secretary-General, did it again. He proposed to improve the operational capacity of the UN by creating yet another department: the Department of Field Support, whose core was taken away from DPKO. However, neither this new department nor the PSO will make any significant difference in terms of increasing the UN's capacity to deal with post-conflict economic reconstruction if they function "within existing resources and expertise". The UN desperately needs new ideas and expertise to deal successfully with post-conflict reconstruction.

STRENGTHENING UN OPERATIONAL CAPACITY TO CARRY OUT POST-CONFLICT RECONSTRUCTION

If the UN is to lead post-conflict economic reconstruction—as I argue it is in principle well placed to do in most cases (premise 5)—it needs to acquire the right expertise and ensure that a properly equipped Post-Conflict Reconstruction Unit (PCRU) is established in the UN Secretariat (Figure 2). Because of the political nature of post-conflict economic reconstruction, the PCRU should be located in the DPA, with strong links to the DPKO and the DESA, with each of these departments having a Post-Conflict Reconstruction Coordinator (PCRC).[17]

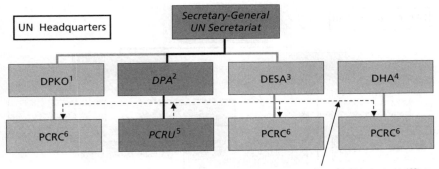

Figure 2. Proposed UN Secretariat organizational chart for effective economic reconstruction

Notes: 1. Department of Peacekeeping Operations; 2. Department for Political Affairs; 3. Department for Economic and Social Affairs; 4. Department of Humanitarian Affairs; 5. Post-Conflict Reconstruction Unit; 6. Post-Conflict Reconstruction Coordinators.

The creation of the PCRU would provide leadership, support, and operational guidelines from headquarters to a counterpart National Reconstruction Coordinator Office (NRCO) in the UN peacebuilding (or integrated) mission in the field (Figure 3). The NRCO would be under the Deputy Special Representative of the Secretary-General (DSRSG) for Economics and Finance. Large peacebuilding operations could have two deputies under the SRSG, one for political and security affairs, and the other for economic and financial affairs.[18] The latter would have two offices, the first for reconstruction and the second for administrative and budgetary issues related to the UN mission itself. While the SRSG should be selected for his diplomatic, political, and negotiating skills, the Deputy with responsibility for economics and finance should be a good manager, with strong qualifications and experience in economic, administrative, and financial issues. In small operations with only one DSRSG for Political Affairs, the National Reconstruction Coordinator could come directly under the SRSG and be his top adviser on all reconstruction issues.

Both the PCRU at headquarters and the NRCO in the mission will have to be headed at a high level. They will also have to have staff that is, at the same time, fully versed in both economic and financial issues related to reconstruction, and fully aware and up to date with the political and security issues constraining reconstruction. This can be achieved only through rigorous hiring and intensive training policies and practices, including at the highest level. Having this expertise could facilitate dialogue with the IFIs, which, as discussed below, play a critical role in post-conflict reconstruction.

At the field level, the NRCO should include four units, each one headed by a Policy and Strategy Coordinator, an Aid Coordinator, an IFIs Coordinator,

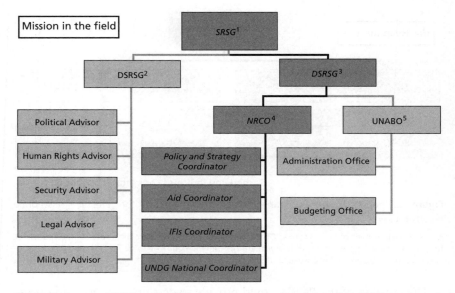

Figure 3. Proposed UN Peacebuilding Mission organizational chart for effective economic reconstruction

Notes: 1. Special Representative of the Secretary-General; 2. Deputy Special Representative of the Secretary-General for Political Affairs; 3. Deputy Special Representative of the Secretary-General for Economics and Finance; 4. National Reconstruction Coordinator Office headed by the National Reconstruction Coordinator (NRC); 5. UN Administration and Budgeting Office.

and a UNDG National Coordinator.[19] The Policy and Strategy Coordinator would coordinate all the substantive work on reconstruction, assist countries in the design of the reconstruction strategy, and coordinate with them the assistance of the international community. The Aid Coordinator would centralize all data and information related to donors' assistance, including from the IFIs, in order to avoid duplication and working at cross purposes, and would have major responsibility for fundraising activities, including the preparation and presentation of financing requests for donors' conferences.[20] The IFIs Coordinator would centralize relations with the different government bodies relating to the provision of technical assistance and capacity building by the IFIs. The UNDG National Coordinator would coordinate all assistance with UN agencies and programs. For this position, the higher-ranking UNDG official in the country or the head of the agency with the largest and/or most visible program in the country could be selected.

The NRCO under the leadership of the National Reconstruction Coordinator (NRC) should deal solely with the broad range of economic reconstruction issues and have strong links with the PCRU at UN headquarters (Figure 4). This integrated approach would improve the effectiveness of the UN system and the allocation of resources in assisting reconstruction in post-conflict

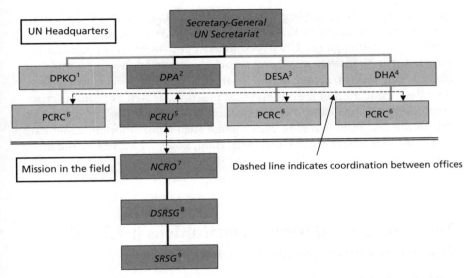

Figure 4. Proposed coordination links between UN Headquarters and the Peacebuilding Mission in the Field for effective economic reconstruction

Notes: 1. Department of Peacekeeping Operations; 2. Department for Political Affairs; 3 Department for Economic and Social Affairs; 4. Department of Humanitarian Affairs; 5. Post-Conflict Reconstruction Unit; 6. Post-Conflict Reconstruction Coordinators; 7. National Reconstruction Coordinator Office; 8. Deputy Special Representative of the Secretary-General for Economics and Finance; 9. Special Representative of the Secretary-General.

countries by enabling the UN mission responsible for peacebuilding to make critical policy, strategy, and operational decisions in close coordination with the government and other actors involved. It would also facilitate the integration of the economic and social transitions, on the one hand, with the political and security transitions on the other. Just as importantly, once the peacekeeping/peacebuilding mission is dismantled, the UNDG National Coordinator would provide the essential link to the "development as usual" functions of the UN system. At this stage, he or she would become UNDG Resident Coordinator, ensuring continuity between the peace and development processes.

The institutional memory of the UN in post-conflict reconstruction should be part of the PCRU at headquarters, with the support of the NRCO at the field level.[21] Unless such a memory exists, the parties to peace agreements or other political arrangements might find it to their advantage to wriggle out of or distort previous economic and social commitments to which they may have agreed only reluctantly. The problem of frequently changing staff and lack of institutional memory mechanisms was evident in El Salvador—the first UN multidisciplinary PKO—as it has been in every subsequent operation. It would greatly facilitate reconstruction not only to ensure recruitment of qualified experts from the beginning of the operation, but also to have over-lapping contracts to ensure that institutional memory is not lost.

Moreover, although the UN has conducted post-mortems of political and military operations, systematic evaluations during and following completion of economic reconstruction should be greatly encouraged. This would facilitate the formulation of lessons and best practices, as well as promote cross-fertilization among different reconstruction experiences. The UN did not do this in the case of El Salvador, even though such a post-mortem could have facilitated later operations in Guatemala, Haiti, Kosovo, East Timor, and many other places.

The international financial institutions (IFIs) and the economic framework

The UN often mediates peace agreements that have serious economic consequences and require large amounts of technical assistance and financing. The IFIs, which include the Bretton Woods institutions–the IMF and the World Bank—and the regional development banks, play a critical role in establishing the economic and financial framework for the transition to peace. These institutions become involved in post-conflict economic reconstruction in different ways and at different stages. They assist countries in normal times, and they, in general, cease operating in countries at war, renewing their relationship as soon as security conditions permit and a credible government is in place.[22]

As the Asian Development Bank (ADB 2002b) puts it, economic reconstruction is much more than building roads, bridges, and schools: it is largely about building capacity for market-based recovery and sustainable growth. This is where the IFIs and other development organizations play a major supportive role. They carry out this role through four channels: policy advice, technical assistance and capacity building, financing reconstruction, and catalyzing financing from other donors. All of these activities are important since, for the reasons I discussed earlier, financial stability and the reactivation of growth and employment are decisive in the transition to peace.

There is abundant evidence that donors are not likely to be generous with countries that are not putting their economies in order and doing their best to help themselves. In general, donors will provide large flows of aid only if they think that their financial resources will be used effectively and transparently and that recipient government policies are consistent with financial stability. Moreover, the IMF's blessing through a formal or informal program to ensure financial stability and the reactivation of growth has proved to be a de facto if not *de jure* requirement for assistance from the World Bank, the regional development banks, and often even from bilateral donors.[23] This, however, is beginning to change, as discussed later.

Policy advice and technical assistance from the IFIs has proved particularly important, because countries in the transition to peace need, as a general rule, not only to stabilize their economies but also to establish or modernize their macroeconomic institutions and to develop adequate policies to deal with the challenges of reconstruction. The IMF's role during the early post-conflict transition is to help countries to reestablish macroeconomic stability and assist with the building of national institutions, particularly in relation to the finance ministry and the central bank. Typically, the IMF focuses technical assistance on rebuilding capacity in the fiscal, monetary, exchange, and statistical areas.[24] Policy advice focuses on budget preparation to ensure that it is consistent with available national and international resources, that inflationary pressures subside, that the external position is strengthened, that new quick-yielding revenue measures are developed, and that the system of payments, credit, and exchange operations is restored and functioning properly. The latter is essential to ensure effective use of aid resources and facilitate payments to civil servants, who in some cases have not received wages for long periods.

As the 2007 *Report of the External Review Committee on Bank-Fund Collaboration*, known as the *Malan Report*, notes, close collaboration between the World Bank and the IMF is vital because, while they have separate mandates, they are inherently linked. For example, the Fund's efforts at macroeconomic stabilization will not be sustained unless they are linked to supply-side measures to promote investment, growth, and improvement in the quality of public spending, which is a major Bank concern (IMF and World Bank 2007: 6, 24–5).[25] In other words, the reestablishment of a stable macroeconomic policy framework supported primarily by the IMF is a necessary, but not sufficient, condition for the reactivation of growth and the creation of employment. It must be accompanied by a focus on the supply-side or micro-foundations of investment and growth (rehabilitation of infrastructure and human resources, improvement of the business climate, and poverty alleviation)—the domain of the Bank and other development organizations, such as the UNDP, the regional development banks, and other UN agencies. These institutions also provide technical assistance and support for the development of specific sectors, including energy, agriculture, industry, and the financial sector.[26] Since 1994, following its first experience in Uganda, the World Bank has also been increasingly involved in mine clearance and in demobilization and reintegration of former combatants and other groups affected by the conflict (World Bank 1998a, 1998b).

In countries under normal development, the Fund and the Bank provide assistance at the request of member states and with their consent. Their activities in UN and US protectorates in Kosovo, East Timor, and Iraq, as well as in countries with weak governments like Afghanistan, have been rather intrusive. According to Boon (2007: 526–33), these institutions have assumed "quasi-legislative functions." Boon argues that the Security Council has become an institutional enabler for the Bretton Woods institutions (through the issuance of Chapter VII resolutions) and that these organizations had to undertake significant interpretive leaps with regard to their Articles of Agreement, revealing an important new expansion in their mandates.[27]

In 1997, the World Bank adopted a framework for its involvement in post-conflict reconstruction (World Bank 1998a) to draw on best practices of their operations up to that time and to sketch guidelines for their future operations. The Bank also established a special Post-Conflict Unit to act as a focal point to provide assistance to countries in the transition to peace.[28] Member states provided staff on secondment to this unit so that it could acquire talent and expertise not available at the Bank at the time.[29]

Soon afterwards, the World Bank started collaborating with the UNDG in preparing and carrying out Post-Conflict Needs Assessments (PCNA). The UNDP and other UN agencies are often present in the country throughout the war and thus can play a valuable role in this process. The PCNA involves the technical assessment of initial conditions to ascertain the reconstruction needs as well as the national capabilities constraints that will jointly determine the post-conflict reconstruction strategy. The process of analysis, consultation, and negotiation that starts with the PCNA allows national and international actors to discuss priorities, define commitments, and plan for action.

Despite collaboration with the UNDG, difficulties with the PCNAs led the Bank in 2001 to issue formal directives on Operational Policies and Bank Procedures. Through this framework paper, the Bank formalized several instruments for analyzing the problems of countries in conflict, including the Watching Briefs and the Transitional Support Strategy (TSS).[30] In late 2001, the Bank adopted the Low-Income Countries under Stress (LICUS) Initiative.[31]

In 2003, the Bank finally accepted that "the main objective over the short- to medium-term must be to consolidate peace" (Boyce 2004). This was indeed a major change from its position a decade earlier in El Salvador, which is discussed in the case study in Chapter 7. How this realization has affected the Bank's operational work since then remains an open question that it is too early to evaluate. Events at the Bank over the last two years, leading to the resignation of the President in May 2007, have thrown the Bank into disarray and impaired its functions. New leadership in 2007, not only at the World Bank under Robert B. Zoellick, but also at the IMF under Dominique Strauss-Khan, would hopefully allow these institutions to play a renewed and more effective overall role in post-conflict reconstruction. Member states should ensure that this is the case.

Although the IFIs provide some of their own resources to support economic programs, countries are often not eligible for them in the immediate war-to-peace transition because of debt arrears with these institutions. Moreover, some post-conflict countries are not eligible to borrow at concessional (better than normal) terms from these institutions, either. This is because, on the one hand, they must have an income per capita that puts them below a maximum level, and, on the other, they need to establish a track record before they qualify.[32] At the same time, most post-conflict countries are unable to afford the normal lending terms of the IFIs. This catch-22 process will be discussed separately below.

In cases in which post-conflict reconstruction takes place in provinces or in countries that are not members, the IFIs cannot in principle lend to them but can provide technical assistance. Serbia and Montenegro, a non-member, and Kosovo, a province, were cases in point. Nevertheless, the IFIs have shown flexibility in emergency situations.[33] Both the Fund and the Bank have been involved in countries that were yet to complete the financial normalization and membership process. In 1996, the Bank, for example, approved sixteen emergency infrastructure and social projects for Bosnia and Herzegovina (World Bank 1998b: 11).

The World Bank—often in collaboration with the UNDP and the regional development banks—has played the most important role as a catalyst for financing in post-conflict situations. In this capacity, the Bank organizes and leads consultative group meetings for countries, often even before the country achieves peace. This was the case, for example, in El Salvador and in Bosnia and Herzegovina. For other countries, the UNDP sponsors roundtables with donors. This was the case, for example, in Angola, Rwanda, Sierra Leone, and elsewhere.[34]

THE EVOLVING ROLE OF THE BRETTON WOODS INSTITUTIONS IN FINANCING RECONSTRUCTION

In financing post-conflict countries, the Bretton Woods institutions initially used the same facilities (financing mechanisms) that they used for countries undergoing normal development. Thus, countries like El Salvador and Bosnia and Herzegovina negotiated stand-by arrangements (SBAs) of 12 to 18 months with the IMF at normal (non-concessional) terms. As a result, post-conflict countries often did not draw funds, instead using the facility as a "precautionary" arrangement. Having an SBA, however, facilitated access to other types of financing, including from the World Bank. The Bank lent under the Structural Adjustment Loan (SAL) facility, which allowed countries to carry out reforms to increase their productive capacity. This facility was approved in 1980. Turkey was the first country to use it to finance high priority imports to improve its capacity in agriculture and industry.

In 1994, the IMF Interim Committee recognized for the first time the special needs and problems of countries emerging from conflict and requested the Executive Board to make recommendations in this area. As a result, in 1995 the Fund expanded the scope of its emergency assistance facility to include post-conflict countries, in addition to those recovering from natural disasters. This facility is supported by policy advice and in many cases by technical assistance to rebuild the capacity for macroeconomic policymaking.

For a country to be eligible for Emergency Post-Conflict Assistance (EPCA), certain conditions must be present: disruption of institutional and administrative capacity, sufficient capacity for planning and policy implementation, and urgent balance-of-payments needs. The country must also show a commitment to carrying out an IMF-supported program under an SBA, or extended fund facility (EFF). IMF financing would help the country directly and by catalyzing support from other donors, since Fund support must be part of a concerted international effort. These conditions limited eligibility for EPCA to countries in the transition to peace.[35]

More importantly, a country can have access to EPCA only if it is current with its obligations to the Fund (that is, it has no outstanding arrears). In some cases, EPCA is used to repay bridge loans drawn to pay arrears to the Fund, and in some countries, loans had to wait until the country's membership procedures were finalized.[36]

Given the tragic economic and social conditions that often prevail in post-conflict countries, the terms of EPCA and its use to pay arrears to the Fund seem odd and are topics that deserve urgent public debate. Although the EPCA involves quick disbursement of funds and does not impose performance criteria (conditionality), it does not offer concessional terms and it was originally limited to only 25 percent of the member's quota. As a result, this facility has proved inadequate for the immediate needs of countries in the transition to peace, because the percentage was too low and the logic of the assistance mechanism is reversed. At a critical point when peace-related programs may make the difference between giving peace a chance and reverting to war, the country has to pay normal (non-concessional) rates to borrow from the Fund and has to repay the emergency loan within $3^{1}/_{4}$ and 5 years. While servicing the EPCA at these harsh terms, the country is expected simultaneously to establish "a good track record" to qualify for facilities at concessional terms.

Furthermore, establishing a good track record often requires that the country "resist political pressure to increase spending ahead of...elections, and to sustain and deepen the effort to contain the wage bill, given the large share of public expenditure absorbed by salary payments."[37] The dogmatism and the "development as usual" approach to policymaking that the IMF has often preached have not contributed to national reconciliation, and have even endangered peace. Even in cases where it would be difficult for a country to increase wages, it is the wrong approach for the IMF to say it. It is up to governments to decide on their spending priorities for there is nothing as important in the immediate post-conflict transition as to improve the well-being of public servants and other groups that need to feel part of the peace process and have a stake in it. If the population at large does not perceive a "peace dividend" in terms of improved living conditions, the transition will not be sustainable. Indeed, the EPCA facility's lack of concessional terms implies that it often takes a few years for countries in the transition to peace to become beneficiaries of concessional terms, which often delays implementation of critical peace-related programs and poses an additional threat to the transition.[38]

Not surprisingly, since the meetings of the Interim Committee and the Development Committee in April 1998, there have been calls by member states, including by the G-8 at their meeting in Birmingham in May of that year, for additional and timely assistance to post-conflict countries. Despite these calls, little has been done to improve the terms, conditions, and timing of financing to post-conflict countries in the immediate transition to peace. In fact, changes took place only with regard to facilities for which post-conflict countries had to establish a track record. Thus, in early 2001, an administered account was established at the Fund to subsidize the rate of charge on EPCA, but only to members eligible for the Poverty Reduction and Growth Facility (PRGF).[39]

Since the late 1990s, several post-conflict countries became potentially eligible for debt reduction under the HIPC Initiative, but in order to qualify they also needed to establish a track record under the IMF- and International Development Association (IDA)-supported programs (IDA is the concessional lending arm of the World Bank for the world's poorest countries).[40] Moreover, the EPCA facility remains inadequate for the needs of post-conflict countries. In 2004, the IMF extended it for up to three years, with an increase in resources up to 50 percent of quota, although with an annual limit of 25 percent as of end-2006.[41]

Since the mid-1990s, financing of post-conflict reconstruction has increasingly taken place through the establishments of Trust Funds, often administered by the World Bank.[42] In addition to the regular performance-based IDA allocations, the World Bank created a Post-Conflict Fund (PCF), the LICUS Implementation Trust Fund, and a Multi-Donor Trust Fund to deal with post-conflict and LICUS countries. Through different trusts, the World Bank has channeled grants—as opposed to loans—for short-term budget support and emergency projects. Nevertheless, UNDP and the UN agencies continue to be a more important source of grants to these countries. These organizations are funded by voluntary contributions from member states and, since they provide grants rather than loans, have a strong presence in failed states and other low income countries.

The Trust Fund for Bosnia and Herzegovina created a precedent, since the Bank did not wait for its membership and normalization of arrears. Given the country's needs and special circumstances in its transition to peace, a series of emergency projects to help jump-start the reconstruction effort were to be financed with a $150 million trust fund in February 1996.[43]

In March 2002, the Afghan Reconstruction Trust Fund (ARTF) was created to provide a coordinated financing mechanism to enable Afghanistan's interim administration to finance budgetary and other priority expenditure, as well as specific investment projects that are crucial for the country. The World Bank administered this fund—which covered more than half of the funding required for the operating budget—under the supervision of a management committee comprising the ADB, the IsDB, and the UNDP.

In January 2004, the World Bank and the UNDP (representing the UNDG) launched the International Reconstruction Fund Facility for Iraq (IRFFI) to facilitate the channeling of donors' funding and coordinate other support for reconstruction and development. This was the first time that the two organizations administered a multi-donor reconstruction trust fund. However, because of security and other problems, reconstruction has lagged in Iraq, so experience with this fund does not allow us to draw any conclusion on whether it is the right trust fund model for the future.

The development of trust funds under concessional terms has been a welcome development, particularly since it has allowed financing of critical recurrent expenses such as civil servants' salaries and pensions. These expenses were difficult to finance in the past, owing to donors' reluctance to provide budgetary support for recurrent expenditure.

Increased collaboration between the UN and the Bretton Woods institutions

When de Soto and I wrote our *Foreign Policy* article in the early 1990s, our objective was to call attention to the fact that separate, simultaneous political and economic activities overseen by the UN and the Bretton Woods institutions in El Salvador—the first comprehensive UN peacebuilding operation— were on a collision course. We argued that the lack of operational integration had put peace at risk soon after the signature of the peace agreement in January 1992. We favored Boutros-Ghali's integrated approach to human security, according to which military, political, economic, and social issues would be addressed jointly and coherently rather than separately, as was the practice at the time.[44]

Since then, the situation has clearly changed for the better. In the summer of 1993, the Secretary-General and the Managing Director of the IMF Michel Camdessus, agreed to promote a coordinated effort in post-conflict peacebuilding on the basis of *An Agenda for Peace*, focusing on cases where this was required imminently or in the near future. Cambodia, Haiti, and Mozambique were specifically mentioned. A meeting between the UN and the IMF took place in October to discuss the follow-up to the agreement between the heads of the two organizations. In preparation for this, the Secretary-General asked the head of the DESA to convene and chair an interdepartmental task force for the purpose of drawing up an *Inventory of Post-Conflict Peacebuilding Activities*, identifying activities and techniques relevant to post-conflict situations, as well as agencies with the required expertise. Despite the importance of economic and social issues, the *Inventory* included other peacebuilding activities in the political, legal, and institutional fields.

In 1995, after the Interim Committee recognized the special needs of post-conflict countries, the G-7 Summit in Halifax called on the Bretton Woods institutions and the UN to establish a new coordination procedure. This was necessary to facilitate a smooth transition from the emergency to the rehabilitation phase of crises and to cooperate more effectively with donor countries. After the poor experience in El Salvador, by mid-1995 the UN, the IMF, and the World Bank were working closely in peace processes in Guatemala and in Angola. In Guatemala, contrary to what had occurred earlier in El Salvador, the IMF was involved in the peace process from the very beginning, with its staff maintaining relationship with the Secretary-General's envoy, the UN Secretariat in New York, and the UNDP in the field. Consultations were particularly intensive prior to the signing of the peace agreement in 1996.[45]

In the case of Angola in the mid-1990s, the IMF also collaborated closely with the UN, both in New York and in the field. At the same time, the Fund and the UNDP jointly financed technical assistance throughout a difficult period to improve the country's management of its economic and financial resources. The IMF staff participated in the 1995 UNDP-sponsored roundtable conference convened for Angola in Brussels, and in turn organized a follow-up meeting during the IMF–World Bank Annual meetings in October 1995.

The more cooperative and integrated approach between the Bretton Woods institutions and the UN in post-conflict situations has continued in matters in which human security is at risk.[46] Correspondence between successive Secretary-Generals (first Boutros-Ghali and later Annan) and the heads of the Bretton Woods institutions from 1994 to 1997 showed close collaboration on Guatemala, Angola, and Haiti, which had been lacking in the case of El Salvador.[47]

By the turn of the century, close collaboration was taking place in Kosovo and East Timor, and even during peace negotiations, such as those in Cyprus. This is as it should be, since peace-related programs have financial implications that must be considered early on in designing peace agreements and reconstruction strategies. As a result of the problems faced in El Salvador, the UN became more aware of this, and acknowledged that peace requires macroeconomic stability.[48] At the same time, the Fund explicitly recognized the need for increased flexibility in setting economic objectives and targets to allow for peace-related expenditure, including through access to some domestic financing, despite its potentially inflationary impact.[49]

However, a truly integrated approach between these organizations has remained difficult to achieve, despite the significant improvements in their collaboration over the years. This was reflected in the position taken by World Bank President James Wolfensohn when he participated for the first time in the High-Level Segment of the ECOSOC in 1995. According to Wolfensohn, he was all for cooperation, but not for being coordinated.[50]

Cooperation and coordination within the UN System

Many analysts have long argued that member states need to rethink conceptually and operationally the involvement of the UN system as a whole in the humanitarian and development fields. Despite much talk about UN reform, only changes at the margin have been achieved so far. Under normal development conditions, most countries house several UN bodies—each with its own program and budget—most of which respond to their own headquarters, board, or governing council. Overall planning and coordination between these bodies is often discussed, but very little of it actually occurs. Each institution often designs its national programs following a general model, with little concern for the particular nature or idiosyncrasy of the case at hand, or for what other institutions are doing in the country. The problems that this creates have been tremendous, both in the field and in competing for donors' funding.[51]

The need to rethink conceptually and operationally the involvement of the UN system is even more urgent in countries in transition from war to peace, where the link between peace and development is critical. It is in these countries where the international community's involvement is at its highest and, for that reason, the potential distortions and inefficiencies are greatest. A large UN presence burdens the capacity of the national authorities to deal separately with the different agencies, creates all kinds of distortions in the national economy, and is a waste of taxpayers' money due to duplication and overlapping mandates. Moreover, endless turf battles and competition for funding at donors' meetings is the rule rather than the exception. The UN system often spreads its resources so thinly that they hardly make a difference, rather than pooling them strategically according to the specific comparative advantages of the different programs and agencies. All this has contributed to the misallocation of resources in post-conflict countries—both human and financial.

As a rule, the larger the international support for a peacebuilding operation, the greater the distortions of the international presence in the post-conflict economy. This is inevitable due to the presence, not only of officials from the UN system, but also of expatriates from other multilateral agencies, bilateral donors, and NGOs. These expatriates, with access to large foreign exchange resources, bid for a limited number of qualified local professionals and other workers, viable office space, and housing, food, and all types of services. In doing so, they drive up prices, rents, and wages and deprive the national civil service of their most qualified people. Just as worrisome, by not doing what they were trained to do, qualified people would lose their skills and this would affect the future productive capacity of the country. Engineers or doctors, for example, working as drivers or translators for the UN for many years, may find it difficult to go back to their professions. For the transition to be effective, these distortions have to be kept to a minimum. Otherwise, nationals in post-conflict countries will resent the international presence and make the transition more difficult.[52]

Only an integrated approach to human security—as proposed by Secretary-General Boutros-Ghali in his *Agenda for Peace*—can avoid the distortions and inefficiencies that have plagued the UN system. In 1992, as a first step, the Secretary-General created UN Interim Offices in seven former Soviet republics to facilitate the transition to democracy and a market economy in those countries by providing a unified UN presence. The idea behind integrated offices was that the UN Resident Representative would be the only high-level UN representative in the country. All other programs and agencies would be represented within the same office, at a lower technical level. However, when he tried to extend his policy of integrated offices to other countries, he failed, in what one of his close advisors referred to as a "finger-burning experience."[53]

Secretary-General Annan also made efforts to improve coordination at the field level. His efforts included a much less ambitious model. In 1997, the Secretary-General created the UNDG, bringing together the operational agencies and UN departments working on development. Its purpose was to establish, in a coordinated way, policies and procedures to allow the UN system to work together and to support strategies and programs aimed at poverty alleviation and other development goals. In particular, the UNDG is geared towards the achievement of the Millennium Development Goals (MDGs), and thus is not an appropriate coordination mechanism for post-conflict countries, which have special needs and face mostly political challenges. In fact, the Secretary-General never clearly specified the mechanism for the UNDG and the peacekeeping or peacebuilding missions in the field to collaborate in matters of peace and development, leaving the seat of responsibility for post-conflict reconstruction adrift.

At the same time, some of the UN Interim Offices became UN Houses in the new millennium, after agencies joined under a single roof. The Secretary-General created a few new UN Houses as well. However, although physical integration may improve the situation marginally, it does not eliminate the other problems and distortions created by the large number of UN agencies and programs in the field, which put tremendous strain on the capacity of weak governments in developing countries to deal with them.

Ad hoc institutional structures were established in different post-conflict countries when a peacekeeping or peacebuilding operation was put in place. In some cases, one of the deputies SRSG was appointed from UNDP to also carry out the Resident Coordinator's functions. As I mentioned earlier this is the case in Haiti and Liberia, among others. In other cases, as for example, Sierra Leone (see Figure 1), the head of mission has the UNDG directly under him, without someone with the right credentials making the link between the political and economic objectives of the transition. Both structures promote a "development as usual" approach to reconstruction rather than an integrated approach to human security.

In November 2003, soon after the tragedy of the attack on the UN in Baghdad, the Security Council brought UNAMI (UN Assistant Mission for Iraq) to a minimum. At the same time, the UNDG started an integrated team approach, "with the lightest footprint in Iraq" to avoid terrorist attacks. The purpose was to minimize the UN presence in the country, by engaging more closely with a network of Iraqi partners that UN agencies had built over the years. By early 2004, the UN country team (UNCT) had prepared a comprehensive Strategic Plan for Assistance to Iraq. Innovative aspects of this plan included grouping areas of assistance into ten clusters for joint planning, programming and implementation; sharing premises, transportation, communications, procurement, and administration; and strengthening advice, support, and assistance to the UN national staff members who continued to work across the country. The so-called "UN cluster approach" was a way to provide assistance to key Iraqi ministries such as the Ministry of Planning and Development Cooperation. In the organizational chart of UNAMI, the SRSG has two deputies, one for political matters and the other for humanitarian coordination. No institutional arrangement exists, though, to deal with economic reconstruction per se (UNAMI 2004).[54]

For Iraq and other governments in such situations, to be able to work with the UNCT as one entity is indeed a welcome development. What is clearly missing in UNAMI's structure is a way to integrate the work of the UNCT with the political work of UNAMI, all under the SRSG leadership. First, by having a DSRSG for humanitarian affairs coordinate work on economic reconstruction, the UN is conflating activities that are clearly distinct, and should be done by different actors. As I will discuss in detail in Chapter 6, humanitarian assistance is for consumption purposes (and hence humanitarian) and only reconstruction activities can create sustainable investment and employment in the country. This distinction is critical in avoiding aid dependency in the future. Second, the SRSG will need to rule if the political and economic objectives ever clash, as they often do. Since SRSGs are generally selected for their political and diplomatic skills, they will need good advice on economic reconstruction, which the current institutional organization does not contemplate. Unless the SRSG has this capacity, he or she will not be able to provide effective support to the government in this area. At any rate, the capacity of missions to deal with economic reconstruction should be institutionalized rather than being dependent on the personal qualifications and experience of the SRSG.

In November 2006, the newly established High-Level Panel on System-Wide Coherence recommended that, in order to carry out its "development functions," the UN should "deliver as one" at country level, with one leader, one program, one budget, and, where appropriate, one office, along the lines proposed by Boutros-Ghali. According to this latest proposal, should the country want it, all UN program activities are to be consolidated at the country level. An empowered Resident Coordinator should manage the "One UN" country program. The proposal also contemplates restructuring the UNDP to strengthen its operational work and focus it on policy coherence and positioning of the UN country team, while withdrawing from sector-focused policy and capacity work carried out by other UN organizations.

A year later, in November 2007, the government and the UN system in Rwanda signed the first "One UN" program. By signing this pact, sixteen UN agencies operating in Rwanda will commit to creating a more efficient and cost effective UN to speed up the work towards achieving the Millennium Development Goals and improve the lives of Rwandans. Seven other countries are likely to adopt the One UN soon. Although it is still too soon to be overly optimistic, this new reform is certainly in the right direction to minimize the UN presence and avoid the large distortions that it otherwise creates.

But, the One UN program is not enough for an integrated approach to human security, as Boutros-Ghali proposed. Although this program would allow minimization of the UN presence and the distortions it creates, it is not, by itself, enough to enable the UN to integrate the political and economic objectives of the transition from war to peace. The latter could only be done effectively by giving the peacekeeping or peacebuilding mission in the field, and its SRSG, the capacity to deal with the technical aspects of economic reconstruction. Thus, my proposal to create a National Reconstruction Coordination Office (NRCO) (see Figure 3) would provide the institutional capacity through which the SRSG can follow an integrated strategy to human security.

6 Issues for debate on international assistance

> "Along with the great problem of maintaining the peace, we must solve the problem of the pittance of food and coal and homes. Neither of these problems can be solved alone."
>
> George C. Marshall, November 1945[1]

As discussed in Chapter 2, the type of wide-ranging debate that took place after the two world wars concerning economic reconstruction has been largely absent following the Cold War. Given the large demand and the increasingly troubling record with economic reconstruction, it is never too late to initiate a serious public discussion about how to improve the international community's capacity in this regard. Stronger capacity for international assistance, in conjunction with a sound strategy at the country level—the topic of Part V of this book—would greatly improve the countries' chances of success in consolidating peace and fully devoting their resources and energies to the normal challenges of development and poverty alleviation.

To be sure, the debate stimulated by our *Foreign Policy* article on the need to integrate the political and economic aspects of peacebuilding, discussed in Chapter 5, resulted in much-improved coordination between the United Nations and the international financial institutions (IFIs). Some mechanisms such as the creation of the UNDG and the One UN, discussed in Chapter 5, have also sought to improve coordination among UN agencies. However, coordination has proved to be a necessary but not a sufficient condition for successful reconstruction. Two other factors are critical. On one hand, there is a need for greater flexibility and more aid mechanisms on concessional terms from the IFIs and other donors. On the other hand, post-conflict countries must assume greater responsibility and accountability for dealing with aid and reconstruction issues. Thus, the purpose of this chapter is to discuss issues of aid, budgets, debt, conditionality, concessionality, and technical assistance related to economic reconstruction and to propose measures to improve the mechanisms and capabilities of the international system as a whole to carry out effective reconstruction in the future.

Official aid flows

Countries coming out of armed conflict or socio-political upheaval find it particularly difficult to foster domestic savings or to attract private capital in the short run. At the same time, the so-called "peace dividend"—which in fiscal terms relates to the possibility of releasing resources for non-military purposes resulting from the fall in military expenditure—is usually limited in countries where conflict has been basically foreign-financed. This is because financing will wither as the conflict winds down.

For this reason, post-conflict countries rely primarily on official aid flows, from both bilateral and multilateral donors.[2] Financing is unquestionably a critical ingredient of, and constraint on, economic reconstruction. Foreign governments often spend large amounts of money to support one side or another during a conflict, or on their own military, if they lead an invasion and occupation of the country, as with the United States in Afghanistan and Iraq.[3] By contrast, financing for peacetime is often not so forthcoming. However, financing reconstruction could be a good investment for the international community if it helps the country avoid relapsing into conflict.

There is an increasingly high demand for official flows, mostly in the form of grants, for development and environmental issues ranging from the fight against HIV/AIDS to poverty alleviation to climate change.[4] This, in conjunction with the fiscal constraints and the recessionary and inflationary pressures faced by major donor countries, resulting from the 2007 banking and liquidity crisis as well as the increase in the price of oil, makes them more likely than ever to cut their financial and technical support and shift their attention elsewhere as soon as the conflict winds down—and certainly before peace is consolidated. Because foreign financing and technical assistance are such an essential element of post-conflict economic reconstruction, the international community should recognize that, by not supporting a country in this critical transition, it may lose its investment of time and resources in ending the conflict. Indeed, the cost of reconstruction is but a fraction of what would be required for humanitarian assistance, military intervention, and peacekeeping operations in case the country reverts to war. Nowhere has this been more vividly demonstrated in recent years than in Timor-Leste, Iraq, and Lebanon.[5]

An emphasis on the role and responsibility of the international community in supporting economic reconstruction, should not, however, detract from the responsibility of governments and other domestic actors to use aid effectively and transparently. Nor should it detract from the responsibility of governments to provide appropriate legal, fiscal, judicial, and institutional frameworks essential to fostering domestic savings and attracting private capital inflows as soon as possible. Although such frameworks take time to develop, without them a country will be unable permanently to reintegrate large numbers of people into productive activities, let alone move onto a development path, regardless of how much foreign money is poured into its economy. As discussed in the case of Kosovo, aid dependency should be avoided, which implies that reactivation of growth and employment should take priority.

"TIED" AID

Donors often require a quid pro quo for their assistance in the form of recruiting their own people for the implementation of projects or requiring the purchase of inputs from their own countries. This is known as "tied aid," and it is often motivated by political considerations, in addition to economic interests. The case studies in the following chapters will discuss experiences in which tied aid, not only slowed down and complicated post-conflict reconstruction, but also led to programs that the country did not want and to employment of foreign experts for tasks that nationals should have carried out.

The Marshall Plan offers interesting insights with respect to this and other aid issues. In raising support for the Plan, Dulles (1993: 81–7) argued that "outright gifts" were unwise. In his view, the US should not give away the nation's assets without obtaining in return what they could reasonably require from the receiving governments. However, in addition to tying part of the aid to goods and services provided by the United States, the Marshall Plan included a monetary quid pro quo for part of recipient countries' debt, which is usually absent from current reconstruction assistance, as it is from development aid.

The issue of a monetary quid pro quo was widely debated at the time. As a result, the Foreign Aid Act of 1947 specified that countries that received aid from the US and could not pay for the assistance in dollars should set aside a "commensurate amount in local currency at the going rate of exchange of the value of the goods delivered, irrespective of the price at which they may be sold." This special account would be used within the country, subject to United States approval, for relief purposes, including American expenses related to the provision of such aid, or other expenditure required by the US government (embassies, educational grants). It would also be used for the production and purchase of strategic raw materials (mostly from undeveloped resources in colonial territories) that the US sought to stockpile, and to provide technical assistance to support reconstruction efforts in the country. President Harry Truman's 1947 report to Congress on the Marshall Plan suggested that the local currency funds could also be used to assist financial reform and currency stabilization, retire national debt, and cover local currency costs of projects sponsored by the World Bank.[6]

A quid pro quo in aid to post-conflict countries in the post-Cold War era could improve its effectiveness and should be a matter for debate. While humanitarian aid could be provided through grants, a quid pro quo could be demanded from reconstruction aid. This would give donors an incentive to extend and sustain aid flows and would create a larger incentive among recipient countries to use aid productively. It would also contribute to reactivating the local economies, although this requires discipline to avoid excessive inflationary pressures. Furthermore, many countries in reconstruction are rich in natural resources, and donors could use domestic accounts to help them explore and reactivate production of commodities and minerals in exchange for long-term contracts to purchase such goods at international market prices, as occurred in the context of the Marshall Plan. This could serve to enlarge the donor community, particularly by including resource-hungry countries such as China and India, into a more transparent and accountable system.

POST-CONFLICT AID VERSUS DEVELOPMENT AID

In a study that stands out from much of the IMF's "development as usual" research, Demekas, McHugh, and Kosma (2002b) correctly argue that "post-conflict aid" is different from conventional "development aid" because of these countries' environment and circumstances. They also correctly argue that conflict normally redirects economic activity towards rent-seeking and criminality, while productive activity collapses and needs to be revived in the post-conflict phase.

As they point out, there are two types of aid in post-conflict situations, each with clear objectives. First, "humanitarian aid," which provides for a minimum level of basic consumption, is necessary to address the humanitarian crisis that normally follows the aftermath of war. Second, "reconstruction aid" is necessary to address the rehabilitation of basic infrastructure and services, to improve security and law enforcement, as well as to implement other measures aimed at strengthening the country's institutional framework. Thus, the objectives of these two types of aid are fundamentally different from the objective of "development aid," which is to supplement domestic savings, boost long-term growth, and reduce poverty.[7] As discussed in Chapter 3, development aid also exhibits a stable pattern, with humanitarian and reconstruction assistance often reaching a peak during or soon after the transition to peace, and falling drastically soon after. As Demekas *et al.* (p. 4) starkly put it, post-conflict aid comes in a large sudden burst, whereas development aid is a steady trickle.[8]

The authors also rightly argue that, for two reasons, post-conflict humanitarian and reconstruction aid can be expected to have a different impact on recipient countries. First, humanitarian aid, provided mostly at the early stages of the transition to peace, is used to support basic consumption needs (food, shelter, medical care). Thus, this type of aid should wither as soon as the population reaches minimum levels of consumption. Second, because reconstruction aid is used to rehabilitate infrastructure (including public utilities) and establish the basic legal, regulatory, and institutional framework, it contributes directly to improve productivity and hence increases the country's productive capacity.

These findings suggest important policy implications. First, while humanitarian aid improves welfare in the short run, it will not lead to investment and capital accumulation in the long run, since it is consumed rather than saved. Furthermore, by providing goods rather than helping countries to produce them, humanitarian aid is likely to create distortions and dependencies, and thus should be restricted in time. Second, the economic consequences of reconstruction aid are more complex, and depend on how much of it is saved, how productively it is invested, and the impact it has on labor supply and on the exchange rate. In this regard, reconstruction aid should be targeted at improving infrastructure and basic services, as well as creating employment. Humanitarian aid should be provided up to the point where it does not create a disincentive for people to work. Moreover, the so-called Dutch disease—the impact that aid flows in foreign exchange have on the appreciation of national currencies—needs to be managed to avoid a sharp decrease in countries' export competitiveness. These issues, critical in the design of an effective post-conflict reconstruction strategy, will be discussed in Parts IV and V.

Although Demekas *et al.* provide additional support for my argument that post-conflict reconstruction is not normal development, their final conclusion is not consistent with it. I fully share their conclusion that, under normal development conditions, aid should give high priority to investment in infrastructure, institutions that boost international trade, and public services that facilitate private-sector development. However, I argue that post-conflict economic reconstruction and normal development are strikingly different because, in addition to setting the framework for growth and development, effective reconstruction must above all promote national reconciliation and the consolidation of peace. Thus, I strongly question their recommendation to give lower priority to projects that do not promote the production of tradable goods, such as, for example, "sports, religious, or cultural facilities." In post-conflict countries, the rate of return of investing reconstruction aid in social and cultural activities, as well as in strengthening civilian police forces, disarmament, demobilization, and reintegration of former combatants, and confidence-building measures among warring factions, is likely to be high.

Many analysts argue that, like development aid, reconstruction aid is more effective once the country has improved its managerial and absorptive capacity. In fact, some claim that aid is more effective after 3–5 years, at a time when it is likely to fall.[9] In post-conflict conditions, this would mean serious delays that could have tragic consequences. Staines (2004: 6), for example, provides evidence that the productivity of reconstruction aid can be high in the initial post-conflict period, when the government is committed to following sound macroeconomic policies, particularly if assistance is provided to the budget in support of stabilization. In his view, direct budgetary assistance could be provided while meeting concerns over governance, through donor trust funds to help pay for the civil service wage bill, debt servicing, and other recurrent expenditures. As the case studies will show, although this can facilitate the difficult immediate transition to peace, it is still resisted by donors. While aid flows are normally largest in the first three years, the immediate transition is often difficult to finance.[10]

CASH VERSUS IN-KIND AID, AND GRANTS VERSUS LOANS

The experience of the Marshall Plan is also relevant to the discussion of different types of aid and their policy implications. Aid is often given not in cash but in kind. If aid is in kind, transportation costs and logistics become an important issue. Moreover, if aid is given in terms of basic grains, for example, the impact on prices of local production will need to be considered so as not to discourage it. Taking these considerations into account, donor and recipient countries must decide what type of assistance is best, and whether it should be through grants or loans.[11]

When the United States (as the main donor country) and the sixteen European countries planned economic reconstruction of Europe after World War II, it was decided that the "three F's" (food, fuel, and fertilizer) were critical "to keep body and soul together, so that there will be men and women in Europe with the strength and the will to work." But humanitarian aid alone would have created long-term dependency on the United States. Thus, the strategy financed by the Marshall Plan contemplated an initial aid phase in which the three F's were provided jointly with tools (farm implements, mining machinery, trucks, and transportation equipment) so that Europeans could increase their own production of these goods. Some commodities, such as cotton, and some incentive goods, such as tobacco, were also judged to be necessary imports (although many argued that this policy was merely an excuse to support the tobacco interests in the United States).

In the reconstruction phase that followed, capital goods needed for rehabilitation of European industry and utilities (including power plants), transport and other equipment, as well as some basic commodities had to be imported as well. This is where the World Bank and the private sector were heavily involved. The Marshall Plan provided incentives to private-sector involvement by providing some guarantees for political risk, but imports in general were financed through loans rather than grants.[12]

The current context is different from that of the Marshall Plan in one important way. While the Plan contemplated the reconstruction of Europe and eventually the creation of a large market for US goods, at the same time the Plan was building Europe's competitiveness to the detriment of that of the United States. This aid dilemma is nowhere present nowadays. Poor, developing countries will not become competitive with donor countries in world markets, or even in their own. On the contrary, post-conflict countries in the developing world often produce critical commodities that can be exported to donor countries in exchange for capital and other goods. In fact, by helping post-conflict countries develop their own natural resources, donors could benefit in terms of the availability and cost of such resources. Thus, except in a few cases, such as textiles, donor countries would not be building competitiveness in these countries at the expense of their own. Indeed, as these countries recover they will become new markets for donor countries' exports.

AID DEPENDENCY

In the current context of post-conflict reconstruction in low-development areas, countries are more prone to aid dependency than European countries were at the time of the Marshall Plan. This reflects the significantly higher amount of aid relative to GDP in the post-Cold War period than was the case at the time of the Marshall Plan, when it amounted to slightly over 2 percent of recipient countries' GDPs.[13] A large amount of aid, like in the case of Kosovo, where grants amounted to 45 percent of GDP in 2001–2, normally leads to aid dependency rather than sustained growth.

President Truman's assessment that no aid can bring recovery unless countries take charge of their production and trade effectively remains valid today. Aid dependency must be avoided, and aid should thus be discontinued where countries do not use it responsibly. Only countries that are willing to do their part can enlarge their post-conflict growth possibilities and improve their prospects of resolving future conflicts peacefully. Corrupt and ineffective use of aid will not be Pareto optimal (welfare-improving) for the country itself, and may even lead to further conflict by increasing discontent and exacerbating the income gap, while at the same time depriving other countries of resources.

Conditionality

Conditionality is often discussed in relation to the IFIs, but bilateral donors have also imposed it over the years to ensure proper and productive use of their aid. In the case of the Marshall Plan, each of the countries receiving aid was required to enter into a contract with the United States. Recipients pledged to increase industrial and agricultural production, stabilize currencies, establish proper exchange rates and restore confidence in the monetary system, reduce trade barriers, and make efficient use of aid received within the framework of a joint program for economic recovery in Europe. They also promised to stimulate production and procurement of specified raw materials for stock-piling purposes in the United States; set aside the local-currency equivalent of aid furnished in the form of grants to be used in a manner agreed with the United States; and inform the United States about how aid was used. The report on the Marshall Plan that Truman sent to Congress enumerated these points (Dulles, 1993: 79–80).

Dulles also noted that the United States was not telling the countries of Europe what kind of government or social structure they should adopt. Nor did the United States explicitly say what it would do if beneficiary countries adopted a policy that the United States would not support, such as national-izing an industry. To do either would have been construed as direct political interference in the domestic affairs of these countries. However, the Foreign Aid Act of 1947 gave the US president discretion to terminate aid whenever he found that conditions had changed, that it was not being used effectively, or that it was no longer consistent with national interests.

ECONOMIC CONDITIONALITY

Of course, the IFIs also impose conditionality. IMF conditionality refers to the commitment that countries make to follow economic and financial policies—specified in an IMF-sponsored economic program (a "policy program")—if they want to borrow from the Fund. The program is described in a Letter of Intent, which often has a Memorandum of Economic and Financial Policies attached to it, that accompanies the country's request for IMF financing. Most loans contemplate phased disbursements to ensure that countries comply with their commitments. For monitoring purposes, the Fund relies on "prior actions" (measures that the country agrees to take prior to the approval or renewal of the IMF loan) and "performance criteria" (which have to be met for the disbursement to take place). The performance criteria are either "quanti-tative" (macroeconomic variables such as the level of international reserves, monetary or credit aggregates, the fiscal balance, and external borrowing) or "structural" measures that are critical to the program's success. The latter include, inter alia, financial sector reform, social security reform, and the restructuring of critical sectors. Even if the country does not borrow from the Fund, but only wants to use the program as a "precautionary" facility, funds will be potentially available only as long as the country satisfies the conditions.

The IMF argues that, given the revolving financing mechanism involved, conditionality is needed to ensure that its loans are well used and that countries will be able to repay them, so that it can lend to other members in need. At the same time, the Fund provides assurances to borrowers that if they comply with the specified conditionality, the Fund will continue supporting their programs, including through additional lending. However, critics of the IMF, most notably Nobel Laureate Joseph Stiglitz, argue that conditionality is a way for the Fund to impose its policies—often the wrong ones—on countries in balance-of-payments crises.[14]

In response to criticism, the IMF established new conditionality guidelines in 2002, replacing its guidelines from 1979. In the Fund's view, the new guidelines focus and streamline conditionality to promote national ownership of economic and financial policies, limit it to the minimum necessary to ensure the achievement of program objectives, and tailor policies more closely to members' circumstances. However, the new guidelines do not make any reference to post-conflict countries, although it would seem reasonable that conditionality for countries coming out of war should take this into account and be more flexible.

World Bank conditionality has also evolved. Like the IMF, the Bank increasingly recognizes the need for country ownership to carry out effective development policies, and has streamlined conditionality to actions critical for achieving desired results. At the same time, the Bank's focus has shifted from short-term economic distortions to a medium-term institutional and social agenda, thus de-emphasizing state-owned enterprise restructuring and privatization, policies that the Bank pursued in the 1990s. World Bank conditionality also depends on the level of country development, focusing on structural policies in better performers and on basic public-sector variables in countries that perform more poorly.

POLITICAL CONDITIONALITY

It is interesting that some analysts who have criticized Bretton Woods economic conditionality as too harsh, and would have preferred stabilization to proceed at a slower pace in post-conflict situations, have advocated empowering these institutions further with political conditionality. In a study by Boyce *et al.* (1995: 83–9) on El Salvador, the authors criticized the IFIs for not conditioning their assistance specifically in support of the peace agreements—what they labeled "peace conditionality"—through either formal performance criteria and/or informal policy dialogue. They argued that the Bretton Woods institutions could have pressed the government more aggressively to pursue domestic resource mobilization and increases in the tax burden, as well as shifts in the composition of public expenditures away from the military and in favor of health, education, and peace-related programs.[15]

The World Bank Operations Evaluation Department (2000) argued against peace conditionality on the grounds that the Bank's Articles of Agreement specify that the proceeds of Bank financing are to be "without regard to political or other non-economic influence or consideration."[16] However, it also concluded that "if tax effort and the pattern of public expenditures have a direct bearing on post-conflict reconstruction, as they did in El Salvador, it is legitimate to include these parameters in the conditionality agenda."[17] Boyce (2004) reports evidence on peace conditionality by the Bretton Woods institutions in the case of Croatia, where loans were withheld until the government surrendered ten war-crime suspects indicted by the International Criminal Tribunal for the Former Yugoslavia (ICTY) in The Hague. In fact, an ongoing EFF program, in which all economic conditions had been met, was discontinued at the insistence of the United States.

There are two important factors, in my view, that militate against the general imposition of peace conditionality. First, these institutions do not have the political expertise to judge and monitor whether the government and former guerrilla groups are complying with peace agreements in matters of human rights, military behavior, police and judicial reform, and similar areas. Second, if compliance is measured in terms of explicit economic targets (for example, tax revenue or public expenditure) or political targets (for example, extradition of war criminals), non-compliance may derail economic programs necessary for a successful war-to-peace transition that the Bretton Woods institutions would otherwise have been able to support.

In Guatemala, for example, where the peace agreements ended a war spanning close to four decades, the accords envisaged important political, social, and economic changes, including substantial increases in tax collection that would support higher public spending in the social sectors. The UN-brokered agreement contemplated an increase in tax revenue from 8.5 percent of GDP in 1996 to 12 percent by the year 2000 (later on extended to 2002). Because the Fund insisted that the country comply with the tax revenue increase specified in the peace agreement (in fact imposing peace conditionality), and the government failed to achieve this target, relations were strained in subsequent years and an agreement with the Fund could not be reached until 2002. Without there being a viable economic program, donor countries and multilateral institutions reduced financing commitments. As a result, financing for the peace process was short, particularly given the high expectations that the peace agreement had created.[18]

The agreement in Guatemala was much more ambitious than that of El Salvador where benefits of the peace agreements had been restricted to former combatants of both sides and their supporters who had occupied land during the war. By contrast, the Guatemala agreement contemplated major economic and social reform, encompassing not only the groups directly affected by the war, but the overall indigenous population which accounted for about 60 percent of the total. This would have required huge resources. Because an IMF-supported program was often a prerequisite for other international assistance, IMF-imposed peace conditionality made the implementation of the peace agreement more difficult without improving the chances of achieving the revenue objectives necessary for economic and social development. Even at the end of 2006, tax revenue remained below 10.5 percent of GDP.

While in the next chapter I will discuss in detail how stringent economic conditionality imposed by the IFIs in the early part of the Salvadoran transition to peace endangered the peace process, economic conditionality imposed by the UN in the Guatemalan peace agreement endangered its implementation. Thus, although it is unquestionably desirable that the Bretton Woods institutions support the peace process, explicit peace conditionality may impede their normal policy dialogue with the authorities and their support for economic programs. Because, as discussed earlier, an IMF-supported program has so far been an implicit condition for other assistance, failure to conclude a program has often had a negative impact on the population, creating an additional burden in post-conflict situations, in which reactivation of growth and employment creation are imperative.

A better proposal might be to adopt a mechanism like the one that the new IMF conditionality guidelines contemplate with regard to coordination between the Fund and the World Bank. This mechanism is based on the concept of "lead agency," according to which each agency takes the analytical lead within its core areas. When conditions in Fund-supported programs apply to areas of World Bank competence, the design and monitoring of such conditions are to be based on the Bank's advice as much as possible.

Along the same lines, Bretton Woods peace conditionality could be coordinated with the UN—perhaps through the Security Council. Thus, any such conditionality that the Bretton Woods institutions would want to impose on post-conflict countries would have to be coordinated with the UN as the lead agency. According to this system, the UN would advise these institutions on whether the country is complying with specific political commitments and peace-related programs.[19] This system would have two advantages. First, the Fund and the Bank would not have to make decisions on issues well beyond their competence and capabilities. Second, it would increase collaboration and help integrate the activities of the UN and the Bretton Woods institutions in post-conflict situations.

Following the same logic, the UN should not impose economic conditionality, as it did in Guatemala, even if it is in favor of the peace process. The IFIs are in a much better position to judge what is feasible from an economic point of view. Under their leadership—and in consultation with the UN—economic conditionality could be targeted towards building a healthy fiscal position, which would allow financial support for the peace process.

AN END TO PROGRAM CONDITIONALITY?

Although an IMF-supported program has so far been a precondition for financing from other institutions, developments in the world economy related to financial crises in the new millenium and increased globalization are changing the character of financing mechanisms, including conditionality. The pattern—closely analyzed in the case study on El Salvador—where countries had to enter into an IMF-sponsored program, even if they were going to use it for precautionary purposes only, seems to be changing a decade and a half later. The reason for this was that IMF-sponsored programs were a precondition for financing from the World Bank, the regional development banks, and often even from bilateral donors (including the Paris Club).[20] Although countries in general have been repaying the Fund and moving away from IMF programs[21] (with serious consequences for IMF finances as the organization ran a deficit in 2006 for the first time in its history), it remains to be seen what longer-term impact this may have on post-conflict countries. While there is not a repetition of the financial crises of the early 2000s, the IMF could well allocate more financing to post-conflict reconstruction in countries that have no access to the international capital markets.[22]

Changes in program conditionality can also affect the issue of debt relief from the Paris Club. Conditionality in the form of an IMF-supported program demonstrating the need for debt relief and measures to deal with debt problems has been attached to all Paris Club reschedulings since 1956, when Argentina agreed to meet its official creditors in Paris. Argentina has always been at the vanguard of debt default and restructuring issues and it might be setting a new precedent soon. After defaulting on its debt to private creditors in 2002, Argentina pre-paid all debts to the IMF in 2005, thus effectively concluding its IMF-supported economic program. In late 2006, Paris Club members agreed to negotiate debt restructuring with Argentina without an IMF program in place.[23] This has created precedent and is likely to be a harbinger for the future. This would be a welcome development in the case of post-conflict countries, which operate under more stringent constraints and need additional flexibility to deal with their debt problems.

Foreign debt, debt arrears, and debt relief

Countries at war usually stop paying their debt obligations and run into arrears[24] with the IFIs as well as with other creditors. The situation, however, is quite different with regard to the IFIs than it is in regard to other creditors. While other creditors—including Paris Club members and other bilateral donors and the NGOs—can decide to start lending to countries in the transition to peace, even if such countries are in arrears on outstanding debt, the IFIs cannot do so. In fact, countries need to eliminate arrears before these institutions can start lending back to them. In cases of protracted arrears, the IFIs even suspend the country's voting and related rights.[25]

Although they cannot lend in arrears, these institutions can, however, provide technical assistance, particularly in regard to solving arrears and other economic and financial problems post-conflict countries may have. The international community often gets together in solving the arrears problems of countries in the war-to-peace transitions. This happened in Haiti, Afghanistan, and many other such transitions. The IFIs are "preferred creditors" which means that, when countries start clearing arrears, they should do so with the IFIs first.

Even after the country solves the arrears problem with the IFIs, these organizations continue to support an overall solution to this problem. Despite the fact that bilateral donors may choose to finance countries in arrears, an eventual solution to the arrears problem has proved important if post-conflict reconstruction is to proceed successfully. Countries that are in arrears do not have easy access to commercial flows (suppliers' credits, other trade flows, and foreign investment). Though this may not be important in the short run when private flows are not likely at any rate, it will make reactivation of the economy difficult and unsustainable, particularly in cases where the country will have to bear in large part the cost of reconstruction. This, it could be argued, is the case in Angola, Iraq, and the DRC, resource-rich countries, with large populations and large demands for reconstruction.[26]

With respect to the solution to the arrears problem, scholars and practitioners need to debate a number of issues to determine what should be "best practice". First, the issue of timing is important. Is the immediate transition to peace the best time to find a solution to the arrears problem? On the one hand, countries undergoing reconstruction can expect to have a goodwill response from the international community to debt restructuring at this time. On the other hand, because the economy may be in a weak political and security situation, and peace-related activities may be so critical and expensive, any debt payments and fees paid to legal and financial advisors would most likely divert key resources from other most important activities. This could, and would probably, be interpreted by the population at large as a poor choice of resource allocation—as it is indeed likely to be—at such a critical point in the country's life.

Furthermore, in cases where a particular donor is leading reconstruction, such as is the case in Iraq, debt restructuring at this time might be seen as serving the donor's self interest (and that of its private companies or banks), even if that donor contributes to debt forgiveness. Because the case of Iraq illustrates the policy alternatives and the dilemmas of resolving debt arrears with the Paris Club members—which will have implications for future debt restructuring and write-offs in countries such as the DRC and other resource-rich countries—it will be discussed in Chapter 10.

Another issue to be debated is whether post-conflict countries should repay their debts at all as they move from war to peace. Many argue in favor of the application of the doctrine of "odious debt," developed in relation to the Spanish-American war in the late 19th century.[27] Others, like myself, are more inclined to find some innovative approaches to facilitate the war-to-peace transition, rather than the full elimination of previous debt which would have moral hazard implications. In this sense, a grace period and a partial forgiveness could be more effective. Countries should not get a blank check.

One possibility would be to put the debt issue (both relating to the stock of debt as well as debt arrears) on hold, for say, three years. If during those three years the country makes progress in economic reconstruction and uses new financing effectively and transparently, creditors could agree to condone, say, 65–80 percent of outstanding debt, depending on the conditions, needs, resources, and performance of the country. The rest the country could pay in domestic currency into an account under the creditors' names in one of the local banks, as was the case with aid during the Marshall Plan. Creditors could then use those funds to pay for their activities in the country (embassies, local staff salaries, purchases of local goods and services) or to support local institutions (schools, hospitals, human rights organizations, civilian police forces).

If, on the other hand, countries failed to advance the peace process, disregarded governance, and/or allowed corruption, new financing would be seriously restricted to humanitarian purposes and the country would still be liable for past outstanding debts as well as arrears. Thus, there would be incentives to good performance in the future without the moral hazard of debt forgiveness.

A third issue that needs to be debated is what countries should do if their creditors are not willing to grant some form of debt forgiveness. This is precisely the situation Iraq has with its non-Paris Club creditors. Could countries simply selectively default on their debts? In the past, countries have avoided debt default in an effort to maintain access to capital and commodity flows. However, the recent experience of Argentina has shown that creditors have a short memory. Despite the 2002 default and a so-called haircut of $80 billion (representing a debt reduction of about 75 percent), the country is not only back in the international capital markets but the spread the country has to pay to borrow reached a historical low in early 2007.[28] The Argentinian spread was not only below 200 basis points but it was only slightly higher than countries that restructured their debt without the haircut. Argentina is once again likely to set a precedent in this regard and be a harbinger of more defaults in the future.

Changing the IFI's aid and debt logic

Despite increasing efforts by the IMF to support post-conflict countries by establishing emergency assistance loans, which are usually quick disbursing and do not involve adherence to performance criteria, Fund conditions remain too tough. In particular, the need to solve in the early transition to peace arrears that have been accumulated for a long time seems unreasonable. Furthermore, there seems to be a reverse logic to their lending practices in post-conflict countries. Rather than giving concessional assistance to countries that have made the difficult decision to end the war, the Fund's Emergency Post-Conflict Assistance (EPCA) resources rely on regular financing rather than on concessional terms. Concessionality would facilitate the disarming and demobilization of former combatants and rehabilitation of basic services and infrastructure at this critical juncture.

At the present time, countries in a fragile phase as the immediate transition from war to peace is, need first to solve the question of arrears to the Fund and second, to negotiate an IMF-supported program to have access to emergency loans on non-concessional terms. From there, countries need to build up a track record and credibility in policymaking to have access to concessional resources under the Poverty Reduction and Growth Facility (PRGF). Once they do that, the countries may use the PRGF resources to repay the non-concessional emergency loan. Countries also need to build up a track record before they have access to debt relief under the Highly Indebted Poor Countries (HIPC) Initiative.[29] This puts unnecessary pressure on governments at a critical breaking- or making-point in their transition from war.

Not only is the EPCA facility expensive but countries use its resources largely to normalize relations with other creditors and remain current on external debt service. This means that positive net transfers from the Fund to post-conflict countries can be very low in the immediate aftermath of conflict. Besides the inadequacy of resources and their high cost, the whole process is burdensome for countries coming out of conflict with limited administrative and negotiating capacity.

World Bank assistance in the form of grants from the Post-Conflict Fund (PCF) and the LICUS Fund (rather than from regular Bank resources) is very limited in the immediate post-conflict period. In countries in arrears, these grants are only provided for analytical and technical assistance purposes. Furthermore, Bank disbursement is slow, both because of complex internal procedures and because of consultation with national governments. Although the issue of ownership is critical in "normal development," in "post-conflict" such a consultative process may allow the government to drag its feet in implementing certain projects. This may be the case in relation to projects that the government agreed to only reluctantly in the peace accords, and which the

UN has to monitor to ensure that other adherents to the peace accords get what they bargained for.

Thus, the whole system of IFI's aid to post-conflict countries needs to be rethought and debated. Although it is unquestionably true that aid will be more effective after governments build up capacity and the institutional framework for its utilization, aid in the immediate transition to peace may be essential for peace to have a chance.

Part IV

Lessons from Case Studies

"Access to a career and to a livelihood in society's mainstream economy is again a topic of discussion among economists and sociologists. Great value is placed on working-age people having the opportunity to obtain rewarding work in the formal economy and to earn enough in such jobs to be self-sufficient. These are the twin conditions for what is sometimes termed social inclusion, or, more aptly, economic inclusion."

Edmund S. Phelps, 2006 Nobel Laureate in Economics, in his Introduction to *Designing Inclusion* (2003)

Justification for case selection

The selection of case studies is based on the special characteristics of the post-conflict transition and how they determined policy choices for economic reconstruction. The selection was influenced by personal involvement, and the number of cases was restricted in order to isolate experiences that were strikingly different from each other, while at the same time covering all relevant issues. All case studies focus on the issue of job creation and social inclusion, a *sine qua non* for effective economic reconstruction. Table 2 shows the important differences among the selected cases with respect to a number of variables.

The case studies aim to illustrate the variety of operational, institutional, administrative, managerial, and financial challenges that countries and the international community face in reconstruction, as well as to provide important policy lessons, derive best practices, and establish policy guidelines for countries, such as Lebanon, the Palestinian territories, Sudan, or Colombia, that are or may soon be starting economic reconstruction. The analysis will

Table 2. Comparison of Post-Conflict Economic Reconstruction (PER) in case studies

Characteristics	El Salvador	Kosovo	Afghanistan	Iraq
Nature of the conflict	Cold war ideological and class confrontation	Ethnic rivalries	Tribal rivalries and foreign intervention	Religious, sectarian
Length of conflict	Longest formal, high intensity civil war in Latin America	Short and intensive war following long-term internal and regional conflict	Short US military intervention after 30 years of internal and external conflict	Short US military invasion after years of war, sanctions, internal and external conflict
Sanctions	None	UN arms embargo and on remittances to pay for arms	None	Comprehensive US-imposed sanctions
Destruction	Localized infrastructural damage (estimated at $1.5 billion to $2.0 billion)	Large infrastructural and housing damage from Serb attacks, NATO bombing and years of underinvestment	Caused by foreign occupation, years of war and lack of investment	Caused by years of sanctions and lack of investment
Ceasefire/security	CF fully respected throughout the country; high common crime	Ethnic violence at various points broke ceasefire	Large parts of the territory lacking security and under the control of warlords or Taliban	Basically fell into civil war in mid-2006; some improvement at end-2007
State/Province	Sovereign State	Province of Serbia; Interim UN-protectorate	Sovereign State: strong involvement of donors, weak government	Occupied state (Mar. 2003–Jun. 2004); Elected government (May. 2006)
Post-Conflict Economic Reconstruction (PER)	UN-led following UN-led Peace Agreement (Jan. 1992)	UN-led following NATO bombing to stop Serb aggression (Mar. 1999), not approved but condoned by Security Council	UN-led following US-led military intervention in search of Taliban regime change	US-led following US-led military intervention in search of Hussein regime change and occupation by the Coalition Provisional Authority (CPA)
Executive/legislative decisions with regard to PER	Government of El Salvador and Congress–strong ownership. UN supportive role	UNMIK(Jul. 1999–present) exercised all PER decisions in the early transition. UN intrusive role	Government (led by few officials)–weak ownership. UN light footprint	CPA exercised all PER decisions in the early transition. UN marginal role
Government	Government (GOES) Free elections: 1990, 1994, 1998, 2002 (Arena party)	Joint Interim Administrative Structure (JIAS): Dec. 1999 to share in provisional administration with UNMIK	Interim (AIA): Dec. 2001 Transitional (ATA): Jun. 2003 Elections: Oct. 2004	CPA: May 2003–Jun. 2004 Interim: Jun. 2004 Transitional: May 2005 Elected government: Jan. 2006
Main donor/Aid channel	US/GOES	EU/UNMIK	Several/UN agencies, NGOs	US/foreign contractors
GDP per capita	$1,100	NA	$200	$800
Natural resources/crops	Coffee	Lead and zinc	Poppies	Oil
Human Development Index	110th out of 173 countries	NA	169th out of 174 countries	126th place of 175 countries

also be relevant to countries such as Afghanistan, Iraq, the DRC, Timor-Leste, Sierra Leone, and many others that need to revise their strategy to create employment and social inclusion if economic reconstruction is to succeed at all. Finally, a number of issues are also raised with the purpose of creating debate among policymakers, academics, and other practitioners on possible options and solutions.

EL SALVADOR

The political science literature and different organizations have widely analyzed and researched El Salvador's experience with UN-led reconstruction, following UN-led peace negotiations. Its inclusion in Chapter 7 for analyzing economic reconstruction issues throughout the implementation of the peace agreements is justified for several reasons.

First, many analysts consider El Salvador's war-to-peace transition as perhaps the most successful in the post-Cold War period, owing mainly to its emphasis on efforts to reintegrate former combatants, their supporters, and other war-affected people into productive activities. El Salvador was considered a success story in the 1990s, and it appears in an even more favorable light today, following more recent experiences in Kosovo, Timor-Leste, Afghanistan, and Iraq.

Second, for the first time, the UN mediated the peace agreements and played a major supporting role throughout the peacebuilding phase, including verification of agreements and the provision of good offices relating to political, humanitarian, military, police, human rights, and economic and social issues.

Third, after having been a signatory to the peace agreements, El Salvador's elected government made all executive decisions and set priorities for economic reconstruction and all other peace-related issues, many of which an elected congress had to approve. At the same time, the agreements contemplated consultation with the other signatory to the agreements, the FMLN, and with civil society.

Fourth, the UN Security Council's mandate for ONUSAL (UN Observer Mission in El Salvador) had a clear exit strategy. ONUSAL would end as soon as the UN could certify compliance with all peace agreements. The Security Council, acting under Chapter VI of the UN Charter, established ONUSAL by Security Council Resolution (SCR) 693 of July 1991. ONUSAL was directed and supported by the Department of Peacekeeping Operations (DPKO). In contrast to Chapter VII operations, Chapter VI operations do not contemplate "enforcement" and are only carried out at the request of member states.

Fifth, El Salvador is one of the few countries in the post-Cold War period that, five years after the signature of the Peace Agreement of 1992, had successfully completed its implementation and had moved onto a path of normal development. An analysis of this new transition—from post-conflict reconstruction to normal development—will allow us to draw some important lessons for future experiences.

Sixth, most previous studies of the Salvadoran peace transition have focused largely on its political, police, human rights, and military aspects, with only cursory analysis of the economic and financial aspects, particularly how the interrelation between the IMF-sponsored economic program and the UN-sponsored peace agreement affected economic reconstruction.

Seventh, while most countries enter the war-to-peace transition amid large-scale economic mismanagement and disequilibria that need to be addressed right away, El Salvador was unusual insofar as economic stabilization and structural reform had started two years earlier, while war was still raging.

Finally, the Salvadoran experience is illustrative of the many coordination problems faced by the UN system, particularly between the UN and the international financial institutions (IFIs). These difficulties led to a broad-based debate and created a precedent that influenced future relations between these organizations.

KOSOVO

The UN-led reconstruction that followed the NATO-led military intervention in Kosovo in 1999, which is analyzed in Chapter 8, provides not only a striking contrast to the case of El Salvador, but also exhibits important similarities and differences with Afghanistan and Iraq.

First, Kosovo was a province of Serbia rather than an independent country, and the Security Council asked the UN to govern it as an interim open-ended protectorate. Thus, in Kosovo, the UN would for the first time perform civil administration functions that are normally the sole prerogative of a sovereign government. The fact that Kosovo was not a sovereign country led to special challenges in policymaking for economic reconstruction, particularly concerning tax and customs revenue collection, financing from the IFIs, money creation, debt, as well as in many other areas. In this sense, Kosovo set a precedent for East Timor (which later became independent using its Portuguese name: Timor-Leste).

Second, the Security Council, acting under Chapter VII of the UN Charter, established UNMIK (UN Interim Administration Mission in Kosovo) by SCR 1244 of June 1999. UNMIK was directed and supported by the DPKO. The Resolution gave UNMIK an open-ended mandate, since the path to a political solution was not clear. In fact, nine years after UNMIK's establishment, the political status of Kosovo is still unresolved. This created further policymaking challenges that were not present in the later case of East Timor, where the political path to independence was clear from the start. These challenges related mainly to issues of legitimacy, which affected property rights and created uncertainty about policies for privatization of publicly and socially owned enterprises, negatively affecting investment and growth. Legitimacy issues were also present in Iraq following the US-led invasion and occupation.

Third, as a result of the overwhelming Security Council mandate, the UN established, for the first time, an integrated operation with four different functional pillars. Some of these pillars where led by stronger organizations—most notably the EU in the pillar for economic reconstruction—which created a new challenge for UN leadership, and clearly brought up its weaknesses.

Fourth, the fact that Kosovo is in Europe led to large-scale economic assistance, both financial and technical. At the same time, the large international presence in Kosovo led to severe distortions that need to be avoided in future transitions.

Finally, the case of Kosovo illustrates the danger of aid dependency and the problem of "development as usual" policies that impede the quick reactivation of employment, with unrealistic and misconceived economic policies failing to put the province on a sound economic footing, even many years after the transition began.

Despite all these sharp differences, Kosovo and El Salvador were similar in two aspects. First, in both operations, the UN's shortcomings in leading or coordinating the economic and financial aspects of post-conflict economic reconstruction became clear from the very beginning.

Second, in both cases economic conditions were positively affected by the large inflows of remittances from the diaspora—in the case of El Salvador from Salvadorans in the United States and in the case of Kosovo from Kosovars in Germany and other European countries. In both cases, remittances enlarged the consumption possibilities of families during economic reconstruction and were an important factor in poverty alleviation, both during and particularly after the war.

AFGHANISTAN AND IRAQ

In Afghanistan and in Iraq, the US-led invasion pursued regime change, which was framed as part of the broader "war on terror." Contrary to the case of Afghanistan, where the international community at large was fully involved in humanitarian and reconstruction activities following the US-led invasion, post-conflict economic reconstruction in Iraq was clearly led by the US government, including the US Agency for International Development (USAID) and the US Treasury. Both countries' reconstruction experiences have been quite different from those of the UN-led efforts of El Salvador and Kosovo.

In Afghanistan, the Security Council established, under Chapter VI of the Charter, UNAMA (Assistance Mission in Afghanistan) by SCR 1244 of June 1999. UNAMA was established as a Political Mission directed and supported by the DPKO. In Iraq, the Security Council established under SCR 1500 of August 2003 UNAMI (Assistance Mission for Iraq), to carry out a mandate specified, under Chapter VII, in SCR 1483 of May 2003. Contrary to UNAMA, UNAMI is directed and supported by the Department of Political Affairs (DPA).

Afghanistan and Iraq are roughly the same size in terms of population (about 22 million to 26 million) and hence had much larger needs than El Salvador and Kosovo. Afghanistan and Iraq differ, however, in terms of natural resources. While oil is a major factor in the reactivation of the legal economy in Iraq, poppy production and cannabis are the main factors in the reactivation of Afghanistan's economy, albeit illegal and hence excluded from the country's official statistics.[1]

Since the experiences of both Afghanistan and Iraq have been extensively analyzed in the recent literature by researchers with close involvement in these countries, I will not follow the step-by-step approach used for El Salvador and Kosovo. Rather, after a cursory discussion of the political and security issues under which post-conflict economic reconstruction has taken place in each country, I will focus on particular issues that need to be considered for successful reconstruction and those that need to be avoided or rethought in future cases.

In the case of Afghanistan, several issues for debate will be identified. First, the Afghan case highlights the question of whether a reconstruction strategy in a country with such limited human resources, weak institutions, and low capacity to absorb aid requires a sophisticated legal, institutional, and regulatory framework. I will argue that the international community, particularly the IFIs, USAID, and the US Treasury, spent a lot of time and money designing overly complicated frameworks. On one hand, the design of such frameworks did not take sufficient account of national preferences or cultural and local idiosyncrasies; on the other hand, it detracted from efforts at rehabilitation and social policies that would have facilitated peace consolidation in the short run by improving the welfare of the population.

Second, the issue of aid to Afghanistan contrasts sharply with that of Kosovo. Whether aid was scant, as many analysts argue, is a debatable issue since the low capacity of the country to absorb it might have been a constraint to larger assistance. However, the utilization of aid was indeed an issue, since it was used to a large extent to finance foreign experts. Despite this, there was not enough emphasis on capacity building as there should have been. Furthermore, aid was channeled through a large number of different trust funds, which created serious administrative problems and led to inefficiencies.

By bypassing the government in many areas, aid also failed to strengthen and legitimize the government.

Third, the increase in drug production has become a serious problem for effective reconstruction. Eliminating poppy plantations without a viable economic alternative has been a source of conflict rather than a peace-supporting strategy. Efforts by the US government to eradicate drug plantations without viable alternatives for local livelihoods have led to a resurgence of the Taliban which is back in control of large parts of the territory.

Given the serious deterioration in political and security conditions in Iraq in 2006 and increasingly in Afghanistan, and little progress on economic reconstruction in either country, it could be argued that these countries are no longer post-conflict countries, and hence they do not belong in this book. However, an analysis of what went wrong is needed if the international community is to make progress on reconstruction in the future. Furthermore, an improved security situation and the willingness of the US government to revise its policies in Iraq in late 2007 may give reconstruction a new impetus. At the same time, there has been discussion that the government of Afghanistan and the government of the United Kingdom are thinking about revising their strategy in Afghanistan and the G-7 have made new pledges to increase troops and equipment to improve security. This, in conjunction with concrete proposals for helping Afghanistan stand on its own feet by promoting alternatives to drug production (Phelps and del Castillo 2008), may also lead to renewed efforts at economic reconstruction in the country.

With regard to Iraq, while the political issues related to the US invasion itself will be left aside, the country will be used to highlight several issues. First, the absence of legitimacy associated with US occupation and the Coalition Provisional Authority (CPA) policymaking in the early period led to uncertainty about property rights and other shortcomings. USAID's early strategy for economic governance and reconstruction—including proposals for privatization of the oil industry—was a major factor in the reaction against US-led occupation.

Second, the involvement of the UN in reconstruction as an afterthought did not resolve the legitimacy problem, particularly since reconstruction was clearly led by USAID. Furthermore, in a country where the UN had imposed comprehensive sanctions for twelve years, with a dramatic impact on large segments of the population—it was naive to think that the UN would be received with open arms.

Third, because of the importance of debt arrears in post-conflict reconstruction, the Iraqi case should stimulate debate on whether debt arrears are best resolved in the immediate transition from war. The alternative is to leave debt restructuring for later, as the national authorities gain legitimacy, the living conditions of the population improve, and peace and security get better.

Finally, the case of Iraq provides a platform to discuss the significance of corruption and inefficiencies in procurement, construction, and other areas, as well as the need to use domestic companies for reconstruction purposes as much as possible to create domestic employment. This may be particularly true in countries such as Iraq, which over the years has proved its resourcefulness in overcoming the technological and manufacturing challenges posed by sanctions, especially in the oil sector.

7 UN-led reconstruction following UN-led negotiations: El Salvador²

Introduction³

After a decade-long war, with over 100,000 estimated dead and serious damage to human capital and physical infrastructure, a Peace Agreement between the government of El Salvador and the Frente Farabundo Martí para la Liberación Nacional (FMLN), signed on January 16, 1992, in the Chapultepec Castle in Mexico City, created high expectations.⁴ While El Salvador is considered, by any standard, to be one of the most successful UN peace-keeping operations,⁵ the implementation of post-conflict economic reconstruction was plagued with difficulties and complex challenges from the start. With economic reconstruction over and with the country having moved to a path of normal development a decade ago, now is a good time to re-evaluate the strengths and weaknesses of its reconstruction experience, particularly in relation to later experiences elsewhere. This will facilitate the design of future reconstruction strategies by highlighting policy measures that worked, as well as the mistakes to be avoided.

A discussion of El Salvador is relevant and timely in light of both the international community's increasing involvement and disappointing performance in post-conflict reconstruction efforts and the realization that purely military-police peacekeeping operations can be costly and ineffective without a solution to the non-military issues, which are often root causes of conflict. In this regard, an improvement of the economic and social conditions of those who played an active role in the war, as well as the strengthening of national institutions to facilitate peaceful resolution of future problems, proved particularly important in fostering peace in El Salvador.

Although conflict is not likely to recur, and the war-to-peace transition can, on these grounds, be considered a "success story," many of the problems and inefficiencies that were identified during the Salvadoran reconstruction process, particularly in relation to UN participation and leadership, have not been addressed. Because of the lack of UN action in many areas—particularly human resources and institutional arrangements—the opportunity was missed to provide a truly "integrated approach to human security," as advocated in Secretary-General Boutros-Ghali's *An Agenda for Peace.*

In particular, the UN failed to provide sustained support to former combatants and other groups affected by the conflict. As a result, many of the peace-related programs were not sustainable. This contributed to the growing insecurity that has existed in El Salvador during the last decade, and that has been a major deterrent to investment in the country. More importantly for the large number of countries that have achieved a tenuous peace and need to embark on post-conflict economic reconstruction, the high cost and unsustainability of these programs made donors increasingly reluctant to support such programs elsewhere.

After the conclusion of the peace agreements, El Salvador embarked on a complex war-to-peace transition. At the time, El Salvador, like Mozambique and Angola, belonged to a new breed of UN operations that were multidisciplinary in nature and sought to address the root causes of conflict in a comprehensive and integrated manner.

The country moved a long way in this transition. Although successive Salvadoran presidents have continued to be elected from the *Alianza Republicana Nacionalista* (ARENA), in the March 2000 elections, the FMLN won 31 of 84 seats in the unicameral legislative assembly. This was a remarkable achievement for the FMLN, barely eight years after becoming a political party, allowing it to block bills requiring a two-thirds majority. This moved the country further ahead in the political transition. In the municipal elections of 1997, the opposition had won about 80 percent of the largest cities, including the capital.

In an evaluation of the 1992–2004 period, the Inter-American Development Bank (IADB 2005) concluded that Salvadoran society had made a successful transition to peacetime and has gained considerable ground in terms of stability, economic modernization, and poverty reduction. In the IADB's view, it would be hard to find another country that provides such an outstanding example of speedy action and success in addressing a very difficult and complex initial situation. However, in terms of the Human Development Index (HDI), El Salvador has progressed at a snail's pace, from 110th place (out of 173 countries) in 1990, at the peak of the conflict, to 101st place (out of 177 countries) in 2006, 14 years after the Peace Agreement was signed.[6] This pace would have probably been much faster had the international financial institutions (IFIs) and other development organizations been more involved in providing technical assistance to reintegration programs, and had the UN ensured effective and continued support for these and other peace-related programs.

Economic and political background

ROOT CAUSES OF THE CONFLICT

The roots of El Salvador's decade-long civil war extended deep into the nineteenth century. As Torres-Rivas (1997) has pointed out, Salvadoran society systematically generated economic marginalization, social segregation, and political repression. Land tenure was as much a root cause of the conflict that raged throughout the 1980s as was the overbearing power of the armed forces.[7] The two problems were not unrelated: scholars of El Salvador pointed to the armed forces as an instrument created and nurtured by the powerful landed class to protect and preserve its position. Torres-Rivas explains how this alliance arose as a tacit accord following the 1932 peasant uprising and the corresponding massacre, or *Matanza*. In his view, the oligarchic landowners, afraid of another peasant insurrection, allowed the military to retain the reins of government while they maintained their economic and social power.

THE ECONOMY BEFORE THE CONFLICT

Despite political tensions and socio-economic injustice, El Salvador experienced significant economic progress in the 1960s and 1970s. Annual real GDP grew by close to 6 percent in the 1970s, reflecting a stable macroeconomic environment with fiscal discipline and low inflation, an improvement in the terms of trade, and, following the creation of the Central American Common Market (CACM), an expansion of the regional market for manufactured products. Domestic investment increased from 13 percent of GDP in 1967–9 to 22 percent of GDP in 1977–9, just before the conflict started in 1980. This was financed mostly out of national savings, which reached 18 percent of GDP in 1977–9.[8]

Despite healthy economic growth, social progress lagged. Although some gains were achieved in life expectancy, literacy rates, and primary education enrollment, by the time civil war erupted, life expectancy continued to be below 60 and infant mortality rates remained high. At the same time, only 20 percent of the school-age population attended secondary education, and illiteracy was as high as 45 percent of the population (age 15+). Per capita GDP remained low, at slightly over $600, with one of the worst income distributions in the world.

By 1980, in an economy widely perceived as agricultural, this sector accounted for only 28 percent of GDP, compared with 21 percent for industry and 52 percent for services. Agriculture was much more important, however, in terms of employment (over 40 percent) and export revenues (well over 60 percent). Coffee was of primary importance, accounting for about

8 percent of GDP, 37 percent of real value-added in agriculture, and 50 percent of exports.

THE CONFLICT

During the decade-long civil war in El Salvador, in addition to those who died from armed conflict and massacres of civilians, about a half-million persons were displaced, approximately 45,000 became refugees, and more than one million (roughly one-fifth of the population) emigrated, mostly to the United States.[9] Many of the displaced were settled in communities, some of them on abandoned land, creating serious property rights controversies. It was under these conditions that the United States used the carrot-and-stick mechanism: on one hand, it threatened to stop aid if the war continued, and, on the other, it offered generous financial support if a peace accord was reached. Starting in 1990, the parties agreed to negotiate under UN auspices.

THE ECONOMIC CONSEQUENCES OF CIVIL WAR

As in other conflicts, the civil war in El Salvador diverted public resources from investment and the social sectors to military expenditure. The figures are telling.[10] Military expenditure averaged more than 4 percent of GDP in 1988–90 and represented 20 percent of central government expenditure— the highest level in Latin America with the exception of Nicaragua. Central government expenditure on education dropped from 4 percent of GDP in 1980 to less than 2 percent in 1990 (as compared with an average of more than 4 percent for Latin America in both years). By 1990, total health expenditure had fallen to less than 1 percent of GDP (from 2 percent in 1980), which, in per capita terms, represented less than one-third of the average for Latin America.

At the same time, inappropriate economic policies and a deteriorating external environment due to falling terms of trade, high real rates of interest, and world recession, weakened public finances in 1989. As a result, government revenue proportionate to GDP fell sharply. In addition, the colón remained overvalued. The external deficit on goods, services, and income (that is, the current account excluding transfers) widened from less than 4 percent of GDP in 1977–9 to more than 12 percent in 1987–9.[11] By 1989, domestic investment and national savings were down to 15 percent and 6 percent of GDP, from the high pre-war levels reported above. Net international reserves had declined to the equivalent of three months of imports and sizable external payments arrears had accumulated. The situation deteriorated further at the turn of the decade, owing to the intensification of the armed conflict, reconstruction following the devastating earthquake in 1986, a severe drought, and the economic downturn in other Central American countries. As a result, domestic investment and national savings bottomed out in 1990 at 12 and 5 percent, respectively.

Damage to the country's infrastructure as a result of the civil war was estimated at $1.5 billion to $2.0 billion (more than 30 percent of 1990 GDP). War destruction and grinding poverty caused serious environmental problems as well. Real GDP declined by 12 percent during the 1980s, and real per capita income dropped by 25 percent, with 56 percent of the population falling below the poverty level. In a country historically known for its price stability, inflation reached 24 percent at the end of the decade.

Despite some improvement in social indicators, by 1990 El Salvador was in 110th place out of 173 countries in terms of the HDI—just below Nicaragua— a country with an income per capita of about $275, one fourth of that of El Salvador. Infant mortality remained high, at 56 per thousand (compared with an average of 44 per thousand for Latin America), while the daily calorie intake per capita, at 2,155, was about four-fifths of the Latin American average. Furthermore, the adult illiteracy rate of 27 percent was almost twice the average for Latin America, and the average of 4 years of schooling remained extremely low, even by Latin American standards.

One factor that sustained El Salvador's economy during the war years and helped contain the spread of poverty was remittances by migrant workers abroad, particularly from the close to one million Salvadorans who had emigrated to the United States during the war. At the end of the 1980s, remittances represented 5 percent of GDP, growing rapidly in subsequent years, to 12 percent of GDP in 1992–5.

IMF and UN involvement in El Salvador before the end of the conflict

Upon taking office in June 1989, President Alfredo Cristiani set three main goals for his Administration (1989–94): end the civil war and initiate a national reconstruction and reconciliation effort; carry out stabilization and structural reforms necessary to put the economy back on a path of sustainable growth and development; and reduce poverty.

The Cristiani administration decided to adopt a new macroeconomic framework, despite the raging war. The new framework relied on macro-economic stability and market-based reforms, including liberalization of the domestic economy and of foreign trade and investment. At the same time, the government would focus on providing the regulatory, legal, institutional, and infrastructural framework necessary to foster an environment conducive to investment and growth, and rely on the private sector for the provision of most services.[12]

Negotiations with the IMF on an economic program, to be supported by a 12-month stand-by arrangement (SBA), began in November 1989, but were interrupted by a major FMLN offensive in San Salvador. In addition, a series of external shocks, particularly the dramatic fall in coffee prices after the breakdown of the International Coffee Agreement in June 1989, aggravated the financial situation. Notwithstanding these adverse developments, President Cristiani reached an agreement with the Fund on an economic program in August 1990, at the peak of the armed conflict.[13] Economic activity was disrupted by acts of sabotage of electric power and other infrastructure, and disruption of harvests. During this period, official transfers (grants) began to decline (from close to 6 percent of GDP in 1989 to 3 percent in 1991), though private transfers (remittances from Salvadorans abroad) increased (from about 5 percent of GDP in 1987–9 to more than 7 percent in 1990–1).

While the Fund supported stabilization amid civil war (1989–92), the UN negotiated a Peace Agreement (1990–2), oblivious of the economic consequences of peacetime. The FMLN offensive in November 1989 was the largest of the civil war, affecting large parts of San Salvador and other major cities for the first time. Six Jesuit priests thought to be connected to the guerrillas were murdered, and the killers were widely believed to be closely associated with the military. Domestic and international pressure on the government and the FMLN to end their hostilities grew. The violence of 1989 not only claimed hundreds of lives and caused severe physical damage; it also demonstrated the impossibility of military victory by either side, and set the stage for a negotiated solution.

By early 1990, the FMLN and the government had separately requested UN Secretary-General Javier Pérez de Cuéllar to help negotiate a solution to the military conflict. The agenda agreed for the negotiations made clear that ending the conflict required addressing its root causes. After two years of long, complex, and painstaking negotiations, and a series of partial agreements, the formal signing of the El Salvador Peace Accord took place on January 16, 1992, at Chapultepec Castle, marking the beginning of the long, ambitious, and arduous war-to-peace transition in El Salvador.

A synopsis of the peace agreements[14]

The parties set themselves a fourfold goal for the political transition: ending the armed conflict by political means as speedily as possible, promoting democratization, guaranteeing respect for human rights, and reunifying

Salvadoran society. A key aim of the UN-led peace negotiations was to reintegrate members of the armed forces, the FMLN, and their political supporters into productive activities. The peace agreements would establish the necessary guarantees and conditions for reintegrating these groups, within a framework of full legality, into the civil, institutional, and political life of the country. The reintegration of the FMLN would take place through three main economic and political channels: agricultural production, the new National Civil Police (known by its Spanish initials PNC), and political activities.[15]

The Peace Agreement (also known as the "Chapultepec Agreement") was the culmination of a series of accords encompassing a wide-ranging agenda— human rights, the armed forces, the judicial system, the electoral system, economic and social questions, and constitutional reform. The first substantive agreement, the San José Agreement, signed in Costa Rica on July 21, 1990, concerned human rights.

On April 27, 1991, the parties agreed to a number of constitutional reforms that became known as the Mexico Agreements. The most radical reforms, and the most difficult to negotiate, strengthened civilian authority and circumscribed the armed forces' role, almost completely eliminating their responsibility for the maintenance of public order. The constitutional reform provided for the disbanding of several military-dominated police bodies, replacing them with a single, nationwide corps, strictly civilian in character, structure, management, and doctrine. The parties also agreed to overhaul the judiciary, making it more independent; to liberalize the electoral system to include a broader spectrum of political parties; to create a national human rights prosecutor, and to establish a Truth Commission. The purpose of the Truth Commission, composed of three eminent persons (all non-Salvadoran) appointed by the Secretary-General, was to examine the most notorious cases of violence from the decade-long war and to make recommendations to prevent their recurrence.

The New York Agreement, signed on September 25, 1991, created the multiparty National Commission for the Consolidation of Peace (COPAZ) as a mechanism for enabling key groups, including the still illegal FMLN, to monitor and participate in the peace process. COPAZ was composed of two representatives of the government, including a member of the armed forces, two representatives of the FMLN, and one representative of each of the parties or coalitions represented in the Legislative Assembly.

The final agreement signed at Chapultepec provided for broad reforms of the armed forces, including a purge ("*depuración*") of the officer corps based on recommendations by an independent civilian panel, known as the Ad Hoc Commission, and detailed provisions for a ceasefire and separation of forces. The agreement also included an intricate calendar to synchronize the dismantling of the FMLN military structure with the implementation of the economic and social reforms agreed to by the government. Except for the human rights agreement, which entered into force before the signing of the Chapultepec Agreement, the calendar's approval would trigger implementation of the whole package of agreements, as well as economic and social measures to facilitate the reintegration of ex-combatants into the productive life of the country.

Two of the most prominent measures of the Peace Agreement were the creation of the PNC and the provision of credit for land purchases to former combatants on both sides, and supporters of the FMLN who had occupied land in the war zones. There are several reasons for singling out the PNC and the land program. First, these programs were among the most innovative features of a pioneering foray into a new generation of UN peace ventures. Second, the entire peace process and its long-term sustainability depended on their success. Third, both programs encountered serious difficulties and suffered distortions that at times endangered the peace process.

The war-to-peace transition

El Salvador illustrates the experience of a country entering the complexities of a war-to-peace transition after the conclusion of UN-sponsored peace accords between the government and guerrilla or rebel groups, as was later the case in Guatemala. The agreements negotiated through 1990 and 1991 brought the decade-long civil war in El Salvador to an end in an impeccably observed ceasefire. In light of their extraordinary breadth and scope, the reforms were aptly described by Secretary-General Boutros-Ghali as a "revolution achieved by negotiation," since they aimed at nothing less than eliminating the causes of the conflict: a militarized society, profound economic and social injustice, and a closed, non-participatory political system.[16] The implementation of the agreements took a long-suffering nation a great distance: El Salvador became a democratic society capable of solving its own problems through civilized discourse. Previously unthinkable transformations occurred, including far-reaching constitutional reforms, attained for the first time in El Salvador's history through peaceful means. Moreover, former guerrillas were elected in significant numbers to public office.

The economic consequences of peacetime: 1992–7

El Salvador's civil war was costly, but so were the economic consequences of peace. Moreover, the latter were difficult to finance owing to the fact that foreign financing dried up after the end of the Cold War. Since the war in

El Salvador was largely foreign-financed, there was hardly any peace dividend in fiscal terms—that is, resources that could be released from military to non-military purposes—during the transition to peace.[17]

Peace could be sustained only at a relatively high cost. Rebuilding damaged infrastructure, restoring basic social services, reintegrating former combatants, and reactivating growth entailed financial costs that far exceeded the country's resources and thus required generous assistance from the international community. As part of the peace negotiations, a number of programs were to be implemented in the financial framework of the National Reconstruction Plan (NRP) for the period 1992–7, at an estimated cost of about $2 billion, or roughly one-third of 1992 GDP. At the same time, the financial implications of the NRP had to be incorporated into and reconciled with the fiscal restrictions imposed by the IMF-supported economic stabilization program. This, as discussed below, imposed a serious constraint on the peace process.

The main objective of the NRP was the satisfaction of the immediate needs of those sectors of the population hardest hit by the conflict, the reconstruction of damaged infrastructure, and the reactivation of economic activity in the former conflict zones. The two most important programs within the NRP were the creation of the PNC, separate and distinct from the armed forces, and the land program to former combatants on both sides and for supporters of the FMLN who had occupied land during the war years. Given that land had been a root cause of the conflict, the land program was the main vehicle for reintegrating those most closely involved in the conflict into productive life.

Other peace-related programs focused on resettlement of displaced persons; reintegration through micro-enterprise development; reduction of the armed forces; creation of a police academy to train the PNC; strengthening the country's democratic institutions (including the judiciary and the electoral system); and rebuilding social and physical infrastructure. In order to facilitate the allocation of resources and the implementation of peace-related programs, the NRP was to be carried out through consensus-building among the government, the FMLN, and other sectors of society.

With the signing of the Chapultepec Agreement, the challenge of attending to the unsatisfied demands of the participants in the conflict, and the fulfillment of basic needs for large segments of the population that had suffered significant declines in their living standards, required the resumption of stability and economic growth. The government was committed to ensuring that reconstruction efforts would be conducted in a framework of macroeconomic stability. Underlying the government's actions was the belief that stability and economic growth could not be sustainable without a lasting peace, and that peace was not durable without high-quality growth.

Post-conflict economic reconstruction: 1992–7

Reconstruction in El Salvador presented a number of challenges to the UN and the IMF, both of which played a critical role in the implementation of the peace agreements. Other international organizations such as the World Bank, the IADB, the UNDP, and a large number of NGOs were involved in specific development programs in the country at the time, some of them dating from before the Peace Agreement. However, their policies had more limited impact on the overall implementation of the agreements, which was clearly led by ONUSAL. Despite their support through donors' coordination, neither the UNDP nor the World Bank played the technical assistance role in support of peace-related programs—particularly those focusing on reintegration—that they could have played.[18]

REORIENTATION OF ECONOMIC POLICY

As mentioned earlier, even before peace was attained, the government decided on a major reorientation of economic policy to improve economic performance, including a greater reliance on market forces and a major reform of the exchange and trade system. The multiple exchange-rate regime was replaced by a unified market-determined system, import tariffs were reduced and unified, and exchange restrictions were eliminated. Price controls were reduced and state monopolies in the marketing of agricultural commodities were eliminated. The strengthening of fiscal policy was based on a major tax reform, which included the introduction of a value-added tax (VAT). Greater flexibility in adjusting public-sector prices and improvements in the operating efficiency of state enterprises were also implemented. Credit policy was tightened in the context of dismantling the complex system of credit allocation and a move toward market-determined interest rates.

The medium-term adjustment strategy included a social-sector program aimed at reducing poverty and raising the standards of living, education, and health of the population through investment in social infrastructure. The strategy also provided for temporary employment, income, and food supplements, and expansion of social services. The government developed a social safety net through the development of community projects, supported by the Social Investment Fund (known by its Spanish acronym FIS), designed to channel donors' financing to poverty alleviation projects. Efforts were also made to improve the effectiveness of social expenditure, with health and community school programs designed to expand the coverage and increase the quality of health care and pre-primary and primary education in the poorest areas through community participation. Moreover, remittances from Salvadorans abroad remained a critical factor in poverty alleviation.

Because social progress lagged and the poverty situation remained dismal, there was no room for complacency. In the government's view, social development and poverty alleviation were, however, to be tackled on a longer-term basis. Putting the economy on a sound footing through fiscal discipline was a prerequisite in this endeavor.

ECONOMIC ASSISTANCE[19]

International assistance to El Salvador was strengthened by the government's own effort at increasing domestic savings. Non-financial public sector (NFPS)[20] savings rose from an average of -0.8 percent of GDP (implying public expenditure larger than revenue) in 1989–93 to 2 percent of GDP by 1994–7. At the same time, the deficit of the NFPS (excluding grants), which reflects the borrowing requirements of the government, was reduced from 5 percent to 2 percent of GDP. The improvement was due to an increase in current revenue, which resulted from the introduction of a VAT at a rate of 10 percent, the approval in early-1993 of the Fiscal Crime Law to reduce tax evasion, and the execution of a fiscal package yielding revenue equivalent to 2 percent of GDP. This increase in revenues was accompanied by a shortfall in capital expenditure (including under the NRP) due to implementation problems.

With the achievement of peace, remittances from Salvadoran workers abroad continued on a large scale, averaging over 12 percent of GDP in 1992–5, as mentioned earlier. The government also requested $2 billion specifically for its peace-related programs during the 1992–7 period, mainly in the form of external grants and long-term concessional loans from bilateral and multilateral creditors. The World Bank played an active role as a catalyst for financial support for the country, even while peace negotiations were ongoing. Although no pledges were made at the time, the World Bank, in collaboration with the UNDP, organized a consultative group meeting in May 1991 to familiarize donors with events in El Salvador and the financing and technical assistance needs that the country would face after peace was achieved. Three consultative group meetings, attended by donors, the national authorities, the FMLN, and the UN took place in March 1992, April 1993, and June 1995. The international community provided grants averaging more than 3 percent of GDP in 1992–5. Although donors were supportive of El Salvador's peace efforts, they showed a clear preference for financing specific projects, mostly in infrastructure and the environment. Thus, quick-disbursing external financing for peace-related expenditure such as the reintegration of former combatants, the creation of the PNC, and the promotion of democratic institutions was in short supply.[21]

Challenges to the UN and the IMF in El Salvador

"BUSINESS AS USUAL"

Six days after the signature of the Chapultepec Peace Agreement, the IMF's Executive Board concluded the 1991 Article IV consultations and approved a 14-month stand-by SBA worth SDR42 million.[22] The arrangement called for a mid-term review, to be completed by August 31, 1992, that would provide an opportunity for the incorporation in the program of the NRP's financial requirements. The Salvadoran authorities expected that the Peace Agreement would allow for a reduction in military outlays and make room for an increase in social expenditure. To be able to keep the program on track, however, the government had an understanding with the Fund that peace-related expenditure would have to be financed by additional public savings, reallocation of other public expenditure, or external resources.

A severe slump in international coffee prices, a drought, and the large financial requirements of the NRP complicated macroeconomic management in 1992. While real GDP grew by close to 8 percent, there was a considerable deterioration in the overall deficit of the NFPS (of over 2 percentage points of GDP), in the current account, and in the rate of inflation. At the same time, the accumulation of reserves was lower than contemplated in the IMF program. The review of the program called for under the SBA was not completed, because an agreement could not be reached on policies to return the program to an appropriate path. In light of the shortfalls in external assistance in 1992, the Fund's view was that the government "should take additional fiscal measures or postpone some of the peace-related expenditure" if shortfalls in external assistance recurred in 1993 (IMF 1993). This was a clear violation of my Premise 2 that the political objective should prevail at all times and that peace-related expenditure should have priority in budget allocations.

As discussed earlier, the government of El Salvador had been implementing an IMF-supported economic program since 1990. The signing of the UN-brokered Peace Agreement in early 1992 paved the way for accelerated economic reconstruction and improved social welfare for the entire population. As de Soto and I pointed out in our 1994 *Foreign Policy* article, despite the UN's involvement in the search for peace and the inclusion of the NRP in the agreement, the economic program was formulated and implemented without the UN being informed about either its progress or its constraints.[23]

In the same vein, we noted that the UN did not inform the Bretton Woods institutions about progress in the peace negotiating process, nor did it consult them on the financial implications of the NRP and other programs under negotiation. These institutions were notoriously absent during the negotiation of the economic and social portion (Chapter V) of the Peace Agreement in December 1991, as well as during the negotiations that led to a revised agreement on the land program in October 13, 1992.[24] However, some indirect early collaboration took place in catalyzing foreign assistance. The Fund and the Bank lent full support to the consultative group meeting held in Washington in March 1992, in an effort to secure external assistance to cover outlays under the NRP.[25]

The business-as-usual approach led to misunderstandings and confrontations as the separate economic and peace processes moved forward. In a speech in Bangkok in April 1993, Secretary-General Boutros-Ghali expressed strong concern that the Fund and the UN did not seem to work on a fully coordinated and transparent basis toward the overriding goal of consolidating peace and human security. In his view, implementation of the agreements could not be made conditional on the availability of foreign financing, as the Fund insisted. The Secretary-General argued that it was the government's responsibility to define fiscal policies and public expenditure priorities that would enable it to fulfill its commitment to full implementation of the agreements.[26] The IMF later acknowledged its business-as-usual approach by recognizing that, while cooperation between the UN, the Fund, and the Bank had been instrumental in planning technical assistance and a macroeconomic framework for Rwanda, such coordination had initially not occurred in the negotiation of El Salvador's NRP. As a result, the fiscal impact of the NRP had not been fully assessed when the Peace Agreement was drawn up (IMF 1995g).

INCREASED COOPERATION AND FLEXIBILITY WITHIN A MORE INTEGRATED APPROACH

As pointed out earlier, the IMF's initial reaction to the NRP had been that, in order to keep the 1992 program on track, peace-related expenditure would have to be financed by additional public savings, reallocation of expenditure, or external resources. Beginning in early 1993, however, the Fund worked closely with the government to develop an economic program that would allow for annual NRP expenditure of $250 million in 1993–4 (more than 3 percent of GDP per year). This would cover the indemnity payments related to the demobilization of the military, the establishment of the PNC, health and education facilities in the former conflict areas, and the acquisition of land for ex-combatants. Thus, a compromise scenario was incorporated into the 1993 economic program; by cutting certain expenditure categories and reallocating others, room was made for a significant increase in peace-related expenditure.[27]

As discussions between the Fund and the UN began on a regular basis and a more cooperative and integrated approach was developed, methods were explored to support financing of the higher peace-related expenditure required under the NRP from external resources, higher domestic revenue, expenditure switching, increased bond emissions, and money creation.[28] Despite an uneven pattern in the availability of grants and net external financing, the central government was able to increase nonmilitary expenditure by more than 3 percentage points of GDP in 1992–7 as compared with 1989–91. This can be explained by a decrease in military expenditure of 2 percentage points of GDP, together with an increase in tax revenue of 2.5 percentage points of GDP,[29] which enabled a reduction in the central government fiscal deficit from close to 5 percent of GDP to below 3 percent between these periods.[30]

THE GOVERNMENT'S FISCAL OVER-PERFORMANCE

The performance of the Salvadoran government in managing the economy under a succession of IMF-supported programs and in carrying out peace-related expenditure during the 1989–97 period was remarkable. However, the Salvadoran government often achieved fiscal and other targets under its 1993 and 1994 programs with the Fund with a margin. This means that there was room under fiscal targets and domestic financing ceilings to spend more on peace-related programs, especially on capital expenditure (including under the NRP). By spending less than the program allowed, it could be argued that the Salvadoran authorities were being more royalist than the king. Uncertainty about external financing was one of the reasons for caution on the part of national authorities.

The situation in 1992, however, had been different. Because the expenditure requirements of the NRP had not been incorporated into the 1992 program (they were unknown at the time the program was designed), the NFPS deficit was much higher than programmed (close to 7 percent of GDP, compared with the 2 percent ceiling required by the program). In 1993, with the incorporation of the NRP into the economic program, the NFPS deficit was programmed to reach 6 percent of GDP. This deficit, however, was less than 4 percent in 1993, significantly lower than programmed, reflecting a shortfall in capital expenditure by the central government (including under the NRP) and somewhat higher than expected current revenue. Furthermore, despite a sizable shortfall in programmed net external financing, the net indebtedness of the NFPS was unchanged in 1993, compared with a program limit of close to 1 percent of GDP.

At the same time, current expenditure by the central government was higher than programmed, with lower expenditure on goods and services more than offset by higher than anticipated transfers to local governments for expenditure on health, education, and the reintegration of ex-combatants. However, capital expenditure was about 3 percent of GDP, compared with more than 4 percent allowed under the program. Capital expenditure in 1994 was also lower than programmed (less than 3 percent of GDP, compared with more than 4 percent allowed by the program).

Reintegration of former combatants into civilian life

Perhaps the most daunting challenge of post-conflict economic recons-truction—and the one for which national governments and the international community still lack adequate mechanisms and proven strategies—is the rein-tegration of groups marginalized during years of conflict into the productive, civil, and institutional life of the country. These groups include not only former combatants and war-disabled people, but often a large number of returning refugees and displaced persons.

The Peace Agreement provided for reintegration to take place through three channels: participation in political life, admission to the PNC, and access to productive activities. As envisaged in the agreement, the agricultural sector would absorb not only the bulk of ex-combatants on both sides, but also a large number of civilian supporters of the FMLN—the so-called landholders (*tenedores* in Salvadoran parlance)—who had taken over and worked the land in conflict areas throughout the war years.[31]

Although the Peace Agreement made references to this program as a simple "land transfer," it was much more complex than that. It involved provid-ing credit (and hence creating indebtedness) to former combatants on both sides and to *tenedores* to provide them with a viable livelihood and a stake, however tiny, in the country's wealth. Because it involved "disarmament and demobilization" of combatants as a precondition for eligibility, this program was characterized as an "arms-for-land" exchange (de Soto and del Castillo 1994).

It is not surprising that land became the main vehicle for reintegration. Because of the dismally inequitable distribution of land in El Salvador and its importance to the overall economy, land had been one of the root causes of the conflict. However, the agreement stopped short of attempting to solve the overall problem of land tenure or distribution as such. Though it was quite restricted in its objective, the land program proved to be the most difficult of all the peace agreements to implement, owing to its short-run cost and the complex technical, administrative, and legal issues involved. Another difficulty reflected the reluctance of many, including public employees, to—as they saw it—increase the economic and political power of the FMLN. Moreover, the

FMLN faced its own difficulties in satisfying many of the requirements of the program, and in converting former young combatants into agricultural producers overnight, especially given the overall trend for young people to move from rural areas to urban centers.

The land problem[32]

El Salvador, the smallest country in the continental Americas, has a geographical area of barely 8,620 square miles (roughly 22,000 square kilometers), with agricultural land accounting for about 40 percent of the total. Its population more than doubled in 30 years, to close to 5.5 million in the early 1990s, making the country by far the most densely populated in all of Latin America, with about 260 inhabitants per square kiliometer. With a GDP of about $6 billion in 1991, average income per capita was around $1,100. This made El Salvador ineligible for most concessional programs of the IFIs involved in the country, mainly the Bretton Woods institutions and the IADB.[33] However, the country's income and wealth were highly concentrated. It was often heard that about 85 percent of the land belonged to 14 families. Despite an agrarian reform program that started in 1980, in the early 1990s it was estimated that there were about 300,000 families of *campesinos* (small farmers) who still had no land.

Rapid economic recovery followed the implementation of a rigorous economic stabilization and structural reform program adopted at the inception of the Cristiani administration, but agricultural production lagged. The most important external shock affecting the country during this period was the dramatic fall in the price of coffee, particularly after the breakdown of the International Coffee Agreement in June 1989. This imposed serious constraints on government finances. Moreover, with the country having one of the most diminished natural resource bases in Latin America, serious ecological problems aggravated the effects of the fall in coffee prices. According to a 1993 IADB report, almost half of El Salvador's agricultural land was worked in a manner that downgraded its productive capacity, owing to misallocation and overuse.

The land situation in the conflict zones was very complex. Production had been virtually paralyzed during the war and infrastructure was seriously damaged. As landowners abandoned or were forced off their land, landless peasants had moved in. During the peace negotiations, the FMLN had insisted on the legalization of the landholders' precarious tenure as a reward for their crucial support to the FMLN's largely rural-based guerrilla movement. The landholders were also expected to provide electoral support for the FMLN's post-conflict political ambitions. Moreover, the problem had to be addressed in any case, regardless of the FMLN position, lest it remain as a potential source of instability as landowners tried to recover their land.

The "arms-for-land" program[34]

The objective of the "arms-for-land" program—which was of central importance to the maintenance of the ceasefire—was to provide demobilizing combatants with the means for reintegration into the productive economy by providing credit to potential beneficiaries to purchase land. The agreement also contemplated supplementary short-term programs (agricultural training, distribution of agricultural tools, basic household goods, and academic instruction) and medium-term programs (credit for production purposes, housing, and technical assistance).

Curiously, provisions of the Chapultepec Agreement itself complicated the implementation of these initiatives. While the chapters dealing with legal and institutional reforms were negotiated in detail, negotiations on economic and social issues, of which reintegration was a crucial part, took place literally at the last minute. Negotiators came under pressure to strike a deal before the expiration of UN Secretary-General Javier Pérez de Cuéllar's term in office at midnight on December 31, 1991. The inadequacy of the agreement also reflected the lack of technical expertise on the part of the FMLN—and even on the part of the UN negotiating team—concerning economic reconstruction issues, as well as the government's reluctance to offer major socio-economic concessions.

The important differences between the arms-for-land program and that of the 1980 agrarian reform escaped many serious analysts throughout the process, creating chronic confusion and misunderstanding. On certain land transfer issues, Chapter V of the Peace Agreement was excessively precise, posing severe constraints on its implementation. It stipulated that private land to be transferred had to be "voluntarily offered for sale by its owners" and that transactions had to be concluded at "market prices." It also stipulated that beneficiaries would repay government loans in accordance with the agrarian reform's terms of payment (over 30 years, with a 4-year grace period for principal and interest, and a fixed annual interest rate of 6 percent). At the same time, preference would be given to ex-combatants on both sides, while landholders would not be evicted until a satisfactory legal solution for their land-tenure problem was found.

Under agrarian reform programs in the early 1980s, land in El Salvador had been expropriated and owners had been paid with government bonds. Furthermore, the Agrarian Reform Law of 1980 established that landowners would be paid for their land at the value they had declared for tax purposes, which allowed the government to obtain land at a significant discount on market prices. Thus, the fact that the 1992 Peace Agreement stipulated that owners had to offer their land "voluntarily" for sale at "market prices" created tremendous difficulties for both the acquisition and financing of land purchases. Difficulties also resulted from repayment terms, which were comparable to those of the agrarian reform program. The situation was aggravated by the fact that the government had not honored most of the bonds issued to finance agrarian reform in the past; hence bond financing for the arms-for-land program was impossible.

The Agreement stipulated further that the FMLN would submit an inventory of affected lands in the conflict zones within 30 days of the signing of the Agreement.[35] Legalization of land tenure in these zones was to be completed within six months, that is, by July 31, 1992 (this date was later put off until August 31 in the context of an overall recalendarization). Before starting the program, COPAZ would set up a special unit to verify the inventory of lands presented by the FMLN to determine, among other things, the number of landholders occupying them.

However, despite the precision of Chapter V (Section 3) on certain issues, it completely ignored crucial parameters such as the total number of potential beneficiaries; the size of the plots to which they would be entitled; and the amount of credit that the government would make available to them. Nor did the agreement determine the practical arrangements under which the transfer of land would take place.

Return to the brink of war

The vagueness of the Chapultepec Agreement regarding economic and social issues gave rise to differing expectations on the part of the many players. By the end of September 1992, these differences were so acute that land transfer had become one of the most contentious issues in the implementation of the Agreement, and had actually led the FMLN to suspend its military demobilization. In early October, the FMLN, holding the government responsible for not having started the arms-for-land program, unilaterally halted the third phase of its five-phase demobilization (each phase was to demobilize 20 percent of its forces). The FMLN's negotiating position in resolving this controversy was quite strong, since its supporters occupied the land in question and the Chapultepec Agreement protected them from eviction.[36]

As days went by, positions hardened and the gap between the FMLN's demands and the government's offers widened. The government insisted that the acreage to be transferred should be determined by the availability of land

and financing, and that a ceiling in domestic currency (colón) was to be imposed on the amount of credit that it would provide to ex-combatants and landholders. This implied that if the colón depreciated or the price of land rose during the implementation of the program, beneficiaries would be able to afford only smaller-size plots. Predictably, the land-owning class resisted the transfer of land to the FMLN and its supporters. Many viewed it as a way of increasing the FMLN's political appeal, which was certainly the FMLN's intention.

The FMLN contended that arguments about the availability of land and financing were irrelevant, and that both could be found if the government had the political will. In the FMLN's view, the government, having agreed to facilitate the transfer of land in exchange for demobilization, was simply obliged to deliver.

The positions taken by the FMLN and the government jeopardized the entire peace process, since the reduction and purge of the armed forces and the disbanding of strategic military units were contingent on the FMLN's demobilization. Removing the obstacles to the land program therefore took on great urgency with the belligerents cantoned, fully armed, and massed in an archipelago of concentration areas in the tiny country.

The October 13, 1992, Land Agreement

After intensive consultations with the two parties, the Secretary-General presented a land program that he knew would not fully satisfy either side, but that he asked them to accept, as a package and without amendment, as a fair and reasonable compromise.[37] With its acceptance by the parties a few days later, the so-called October 13, 1992, Land Agreement became, in effect, a supplement to the Chapultepec Agreement.[38] The Land Agreement removed a major roadblock to the demobilization of the FMLN and hence to the reform of the armed forces and the implementation of the agreements as a whole.[39]

Under the terms of the Secretary-General's compromise land proposal, as accepted by the parties, while the size of plots to which beneficiaries could aspire was smaller than the FMLN expected, the government agreed not to press for a ceiling on the amount of credit to be granted to beneficiaries for land acquisition. In practical terms, this meant that the government was assuming both the foreign exchange risk and the risk of land price speculation. The bottom line was that under this Agreement, beneficiaries were guaranteed a fixed amount of a particular type of land, irrespective of its price or possible foreign exchange fluctuation.

The program was designed to ensure the early and rapid transfer of substantial quantities of land to ex-combatants of the FMLN and the armed forces and the legalization of tenure or, if necessary, the relocation of landholders in the conflict zones. It provided for a maximum number of 47,500 beneficiaries, consisting of 7,500 ex-combatants from the FMLN, 15,000 from the armed forces, and 25,000 landholders in the former conflict zones. The amount of land to which each ex-combatant was entitled was determined by the agrarian reform criteria of the Land Institute (*Instituto Salvadoreño de Transformación Agraria*, ISTA) according to the different types of soil.

If owners of occupied land were willing to sell, the landholders would remain on their plots with a maximum size of land equal to that of ex-combatants and a minimum size of half that amount. If owners did not sell, relocation of landholders to land under comparable conditions would await the end of the program. Since the government could not evict landholders, relocation was necessarily to be left for the end. Landowners thus faced the following dilemma: sell their occupied land for cash at current market prices (obviously below the market price of unoccupied land) or hold out and wait until the government could relocate landholders currently occupying their land. Given the government's lack of financing to complete the land program and the existing land constraints, relocation could well take a long time. Thus, putting off relocation was intended to encourage owners to sell and thereby to put downward pressure on prices.[40]

Assuming that beneficiaries would receive on average 5 mz of an average type of land at an average cost of $600 per mz, it was estimated that 175,000–235,000 mz would be required for the arms-for-land program. In total, the program would cost between $105 million and $143 million (equivalent to 1.8–2.4 percent of GDP).[41]

The program was divided into three phases, reflecting the availability of land and financing. For the first emergency phase, resources would be made available between October 1992 and January 1993, when the government would provide state lands and USAID would donate financial resources to cover the needs of more than 15,000 beneficiaries. In this phase, priority was to be given to former FMLN combatants as they demobilized and to landholders on the transferred lands. We anticipated that, although the required resources would be available, the implementation of this phase would take significantly longer because of the practical, legal, and logistical difficulties involved.

In a second phase (February–March 1993), the EU would provide additional resources. Bilateral donors often have different conditionalities for their assistance. According to EU conditionality, this phase would benefit former combatants from the FMLN and the armed forces in equal numbers. Since it excluded landholders, this phase was to take place simultaneously with the first phase, so that landholders could also be legalized. It would be completed only when enough land could be negotiated for about 4,000 beneficiaries.

The timing of the third phase, which was to cover the needs of about 60 percent of the beneficiaries (roughly 28,000 people), was open-ended, since there were neither financial resources nor enough available land to satisfy the requirements for them. Nor was it possible to predict with any degree of certainty when sufficient land and resources would become available.[42]

Interestingly, a national survey conducted in October 1992 by the University of Central America—at a time when the purification of the armed forces and the demobilization of the FMLN were still pending—revealed that almost 40 percent of Salvadorans considered the land program to be the most difficult agreement to implement.[43] Only 20 percent thought that the most difficult requirement to meet was demobilization of the FMLN.

Implementation of the "arms-for-land" program

The agonizing difficulties and frustrations in implementing the arms-for-land program have been well documented elsewhere.[44] The serious delays in its implementation, for which both the government and the FMLN were responsible, created much tension. Many of the delays stemmed from administrative, bureaucratic, and technical difficulties. Others were due simply to the unwillingness of lower-ranking government officials to facilitate the transfer of land to FMLN ex-combatants and their supporters, and the reluctance of FMLN supporters to comply faithfully with the undertaking of their leaders. In the meantime, for many potential beneficiaries, the lack of land titles precluded access to credit for housing and agricultural production, thus impeding their effective reintegration into productive activities. Because of the delays, farmers missed the planting seasons in 1993 and 1994, which meant that El Salvador required more international food assistance than originally planned.

Although the October 13 Agreement was considered a breakthrough at the time, the land program remained at a virtual standstill until late 1993. Given the pace of progress reported up to that time (slightly more than eight beneficiaries a day), I calculated that it would take $9\frac{1}{2}$ years to complete the program. This led to an Acceleration Plan in August 1993. By the end of 1994, however, only 17,200 titles had been issued, covering slightly more than 40 percent of potential beneficiaries.

By the end of ONUSAL's mandate in April 1995, only 45 percent of potential beneficiaries had received land titles. Slow progress in the land program continued throughout 1995. Although the Chapultepec Agreement contemplated that the legalization of land tenure in the former conflict zones would be completed by July 31, 1995, by September 1995, only 74 percent of the potential beneficiaries had received land titles. At that time, however, the UN was surprised to learn that only 25 percent of these beneficiaries had had their titles filed with the land registry (UN A/50/517, October 6).

Three years of post-conflict economic reconstruction: 1992–4

While problems with reintegration had brought the peace process to the verge of collapse in September 1992, stabilization and structural reform under IMF and World Bank leadership proceeded smoothly, lowering inflation and reactivating economic growth. The improved economic performance reflected a strengthening of public finances. It was facilitated by the implementation of structural reforms that increased market allocation of resources, laying the basis for medium-term balance of payments viability and sustained growth. By mid-1990, the government had unified the exchange rate and had introduced a flexible exchange rate system, with the value of the colón depreciating in real effective terms by close to 20 percent. A more realistic exchange rate and structural reform, in conjunction with the peace agreements, improved investor confidence, which in turn underpinned an inflow of private capital (mostly a return of capital flight during the war). This, together with official transfers and debt rescheduling with bilateral creditors, including the Paris Club, allowed for a decrease in external debt arrears.

In evaluating both the obstacles and the achievements of post-conflict economic reconstruction, it is important to distinguish between the short- and long-run developments. By the time of the general election during the first half of 1994—the first in peacetime in decades—most observers, and certainly public opinion, had already filed away El Salvador as a success story.[45] The election was viewed as an important test of El Salvador's political maturity following a long war and decades of violence, but it was never expected to represent the end of the peace process. On the contrary, important portions of the peace accords remained to be implemented before the peace could be deemed irreversible. Regrettably, however, UN Secretary-General Boutros-Ghali's proclamation of success in mid-1994 was premature and removed pressure needed to complete important "unfinished business."[46] In addition to the problems related to the arms-for-land program, nagging problems continued to afflict the new PNC. These two programs were crucial to the success of the entire process.

The election both diverted attention from the peace process and politicized it, giving rise to a false analogy with Cambodia, where, in accordance with the Paris agreement, the holding of elections and the establishment of a new government largely concluded the UN's peacekeeping involvement.[47] Such a schedule was never intended for El Salvador. Even under the original schedule, the implementation of the El Salvador peace agreements would have lasted through 1994. Furthermore, with the waning of the Cristiani administration, the second half of 1993 saw a loss of momentum in the implementation of the agreements, on which the reintegration of impatient former combatants and their supporters depended.

The fact that elections were held peacefully and on schedule led to complacency in the international community about the state of affairs in El Salvador, and discussion began about establishing a sunset clause for ONUSAL. The Security Council wisely decided against this course when it renewed ONUSAL's mandate for six months in May 1994, thereby choosing to maintain pressure for the full implementation of the agreements. One more such extension took place in November.

Because of delays in the land and other programs and the need for the UN to complete verification of compliance with pending peace-related programs, a small team would still be necessary after ONUSAL's Security Council mandate finally concluded at the end of April 1995. At the time, the parties to the Chapultepec Peace Accord signed a protocol for the completion of all remaining programs (UN S/1995/407). On the following day, the Security Council adopted SCR 991 (1995), formally putting an end to ONUSAL and initiating a new mission, appropriately called MINUSAL (United Nations Mission in El Salvador) because of its reduced form. The new mission, which enabled the Secretary-General to report to the General Assembly and keep the Security Council informed, was created to continue to provide good offices and verify the implementation of remaining programs. However, it was considerably less visible than its predecessor, given that it was not under the magnifying glass of the Security Council.[48]

"Exit" from reconstruction into normal development: 1995–7

LOSS OF SECURITY COUNCIL CLOUT

The question that arose in mid-1995 was how to "exit" from post-conflict reconstruction amid a peacekeeping operation *strictu sensu* (with military and police personnel), to an operation in which the UN continued discharging its verification and good offices responsibilities and the economy could start the transition toward normal development. The challenge for the UN was to continue implementing its mandate under the peace agreements without losing the momentum provided by pressure from the international community through the Security Council. This had given ONUSAL a strong leadership role, as well as leverage with the programs and agencies of the UN system, in working towards the goal of peace consolidation. This was particularly true vis-à-vis the UNDP, whose local representative, under normal development situations, acts in the dual role of UNDP Resident Representative and Resident Coordinator of the UN System.

OVEREXTENSION OF THE UN

No other UN organ or body has the Security Council's clout. It can keep pressure on the implementation of peace agreements. The Council, however, is normally reluctant to take on or renew open-ended peacekeeping commitments that are financed through assessed contributions, in which permanent members pay a larger share than under the regular budget in order to give poor countries a discount in such financing.[49] One has to reckon with this reality, as well as with the growing pressure to set time limits on peacekeeping operations that goes with it. But, at the time, scarce financial resources were only part of the problem; there was a broader and understandable concern about overextension in general. This led to terminating operations very shortly after the mandate, as originally conceived, had been discharged.

This approach had worked well in Namibia. But the situation in El Salvador was conceptually and practically different from that of Namibia, and even that of Cambodia or Mozambique, where UN peacekeeping operations were ongoing at the time. In El Salvador, the UN was committed to verifying the implementation of all agreements signed by the two parties, a mandate that made no distinction between the military and police portions of the agreements and economic reconstruction.

The question of how the UN would continue to discharge its verification responsibilities was a matter of great debate. Many thought that verification required that the UN have a political office, and that no blue helmets, blue berets, or police monitors were necessary any longer. Instead, what was needed were political observers and good officers with sufficient technical capability—economic, legal, and otherwise—to follow and encourage implementation of complex accords and, above all, to enable the UN to keep a watchful eye trained on the process of consolidation of peace and prevention of future conflict.

Others thought that responsibilities of this nature could be transferred to field missions of development agencies. This is what eventually happened, and the UNDP's office assumed responsibility for all "unfinished business."

FAILURE TO ACHIEVE AN "INTEGRATED APPROACH TO HUMAN SECURITY"

By early 1995, the experience in El Salvador had had its positive impact on relations between the UN and the IMF. Furthermore, the UN had finally seen the need for a coordinated approach with the IFIs in peacebuilding. In his *Supplement to An Agenda for Peace* (January 1995), Secretary-General Boutros-Ghali acknowledged that "in putting together the peacebuilding elements in a comprehensive settlement plan, the UN should consult the IFIs in good time to ensure that the cost of implementing the plan is taken into account in the design of the economic plans of the government concerned." This had never been done before and, in my view, it represented a landmark in the history of the UN.

Ironically—and sadly—the intellectual father of the "integrated approach to human security" failed to take a small practical step to start putting the approach into practice. Despite Boutros-Ghali's earlier contention in his *Agenda for Peace* that the Secretary-General should be able to "mobilize the resources needed for ... positive leverage and engage the collective efforts of the UN system for the peaceful resolution of a conflict," he did not follow through with action aimed at achieving this goal. In fact, he rejected the Salvadoran President's request to appoint a UN staff member who had the necessary expertise, and had been fully involved in the agreements' implementation, to serve as the UNDP's interim head until the UN could certify that the land program and other socio-economic programs were completed.[50]

Had Boutros-Ghali believed that the person proposed by the government was not right for the job, or that he needed this person at Headquarters for some particular reason, he could still have discussed the government's valid request with his advisers to propose an alternative candidate. Doing so would have avoided placing a new obstacle in the path of implementation of the Peace Agreement. Instead, by ignoring the recommendation of his close advisers and dissociating the UN from the UNDP's recruiting process at this critical stage, he did a disservice to the successful completion of the process. This became particularly true *ex post*, when there was plenty of evidence that the UNDP's "business-as-usual" selection process was wrong for the purpose of peace consolidation in El Salvador.

The peace process in general, and the implementation of economic reconstruction in particular, withered from the end of 1995 to 1997, when the NRP came to an end. Lack of financial and technical support for the beneficiaries of the land and other reintegration programs forced many of them to abandon their newly acquired stake in the Salvadoran economy, with tragic security consequences. At the same time, the strong support of some of the critical donors waned as well. This is perhaps best documented in a report by Gunnarsson *et al.* (2004) evaluating the relationship of the Swedish International Development Cooperation Agency (SIDA) with El Salvador in 1979–2001. Sweden, one of the donors that most consistently supported El Salvador throughout this period, had, since the Peace Agreement in 1992, channeled about 80 percent of its aid through the UNDP, but stopped doing so in 1996.

The SIDA study documents how UNDP selection procedures had miserably failed to recruit the right person to lead in a critical phase of the implementation of the agreements, when support for the completion of peace-related programs was needed to ensure their sustainability. The study described how relations with the UNDP deteriorated after the new UNDP Resident Representative and Coordinator of the UN System was appointed in late 1995. The UN gave the UNDP responsibility for dealing with "unfinished business" related to the peace process. According to the authors, the new Representative, who came from a post in Africa and had long experience in countries where the UNDP's main work was to collaborate with governments in relatively uncontroversial projects, was not flexible or able to assume the more "political role" required to support the peace process. In their opinion, the UNDP stopped acting in support of the peace process. Thus, when Sweden's efforts to avoid this shift failed, SIDA decided to stop financing the UNDP.[51]

MISSING THE APRIL 30, 1996, DEADLINE

The UNDP's "development as usual" attitude, the reduced involvement of critical donors, and the inadequate resources of MINUSAL all acted to the detriment of the peace process and its sustainability. After missing a half-dozen successive deadlines for the final completion of the Peace Agreement, missing the April 30, 1996, deadline implied a new extension for MINUSAL. In his letter of January 25, 1996, on the Status of the Implementation of the Peace Accord, the Secretary-General gave a grim assessment, not only on the economic and social issues, but on the police and judiciary reforms as well.

Prospects for completion of the land and other reintegration programs in 1996 were, in the words of the Secretary-General "dim." Although about 87 percent of the potential beneficiaries had received title to their land, only about one-third of those titles had been registered.[52] More worryingly, he noted,

It is a growing concern that the integration of former combatants and their supporters into productive activities... may not be viable in the medium and long term.... The inadequacy and harshness of the terms of credit, as well as scarcity of technical assistance, is threatening most beneficiaries' ability to service their debt. Inability to service their debt excludes potential beneficiaries from further access to credit necessary for agricultural products and other basic needs. The transfer of these settlements' productive and social infrastructure, as well as housing, to their current occupants remains a particularly sensitive issue which could exacerbate social turmoil in the regions where they are located.[53]

Only in 2000, Secretary-General Annan reported to the General Assembly that issues related to land had been resolved to the point where the responsible institution, the Land Bank, had been dissolved and residual responsibilities transferred to the ISTA. The Secretary-General also noted that working with peasant associations and UNDP staff, the ISTA had shepherded the process nearly to completion.

THE END OF THE NRP

By the end of the NRP in 1997, the UN had certified compliance with most commitments of the peace agreements, and the expenditure associated with the required institutional reforms had been incorporated into the consolidated government budget.[54]

The performance of the economy and the structural reforms adopted during the NRP were impressive. Only five years after the Peace Agreement was signed, El Salvador received an investment grade rating from Moody's and a rating only one notch below investment grade (BB+) from Standard & Poor's (which, in Latin America, gave investment grade ratings at the time only to Chile and Uruguay). This meant that the country had made significant improvements in its debt situation and could start tapping international markets for funding. Real GDP growth averaged about 6 percent during 1992–7, and the rate of inflation fell to 10 percent. There was a marked strengthening of the balance of payments, which permitted the accumulation of reserves equivalent to six months of imports. The improvement in economic performance reflected a major reorientation of economic policy, including a greater reliance on market forces and a major reform of the exchange and trade systems.[55]

"NORMAL DEVELOPMENT": 1997 ONWARDS

With the full implementation of the NRP at the end of 1997, and with the expenditure associated with the institutional and other peace-related reforms incorporated into the consolidated government budget, it can be argued that by 1998 El Salvador had started a new transition towards normal development. Although this is well beyond the topic of this book, since the other countries studied here have not reached this stage, a few comments are useful in order to understand how it is different from the war-to-peace transition.

During this period, El Salvador had to continue carrying out necessary reforms and maintaining macroeconomic stability. Weak public finances, with a narrow tax base of about 11 percent of GDP, were a serious constraint for a country with El Salvador's social and infrastructure needs. An inadequate revenue base and extra expenditure, owing to the two devastating earthquakes in early 2001, put further pressure on the fiscal accounts. This took place soon after the dollar became legal tender and the use of the colón was phased out, a policy known as "dollarization." The new reconstruction budget—this time for expenditure related to disaster relief rather than post-conflict measures—increased the fiscal deficit by about 1 percent of GDP.[56] Rapid and sustained growth has also been impaired by low levels of domestic savings and investment, as well as weak competitiveness, related mostly to a poor business climate, including low levels of education and other human development indicators, complex bureaucratic procedures, and other factors that discourage investment.[57]

Despite the many problems, basic economic and political reform during post-conflict reconstruction, as well as reconciliation and reintegration into society of groups most affected by the war, facilitated the pursuit of long-term development goals, significantly reducing the probability that El Salvador will revert to war. However, many development challenges remain to be addressed.[58] Although El Salvador's government is committed to achieving the UN's Millennium Development Goals—some of which have already been achieved or are achievable—many remain elusive. The development challenge is how to make all of them achievable in a reasonable period, taking into account the fact that grants and other concessionary financing will be much restricted during this period, in comparison with the reconstruction one.[59]

An evaluation of the UN and ONUSAL

STAFFING ISSUES

One of the most exciting experiences for me in moving from the office of the Director-General for International Economic Development and Cooperation to that of the Secretary-General was involvement in peacebuilding operations. I was amazed upon visiting ONUSAL at the staff's expertise and commitment. Although conditions were not as harsh as they were in subsequent peacebuilding missions in Kosovo, East Timor, Afghanistan, Iraq, and many countries in Africa, it was a no-family post and hence staff members lived away from their families for long periods. Weekends were just as work-intensive as any other day. Conditions in the local offices throughout the former war zones were precarious. There was a sense of purpose and dedication among the staff that—despite the large number of exceptions—were generally lacking at Headquarters in New York.

As the father of the peace process, Assistant Secretary-General de Soto, who had become Boutros-Ghali's political adviser in the Cabinet, was involved in all aspects of the operation and had managed to entice top people to ONUSAL in the areas of human rights, the military, and the police. Under the leadership of the special representative, these experts performed exceptionally well.[60] Iqbal Riza, the veteran UN official who played a critical role in setting up ONUSAL, was later replaced by Augusto Ramírez-Ocampo and Enrique ter Horst, two impressive and well respected Latin Americans who helped maintain interest in and support for the operation. Periodic intervention and frequent visits by Under-Secretary-General for Peacekeeping Operations— and later for Political Affairs—Marrack Goulding was critical in moving the peace process forward.

The UN had major staffing problems, however, in carrying out anything related to economic reconstruction and coordination with the IFIs. In my view, this had to do with the fact that analytical economists at the UN were writing reports for the Economic and Social Council (ECOSOC), oblivious to the political work of the Organization. The Director-General's Office, which had been best placed to link the economic and political sides of the organization, had been dismantled at the time Boutros-Ghali came into office. Before this happened, under the superb leadership of Enrique ter Horst, who was the second in command in that office, we had carried out activities where the link with the IFIs was strong. These included the promotion and coordination of support for the Commonwealth of Independent States (CIS) countries after the fall of the Berlin Wall, as well as analytical work on compensation and sanctions related to Iraq's invasion of Kuwait. Since January 1992, the newly created Department of Economic and Social Information and Policy Analysis (DESIPA, now DESA) had been headed by the previous head of technical assistance, and had lost the political clout, expertise, or interest in this link that the Director General's office had. Despite a change of leadership a few years later, this Department did not regain any of these capacities or responsibilities.

The UN, both at headquarters and at the field level, found it difficult to attract economists able to deal with economic reconstruction issues. At the time, being a UN economist working on political economy issues was not highly regarded by fellow economists, who did not consider such issues as intellectually or empirically interesting as they do today, following years of constant coverage by the *Financial Times*, *Le Monde*, the *Wall Street Journal*, *The Economist*, and other leading publications.[61]

The lack of the right expertise made implementation of some complex programs, particularly the land program, difficult. ONUSAL had neither a permanent team of economists to deal with reconstruction, nor a special unit to deal with these issues.[62] Instead, it relied on staff who were appointed on short-term secondment from the Economic Commission for Latin America and the Caribbean (ECLAC/CEPAL). Regrettably, the UN never explored the possibility of longer-term secondment from the IFIs or from donor countries. As ONUSAL moved along, it became clear that neither the DPA nor the DPKO departments possessed the expertise to deal with these issues, which both departments viewed as somewhat beyond their mandate. At the same time, the DESIPA was never even consulted.[63] Under these circumstances, most of the important issues, particularly those for the Security Council, were dealt with in the Secretary-General's Office, which created problems with the functional departments.[64] Furthermore, there was an unclear division of responsibilities between ONUSAL and UN Headquarters, creating another source of chronic friction.

THE UN AND THE BRETTON WOODS INSTITUTIONS

As I showed earlier, the relationship between the UN and the IMF improved after a rocky start. "Rapprochement" led to regular consultations and exchange of information starting late in 1993. This proved useful in the later cases of Angola and Guatemala, where the UN began including the Fund and the World Bank in their consultations from the inception and kept them regularly informed about progress toward peace. The Bretton Woods institutions reciprocated by keeping the UN informed of economic and social developments, and particularly about financing prospects for the respective peace processes. Given this experience, staff on secondment from these institutions, particularly from the World Bank, clearly could have helped in the implementation of economic and social programs in El Salvador.

ONUSAL'S RELATIONS WITH UN AGENCIES

While ONUSAL existed, its relationship with the UN agencies was relatively good. Nevertheless, there was constant infighting for scarce resources, particularly at the consultative group meetings. Furthermore, it was not always easy to involve the programs and agencies of the UN system in the specific projects to which the UN gave top priority from a political point of view, namely those related to land and the police. The UNDP and the specialized agencies had their own country agenda and went along independently, making an integrated approach elusive in practical terms, although many often played lip service to the concept. Most notoriously, the UNDP, like the World Bank, was always reluctant to get involved in facilitating the land program. Both institutions were uniquely qualified to provide credit and technical assistance to beneficiaries of this program, but failed to do so, which seriously affected its sustainability.[65]

UN PERSONNEL POLICIES

UN recruitment contrasts sharply with that of institutions, such as the IMF, which are recognized as having staff who are competent in their fields. At the IMF, the human resources staff comprises qualified economists with many years of experience in both the functional and regional departments. Furthermore, the selection of new personnel involves day-long panel interviews with heads of departments and other staff from the relevant regional and functional departments. At the UN, however, recruiting officers have often been administrative staff who passed a General Services to Professional exam (known as the "G to P" exam). Thus, such officers in general lack substantive or technical expertise and often even a relevant academic degree. This made it impossible for them to identify "talent," let alone recognize "expertise" or "educational background."[66] In no area has this been more notorious than in the economic field, since political experts were better known or recognized at the UN. Recruiting officers at the UN often compare candidates based on the degree they have (irrespective of the university they attended) and on the number of years they have worked (irrespective of the relevance of the experience). This has seriously affected the recruitment of economists and other financial experts at the UN over the years.[67]

In addition to incompetence, there were serious governance issues that also affected the capacity of the UN to deal with peacebuilding. This is clear from *Good Intentions Corrupted: The Oil-for-Food Scandal and the Threat to the UN* (Meyer and Califano 2006: 235), which summarizes the findings and recommendations of the Independent Inquiry Committee chaired by Paul Volcker. In recording the performance of UN staff, the Committee concluded that the organization appears to be pervaded by a culture of resistance to accountability. Reform of personnel recruitment policies, as well as technical and governance training for staff will be critical in ensuring that UN staff are competent and accountable, and can improve their performance in post-conflict reconstruction.

Lessons from El Salvador

Post-conflict reconstruction in El Salvador highlights five lessons that could help national governments and the international community create and implement strategies for facing similar challenges in the future.

DESIGNING PEACE AGREEMENTS AND RECONSTRUCTION STRATEGIES CAREFULLY

An important lesson from the Salvadoran experience is that the design of the economic and social sections of a peace agreement is critical to its successful implementation. For this reason, careful thought and appropriate professional and technical expertise at the UN, as well as on negotiating teams, are needed in order to facilitate the elaboration of realistic peace agreements. In cases where peace does not follow a peace agreement, the same considerations should apply to the elaboration of the post-conflict economic reconstruction strategy.

Both in the design of peace agreements and in the design of the strategy for post-conflict economic reconstruction, the pros and cons of specificity versus vagueness must be weighed. The letter of the agreement and of the strategy itself, particularly concerning the national reconstruction plan, can determine the ease or difficulty with which the resulting programs will be implemented. The operational difficulties encountered in the implementation of the land program in El Salvador, for example, stemmed from both the specificity and the vagueness of the Chapultepec Peace Agreement.[68]

Moreover, peace agreements or reconstruction strategies should not create unrealistic expectations about what peace will bring. Unfulfilled expectations of disgruntled groups can seriously endanger a war-to-peace transition. As a result, policymakers and the international community that support post-conflict economic reconstruction must make an effort at communicating to the population what can be expected in the short, medium, and long term.[69]

ADOPTING AN INTEGRATED APPROACH TO ECONOMIC RECONSTRUCTION

The UN and the IMF, in conjunction with other national and international actors, must work together closely to provide an integrated approach (as opposed to a merely coordinated one) to matters of peace and economic stability. Each organization should use its own comparative advantage while taking into consideration and contemplating the needs of the others. By their doing so, many mistakes that led to parallel but largely unconnected and sometimes conflicting operations in the early stages of the Salvadoran transition, as well as to unfinished business in the implementation of many of its programs, could well have been avoided.

The experience of El Salvador demonstrates the importance of a combination of factors in creating an integrated approach to economic reconstruction.

First, the UN must design peace agreements that accord with the country's financial and technical capacity to implement them. Second, the different organizations must have the right kind and mix of multidisciplinary expertise to carry out economic reconstruction. Third, the programs critical to the successful implementation of the peace process must be adequately funded early on in the process. Finally, the government must not use conditions imposed by an IMF-sponsored economic program as an excuse to avoid making difficult political decisions that are essential to a successful transition.

ENSURING THE REINTEGRATION OF FORMER COMBATANTS AND THEIR SUPPORTERS

The war between Israel and Hezbollah in the summer of 2006 was a stark reminder that the disarmament, demobilization, and reintegration (DDR) of former combatants and militia groups is a *sine qua non* for making a war-to-peace transition irreversible. El Salvador's experience with reintegration—particularly with the arms-for-land deal—was successful in the sense that it helped maintain the ceasefire and lock in the peace process. However, the lack of sustained support through technical assistance and credit to the beneficiaries of the land program was a serious flaw that resulted in considerable public insecurity, as many beneficiaries abandoned the land and lacked a viable source of income.[70] The international community should not underestimate the importance of supporting post-conflict economic reconstruction in a sustained manner. As Secretary-General Boutros-Ghali noted in a March 1995 report, the *Plan 600* for medium-level FMLN former commanders, who received more training, orientation, and technical assistance, showed much better results than the land program in terms of investment and repayment.

FOCUSING ON ECONOMIC RECOVERY AND JOB CREATION TO AVOID AID DEPENDENCY

The success of reintegration and other reconstruction programs is often dependent on post-conflict economic recovery. Reintegration becomes particularly difficult in stagnant economies and in countries undergoing necessary but rigorous economic stabilization and structural reforms programs that follow a "development as usual" approach. This is because the financial implications of peace-related programs often conflict with the objectives of economic stabilization. In this regard, it is particularly important that the UN, the IFIs, and bilateral donors work together closely in support of the economic program, particularly to ensure domestic and foreign financing for all peace-related programs. Efforts by the Cristiani and Calderón Sol administrations, aimed at macroeconomic management and at financing part of the peace-related programs domestically through expenditure reallocation, facilitated foreign financing. The lesson from this experience is that donors are much more likely to support countries that do their best to help themselves. If countries do not do enough to adopt sound economic and financial policies, aid dependency will likely impede the course of their reconstruction and development.

ENSURING SUPPORT FOR THE TRANSITION TO NORMAL DEVELOPMENT

In its effort to get out of El Salvador in a speedy fashion—and to end its permanent members' assessed contributions—the Security Council neglected "unfinished business" concerning reintegration and other economic and social programs for former combatants. A modus operandi should have been worked out between the UN and the UNDP to ensure sustained support of beneficiaries of the peace process so that the programs could succeed over the medium and long term. Instead, programs that served the short-term purpose of supporting peace did not lead to longer-term development. In future operations, particularly those in which national authorities have relied so heavily on UN support for peace consolidation, such backing should be long-lasting. This does not mean that peacebuilding operations should remain indefinitely. It means that a working relationship—and the right kind of expertise—should be established with the UNDP and other UN programs and agencies to ensure that the political objectives are not overlooked, and that support for peace-related programs is not prematurely withdrawn by moving to a "development as usual" approach too quickly.

8 UN-led reconstruction following NATO-led military intervention: Kosovo

Economic and political background[1]

Post-conflict economic reconstruction in Kosovo has been determined largely by the conflict in the early 1990s between the majority ethnic Albanians (K-Albanians) and the ruling minority Serbs (K-Serbs), supported by Serbia. This conflict eventually evolved into a violent secessionist offensive in 1998–9, following the disintegration of the Socialist Federal Republic of Yugoslavia (SFRY).[2] In the spring of 1999, NATO launched air strikes—which the UN Security Council had not authorized but in practice condoned—against Serbia and its forces in Kosovo.[3] Following the military intervention, a Security Council resolution (SCR 1244) of June 1999 paved the way for economic reconstruction in Kosovo. While the UN led the transition to peace, K-Albanians saw the United States as "their great liberator."

BEFORE THE CONFLICT

Soon after he became President of Serbia, Slobodan Milosevic started a campaign to revoke the autonomy granted by the 1974 SFRY constitution to the provinces of Kosovo and Vojvodina.[4] In response, the K-Albanians called for Kosovo's secession from Serbia, with the aim of becoming an independent republic of Yugoslavia. In July 1990, the Serbian parliament dissolved Kosovo's predominantly K-Albanian legislature and government. Two months later, a newly adopted Serbian constitution revoked Kosovo's autonomy and provided for its direct rule from Belgrade, replacing the vast majority of K-Albanians in public service with K-Serbs. This led to the establishment of the shadow "Kosovo Republic," a parallel government under the leadership of Ibrahim Rugova.

With an area of less than 11,000 square kilometers (about half the size of El Salvador) and a mountainous landscape, the landlocked province of Kosovo was home to about 2.2 million people before the 1998–9 events. Of these, about 85 percent were ethnic Albanians and 10 percent were Serbs. Smaller groups included Roma (Gypsies), Bosniaks (Muslim Slavs), and Turks.

In the 1960s and 1970s, a string of factories were built in Kosovo in an effort to industrialize and diversify the mainly agricultural economy and provide downstream outlets for the large Trepca mining and metallurgical complex.[5] This strategy, however, neither created a strong industrial export base nor increased foreign exchange reserves. It did, however, lead to national bankruptcy and a large foreign debt, estimated at about $20 billion in the 1980s.

Economic data on Kosovo before the conflict are scant and unreliable. An estimated 60 percent of pre-1998 employment was created by agricultural activities (including forestry and agro-business). The means of production were predominantly socially owned. As part of the process of centralization, Milosevic dispossessed the K-Albanians of their equity in most socially owned enterprises "through a rigged process of privatization" (Dobbins *et al.* 2003: 111).

Indeed, while Kosovo was always the SFRY's poorest province, the Milosevic regime's policies of systematic discrimination and exclusion deepened Kosovo's socioeconomic underdevelopment, massive unemployment, and widening inter-ethnic inequalities. It has been estimated that Kosovo's economic activity contracted by about 50 percent in the five years following the imposition of Milosevic's rule, and a further 20 percent following the violent events of 1998–9.[6] Throughout this period, the brain drain accelerated, with many K-Albanians emigrating to other European countries, particularly Germany and Switzerland, thus establishing a large diaspora, which would play an important role in political and economic developments in Kosovo through the large amount of remittances they sent home.

Advocating peaceful resistance to the regime in Belgrade and economically sustained by the widespread informal economy and significant diaspora remittances, Rugova's shadow government carried out basic services for the K-Albanians and provided a considerable measure of order and restraint until the mid-1990s. According to Yannis (2003), the decision of the Kosovo Liberation Army (KLA), the underground paramilitary structure of K-Albanians, to mobilize against the Serbian state was triggered by the Dayton Accord of 1995 and by state collapse in neighboring Albania. In his view, the Dayton Accord rewarded those who had forcibly redrawn the ethnic and political map of neighboring Bosnia and Herzegovina. Thus, remittances, which had been used productively by the "Kosovo Republic" to provide services and had supposedly played a "conflict-averting" role, were increasingly captured by the KLA as their popular support increased. This allowed the KLA to purchase arms from neighboring Albania as that country sank into chaos. The KLA's military power grew *pari passu* with its control of the shadow economy, remittances, and a growing cross-border smuggling and drugs network.[7]

THE CONFLICT

Following the failure of diplomatic efforts aimed at putting pressure on Milosevic to cease repression and restore autonomy to Kosovo, the UN Security Council (UNSC) imposed an arms embargo on the Federal Republic of Yugoslavia (FRY), comprising Montenegro and Serbia, including Kosovo (SCR 1160 of March 31, 1998). A subsequent resolution in September 1998 (SCR 1199) requested states to pursue all means to stop remittances from their countries that could be used to contravene SCR 1160.

The increasing deterioration of the situation on the ground led the international Contact Group to agree on a draft peace plan for Kosovo.[8] In February 1999, the Contact Group invited the two sides to Rambouillet, near Paris, to start peace talks based on the draft plan. Moreover, a day after the Contact Group agreed on the draft plan in January, the North Atlantic Council authorized NATO to launch air strikes against targets in Serbia, in case the Serbs rejected it. The plan called for a three-year interim settlement in which Kosovo would have greater autonomy within Yugoslavia, as it had under Tito. It also contemplated the deployment of a NATO-led international military force. The draft plan was signed by the K-Albanian delegation on March 18, but the Serb delegation rejected it. On March 24, NATO began air strikes on the FRY.[9] Yugoslav forces moved rapidly to expel K-Albanians from their homes and atrocities were committed in the process.

The human and economic consequences of the 1998–9 conflict were overwhelming. An estimated 50 to 75 percent of houses were either looted and burned or destroyed by Yugoslav forces and NATO's air strikes. The OSCE estimated that about 900,000 K-Albanians, almost half the prewar population of Kosovo, fled to Albania, the Former Yugoslav Republic of Macedonia, and Bosnia, in an effort to avoid being abused, tortured, raped, or killed by Yugoslav forces.

THE WAR-TO-PEACE TRANSITION

On June 3, 1999, after 78 days of increasingly intense air strikes that inflicted damage on Yugoslavia's infrastructure and armed forces, in conjunction with a serious threat of a ground offensive to follow, Milosevic agreed to a peace plan based on NATO demands and a proposal from the Group of Eight.[10] The plan called for the withdrawal of all Yugoslav forces from Kosovo; the deployment of an international peacekeeping force with NATO at its core; and an open-ended UN administration of Kosovo, leading first to elected interim institutions and eventually to negotiations on Kosovo's final status.

On June 10, SCR 1244 opened the way to Kosovo's complex multi-pronged transition to peace: from war to public security; from Belgrade's political control to a UN-administered interim protectorate; from ethnic exclusion to national reconciliation; and from a state-controlled to a market-oriented economy.[11] Difficulties in this transition as well as uncertainty about a future political settlement for Kosovo have constrained economic policy-making and deterred investment. The very tense and volatile political and security situation in the ethnically divided city of Mitrovica and other Serb enclaves has, at various times since 1999, fuelled speculation about a possible partition of the territory, thus adding to the uncertainty. The non-participation of members of the K-Serb minority in municipal and parliamentary elections has also undermined security and destabilized the political situation.

According to SCR 1244, negotiations on Kosovo's "final status" must involve Belgrade. The talks only started on February 2006 and concluded in December 2007 without resolving the issue. On February 17, 2008, K-Albanians declared unilateral independence, with support from the United States and the larger members of the EU, but with strong opposition of Serbia, Russia, and several members of the EU.

AN INTERIM OPEN-ENDED UN PROTECTORATE

Because Kosovo remained a province of Serbia—with the political transition leading to national sovereignty or some other arrangement indefinitely delayed—its eight-year post-conflict transition has been unique and particularly troublesome.[12] As per SCR 1244, the UN Interim Administration in Kosovo (UNMIK) has had to perform civil administration functions that are usually the sole prerogative of a sovereign government. All legislative and executive powers to carry out such a mandate were vested in UNMIK and exercised by the Special Representative of the Secretary-General (SRSG) through the issuance of "Regulations" until Kosovo's final status could be determined. This was the first time that the UN was given such broad government responsibilities.[13] To perform these functions, the UN led, for the first time, "an integrated operation" as advocated by Boutros-Ghali in the early 1990s, in which the UN set priorities and coordinated humanitarian, civil administration, democratization, and economic reconstruction activities. A senior official of a different organization headed each of these four functional "pillars."[14]

UN UNPREPAREDNESS

The fact that K-Albanians had been used to running educational, health, and other services was a critical element in their readiness to perform civil functions after the NATO war ended. Thus, while the international community got organized—which required considerable time, reflecting the UN's organizational capacity and the lack of human and financial resources—the K-Albanians took it upon themselves to carry out a number of activities.[15] This was an important factor behind the difficulties encountered by UNMIK to perform the functions mandated by the Security Council, particularly early on in the transition. Not only did the KLA carry out civil functions in the period immediately following NATO's bombing, but they financed them through increasing involvement in illicit and criminal activities. As a result, it was difficult to eradicate these activities—which should be a priority of every war-to-peace transition—and lawlessness became a permanent feature of economic reconstruction in Kosovo.

GOVERNANCE

By August 1999, UNMIK slowly started adopting "Resolutions" and carrying out economic reconstruction functions. Security Council Resolution 1244 had tasked UNMIK with gradually transferring its administrative responsibilities to elected, interim autonomous government institutions, while retaining an oversight role. Ultimately, UNMIK would oversee the transfer of authority from the interim autonomous institutions to permanent institutions, after Kosovo's final status was determined.

By February 2000, UNMIK had established the Joint Interim Administrative Structure (JIAS) to allow Kosovars to share in the provisional administration of Kosovo with UNMIK. The JIAS included K-Albanians and K-Serbian leaders, but Kosovars did not yet exercise decision-making authority in them. Kosovars took the first steps in establishing their own elected institutions on October 26, 2000, when OSCE-supervised municipal elections were held.

In May 2001, UNMIK issued a "Constitutional Framework" for Kosovo, providing for an elected legislature and an autonomous government with limited powers. The framework established that UNMIK would share responsibility for administering Kosovo with the Provisional Institutions of Self Government (PISG).[16] Elections to the Kosovo assembly were held on November 17, 2001. Slightly less than half of eligible Serb voters participated in the vote.[17] The formation of the government was delayed for months due to political infighting. Three leading ethnic Albanian parties were represented in the PISG, which finally took office in April 2002.[18] Serbs gained control of one ministry, while another represented non-Serb minorities (mostly Roma, Bosniaks, and Turks).

While the final status of Kosovo remained in limbo, SRSG Michael Steiner announced in April 2002 a policy of "standards before status," with a number of benchmarks needed to be satisfied before any negotiation on final status took place.[19] The Security Council endorsed these benchmarks and a progress report was presented at the end of 2005. At that time, the Secretary-General appointed former President of Finland Martti Ahtisaari as his Special Envoy. During a trip throughout Kosovo and the region in December, Ahtisaari argued that final status presupposed meeting the standards, and that more concrete progress was needed in implementing them (UNMIK 2005).

In February 2006, Serbs and K-Albanians started UN-mediated talks on the future status of Kosovo in Vienna. In July, the President and Prime Minister of Serbia met Kosovo's authorities for the first time.[20] Talks were complicated in August 2006, as the Serbs accused Ahtisaari of being biased against them. In the following months, there was little progress or compromise, and independence did not come about before the end of the year, as some expected. Violent clashes in mid-February 2007 between the police and demonstrators, in which at least two people died, were a harbinger of the difficulties ahead. In March 2007, Athisaari put forward a UN plan that granted Kosovo "supervised independence" under EU tutelage and NATO protection. Although K-Albanians accepted the plan, Serbia rejected it, leading to renewed violence.

The UN mandated the Troika (the EU, Russia, and the United States) to mediate a negotiated agreement between Serbia and the K-Albanians by December 10, 2007. The K-Albanians had said that if no agreement was reached, they would declare unilateral independence, with the US informally signaling its subsequent official recognition, although the degree of supervision, if any, remained unclear (*Financial Times Editorial* 2007a). Slovenian Prime Minister Janez Janca, whose country was going to assume the EU's rotating presidency in January 2008, indicated three weeks before the deadline that the EU would accept conditional independence, provided the K-Albanians accepted international supervision and guarantees for the Serb minority. As Janca envisaged it, this proposal would include tougher limits on Kosovo's independence than were contained in Ahtisaari's Plan (Wagstyl and Studemann 2007). Despite Janca's declaration, members of the EU, most clearly Cyprus, have opposed an independent Kosovo. Other members of the EU like Spain, Romania, Slovakia, and Greece have also expressed concerns about Kosovo's independence because of the boost it would give to their minorities (Blitz 2007a; Wagstyl 2007).

The December 10th deadline passed without an agreement. On the positive side, the K-Albanians declared that they would not press ahead with a declaration of independence without coordinating the move with the EU and the

United States, and were prepared to delay the move until early 2008. Given that the EU is their main donor, Hashim Thaci, former KLA leader declared that for them recognition was as important as independence (MacDonald and Blitz 2007; Bilefsky 2007).

On January 9, 2008, Thaci was elected Prime Minister and on February 17 Kosovo declared unilateral independence from Serbia. At the same time, Kosovo's authorities have accepted EU supervision along the basic lines envisaged in the Ahtisaari Plan for a phased process, including devolution and protection for minorities and historic buildings. As the book goes to print, it is not clear what will be the legal basis for the transfer of power from UNMIK's protectorate to EU-supervised sovereignty in Kosovo since SCR 1244 is still in force.[21]

Some fear that the move toward "supervised sovereignty" may lead to secession of the Mitrovica region in the north and to fighting over what Serbs consider their cultural heartland, which includes the most sacred sites of the Serbian Orthodox Church (Wood 2006a; Smith 2007; MacDonald and Blitz 2007). As the EU's representative to the Troika has pointed out, unilateral independence would not heal the wounds of post-Yugoslav conflict, but would instead create a huge new burden for the international community. NATO is prepared to avoid the violence that afflicted Kosovo in 2004, which ended with 19 people dead and 30 churches and monasteries destroyed or damaged. UNHCR and other aid agencies have already made contingency plans for an exodus of 5,000 to 100,000 refugees which would account for most Serbs in Kosovo (Blitz 2007; Kulish 2007; Wood 2007).

Three months after Kosovo's unilateral declaration of independence, the exodus has not yet happened and violence has been contained. It is too early, however, to rule them out. In Serbia, the repudiation of Kosovo's decision is widespread. Despite threatening to impose sanctions on Kosovo, Serbia has not done so yet. While an interruption of trade with Serbia will not be specially damaging on Kosovo since most trade is with the Former Yugoslav Republic of Macedonia, UN officials worry that sanctions could disrupt the supply of electricity. This is because Kosovo's main power plant, providing 75 percent of total electricity, runs on water supplied from the north, where Serbia still retains substantial control. Furthermore, Serbia could also interrupt other sources of electricity by stopping transmission from Europe, which runs on power lines through Serbia. Disruptions of this sort would cause additional problems in the already poor and lagging Kosovo economy where electricity is normally unreliable to start with (Wood 2007; Bilefsky 2008b).

In addition to 16,000 NATO-led troops in Kosovo, the EU leaders agreed to send up to 3,000 police, judges, prosecutors, and customs officials to stabilize Kosovo after its declaration of independence. After a 120-day period for transfer of power from the UN, Kosovo's operation would become the largest civilian crisis management mission of the EU.

Serbia has said that it would consider the EU mission illegal unless it is sanctioned by the Security Council. Given Russia's veto power, this will not probably happen. As a carrot, the EU is offering Serbia an accelerated path to EU membership, assuming that its leaders cooperate with the UN war crimes tribunal in The Hague (Barber 2007; Wagstyl and MacDonald 2008).

Challenges to the UN in Kosovo

The war-to-peace transition in Kosovo posed several challenges for the international community in general and for the UN in particular.

BROAD RESPONSIBILITY IN GOVERNMENT

The first and foremost challenge for the UN was the need to exercise government functions that are normally the responsibility of national authorities. Having such broad responsibility of government was indeed the main challenge for the UN, particularly since it had neither the executive nor the managerial capacity to exercise it.[22]

LEADING AN INTEGRATED OPERATION

The second challenge stemmed from UNMIK's establishment as an integrated operation. Although this was certainly a welcome innovation, it was a risky one for the UN. In the process of setting priorities and coordinating all activities, the UN had to take a leading role over organizations such as the EU and the OSCE which are considered to have better resources and management. Not surprisingly, working harmoniously with these organizations, as well as with UNHCR and other UN agencies, was particularly difficult at the early stages. Each institution had its own charter, budget, and governing body to which it had to respond. Furthermore, maintenance and enforcement of law and order was under the control of KFOR, with NATO the only organization not subordinated to the UN. NATO would also provide support for civilian operations (particularly in the humanitarian and reconstruction areas) in the early transition; hence the issue of cooperation and coordination between UNMIK and NATO also became quite a challenge early on.

KOSOVAR INVOLVEMENT IN GOVERNMENT

It was clear from the beginning that to be able to govern effectively, the UN had to have the support of Kosovo's people and had to build a consensus for reconstruction. To succeed, the civil administration system that UNMIK established had to conform as much as possible to what Kosovo's people wanted in the medium and long term.

The debate about economic and political reconstruction in the summer of 1999 was clearly dominated by K-Albanians, given that fewer than 100,000 of the pre-war Serb community of approximately 200,000 remained in Kosovo.[23] Furthermore, there were deep divisions between those who wanted to return to the pre-1990 situation, before Kosovo's autonomy was eliminated and social ownership of the means of production was the rule, and those who wanted to establish a modern, market-oriented economy, closely integrated with the rest of Europe, as UNMIK had in mind. Despite the sharp contrast between these positions, K-Albanians were united in rejecting an economic policy framework and the establishment of a civil administration conforming to FRY laws.

The third challenge for UNMIK was thus to build a consensus among K-Albanians and gradually to involve them in government, while incorporating the K-Serbs as much as possible. This process was particularly difficult throughout, because K-Albanians tried to go as far as they could in the direction of full independence.

THE CHALLENGE OF FINANCING

The fourth challenge was to finance an operation without the involvement of a sovereign country. Given its status as a province, Kosovo was not burdened at the time by repayment of foreign debt, but, at the same time, it has not been able to issue its own currency or borrow money. In particular, Kosovo could not borrow from the IFIs in its transition to peace, as most countries do. Thus, foreign assistance to Kosovo had to take the form of bilateral and multilateral grants.[24]

As soon as SCR 1244 was adopted on June 10, 1999, interim SRSG Sergio Viera de Mello announced his intention of establishing a "quick impact projects trust fund" that would enable the UN mission to respond immediately to emergency needs in a broad spectrum of areas affecting the local population.[25] This was particularly needed in the case of Kosovo, since disbursement of international assistance through normal channels takes time, and Kosovo could not self-finance programs to meet the basic needs of the population. As discussed earlier, Kosovo benefited from the World Bank Post-Conflict Facility (PCF) and the Trust Fund for Kosovo that the Bank created in November 1999.

DESIGNING THE STRATEGY FOR ECONOMIC RECONSTRUCTION

Designing the overall economic reconstruction strategy itself was the fifth challenge. As in other war-to-peace transitions, donors have shown a clear reluctance to finance current expenditure (wages and pensions), except in the very short term.[26] Moreover, bureaucratic restrictions and complicated bidding procedures in the EU, the main donor, added to the problem. These factors negatively affected the design and implementation of the reconstruction strategy, particularly in its early period. On the positive side, however, its strategic position in Europe gave Kosovo access to large financial and technical resources as well as to regional markets for its exports, and resulted in remittances that would be unavailable to other countries in the war-to-peace transition.

Economic reconstruction of Kosovo

Together with the challenges posed by the UN's broad responsibility in government and its weak executive and managerial capabilities, the devastation of the war and lack of investment during a decade of conflict had severely degraded housing, public utilities, and other services. By the time UNMIK was established in June 1999, there was hardly any electrical power or water supply, telephones did not work, schools were closed, food and medicines were in very short supply, and hospitals functioned under very precarious conditions.

RESTORING SERVICES AND HOUSING

Water and electricity supplies were restored on an emergency basis, initially functioning for a few hours each day on an unreliable basis.[27] UN agencies and NGOs, led by UNHCR, were busy throughout the summer and fall providing food assistance and winterizing basic housing. To increase awareness of the housing problems in light of the fast-approaching winter, UNMIK and KFOR organized a helicopter trip for donors in late summer to visit destroyed houses and villages in the Trepre region, in northeast Kosovo (Podujevo), which is 900–1100 meters above sea level. Although housing in this area was insufficient to accommodate people during the winter, inhabitants refused to move to shelters in Mitrovica, a pattern repeated in other villages. We visited the house of a recent war widow with 10 children under 12, including a baby. This situation was not uncommon in Kosovo, providing a window on the demographics of K-Albanians and their bleak prospects for the immediate future. UNHCR and NGOs were already active in the area but much more needed to be done.

There was widespread agreement among UNHCR and other UN staff that distributing local construction materials to villagers was the most efficient way to increase housing quickly. One of the most interesting proposals was to use galvanized steel, which could be produced locally at a nearby Vucitrin factory, to build houses or other buildings. A Swedish/Danish firm that manufactured the machines was offering them at $125,000.[28] It was estimated that eight machines would have sufficed to build what was necessary for the winter. With 10 tons of steel (at $7,500 a ton), it was possible to build four houses of 50 square meters each. Unfortunately, this and other such quick-impact projects were put aside because of EU donors' long bidding processes and restrictions on involving companies from outside their region. This situation led to a short-term solution that provided kits to winterize houses, but that did not address the longer-term housing problem—an example of the distortions, discussed in Chapter 3, often associated with emergency programs that follow different types of crises.

Garbage and rubble were the characteristic feature of Pristina in the early post-war period. One of the most vivid memories of the time I spent there immediately after the war was the yowling of abandoned and starving dogs throughout the night as they searched the garbage dumps for food. Although not a serious problem as in Cambodia, unexploded ordnance, including cluster bombs and mines were nevertheless a lethal threat. Driving through Kosovo, I could once see how these were triggered by cattle roving through fields and forests. The International Committee of the Red Cross (2000) noted that the conflict left behind a severe problem of unexploded remnants of war which would take time to address. De-mining was an issue right after the war since the reactivation of agriculture, a key economic activity, depended on it. Furthermore, these devices made it dangerous for people to move around freely in certain areas.[29]

REACTIVATION OF THE PRIVATE SECTOR

Basic economic activity in the informal sector resumed quickly with the return of about 800,000 refugees. Food, medicine, fuel, and other essential goods that had been scarce in the weeks immediately following the end of NATO bombing were gradually reintroduced into the stores through private-sector initiatives, facilitated by remittances from the diaspora. Pizza shops soon mushroomed—the Italian influence on K-Albanians was indeed strong—and were a mandatory meeting place for expatriates and the few Kosovars who could afford them. Coffee shops, serving good Italian cappuccino, were not only a respite from hard conditions, but also a place to observe how the exchange rate evolved. If you paid in Deutsche Marks (DM), the change normally came in dinars. Although a different amount of change from the previous day often simply meant that the waiter did not have more coins (or so he said), it was also a function of events or news that, in practice, affected the exchange rate. Until banks opened, this was as close to an exchange rate indicator as one could get.

ELIMINATING EXTORTION AND ILLEGAL ACTIVITIES

Without waiting for UNMIK to get firmly established, the KLA appointed its own parallel government and started developing its own legislative framework. More worryingly, exploiting the vacuum created by inevitable delays in the implementation of UNMIK's customs policy, the KLA imposed a system of tax collection, more properly described as extortion, on imports, fuel distribution, and other goods. User fees were also collected on a number of services. The collection of unlawful taxes and fees built up a power base for the KLA, undermined UNMIK's authority, and called into question UNMIK's and KFOR's integrity, because they did not stop it. All this made economic reconstruction more difficult. Although not totally new to Kosovars, extortion and other illegal activities have become deeply ingrained in Kosovo's economy and have been difficult to control.[30]

DEVELOPMENT OF A "MINIMALIST" INSTITUTIONAL AND POLICY FRAMEWORK

Despite the desperate need for resumption of basic services, UNMIK was slow to develop a minimalist institutional and policy framework to start the implementation of its civil administration mandate as soon as possible. This was partly due to difficulties in recruiting personnel and moving decisions through complicated and inefficient bureaucracies.[31]

UNMIK's top priority during the summer of 1999 was the establishment of a policy framework that would allow for vital reconstruction of basic services and the establishment of a sound, operative, and efficient economy. A simple budget, setting spending priorities for the remaining months of 1999, was presented to donor countries in July, in search of financing. But Kosovars eventually needed to be responsible for their own current spending. Therefore, the basis for revenue collection became an urgent matter. As there were practically no production, income, and services to tax, imports had to provide the tax base at an earlier stage.

Since Kosovo could not administer its own customs because of its status as a "province of Serbia", UNMIK had to establish a system of its own—the first UN customs administration ever—with revenue collection earmarked to finance the province's budget. Starting on September 1, a simple system was established with *ad valorem* tariffs imposed at a flat 10 percent rate. The system was supplemented with excise duties and sales taxes levied on all imports. A better and fairer tax system was established within the first year, with excise taxes levied on domestic consumption and a service tax on hotels, food, and beverages, thereby covering the large number of expatriates while not relying exclusively on imports.[32]

To restart the economy and to address another significant source of corruption and distortions, the import, distribution, and sale of petroleum products had to be legalized and regulated as well. Use of the Deutsche Mark, the de facto currency in circulation, was legalized in August, as was the use of all other currencies. The euro replaced the DM in early 2002. Compulsory payments in Yugoslav dinars, which remained legal tender, were discouraged through transaction fees.

Because of the absence of a banking system, Kosovo became a purely cash-based economy as of June 1999. UNMIK, through Pillar IV, and with the assistance of the IMF, worked throughout the summer to develop a modern, market-based payments and banking system. In early September a Cash Payment Office (CPO) provided a safe facility for cash deposits from taxes collected at the border and for handling payments made from the Kosovo budget, including those to public sector employees. UNMIK also established the Banking and Payments Authority of Kosovo (BPK) in November 1999 to supervise all financial institutions and operate close to thirty branches throughout the province. Also in the fall of 1999, with the assistance of the IMF, UNMIK established the Central Fiscal Authority (CFA) to exercise firm control over all aspects of the budget.[33]

To promote the development of the private sector, micro-financing was offered from the very beginning. This was promising, since investment in small and medium-sized enterprises was not confronted with the "property rights" problem that would bog down larger socially owned and publicly owned enterprises, as we shall see below. UNMIK (Pillar IV) started working with the European Bank for Reconstruction and Development (EBRD) in August 1999 to craft a well-formulated proposal for the promotion and financing of micro-enterprises.[34] The EBRD had the technical expertise and the money to implement the program, which was similar to its successful and ongoing micro-financing operations in Russia, Albania, and Bosnia. As soon as UNMIK could provide a minimum legal and regulatory framework for the financial sector, the provision of micro-financing started, using banks in the region, since the EBRD, like other IFIs, could not lend to Kosovo directly.

KOSOVO'S BUDGET

Two budgets were prepared for fiscal year 2000 (FY-2000). The regular budget covered only recurrent expenditures such as the provision of basic goods and services, a minimal social safety net, and rehabilitation of utilities. As Corker, Rehm, and Costial (2001: 9) explain, because defense and debt servicing were not included, recurrent expenditure was kept low, at about 14 percent of GDP. Welfare and social security spending was also low relative to comparable economies, because the government made no payments for public pensions (which were liabilities of the FRY), and because social spending at the time was augmented by sizable off-budget humanitarian assistance. The wage bill, too, was modest, reflecting low public employment levels and the underdevelopment of some functions (for example, military, police, and judicial ones). Spending on health care and education, where employment levels were relatively high, was broadly in line with other countries in the region.

The reconstruction budget was drawn up separately and fully financed by donors. Given that Kosovo would be highly dependent on foreign financing, transparency and good governance in the preparation and execution of its budget was essential. For this reason, UNMIK, supported by the IMF, devoted great effort to establishing the appropriate institutional framework.

STIPENDS TO PUBLIC SECTOR EMPLOYEES

In August, UNMIK paid a small "stipend" (subsistence payments) to health, education, and other public workers who had not had any income for the two months since they had gone back to work. The stipend was financed from the UN Trust Fund, which had been established to support civil administration in Kosovo in 1999, and was paid in a most unusual way. When the Serbs fled Kosovo, they took with them all banking assets, including banks' safe deposit boxes. At the same time, there was no way to change large-denomination DM bills. Hence, a commercial plane chartered by UNMIK arrived from Frankfurt full of 10 and 20 DM bills and 1 and 5 DM coins. Since there were no safe deposits available, the money had to be transferred to a room and guarded by KFOR officers.[35]

The arrival of the money was well known to the population and created great expectations. Pristina's airport was closed and the commercial plane carrying the money was one of the few planes arriving. With the news that the UN would pay stipends, schools and hospitals were filled with people, supposedly working there. There was no way of knowing who was employed and who was not, since records had disappeared. In any case, since the main objective was to restore security and move the political transition forward, everyone present received the small stipend—whether they were entitled to it or not.

DISTORTIONS CREATED BY THE LARGE INTERNATIONAL PRESENCE

From the very beginning, wages paid by the international community as a whole created wage distortions that put serious pressure on budgetary decisions and made it difficult to recruit qualified Kosovars to fill posts in the civil administration. Although this was the case in other post-conflict transitions, it was particularly serious in Kosovo, given the large number of agencies and NGOs involved and the fact that they had more resources than is usually the case in developing countries. Demand by international workers for food, lodging, and other commodities also put upward pressure on prices of non-tradable goods and services and increased the need for humanitarian assistance. The difficulty in setting up an efficient civil service concerned not only the relatively low wages paid, but also the fact that, as in other war-to-peace transitions, the best educated and most able had often been the first to emigrate (and were more likely to stay abroad) or work for the international community for a larger salary.

Thorny issues in Kosovo's reconstruction

The thorny issues in Kosovo's reconstruction were rather distinct from those encountered in other post-conflict situations. While this is, in part, related to its special status as a province, rather than as a sovereign country, as well as to the legacy of socialism in its productive structure, some of the challenges were the result of bad choices in policymaking.

INVESTMENT AND PROPERTY RIGHTS

Early in the transition, UNMIK had to deal with critical and complicated issues. Some of those relating to property rights, for example, were too political and complex to be solved by the UN interim civil administration. Nevertheless, UNMIK established the Housing and Property Directorate to provide overall direction on property rights in Kosovo. The Housing and Property Claims Commission was launched at the same time as an independent organ of the Directorate, and was entrusted with resolving private non-commercial disputes concerning residential property.

Property-rights issues involving commercial property were more complex. This was particularly true of large (in terms of employment and capital) publicly owned enterprises such as Kosovo Electricity Company (KEK), Post and Telecommunications Company (PTK), water, waste, and heating companies, the Pristina airport, as well as larger companies that developed under socialism into socially owned enterprises.

After a decade of neglect and under-investment, property-rights issues became a serious deterrent to investment in many critical areas, and precluded an overall investment strategy for Kosovo. An important component of the patchy investment strategy that was implemented was the long-term reconstruction of the housing stock, more than half of which was estimated to have been destroyed in the 1999 war. Other priority areas included the rehabilitation of infrastructure and the reactivation of agriculture and agro-business activities, particularly through the promotion of small enterprises.

THE TREPCA MINING AND METALLURGICAL COMPLEX

The most notorious socially owned enterprise was the Trepca mining and metallurgical complex, a producer of lead and zinc that had been a source of pride, income, employment, and ethnic conflict in the Mitrovica area for many years. Indeed, many say that control of the complex was the main economic reason for Serbian opposition to Kosovo's independence. UNMIK had to decide whether it made sense to restart its activities, and, if so, how and where to find the financing to do so. Some European companies approached UNMIK in August 1999 with documents showing that the Milosevic government had privatized the complex in the mid-1990s and that they held equity in it. Furthermore, there was uncertainty about future property rights. Would prospective investors be interested in the Trepca complex when it was not clear what would happen to property rights after the UN transitional administration left and Kosovo attained final status?

As in other cases where property rights are unclear, privatization in Kosovo has been a difficult and uncertain option. Investors—except the very risk-prone who often rely on dubious or illicit sources of capital (and as such are undesirable)—are not normally willing to take the risk that a new legitimate government will reverse the policy. This could well be done on the premise that the UN, an interim administration, or an occupying country such as the US in the case of Iraq, for example, had no right to divest of local government assets, or even to lease them.[36]

In the case of the Trepca mines, whether and how to restart operations was not, in itself, a simple matter, because the question could not be decided on simple profit-maximizing criteria. The complex was controlled by some of the few remaining Serbs in Kosovo and was, at the same time, very much a political target of K-Albanians, particularly those who had been fired from the complex in the early 1990s, when Kosovo lost its autonomy from Serbia. Another consideration to take into account in deciding on Trepca's future was that the exploitation of the complex would have serious financing implications. It would require hiring a large number of foreign mining and management experts, as well as substantial back-payment of salaries and pensions to local workers. Environmental considerations needed also to be taken into account, since Trepca had been, and continued to be, a serious environmental threat.[37]

Despite the low mineral prices at the time, operations at Trepca restarted in the summer of 2000. In August, claiming concern about rising levels of atmospheric lead in northern Mitrovica, UNMIK assumed control of the Zvecan smelter, after 3,000 KFOR soldiers stormed and took over the plant at dawn. The same day, UNMIK announced that a contract with ITT Kosovo Consortium Ltd., a consortium of US, French, and Swedish companies, was formed to assess and initiate rehabilitation of the Trepca complex. UNMIK expected that, by employing 2,000 workers from all communities, reviving the Trepca complex could alleviate tensions and promote peaceful coexistence in the Mitrovica area. The move, however, was interpreted by residents of the area and many others as the first step toward handing the most valuable piece of real estate in the Balkans to foreign companies.[38]

UNMIK based its action on SCR 1244 and Regulation 1999/1, which specified that "UNMIK shall administer movable or immovable property, including monies, bank accounts, and other property of, or registered in the name of the Federal Republic of Yugoslavia or the Republic of Serbia or any of its organs, which is in the territory of Kosovo." When the agreement with the Consortium was concluded, UNMIK stated that it was not in a position to determine the validity of any claims of ownership rights or other interests in Trepca, which should be determined by a competent court, based on applicable law (UNMIK/PR/312 of August 17, 2000).

Subsequent lack of progress on Trepca is not surprising.[39] Given that past property rights could not be resolved, that future property rights were uncertain, and that both K-Serbs and some K-Albanians strongly opposed privatization, who would invest in Trepca? The risk that any decision by UNMIK or an interim Kosovo government might be reversed was too high to lure desirable investors.

More generally, UN-led privatization in Kosovo has clearly benefited K-Albanians, creating bitter resentment by K-Serbs. Hence, in this regard, the UN, rather than contributing to reconciliation and peace consolidation, made it more difficult.[40]

DISARMAMENT, DEMOBILIZATION, AND REINTEGRATION (DDR)

As argued earlier, disarmament, demobilization, and reintegration are a *sine qua non* for successful post-conflict economic reconstruction. The DDR of the KLA was particularly troublesome, and in my view unsuccessful, since it was clear from the way it was done that it would become a source of instability.

Disarmament and demobilization were incomplete. A large proportion of KLA members, with the acquiescence of KFOR and UNMIK, remained united and under the same leadership.[41] The new civilian force, the Kosovo Protection Corps (KPC), was established in late 1999 with 3,000 active members and 2,000 reservists. In theory, the KPC would carry out humanitarian and reconstruction functions—akin to a western civil defense group—and would not be involved in the maintenance of law and order. In practice, this force remains a cocooned KLA, ready and organized to become belligerent anew.[42]

Productive reintegration of former combatants did not take place. It is difficult to understand why the UN did not insist that such a large group of demobilized combatants reintegrate into productive activities in the private sector as soon as possible, as was the case in successful peacekeeping operations in El Salvador and Mozambique.[43] Such reintegration would not only have diminished the possibility of their returning to arms, but also would have obviated the financial costs of public job programs, which, once created, are difficult to dismantle.[44] Only 16 percent of the 9,000 demobilized KLA members had habitable homes. Helping the 80,000 dependents of KLA members rebuild their homes became a priority in the effort to consolidate peace, given the security problems that unemployed and disgruntled former combatants could have created. This expense could have been avoided had KLA members been successfully reintegrated into productive activities as they disarmed and demobilized.

Public insecurity could not be controlled. Not surprisingly, poor DDR performance led to sporadic violence and a high murder rate that disproportionately affected K-Serbs. Security measures alone, such as increasing the number of international police or strengthening the Kosovo Police Service (KPS), did not suffice. Eight years later, volatility remained just below the surface. In this area, too, effective disarmament and demobilization of former combatants and their rapid reintegration into productive sectors of the economy would have contributed to conflict resolution and peacebuilding.

Other measures that could have contributed to peacebuilding included an increase in aid to the most vulnerable groups and more dynamic economic rehabilitation of human capital, physical infrastructure, and basic services damaged during the conflict. Likewise, provision of humanitarian assistance, employment opportunities, and education to minorities, particularly the Serbs, the Roma, and the Muslim Slavs, who were subjected to ethnic violence and attempts at ethnic purging, would have helped. But these steps either were not taken or were introduced too late.

Eighteen months into economic reconstruction

Economic reconstruction in Kosovo—more than in any other place—started from scratch, with the first 18 months marked by noteworthy progress in laying the groundwork for a functioning economy, despite serious problems and delays in many other areas. By end-2000, major bottlenecks for economic reconstruction had been addressed, and the legal and institutional framework for a functioning economy had been put in place.[45] UNMIK established a framework and a strict regulatory regime for financial transactions. It established BPK, which essentially has functioned as a central bank, except that it has not been able to issue currency due to Kosovo's lack of sovereignty. The BPK granted licenses to a micro-enterprise bank and to a non-bank micro-finance institution. UNMIK also set up CFA as the fiscal authority, whose structure resembled that of a finance ministry and would operate until the ministry was established. There were also new tax regulations to allow for an increase in the domestic revenue base. Close to half the regular budget of $300 million for FY-2000, covering current expenditure (but excluding investment and reconstruction), was financed with domestic revenues.

More important than the specific progress was the fact that Kosovars were gradually taking ownership of economic policies, despite the broad mandate given to UNMIK. The Joint Interim Administrative Structure (JIAS) was launched in February 2000 to allow Kosovars to share in the provisional administration of Kosovo with UNMIK. Kosovars were appointed to co-head 20 departments, with the understanding that all parallel structures of Kosovo's self-appointed government would cease to exist.[46] The success of the JIAS depended, to a large extent, on the fair representation of all political actors, as well as on the quality of the appointed staff. The positions of local co-heads were distributed among the three major K-Albanian political parties, with Kosovo Serbs and other minorities receiving a few posts.[47]

The international community promoted the increased involvement of all groups in economic and social reconstruction, but largely to no avail. "Ownership" of reforms among the majority K-Albanian population—so critical to the sustainability of economic reconstruction—was to some extent facilitated by UNMIK's wise decision to stop applying the laws of the FRY to Kosovo in August 1999. However, while this decision may have eased the creation of the co-governmental structure that UNMIK put in place, it made it practically impossible for Serbs to participate. Moreover, there were deep divisions among K-Albanians as well. These factors called into question the possibility of a multiethnic society and the consolidation of peace and hence the sustainability of economic reform.

Financial assistance, trade, and growth: From boom to crisis

Post-conflict economic reconstruction in Kosovo was also unique in terms of foreign assistance. According to Dobbins *et al.* (2003: 125),

International assistance for Kosovo's reconstruction proved more generous than for any earlier post-conflict response or any since. The United States and international organizations [sic] spent $1.5 billion on financial assistance to Kosovo in 1999 and 2000, including funding for budgetary assistance, reconstruction and recovery, and peace implementation. In addition to official assistance, Kosovars received an additional $350 million in financial assistance from expatriate family and friends. As a result, economic growth was very strong in 2000 and 2001.[48]

As revenue collection grew, donors' grants financed only about one-third of recurrent budget expenditure (regular budget) in 2001, down from one-half in 2000 (*IMF Survey*, March 19, 2001). The lack of reliable statistics and the large informal sector, however, represent a serious obstacle to analyzing the performance of Kosovo's economy. Furthermore, gross national disposable income (GNDI), a better indicator of income in Kosovo, was lower than GDP in the earlier period because expatriate wages were higher than private remittances until 2004, when the reverse was true (IMF 2005e, Table 4: 9).

Most growth after 1999 occurred in the construction sector, in the reconstruction of infrastructure and basic services, in the trade and retail sectors, and in public administration. It has been estimated that about $450 million was spent on housing repairs and infrastructure in 1999–2000, with about 20 percent of the total spent on local inputs. As in other post-conflict contexts, the reconstruction boom was short-lived, and construction fell to 40 percent of its 2000 high in 2001 and to only 13 percent in 2002. Aside from building materials, furniture production, and a small food-processing sector, hardly any other manufacturing was developed. In Pristina's "industrial zone," the largest in Kosovo, 66 plots were rented out in 2002: only 16 were used for production, all had three employees or fewer, and most produced doors and window frames (ESPIG 2004).

Notwithstanding the large inflows of aid in the first two years of reconstruction, financing was not always timely or addressed to critical projects. For example, confidence-building projects designed by UNMIK Regional Administrators in the summer of 1999 to make Serb and Albanian Kosovars in Mitrovica work together (in a bakery, for example) often could not be implemented, owing to a lack of resources. This was clearly a missed opportunity to get an early start on peacebuilding measures in this volatile region.[49]

As financial assistance from the main donors dried up, the military and civilian presence was reduced, and remittances fell sharply to about half their

2000 level as new emigration to the EU was blocked, the economic boom stalled sharply. While high levels of foreign assistance continued into 2001 ($1,200 million, or close to 50 percent of GDP), inflows dropped to less than 40 percent of GDP in 2002, less than 30 percent in 2003, and about 15 percent in 2004–7 (IMF, Aide-memoire, July 14–25, 2005 and October 3–10, 2007). By 2003, all the signs of aid dependency were already present. Dobbins *et al.* (2003: 126), for example, concluded that

although the province now functions economically, it remains dependent on foreign assistance. Private economic activity, although expanding, has not yet reached the point of independently sustaining economic growth. A substantial share of consumption and investment continues to rely on official and private transfers of funds from abroad.

With GDP being about $2.7 billion in 2003, public expenditure, including donor grants, was significantly higher ($3.5 billion). In three years, however, public expenditure had fallen by about 60 percent, from $5.8 billion in 2000. This partly explains GDP performance, which, after expanding by close to 17 percent in 2001, contracted by over 2 percent annually in 2002–3.[50]

In 2004, five years into the war-to-peace transition, the IMF (2004f) reckoned that foreign assistance and external private inflows (including remittances) remained at over 40 percent of GDP. Moreover, expatriates and peace-building soldiers, through their consumption of local goods and services, contributed a further 20 percent of GDP. Kosovo was highly vulnerable to a sudden reversal of private inflows and/or a rapid withdrawal of the international community which could easily lead to serious retrenchment and instability.

Eight years into economic reconstruction: The "development trap"

Despite the remarkable progress in setting up the institutional framework for economic reconstruction in the first eighteen months of the transition which allowed the resumption of the payments and trade systems, uncertainty about final status and misguided policies led to a development trap.[51] The UN's open-ended mandate which created uncertainty about property rights, the serious security breakdowns in March 2004 and in early 2007, and misguided policies made the reactivation of investment and employment difficult. At the same time, these factors strengthened Kosovo's dependence on financial aid and remittances. After eight years, Kosovo remains as aid- and remittance-dependent as it was in the earlier period, failing to find a path to self-sustaining growth and development.

Vulnerabilities that made growth reactivation difficult included an entrenched high structural unemployment rate, low human development, dilapidated public utilities and other infrastructure,[52] and an alarming external imbalance, which has become increasingly difficult to sustain. The IMF and the World Bank have estimated that the employment rate is about 33 percent, while unemployment in the formal sector remains above 30 percent, with the rest employed in the informal sector.[53] This is obviously a continued source of instability and security risk. The current account deficit, after adjusting for foreign assistance, jumped from 18 percent of GDP in 2004 to an estimated 24 percent of GDP in 2007 (IMF, Aide-Memoire, October 3–10, 2007).

Beginning with the first international conference on Kosovo in 1999, a widely shared policy objective had been to set the stage for private sector-led recovery and long-term growth. Unfortunately, Kosovo's heavy reliance on financial aid and private remittances reflects a hostile business climate. Poor enforcement of property rights, inadequate public security, energy supply problems, and a weak judicial system are serious deterrents to investment, particularly foreign direct investment (FDI).[54] A tax system following the "business as usual" practice of the IMF has proved too effective, acting as an additional disincentive to investment. Lack of employment opportunities for the fast-growing youth population has proved lethal and created another vicious circle of insecurity, low investment, and fewer employment opportunities. By the time it declared unilateral independence in February 2008, Kosovo remained as aid- and remittance-dependent as it had been 5 years earlier, due to sluggish growth, a large current account deficit, and poor prospects for inward FDI.[55]

The macroeconomic framework was also established in a "business as usual" mode, with the performance of Kosovo's economy constantly compared with that of other low-income European countries, rather than postwar countries that have experienced numerous human massacres and require a special effort at national reconciliation. The IMF, for example, states at various points in its reports that "the key issues for expenditure policy include maintaining a lean public sector; avoiding industrial subsidies; avoiding commitments on public pensions that cannot be honored in the future" (*IMF Survey*, March 19, 2001: 93).

The Fund (2004: 6–7) also states that the nearly five-fold increase in tax revenues since 2000 and the slower expansion of expenditure has laid the basis for a strong fiscal position, offering a unique opportunity for fiscal policy to help address Kosovo's development challenges. The tax-to-GDP ratio was close to 30 percent, surpassing initial expectations and tax performance in countries at similar levels of development. Thus, according to the IMF, the liberal carrying forward of unused appropriations and unhealthy competition between reserved (UNMIK) and transferred-power agencies (PISG) have impeded progress toward elaborating a clear fiscal strategy. In the context of plentiful resources and weak expenditure management capacity, this carries the risk of setting fiscal policy on a wasteful and unsustainable course. The IMF goes further in recommending that an appropriate fiscal strategy for the short- and medium-term be based on a two-pronged strategy. First, it should rein in the expansion of current spending to preserve a comfortable current budget surplus, help finance public expenditure, and ensure long-term sustainability. Second, it should step up work on medium-term strategies for education, health, and basic infrastructure, and elaborate a well-prioritized public investment program directed at enhancing physical and, especially, human capital.

Although the second policy recommendation is certainly welcome, one wonders whether, given the large current expenditure Kosovo required in order to consolidate peace, it was reasonable or even desirable to expect a current budget surplus.[56] Most likely, a more liberal spending policy could have allowed for a virtuous circle of higher employment, fewer ethnic tensions, greater security, and higher investment.

Because of the many problems with property rights, privatization of socially owned enterprises has lacked dynamism and has mostly involved small enterprises. The privatization process gained some momentum with the amendments to the Kosovo Trust Agency (KTA) legislation in April 2005, which removed the requirement that the KTA work through all available documentation to determine clearly the status of state-owned enterprises before proceeding to privatization (World Bank 2005c: 1). The main constraint, however, was uncertainty regarding future property rights, after final status was reached. As RIINVEST (2001) rightly pointed out, social ownership represented no obstacle to the privatization process in any of ex-Yugoslavia's republics. It was the legal uncertainty about whether the process would be reversed when Kosovo attained final status that discouraged potential investors.[57]

Because of the lack of investment, Kosovo's economy has become not only seriously aid-dependent, but it also relies largely on low-productivity activities that cannot sustain growth in the long run. The large presence of international staff and the influx of remittances from Kosovars in the diaspora have created serious distortions between tradable and non-tradable goods, by diverting resources towards the latter. These factors are responsible for the large external imbalance and the "development trap" Kosovo finds itself in eight years after starting the war-to-peace transition.

An Evaluation of UNMIK

Given that the UN established for the first time an integrated operation in Kosovo to lead the transition to peace in general, and economic reconstruction in particular, it is imperative to examine its performance in an effort to identify positive experiences that can be emulated in other post-conflict situations, as well as problems that need to be avoided.

The creation of an integrated peacebuilding office (UNMIK) was a welcome development. Management of UNMIK, however, has not been smooth, which has complicated the effective and timely adoption and implementation of reconstruction policies. In the immediate transition to peace, which is the period this case study focuses on, difficulties have arisen mainly due to staffing problems, an unclear division of responsibilities, duplication in functions, and a lack of transparency and cooperation among the UN pillars. The absence of a common strategy between UNMIK and the UN agencies impeded the use of limited financial and technical resources and nurtured internal contradictions and inefficiencies. As a result, priorities were not always chosen with the overriding objective that conflict should not recur and that Kosovo be put on a path of sustainable development.

In particular, inefficiencies associated with the way UNMIK was established and managed, in the context of an unsettled political status, made economic reconstruction extremely difficult and unsuccessful in Kosovo. I had been a strong advocate of integrated missions since my years in Boutros-Ghali's office. This type of operation is particularly important during reconstruction, which is a multifaceted process that requires wide-ranging expertise, in both the political and economic fields. The difficulties faced by UNMIK in leading this type of operation, however, were apparent from the very beginning and related mostly to UN failings.[58] Because of the importance of setting up effective integrated offices in war-to-peace transitions, I will focus on the principal factors that caused UNMIK's difficulties and the policy lessons that should be learned.

STAFFING PROBLEMS

Both recruiting and logistical problems beset UNMIK's operations at its inception. Recruitment at UN headquarters was extremely slow and when experts and other staff were rushed into joining UNMIK, they often found themselves stranded in Skopje, the Former Yugoslav Republic of Macedonia, waiting to be driven by land to Pristina. The arrival of those who finally made it often came as a surprise to the SRSG, who was not expecting them, since there was little consultation on recruitment, at least at the early stage. Furthermore, with inadequate staff in terms of numbers and expertise, uncertainty about future arrivals, and blurred lines of command, UNMIK could not carry out its functions effectively. It took about 6 months before a critical mass (about 50 percent of authorized staff) of experts and administrators was in place in Kosovo. Recruitment was particularly inadequate to provide UNMIK with the economic and financial expertise it required, mostly for Pillar II, in part due to human resource problems at UN headquarters discussed earlier in relation to ONUSAL in Chapter 7.

In addition to problems in recruiting, appropriate training was clearly needed but lacking. The UN had no comprehensive training program for staff working in post-conflict countries. This would have been particularly needed in an operation such as UNMIK where the different Pillars carried out their functions relatively independently rather than in a truly integrated manner where the goals of the transition to peace could have been jointly pursued. The lack of active and specialized training at the UN was in contrast to the situation at the Fund, where the IMF Institute, primarily involved in training government officials in member states, has a continuous program designed to train its own staff on theoretical developments and best practices, as well as in quantitative techniques. This training extends to all staff including those at the highest (Director) level. Given the multidisciplinary nature of the war-to-peace transitions, such training would be especially important for experts and other staff assigned both to the field and to headquarters.

One of the important problems that UNMIK faced early on was the general lack of expertise in technical and managerial tasks. Pillar II was expected to carry out a large number of functions in civil administration, an area in which the UN had never been involved before and for which it did not have the required expertise in-house. This was particularly true in the economic area, including at the sectoral level, where the UN had to run the ministries of trade, industry, agriculture, and others. To perform such overwhelming executive and managerial tasks, the UN needed people who were not only well versed in economic and financial issues, but who were also good managers who could make decisions in a timely and effective way. It is no secret that good managers are not easily found at the UN, but UNMIK should have had easy access to experts on secondment from member states' civil services, particularly at an early stage. Had the UN secured better expertise in these areas, its relationship with Pillar IV would have been much more effective in pursuing economic reconstruction.

UNCLEAR DIVISION OF RESPONSIBILITIES IN THE INTEGRATED PEACEBUILDING OPERATION

At the time UNMIK was set up, there was no clear division of responsibilities between Pillars II (Civil Administration, led by the UN itself) and IV (Economic Reconstruction, led by the EU). An efficient allocation of functions—which would have avoided many turf battles, much duplication, and frequent inefficiencies—should have delegated to Pillar IV the functions of the Ministry of Finance and to Pillar II all other ministries. In performing its functions as Ministry of Finance, Pillar IV should have advised the SRSG on all economic matters.[59] It also should have been responsible for macroeconomic policymaking (including budgetary and financial policies), and been the focal point for donors' financing and for foreign technical assistance to ensure that it was properly coordinated and channeled to high-priority projects. This was not always the case, with the result that Pillars II and IV, as well as some advisers to the SRSG, often disputed over these functions.

In fact, rather than working closely with the Pillars, staff in the SRSG's Office often took responsibility away from them. Consequently, Pillars were not always accountable for what they did or failed to do.[60] Moreover, it was not always clear who was in charge of what, which confused donors and made access to financing more difficult.[61]

CONFUSION ABOUT THE BUDGETARY PROCESS

As is the case in any economy, Pillar II, acting as all spending ministries, should have provided Pillar IV, acting as the Ministry of Finance, with the expenditure needs for education, health, housing, and public services. The UN (Pillar II) was best placed to establish priorities in these areas based on political and security considerations. The EU (Pillar IV) was best placed to establish the budgetary process and allocate resources efficiently, according to economic reconstruction priorities, expected local revenue, and available foreign assistance, given that Kosovo was highly dependent on foreign financing for its budget, particularly from the EU. However, there was much confusion at UNMIK about how the budgetary process should function, particularly in the early period. This confusion unnecessarily delayed the process at a crucial stage, because, until the budget gap was clearly established, donors would not disburse any of their previously committed funds.

UNMIK RELATIONS WITH UN AGENCIES

There were no guidelines to UN agencies on how to interact with UNMIK. As a result, the early transition was rather chaotic. Agencies had their own agendas and competed with UNMIK for financing. Clearly, financing for UN agencies was not "additional" money, but was coming from a relatively fixed—or, in light of the earthquake emergency in Turkey and other crises at the time, even dwindling—pool of resources. UN agencies had obviously built up relationships with donors over the years, and UNMIK—not unlike other peacebuilding operations—was at a clear disadvantage in competing with them for funds.

Coordination of UN agencies was similarly chaotic, with the Deputy Secretary-General and the Administrator of the UNDP jointly appointing a "Coordinator for the UN Development Group" in August 1999. At the same time, there was a Resident Representative of UNDP in Kosovo, who was also acting as Resident Coordinator of the UN System and who was not released of his responsibilities. Despite there being two coordinators, there was clearly more competition than coordination. In normal development, two coordinators is surely one too many. When peace-keeping operations are in place, coordination should take place exclusively under the leadership of the SRSG (through his Deputy for Economics and Finance or the National Reconstruction Coordinator as shown in Figure 3, p. 64).

Lessons from Kosovo

Despite the peculiarities of Kosovo's war-to-peace transition, I want to draw some lessons for post-conflict economic reconstruction in general. The lessons revolve around four issues, three of which are still important for Kosovo, since they call into question not only the sustainability of the peace process, but also the possibility of moving towards a normal development path.

THE IMPORTANCE OF PROPERLY STAFFING INTEGRATED PEACEBUILDING OPERATIONS

As discussed earlier, the creation of UNMIK as an integrated operation was a welcome development and it is the ideal framework for future reconstruction. However, UNMIK also demonstrated the UN's incapacity to set up and staff this kind of operation in a timely and effective way. There are several policy lessons from UNMIK's experience. First, the UN must maintain an updated roster of qualified experts in various fields who can be called upon or consulted at short notice. Second, these experts' recruitment or secondment, travel, and logistical arrangements should be organized by professionals in close cooperation with the SRSG and other high-level officials, in the field and headquarters, in order to ensure that the right technical capabilities are delivered without inefficiency and confusion. Third, there should be ongoing training at all times for all those working on peacebuilding activities, both in the field and at headquarters. Such training should focus on every aspect of the transition, including political, security, economic, and social issues.

FINAL STATUS AND PROPERTY RIGHTS

Although the transition to final status would not have solved all of Kosovo's problems, from a reconstruction perspective, the sooner a final status can be reached, the better the outcome will be. Only final status—and not necessarily the new phase of "supervised sovereignty"—will remove the uncertainties with regard to property rights and other legal and regulatory issues that have had a negative impact on investment and on employment creation. These issues were far too political and complex to be resolved by an interim civil administration, let alone by the UN. They will also be difficult to resolve in light of Serbia's and Russia's opposition to changes in the status quo. In East Timor, for example, a clear path toward independence was drawn early on, which meant that the issue of property rights was not left in limbo. Without clarity about future property rights, investment of any kind and magnitude, particularly FDI, will continue to be low, or the economy will attract only undesirable investors. If the unilateral declaration of independence in Kosovo leads to further violence or keeps Kosovo in the news, this will also discourage investment.

The negative effects of uncertainty about property rights—a major problem in post-conflict situations where economies need to be reactivated—have been particularly severe in Kosovo, given the lack of investment before the war. Although Kosovo, like many post-conflict cases, grew fast in the immediate post-conflict period, this was due to foreign assistance, remittances, the large international presence, and illegal activities. Continued dependence on all of them casts doubt on the sustainability of growth. In 2005–7, with foreign assistance drastically curtailed and with a reduced level of remittances, the Kosovo economy was in crisis.

With the transfer of power from UNMIK to a government supported by a strong presence of the EU and NATO, it will be difficult for Kosovo to overcome the unhealthy and dangerous dependence on the international community that has often permanently crippled economies in the Third World. It will also be difficult to eliminate the economic distortions created by the large international presence. This should be a key consideration not only when the UN and the EU review Kosovo's future under EU tutelage, but also when the Security Council mandates new operations in the future.

DEMOBILIZATION, REINTEGRATION, AND RECONCILIATION

The acquiescence of UNMIK and KFOR to the transformation of the KLA into the KPC (rather than reintegrating their members into productive activities) was a risky move that has proved to be a source of instability and has not contributed to an improvement in Kosovo's security situation. Since the creation of the KPC, armed groups believed to be offshoots of the dismantled KLA have attacked targets inside Serbia and the Former Yugoslav Republic of Macedonia, apparently trying to unite the largely Albanian population of the region.

Because of the shortcomings I discussed earlier, UNMIK also was late or ineffective in encouraging peacebuilding measures and in creating or strengthening institutions and machinery for the peaceful resolution of disputes, particularly those of an inter-ethnic character. The failure of reconciliation has doomed post-conflict economic reconstruction efforts. Moreover, lack of timely financing (in part because of the IMF's fiscal policy-as-usual), in conjunction with complicated bureaucratic requirements (including long EU bidding processes and the requirement to procure materials from EU suppliers), delayed reintegration and reconstruction efforts and failed to support national reconciliation.

MISSED OPPORTUNITIES

Post-conflict economic reconstruction succeeds only if it consolidates peace and leads to sustainable development. Peace is difficult to build when unemployment stands at 30 percent or higher and about half the population is younger than 20. Although macroeconomic and institutional stability is critical in improving competitiveness, such stability is a necessary but not sufficient condition for investment and employment creation. A healthy business climate, including public security, an adequate judicial system, good human and physical infrastructure, reliable public services, a fair tax and regulatory system, certainty about property rights, and other factors that affect investment decisions are imperative for the private sector to thrive. Furthermore, FDI needs to be actively promoted, given tough international competition to attract these flows.

Kosovo missed the opportunity to promote FDI in labor-intensive sectors, as countries like El Salvador, Guatemala, Mexico, and several in Asia have done successfully in the past, in order to employ a large number of low-skilled workers in post-crisis situations. Since their capital investments are small, such investors would not have been affected by property-rights issues and could have been attracted to Kosovo by its young labor force as well as by the trade preferences provided to their exports in EU markets.[62] Foreign investors could produce goods that conform to EU standards while creating much needed low-skilled employment in Kosovo. But, because of a lack of vision and initiative, Kosovo is only taking limited advantage of the vast market opportunities that the EU offers. Similarly, the inability to produce more homegrown food has sustained continued reliance on imports, contributing to the alarming trade deficit while robbing Kosovo of further employment opportunities.

9 UN-led reconstruction following US-led military intervention: Afghanistan

Background[1]

After more than two decades of continuous conflict[2] that killed 1.5 million people, and with the rout of the Taliban in November 2001, Afghanistan embarked on a complex multi-pronged transition. In such a transition, the country needed to move from war to peace; from a repressive, militaristic theocracy to a society based on democratic principles, the rule of law, and respect for human rights; and from a state-controlled, war-torn economy to reconstruction and private sector-led economic development. Vaishnav (2004: 244) referred to Afghanistan as the site of the twenty-first century's first major post-conflict reconstruction. For Leader and Atmar (2004: 166–7), the multi-pronged transition meant nothing less than changing the political economy of the country from one based on unaccountable and arbitrary military rule, oppression, predation, and illicit economic activity to one based on democratic, civilian governance, rule-based authority, a thriving, legal private sector, and political freedom.

Despite high expectations, Afghans feel disappointed by the transition: security in many parts of the country, particularly the south, has deteriorated sharply, to the point that some analysts believe that the country has been sliding back into conflict. Even in more secure areas, human security has not improved and the peace dividend has not materialized (Donini 2006). Furthermore, lack of productive alternatives has driven farmers to turn to growing poppies. By mid-2007 the UN Office on Drugs and Crime (UNODC 2007a, 2007b) presented alarming evidence of the booming illicit economy, with the country growing over 90 percent of the world's poppy production and converting about 90 percent of the opium into heroin within the country. A resurgence of the Taliban followed, with large parts of the national territory returning to their control. A weak government, which has failed to provide basic services and legal employment for the population, has been unable to deal with the burgeoning drug problems and the empowered Taliban.

In 2001, Afghanistan had about 25 million people, a per capita income of less than $200, illiteracy rates of 70 percent, and some of the worst health indicators and widest gender inequality in the world. It also had a destroyed economy, with 80–90 percent of the labor force employed in the informal sector, and a culture of war, armed conflict, and drug trafficking. For these and other reasons, the transition to peace has been an overwhelming challenge—both for the national authorities and for the international community—that will take many years. In the short run, the heart of this transition is the daunting task of post-conflict economic reconstruction amid difficult security and political conditions, a basic objective of which has been to build modern institutions for economic governance and ensure that "legitimate and accountable" political authorities lead them.

In Operation Enduring Freedom, planned immediately after the September 11, 2001 terrorist attacks and launched on October 7, 2001, the Bush administration fought a war against Al Qaeda and the Taliban in Afghanistan with a "coalition of the willing." It also promised to help rebuild Afghanistan in the tradition of the Marshall Plan. In contrast to Iraq, although USAID has played an important role in post-conflict economic reconstruction in Afghanistan, the United States involved the international community. Given the legacy of interference and continuous meddling by Afghanistan's neighbors, outside powers had a major responsibility to put things right, and to assist in economic reconstruction. Reconstruction has required the provision of technical and financial assistance as well as training and capacity building, without taking over the process of policymaking.

Unlike Kosovo and East Timor, Afghanistan was a sovereign country at the time of the transition and thus had to be in charge of its own destiny. However, as a very poor society destroyed by foreign forces (rather than by civil conflict alone), and with a history of humanitarian intervention, Afghanistan has had to fight to chart its reconstruction path and formulate its own economic policies.

However, it was difficult for bilateral and multilateral donors, as well as non-governmental organizations (NGOs), to take the back seat in Afghanistan. Reconstruction in Afghanistan came right after the experiences of Kosovo and East Timor, where the UN exercised all executive and legislative powers by issuing regulations. Under such conditions, donors virtually had a free hand in carrying out their activities, usually after receiving a green light from the UN, but often even without it. The temptation to do things without serious consultation with the government proved especially strong in Afghanistan, where the UN and many of its member states had not recognized the Taliban while it was in power, leaving donors feeling empowered to implement their own humanitarian agendas as they saw fit.

The situation was quite different in 2001. A UN-sponsored Afghan peace conference led to the Bonn Agreement of December 2001 that established the Afghanistan Interim Authority (AIA). UN member states recognized the AIA as the repository of sovereignty, empowered to make decisions about the economic strategy and policy formulation. The UN Security Council authorized the establishment of the 5,000-strong International Security Assistance Force (ISAF), to help the AIA create a secure environment in Kabul, but with a mandate that impeded it from operating outside the capital. Thus, warlords continued to control other parts of the country.[3] Nevertheless, the AIA became donors' first interlocutor in the immediate transition to peace.

Economic reconstruction in Afghanistan has entailed various and complex tasks, including strengthening internal security; building formal economic institutions and a legal system that respects property rights, promoting employment-generating growth as a basis for poverty alleviation; and rehabilitating dilapidated physical infrastructure.[4] Accomplishing these tasks, while simultaneously attending to the humanitarian needs of large segments of the Afghan population, would function best in a framework of macro-economic stability (consistent fiscal, monetary, and exchange rate policies) and good governance (fair and efficient allocation of resources).

The challenge of the complex transition to peace following US-led military intervention in Afghanistan has been widely analyzed by those who have been closely involved in it.[5] Some have set impossible goals for the transition. Donini *et al.* (2004), for example, argue that the underlying objectives of military and regime change intervention were peace, stability, development, and accountable governance. For reasons I explained earlier, "development" is a long-term proposition, particularly in a country as poor and underdeveloped—even before the conflict of the last 30 years—as Afghanistan.[6]

I will therefore focus more specifically on economic reconstruction—quite distinct, as I have argued earlier, from economic development—which I believe should be the goal of the post-conflict transition. The purpose of my analysis is not to provide a comprehensive or thorough examination of the reconstruction effort—as was the case in my discussion of El Salvador and Kosovo—but to address specific issues that did not arise in connection with the other two case studies. The purpose of my analysis is to foster debate about how governments and the international community could improve economic reconstruction in the future. Thus, after a cursory description of the political and security situations, I will focus on specific problems that Afghanistan had to face in some areas, and on particular tasks that it performed as well as possible under the difficult conditions characterizing the country.

The Interim, Transitional, and Elected Authorities

As per the Bonn Agreement, Afghanistan established the AIA in December 2001 for six months, giving it sole and ultimate power on all policymaking decisions in the transition from war to peace. Each of the four major ethnic groups—Pashtuns, Tajiks, Uzbeks, and Hazara—participated in the agreement. Vaishnav (2004: 253) notes that in essence, the Bonn Agreement codified the standing of the warlords and legislated the unworkable relationship between the warlords and the central government.

The AIA, headed by a Pashtun, Hamid Karzai, called a Loya Jirga (grand council of about 1,500 tribal and ethnic leaders), which convened in June 2002. The Loya Jirga in turn appointed the Afghanistan Transitional Authority (ATA) to operate for a period of two years. The ATA, also headed by Karzai, was charged with drafting a new constitution (which was submitted to a constitutional Loya Jirga for ratification in late 2003) and preparing national elections to elect a fully representative government in late 2004. During this period, the ATA was also responsible for economic management and policymaking, and exercised all executive powers. However, since there was no legislative body until after the parliamentary elections in September 2005, the ATA had to adopt laws and regulations by executive decree—not always a simple proposition for a transitional government.

In October 2004, Karzai became the first democratically elected president, winning 55 percent of the eight million votes that were cast. With the support of the international community, he had managed early on to appoint a small group of qualified experts to critical positions, despite the overall weakness of the civil service. An estimated two million refugees had returned to the country in 2002—a sign of confidence and hope in the political transition (Thier 2004: 40).

However, the security and human rights situation was far from optimal. After taking over in December 2001, the Karzai government had to share political power and tax revenue with the warlords that helped the coalition forces to defeat the Taliban. These were the same warlords that had ruled Afghanistan in the 1992–6 mujahedin period—and era of widespread human rights abuses that held terrible memories for many Afghans.[7] Under their rule, violations of human rights continued in some provinces, even after the Bonn Agreement (Donini 2004). Thus, impunity, injustice, and lack of accountability—which countries normally need to address at the beginning of the transition to peace—could not be resolved in Afghanistan. Furthermore, the control by warlords of a large proportion of the tax revenue deprived the government of resources that were critical in performing its basic functions.

The Afghan National Development Framework (NDF)

Admittedly, the ATA had severe limitations. Its control over the national territory was tenuous, its human resources were stretched thin, and, with a negligible tax base or mechanisms for generating revenue, it was overwhelmingly dependent on outside donors and agencies for material resources. Nevertheless, the ATA managed to establish the Afghan Authority for the Coordination of Assistance (AACA) as the proper national mechanism to coordinate with USAID, the IFIs, other donors, UN agencies, and NGOs. It also managed in April 2002 to create a coherent strategic framework for economic growth and development: the Afghan National Development Framework (NDF).

Few countries in post-conflict reconstruction have produced such a well-developed preliminary strategy as the NDF. The problem was not—as in many other cases—a lack of strategy, but whether, given Afghanistan's history and politics, the strategy was realistic and could be implemented. This question reflected the deficiencies of the Afghan civil service and security conditions, as well as the attitude and position of donors, the IFIs, the UN, and NGOs. Although the Minister of Finance, Ashraf Ghani, designed the strategy, few other government officials supported it. Furthermore, there seems to have been little effort to build broader support for it, not only among government officials, but also among the population at large.[8] Indeed, the document was never translated into Dari for wide distribution.

The NDF included three pillars: humanitarian assistance and social policy to create sustainable living conditions and promote human development; external assistance for rebuilding physical infrastructure in order to create an environment conducive to private-sector investment; and a wise emphasis on the private sector, both domestic and foreign, as the major driving force in reactivating the economy, creating employment, and thereby ensuring social inclusion.

The promotion of the private sector required a stable macroeconomic environment, clear rules of the game, an appropriate business climate, and good governance, with the government performing a number of responsibilities across the board.[9] A major shift in economic policies away from those that existed during the Soviet era, and a restructuring of the public sector—including privatization of state-owned enterprises and services—was contemplated as part of this process. The resumption of payments and the reestablishment of the banking and trading systems were top priorities, as was the improvement of public finances, including budget planning and public expenditure management.

Having met all requirements under the Bonn Agreement, the governments of Germany and Afghanistan co-hosted a conference in Berlin at the end of March 2004 entitled Afghanistan and the International Community: A

Partnership for the Future. At this conference, the World Bank presented to donors an updated plan for economic reconstruction of the country entitled Securing Afghanistan's Future (SAF). The Ministry of Finance had prepared the document but had not gained the cabinet's endorsement, revealing serious differences of opinion with respect to the vision for economic reconstruction within the country.[10]

In January 2006, the government approved the Interim Afghanistan National Development Strategy (I-ANDS), a strategy for security, governance, economic growth, and poverty reduction. This five-year strategy followed the 2002 NDF and the SAF exercise of 2004. The Afghanistan Compact of February 2006 between Afghanistan and its international partners complemented the national reconstruction plans.[11]

The international actors

After the collapse of the Soviet-backed regime (1979–92), the takeover of Kabul by the Taliban in 1996 that ended the mujahedin period, and the strengthening of the Taliban's control of the whole country in 1998, the UN launched the Strategic Framework in September 1998. This was one of the first UN attempts to integrate its peacemaking, humanitarian, and human rights activities in a country. As told by Donini (2004: 126), up to that time, there had been several international actors in Afghanistan, but nobody knew whether the assistance they provided was "part of the problem or part of the solution." Furthermore, there was no way to measure the impact that a large number of small-scale projects was having. The Strategic Framework was an attempt to agree on an overall strategy and to speak with one voice.

All UN agencies had agreed to the framework, although some did so reluctantly. Donini mentions in particular the UNHCR, WFP, and UNICEF as being bureaucratically driven to resist coordination, using their specific mandates as an excuse. Donors, on the other hand, supported the Strategic Framework for its potential to improve the accountability and effectiveness of aid flows. The UN Resident Coordinator performed the functions of both a resident and humanitarian coordinator. Thus, the UN Resident Coordinator's Office, supported by donors, UN agencies, and NGOs, assumed the functions of a ministry of planning, providing a framework for the prioritization of the scarce resources for humanitarian and rehabilitation assistance, and a forum for discussion on strategic planning. As many analysts have noted, in Afghanistan, as in other failed states, the international community operated through humanitarian operations owing to the lack of political will to intervene in other significant ways.[12]

Following the US-led military intervention, the United States was also to play an important role in economic reconstruction through the involvement of USAID. Nevertheless, the UN and its agencies, with the assistance of a number of NGOs that had been deeply involved during the Taliban period, remained engaged and led economic reconstruction. The Asian Development Bank, the World Bank, and the IMF were the main IFIs in the country and played an active role. In late 2001, the UNDP established an Emergency Trust Fund, which operated until mid-2002, in order to meet the government's initial needs, including civil service wage payments during the AIA's first six months and the costs of the Loya Jirga (IMF 2002c: 8). The World Bank administers two trust funds: the Afghanistan Reconstruction Trust Fund (ARTF), which has become an increasingly important source of budgetary support, and the Afghanistan window of the Japan Social Development Fund.

After Kabul fell to foreign forces with the assistance of the Northern Alliance in mid-November 2001, the main donors met in Washington, D.C. to plan for Afghanistan's reconstruction. They formed the Afghan Reconstruction Steering Group (ARSG), which met the following month in Brussels in anticipation of the donors meeting in Tokyo in January 2002, where a Kabul-based Implementation Group (IG) was also established. At the same time, Afghanistan's government agreed to meet with donors every year to review the country's development priorities. Since then, annual meetings of the Afghanistan Development Forum (ADF) have taken place.[13]

In November 2001, the Security Council adopted Security Council Resolution (SCR) 1378, affirming the UN's role in the political process and calling for the formation of a government that would be "broad-based, multi-ethnic and fully representative of the Afghan people." In March 2002, the UN established the UNAMA (Assistance Mission in Afghanistan) to support the Bonn Agreement. The Secretary-General appointed Lakhdar Brahimi as his Special Representative (SRSG) to head all UN operations.

Brahimi was a strong advocate of a "light footprint" for the UN in Afghanistan. He did not envisage his position as a powerful international coordinator (like the High Commissioner in Bosnia and Herzegovina), but as a facilitator of the Bonn Agreement's implementation. In Brahimi's view, whereas the UN had been given a mandate to run the reconstruction efforts in Kosovo and East Timor, the role of the UN and other actors in Afghanistan would be to support the interim, transitional, and elected governments. It would be left to the UN agencies, as the main implementing agencies, to lead reconstruction. In theory, these actors would promote Afghan ownership of the reconstruction program and ensure its financing. At the same time, Brahimi opposed the military and security approach of the US Pentagon, an approach known as "nation building light." In fact, Brahimi worked to expand the ISAF.[14]

Like the UN agencies, NGOs had been closely involved in humanitarian affairs in Afghanistan for many years. As O'Brien (2004: 187) recounts, NGOs had become a de facto shadow government running many of the social services that the Taliban and their predecessors were unable or unwilling to provide. In this way, they had become the Afghan people's safety net, fighting for emergency funding at a time when the country exhibited some of the grimmest poverty indices. With the fall of the Taliban, existing NGOs had to adjust to strong media attention, large increases in donors' financing, and loss of qualified staff to agencies that paid better salaries. More troublesome was that NGOs had to abandon their principles of impartiality, independence, and neutrality and rally behind the new government, which needed to prove its legitimacy by providing services that NGOs had supplied in the past. On the one hand, NGOs were concerned about the legitimacy and permanence of the Karzai government and, on the other hand, they worried that, by associating with the government, they would lose their ability to provide humanitarian assistance in areas beyond government control. In adjusting to the new environment, the long-established NGOs also had to compete with new NGOs and private contractors, many of which had no experience in the country and were attracted to it by the prospects of large-scale financing.[15]

The Bonn Agreement created high expectations in Afghanistan. As Thier (2004: 46) points out, the difference between the Bonn Agreement and those of the past, in particular that of 1992, was the new interest in Afghanistan shown by the United States and its political willingness to twist arms to ensure political agreement on contentious issues. In this new environment, the UN and its agencies, as well as the NGOs, struggled to adjust to their new role. During the Taliban's rule, the international community's role was purely humanitarian, with capacity building taking place only in areas—like health, agriculture, and de-mining—where interaction with the authorities would not undermine the rights of the Afghans. This had to change with the establishment of the Karzai administration in December 2001, but many forces were arrayed against a redefinition of roles.

"Success" in context

Many of us had the impression that the US government undertook much planning for war but little planning for post-conflict reconstruction. According to John Taylor, Under-Secretary of Treasury for International Affairs at the time, financial planning for Afghanistan began virtually in tandem with the US military's plans for the war, and contemporaneously with the Treasury's plan, launched in the weeks following 9/11, to combat terrorist financing. As mentioned earlier, post-conflict reconstruction is costly and requires fundraising. Indeed, given the large population, widespread poverty, the danger that NGOs would leave or become inoperative during the war, and the fact that warlords controlled vast territories, levying their own taxes and issuing their own currencies, the magnitude of the task was quite different from that of other recent experiences with reconstruction.[16]

Although governments and the international community can always do things better, several of the activities and measures that are needed in planning, as well as in the immediate transition to peace, were implemented in Afghanistan. First, three of the key international actors carried out an early needs assessment, thereby providing an important macro and micro analysis of the economy and its immediate imperatives. The institutions presented the needs assessment at the donors' conference in Tokyo in January 2002, where pledges were made for the next five years. At the same time, donors and the Afghan government established groups (the ARSG, the IG, and the ADFs) to follow up on pledges and coordinate aid.[17]

Second, the finance ministry, with support from the US Treasury and the IMF, carried out plans to introduce a new currency in an orderly way, despite the immense challenges. Given many existing currencies, the authorities viewed the new Afghani as an important symbol of sovereignty and unity. Thus, they opted to introduce new Afghani bills, issued by the central bank (Da Afghanistan Bank, DAB), rather than adopting the dollar or another foreign currency, as had been done, for example, in Kosovo and East Timor. This was also important for conducting monetary policy, since confidence in the old Afghani had been lost over time, owing to counterfeiting and other problems.[18]

Third, the government made efforts to bring into the national budget customs revenues collected by some of the warlords in border provinces. This was difficult, because warlords and their supporters did not perceive much benefit to them from international assistance to the country, and therefore saw no justification for giving up their own sources of income. While the government made some progress in this regard, the average five-year revenue of the national government (2002–6) was below 5 percent of GDP, posing a serious constraint on its ability to carry out its basic functions.[19]

Finally, yet importantly, some improvement in the rights of women was incipient in the post-conflict transition. During the Taliban years (1996–2001), 95 percent of girls did not attend school. Since then, girls have attended primary school in large numbers, and 40 percent of voters were women in the national election of 2004. Women also began to participate in others aspects of the transition. New legislation established women's rights in general to an extent that had not existed in the near past. Nevertheless, rural areas have yet to experience much progress.

What could have been done differently?

The implementation of the ambitious framework for post-conflict economic reconstruction in Afghanistan has been fraught with problems from the outset. Many factors interfered with the implementation of the NDF. One question concerns the appropriateness of the economic framework developed by the Ministry of Finance with the assistance of the IFIs and the tacit encouragement of the US government (Treasury, USAID). Another obvious shortcoming was the failure to control the opium economy by creating incentives, such as subsidies, credit, and technical assistance for viable alternatives. Moreover, several analysts who have been intimately involved in the aid process have questioned the effectiveness of donors and agencies in the reconstruction of Afghanistan and their relations with the government. Partly owing to the dire social situation and partly because of the "business as usual" attitude, the move from humanitarian assistance to reconstruction was slow, with negative repercussions on Afghanistan's productive and employment capacity.

HOW GENUINE WAS AFGHAN OWNERSHIP OF THE RECONSTRUCTION STRATEGY?

In Afghanistan, most political figures saw the state as a redistributive instrument, funded by foreign donors, to build power through patronage networks. Only a few members of the government shared the vision of the NDF for a small effective state, regulating a market economy, with the private sector as the driving force for development. Similarly, the government's updated plan for economic reconstruction, entitled *Securing Afghanistan's Future* (SAF), lacked broad-based support (and like, the NDF, was not translated into Dari).

Thus, although the strategy designed by the economic authorities, supported by the IFIs, may have been appropriate for a different country in a different context, it did not build on the history and culture of Afghanistan. Nor did it reflect the many political and security constraints that any economic reconstruction plan had to address in order to be effective.

THE ECONOMIC FRAMEWORK FAILED TO "KEEP IT SIMPLE AND FLEXIBLE"

In my view, one of the most serious flaws was the design of policies and institutions that failed to follow Premise 6 for effective reconstruction: "keep it simple and flexible." The simpler the framework in a country, the lower will be the level of expertise necessary to implement it, with fewer opportunities for mismanagement and corruption.

Monetary and fiscal policies designed mostly with the support of the IMF and the World Bank might have been best practice for a country on the normal development path, but they certainly were much too sophisticated for a simple and uneducated country. The complexity of laws and regulations, particularly those concerning taxation, customs, and banking, is burdensome for a weak civil service. It creates opportunities for corruption, and is often an obstacle to the development of micro-enterprises that are needed to generate employment.[20]

Going from an antiquated and inoperative macro- and microeconomic framework to a very sophisticated one, amid all the challenges of the multi-pronged transition to peace, was not realistic. At the end of 2001, both the Ministry of Finance and the central bank had for all practical purposes ceased to operate, and the payments and reporting frameworks, particularly between Kabul and the thirty-two provinces, had broken down. Afghanistan was essentially a cash-based economy with some basic financial services provided mostly through the informal *hawala* system.[21] The six state banks had stopped any intermediation services, as had the licensed commercial banks. The central bank performed deposit and credit operations that are the prerogative of commercial banks in a two-tier banking system (where the central bank and the commercial banks perform different functions). Financial information about banks and the central bank was practically non-existent, and accounting systems were outdated.

At the request of the Afghan authorities, the IMF took an active role in drafting a bank regulation policy. In September 2003, a presidential decree enacted the central bank law and a modern banking law. These laws allowed for central bank modernization by increasing the bank's capacity to conduct monetary and exchange rate policy, to reestablish a basic payments system, and to regulate and supervise commercial banking effectively. The IMF introduced new accounting practices and prepared licensing and prudential regulations for banks in accordance with the Basel Core Principles for Effective Banking Supervision. Despite this, the IMF Institute held its first financial programming course in Afghanistan only in February 2003; thus, capacity building did not start, as it should have, from the very beginning.

At the same time, fiscal policy was primitive, and ministry employees kept budgetary records by hand. Revenue consisted only of customs duties and aid in the form of budgetary support from donors. Expenditure consisted mainly of salaries for government workers, including teachers and the military (Taylor 2007a: 42). To move from such an elementary system to a sophisticated fiscal and budgetary framework at the time of the transition was clearly a mistake, since the government did not have the capacity to implement it in an effective, transparent, and non-corrupt way.

OPTIMAL ECONOMIC POLICIES OFTEN INTERFERE
WITH PEACE CONSOLIDATION

The financial requirements of peace-related programs and macroeconomic stabilization policies are often in conflict, as de Soto and I first argued in our *Foreign Policy* 1994 article in relation to El Salvador. Thus, more worrisome than the lack of simple institutions, policies, and regulations, the macroeconomic framework designed with the assistance of the IMF eliminated any flexibility in policies that could allow for financing of critical peace-related programs, including those necessary to deal with security, drugs, and unemployment. Without these programs, Afghanistan has a high probability of falling back into full conflict. In complex post-conflict transitions, optimum and best-practice economic policies may be attainable but not desirable. This is because the transition to peace is a development-plus challenge (Premise 1), where the political objective should prevail at all times (Premise 2).

Had the government respected these premises for effective reconstruction, it could have made more progress toward reconstruction of infrastructure and services, establishment of police and military forces, and disarming, demobilization, and reintegration of militia fighters. Similarly, the government could have been able to generate more employment and fight drug production and trade, which is eroding what little legitimacy and power the government has. These steps, in turn, would have helped the government consolidate its power and avoid the serious deterioration in security that has occurred in the past year. The potential cost of such policies—delays in bringing inflation to single-digit levels—would have been a risk worth taking.

Instead, macroeconomic orthodoxy imposed its own costs. For example, the central bank law, which enhanced the bank's independence from the government (and enshrined it in the constitution), eliminated the flexibility that Afghanistan could have had in financing peace-related programs. The primary objective of monetary policy was the achievement of price stability and thus the restoration of confidence in the Afghani. The central bank law does not mention the need to control inflation "within a framework of adequate growth and employment," which should be the guiding principle for monetary and exchange rate policies. According to the IMF (2003e: 99), price stability was achievable only by maintaining strict fiscal discipline, including a "no-overdraft" rule for budget financing, and ensuring that the central bank was "independent from any other authority in the pursuit of its objectives and the performance of its tasks." Such dogmatism robbed the government of Afghanistan of any financing flexibility to carry out reconstruction activities.[22]

The central bank law—which entrusts the bank with the tasks of defining, adopting, and implementing monetary and foreign exchange policy—is more orthodox than is the case in higher-income countries such as Brazil, where the bank lacks *de jure* independence. In most countries, the central bank and the finance minister jointly determine exchange rate policies. Even among orthodox economists, central bank independence is controversial, with many experts arguing that the central bank and the government must work together to achieve adequate growth and employment. De facto rather than *de jure* central bank independence—as exists in Brazil and elsewhere—probably would have served Afghanistan better by giving it the flexibility it required in the transition to peace to finance critical, if often unconventional, expenditures.[23]

Growth and employment creation are critical to every nation, but all the more so in post-conflict situations. Even an orthodox central bank like the Bank of England does not establish price stability in the abstract, but within acceptable levels of growth and unemployment. The same is true of the US Federal Reserve. Following the August 2007 sub-prime mortgage crisis, both banks clearly demonstrated their concern for how the crisis would affect growth and employment in their respective economies. While the Fed lowered interest rates three times in 2007, both central banks increased the liquidity of their banking systems to avoid the recessionary impact of the crisis. Indeed, the Fed did so despite the inflationary pressures implied by a rapidly depreciating dollar.

The rigid monetary and fiscal framework designed and supported by the IMF in Afghanistan is particularly surprising, because the Fund's staff is fully aware of the constraints under which macroeconomic management needs to take place. In fact, a July 2006 IMF report explicitly noted the enormous challenges, including enhancing national security and stability outside Kabul by strengthening the police and judicial systems, disarming illegally armed groups, and deepening the political normalization process. Other daunting tasks included combating the opium economy, protecting the vulnerable segments of the population against supply shocks stemming from lingering drought and other natural disasters, and effectively managing the significant inflows of external aid (IMF 2006c: 5–6). Given these conditions, it was at best naive for the IMF, together with the finance minister and a few other national leaders, to believe that a rigid and inflexible framework would work. Such a framework not only made financing basic peace-supporting activities impossible, but also was difficult to implement in light of the Afghan government's weak administrative capacity and scarce human resources.

PLUS ÇA CHANGE, PLUS C'EST LA MÊME CHOSE

Reading IMF documents on Afghanistan is reminiscent of the problems and dilemmas faced by El Salvador in 1992, which almost derailed the peace process. These related to the conflict between the political and security objectives of the UN-brokered peace agreement and the economic objectives specified in the IMF-supported program. For example, after a visit to Kabul in February 2007, the IMF staff declared that, while necessary to tackle the volatile security conditions, "additional expenditures to strengthen adequately the security forces would delay economic objectives." Similarly, the government should "resist" the expansion of recurrent expenditures in the absence of corresponding increases in revenue or at least assurances of durable donor support. This created a catch-22 for the government, as domestic revenue (excluding grants) had averaged about 5 percent of GDP since 2002 (IMF 2007b), owing largely to the security situation, while donors channeled more than 75 percent of aid outside the government budget (Rubin 2006: 36).[24]

This catch-22 situation was reflected at the Joint Coordination and Monitoring Board (JCMB) conference for Afghanistan in Berlin in January 2007, where finance minister Ahady noted that "IMF conditionality on the one hand, and our security and *Millenium Development Goals*...on the other hand, are subjecting us to conflicting pressures." At the same time, the scarcity of employment opportunities and slow improvement in living conditions fueled rising public discontent. The IMF staff worried that, despite significant donors' support, the Afghan authorities' determination to deliver on commitments under IMF-supported programs—which had been strong in the past—might wane.[25] The concern should be, however, that unless quick improvements in these areas take place within a reasonable time span, the country might well slide into chaos. In that case, the cost of adopting a "shock" program of economic stabilization, rather than a more gradual one giving the government more budgetary flexibility, would be large indeed.

THE FAILURE TO PROVIDE ADEQUATE CAPACITY BUILDING AND TRAINING

The IFIs, USAID, and the US Treasury failed to provide enough capacity building, training, and resources to the government for the sophisticated institutions and policies they had created or blessed. In conjunction with the UN agencies and other donors, they also failed to enable the government to carry out the rapid improvement in basic infrastructure and services. For example, Rubin (2007a: 10) reports that in 2005/6[26] the government executed less than half of the reconstruction budget. This is indicative of the government's weak institutional capacity, which seems to have been more of a problem than lack of resources.

Peace creates expectations that need to be satisfied. Both the devastation caused by the war and the lack of investment over the past three decades had resulted in poor housing, health, public utilities, and other services in one of the most deprived countries in the world. In light of the severe conditions, donors managed to ensure that sufficient resources were available to provide basic shelter, food, and medical supplies to the large impoverished segment of Afghanistan's population. However, while the international community managed to avert a humanitarian crisis, the country made little progress with reconstruction, which had important political, security, and economic consequences.

TRANSCENDING THE ILLICIT ECONOMY

Successful reconstruction requires moving away from a largely illicit war economy to one in which the rule of law and legal activities predominate. The move in Afghanistan was in the wrong direction, with drug production becoming entrenched in the post-conflict economy since 2001. By several accounts, the drug economy is huge. The UNODC (2007a) and the IMF estimate that drug production amounted to about 36 percent of non-drug GDP in 2007.

The UNDOC estimates that Afghanistan's share of global opium production rose to more than 90 percent, from just 12 percent in 2001. Estimates also show that opium production increased to more than 8,000 tons, from 3,400 tons in 2002, employing about 150,000 workers. The area under poppy cultivation increased to a record 193,000 hectares, almost double what it had been two years earlier and an area larger than the corresponding total for coca cultivation in Latin America (Colombia, Peru, and Bolivia). Afghans convert most of the opium produced into heroin within the country, with the UNDOC estimating output at about 1,200 metric tons.

The precursors needed to convert opium into heroin are not available in Afghanistan. Thus, while Afghanistan exports opiates, it imports precursors from neighboring countries. Furthermore, as noted by the head of the UNODC, while opium attracts most attention, the significant increase in cannabis cultivation is quite disturbing.[27] Although these figures may not be fully reliable, they nevertheless indicate the tremendous growth in drug production in the immediate war-to-peace transition. The situation seems out of control, with serious repercussions on security conditions in large parts of the country, particularly the south and south-east.

In Colombia and other countries with large illicit drug economies, crop eradication that kills subsistence crops and pollutes water has proven ineffective in controlling production. Moreover, it has enabled criminal and armed groups to extract huge rents (profits). In Afghanistan there has been some progress, most notably in Balkh province, where strong leaders have managed to control production in exchange for promises of aid. However, the aid has not materialized. Having failed to create alternative income for farmers and others involved in the drug trade in these areas, provincial leaders will be unable to sustain such successful efforts.

Budgetary flexibility could have enabled the government to start financing alternative employment programs. Assistance from donors would have followed if the government showed the political will to proceed with these programs. Several agricultural products have been produced in the past, as for example, cotton in Helmand province. Some could also produce certain vegetables, even on small plots. Others, as Rubin (2007b) argues, could produce flowers, herbs, or other fragrance products, including lavender, roses, and basil, for which Afghanistan's soil, climate, and water conditions are well suited. Some of these agricultural activities could produce rents to farmers as high as those in production of poppies and cannabis. To make these options viable, however, would require large amounts of credit and technical assistance as well as improvements in infrastructure and services (better roads, transportation, storage facilities, and processing plants) to bring products to the market.

In the short run, perhaps the only alternative to turn the entrepreneurial spirit of the Afghans away from producing drugs into lawful production is to subsidize production or create price support programs for different crops. For this, donors would have to channel reconstruction aid in the form of budgetary support to allow the government to follow these policies. Donors could also play a role in increasing local industrialization of such crops by providing know-how and credit and by opening their markets with preferential tariff treatment to goods coming from export-processing zones (or "reconstruction zones" as they could be called in post-conflict countries). In the process, donors would not only create a good economy but would help government to consolidate its legitimacy and decrease the appeal of the Taliban (Phelps and del Castillo 2008).

BYPASSING THE SOVEREIGN GOVERNMENT

Donors and humanitarian agencies often ignored the Afghan government's rightful claim to manage and coordinate international assistance in the post-conflict transition. As Donini (2004: 138) described it, although in theory the external actors put themselves behind the new government, in practice, agencies and NGOs continued to act unilaterally, maintaining little contact with national or regional authorities. Although this was partly the result of inertia, it also reflected donors' perception that the government was incapable and lacked the transparency needed to handle large amounts of aid and to implement the necessary humanitarian and rehabilitation tasks. For these reasons, donors, agencies, and NGOs continued to carry on their own programs oblivious to the government's wishes. This undermined the government's popular legitimacy. At the same time, Rubin (2007a: 10), using Ministry of Finance data, notes that donors spent about $500 million on poorly designed and uncoordinated technical assistance that was not a priority for the government.

In addition to not addressing the specific needs of the government in Afghanistan, aid has also put a heavy burden on its weak capacity. As Ghani *et al.* (2007: 154) emphasize, the aid system should be harnessed to maximize the impact of the existing leadership and management. Their first-hand experience in Afghanistan as well as in other post-conflict countries, led them to conclude that the bewildering variety of requirements that the current unharmonized aid system imposes to post-conflict countries requires that the bulk of the energies of people in positions of leadership be devoted to translating the aid pledges into commitments and disbursements, rather than to the creation of wealth and generation of revenues that provide the true basis for sustainability.

With regard to the fundamental differences in financing strategies, Rubin *et al.* (2004: 16) pointed out that in some cases, donors finance an implementing partner—an NGO, a UN agency, or other private organization—to deliver a service. In other cases, donors create a trust fund, such as the Afghanistan Reconstruction Trust Fund (ARTF), that provides budgetary support for the government so that it can recruit the implementing partner of its choice. By enabling the government to increase its own expenditures within the priorities established in its budget, donors strengthen government structures and processes. Furthermore, in such cases, the government will get credit and recognition for the services that it provides and will be accountable for its failure to provide them efficiently. Much more emphasis on the latter strategy will be necessary to build an effective and accountable state in Afghanistan.

Only 16–18 percent of total financing in 2003 was in the form of budgetary support. In 2004/5 the authorities adopted, for the first time, a "core budget" to improve coordination and control over donor flows. Whereas the "operating budget" essentially covers current expenditures, the "core budget" consolidates the operating budget with development expenditures channeled through the treasury's accounts. The "external budget" refers to fiscal operations implemented directly by donors outside the control of the authorities. In the three-year period ending in March 2004, the core budget amounted to about $1 billion, while the external budget was around $3.5 billion. Hence, donors channeled 22 percent of financing through the government during this period. In the fiscal year 2004/5, although total assistance fell to $4 billion, the percentage channeled through the government increased to 35 percent.[28]

OTHER DONOR-RELATED ISSUES

Four other factors seem to have affected aid effectiveness to implement the reconstruction strategy, as specified in the NDF and NDS. First, donors failed to be flexible and to avoid imposing conditionality, while bureaucratic red tape and bidding requirements were often time-consuming and inefficient. By the time donors approved proposed initiatives, conditions had often changed, and earlier plans were no longer optimal or even needed. Because of tied aid practices, donors often required the recruitment of their own people or the purchase of their goods. Given the dismal conditions in Afghanistan and the need for quick-impact humanitarian projects, conditionality was ill conceived.[29] Not only is aid largely channeled outside government control but, as Ghani *et al.* (2007: 156) describe it, "the aid system currently exists as a parallel series of bureaucracies, each with its own revenue, expenditure, and reporting systems. These multiple and fragmented systems are not linked through a budget process that would ensure accountability either to the citizens of donor countries or to the citizens of beneficiaries countries."

Second, even while working within the NDF and NDS frameworks, donors did not coordinate sufficiently among themselves to avoid duplication and overlap. At the same time, donors often engaged in needless competition and turf battles that wasted precious resources, time, and energy.

Third, because of the poor security situation in large parts of the country, and because major combat operations occurred simultaneously with reconstruction, foreign military forces were involved in the provision of relief and reconstruction activities. The so-called Provincial Reconstruction Teams (PRTs) and other civil–military operations were located in dangerous areas, creating a number of problems with aid agencies, NGOs, and the national authorities that need to be addressed in future operations. The perceived or real encroachment by military actors on the operations of humanitarian agencies and NGOs was a problem in Kosovo and East Timor as well. At the same time, because they worked in such dangerous areas, PRTs in Afghanistan did not necessarily achieve their reconstruction objectives (Taylor 2007a: 64–8).[30]

Fourth, in July 2006, Afghanistan reached a debt restructuring agreement under Naples terms with the Paris Club creditors (Russia, Germany, and the United States), after an upfront 80 percent discount on debt disbursed prior to 1992 was applied to Russian debt (by far the largest). Thus, debt fell from about $12 billion to $0.9 billion. Although creditors indicated their intention to provide 100 percent debt relief in the context of the HIPC Initiative for low-income countries, as of end-2007, the country had not yet completed the qualifying process (IMF 2008, 2007c).[31]

The IMF estimated that Afghanistan's external debt was about 150 percent of GDP (IMF 2006b: 9). Given the conditions in the country, instead of negotiating a debt restructuring, creditors should have agreed early in the process to a debt moratorium—including arrears with the IFIs—that would last until Afghanistan was on a sound footing and could begin to restructure and service its debt. In late 2002 and early 2003, Afghanistan settled arrears with the Asian Development Bank, the Fund, and the World Bank, supported by grant contributions from donors. In situations such as the one faced by Afghanistan at the time, those grants should have been used for peace consolidation by promoting security and financing social and economic programs, rather than servicing foreign debt.

SLOW MOVE FROM HUMANITARIAN TO RECONSTRUCTION ASSISTANCE

Because of the dismal social conditions, the large number of returnees, and the low income per capita, reconstruction in Afghanistan had to have a large humanitarian component in the short run.[32] This dire situation reflected three decades of war and several years of severe drought. It unquestionably required large amounts of humanitarian assistance for saving lives and improving livelihoods (Oliker *et al.* 2003: 23).

However, as discussed earlier, in the transition from war to peace, and in the presence of a government that the international community recognizes as representing the interests of the population, humanitarian aid should go hand in hand with reconstruction aid. While humanitarian aid has an impact on consumption, only reconstruction aid would improve the investment and productive capacity of the country, thereby allowing it to create sustainable employment. Because of the large presence of humanitarian agencies and NGOs in the country, donors channeled reconstruction aid through them, although they were not always prepared to use it effectively. As a result, reconstruction lagged, with tragic repercussions.[33]

INADEQUATE RESOURCES AND SLOW DISBURSEMENT

In late 2001, the Asian Development Bank, the World Bank, and the UNDP carried out a needs assessment in preparation for the donors' meeting in Tokyo the following month. This assessment provided a base estimate of reconstruction assistance of about $1.7 billion for the first year, $5 billion for 2.5 years, $10 for 5 years, and $15 for ten years. These estimates were in addition to the humanitarian assistance that the country was receiving at the time. However, of the $4.5 billion pledged for the first five years (but mostly covering the first 2.5 years) and the $1.8 billion pledged for the first year, about one-third provided support to the government's operating budget and about two-thirds was for humanitarian assistance (IMF 2003f).[34]

Rubin *et al.* (2003) argue that in May 2003, after 17 months, donors had spent less than $200 million on reconstruction, out of the about $2 billion pledged for the first year. However, by lumping together reconstruction with humanitarian assistance, donors claimed fulfillment of the Tokyo targets. Furthermore, only 16 percent of the total disbursements (including for humanitarian purposes) had passed through channels in which the government had any control, hence failing to build government capacity or legitimacy.

As became clear soon afterwards, resources pledged at Tokyo were not sufficient for the task. In Tokyo, there was no clear sense yet of what the government would try to achieve. The inadequacy of resources affected reconstruction negatively. Contrary to Kosovo and East Timor, which had small populations, Afghanistan has a large one and hence large needs.[35]

In March 2004, the government prepared its Securing Afghanistan's Future program, updated the initial assessment, and requested $28 billion over a seven-year period. This sum, which looks large, is in fact a mere pittance relative to security spending. According to Vaishnav (2004: 245), for example, the US spent about $1 billion in humanitarian and reconstruction assistance in fiscal year 2003—less than one-tenth of what it spent on military operations in the country.[36] In addition, as security conditions deteriorated, the government has found it difficult to redirect financing to reconstruction, as governments need to do as the transition to peace proceeds over time. Unstable security conditions also discouraged other donors from providing aid, owing to their fear that it would be wasted.

Unfortunately, Afghan leaders, like many others in post-conflict situations, failed to recognize the extent to which donors' fatigue can become a problem. Afghanistan was soon competing with countries such as Iraq and several African countries for scarce resources, as these countries entered peace transitions of their own. Moreover, once the media focus on Afghanistan diminished, fundraising became more difficult.

LARGE DISTORTIONS DESPITE SCARCE RESOURCES AND BRAHIMI'S "LIGHT FOOTPRINT"

Despite inadequate resources and Brahimi's "light footprint," the distortions created by the increased interest of the international community in Afghanistan have been large. UN agencies as well as bilateral actors and NGOs had a "heavy footprint" and bid for a limited number of qualified Afghans, viable office space, housing, food, and all types of services. In the process, although they helped reactivate the economy, they drove up prices, fueled real currency appreciation, and deprived the Afghan civil service of its best people.[37] Misallocation of resources and other distortions also arose from the shortsightedness of international aid agencies and NGOs that attempted to transplant policies, systems, or ideas that were not suitable for Afghanistan.[38]

As an improvement in the wellbeing of the population was not forthcoming, people began to resent the large international presence.[39]

To give some idea of magnitudes, Donini (2004: 136 and footnote 39) notes that before the military intervention in October 2001, there were about 20 UN international staff in Kabul, another 40 outside the capital, and about 200 expatriate NGO personnel in the country. By mid-2003, the UN alone had 700 international staff, costing the international community about $300 million per year and putting strong pressure on the prices of goods and services, including food and housing. Expatriate NGO staff mushroomed as well.

MULTIPLE POWER CENTERS

As Wimmer and Schetter (cited in Leader and Atmar 2004: 169) have pointed out, unless the Afghan state acquires a monopoly of power with respect to basic functions, the country will not be able to break out of the vicious circle of political disintegration, endemic conflict, poverty, and economic collapse. As the government regains control of revenue sources still in the hands of powerful warlords, it will have more resources to improve security, establish macroeconomic stability, and create the right legal and institutional framework to promote an environment conducive to private sector investment, employment generation, and growth. Most importantly, the government must find ways—even unconventional ones—to create alternatives to drug production and trade.

The inability of the government to create such a framework has been one of the most important failures in Afghanistan, particularly in light of donors' fatigue and the shift in attention to Iraq and other countries. M. Ishaq Nadiri of New York University rightly emphasizes that, given Afghans' tremendous entrepreneurial spirit as traders and textile makers, they needed more than aid. They needed ideas and a basic framework to create a thriving private sector, which the government cannot provide without a monopoly of power. And, without the creation of a viable private sector, reconstruction in Afghanistan will not take root (Taylor 2007a: 31).[40]

Moving forward

We need to recognize the blunt fact that Afghanistan will remain a poor country with critical development challenges for years to come, and that international assistance will be imperative for its survival as well as for the maintenance of peace in the region. Without adequate support of the Afghan government to ensure that expectations for a better life are reasonably satisfied, disgruntled groups will continue to endanger the fragile peace.

In 2007, the Taliban resurfaced in force, and the opium economy is thriving. To fight on both fronts requires that the government create viable employment as soon as possible, particularly for Afghanistan's large youth population. It is also imperative that the government give priority to basic reconstruction to ensure the provision of vital housing, health, and other services to the large majority of the population that lacks them. Afghanistan has been, and will continue to be, a rudimentary economy in the immediate future. In designing the market-driven, private-sector-led strategy that the government first proposed in the NDF and later elaborated in the NDS, clear and simple rules for trade and investment and an uncomplicated and fair system of taxation are critically important. Even under the best-case scenario, in which the Afghan government increases its revenue prospects, donors should be prepared to continue covering part of budgetary expenditures. Afghanistan will not be able to cover these costs on its own for quite some time.

With a serious commitment to work in support of the government in rebuilding a simple economy, the international community, UN agencies, IFIs, bilateral donors, and NGOs could also provide much-needed technical assistance and practical macro- and microeconomic training. Capacity building has been insufficient and needs to be implemented on a large scale to build Afghanistan's technical expertise and solid economic and financial institutions.

Without alternatives to drug production and without a rapid and broad-based improvement in the appalling living conditions of the large majority of Afghans, peace and political stability in the entire region may be at stake. This may be particularly true after the death of Benazir Bhutto in Pakistan, which has increased instability in the country as well as the region. The international community can ignore this only at its own peril.

As Rubin (2007a: 1, 6) notes, US policymakers have been underestimating the stakes in Afghanistan for decades—not only since 2001. He warns that a mere course correction will not be enough to prevent the country from sliding into chaos. As Finance Minister Ashraf Ghani warned the international community at the Brussels meeting in March 2003, there were three possible scenarios for Afghanistan: stability and prosperity, state failure, or emergence of a narco-mafia state. While elements of the second and third scenarios were already visible at the time, by end-2007 the probability that one or the other will be realized has become high.[41] The *New York Times* editorial (2007a) welcomed the December agreement of the United States and the EU for a much-needed top-to-bottom review of their strategy. As they point out, it is better late than never. In their view, unless the strategy involves more investment, attention, and troops, the "good war" will go irretrievably bad. I think that what is at stake could not have been put in better words.

Lessons from Afghanistan

As in other post-conflict transitions, a great deal rides on the success or failure of Afghanistan's economic reconstruction. Seven years into the war-to-peace transition, Afghanistan offers several lessons, not only for other countries embarking on this transition, but also for moving the country forward. Two such lessons stand out.

DEVELOPING A SIMPLE AND FLEXIBLE ECONOMIC FRAMEWORK

Good economic management and macroeconomics stability are critical in post-conflict situations. It seems to me, however, that there is no need—and in fact the cost may be high—to move from one extreme to another in policy-making. Afghanistan had been in a situation in which there were no payments or banking system, the government financed its activities with an inflationary tax by printing money, and the civil service lacked basic qualifications. To move quickly to sophisticated laws and regulations that are best practice in higher-income countries, but with neither the capacity to implement them nor the security conditions and judicial system to enforce them, is not optimal. Until the risk of a reversal in the peace process fell and the capacity of the civil service improved, Afghanistan would have been better off with a simple and flexible monetary and fiscal framework. This would have given the government the ability to weather the difficult political and security decisions it had to make on a daily basis. It would have also allowed the government to create temporary employment for the large youth population and create alternative employment to drug production, even if macroeconomic stabilization took longer to achieve.

In particular, central bank independence should not be best practice in post-conflict situations. In fact, the government should have the flexibility to engage in deficit financing if it needs to carry out specific programs that are essential for the maintenance of peace, even if macroeconomic stability suffers in the process. Thus, strict budgetary discipline is not necessarily a virtue in post-conflict situations, especially if it interferes with peace consolidation.

Macroeconomic stability is a necessary but not sufficient condition for effective reconstruction in the transition from war to peace. One thing that becomes clear from the case of Afghanistan is that it is much easier to build economic institutions and good macro policies than it is to build peace. Reading the IMF reports from 2002 to 2007, one is amazed by the progress made in these areas. The currency exchange, for example, was necessary and operated in an exemplary way, despite all the obstacles and bottlenecks that it faced. Nevertheless, Afghanistan may be farther from peace today than it was in 2002. Economic transition cannot take place in a vacuum. Reconstruction can take place only within the prevailing various political, security, and social constraints, not separately from them.

AVOIDING AID DEPENDENCY

To prevent the aid dependency that has characterized Afghanistan from becoming a feature of future efforts, the balance between humanitarian and reconstruction assistance should shift heavily and quickly towards the latter. Furthermore, unless donors use reconstruction aid productively and effectively to strengthen the government, to replace the illegal and drug economy, and to create the basic infrastructure to support private initiatives, Afghanistan's chances of moving onto a sustainable development path will be slim. Private capital will not flow into the country—on the contrary, capital flight will continue—unless the security situation improves, electricity is restored, other basic infrastructure is built, a simple and non-corrupt legal and regulatory framework is in place, and human capital is upgraded.

The earlier the economy shifts from reliance on foreign aid to trade and foreign investment, the better the peace transition's outcome will be. In this regard, donors should open up their markets to Afghan exports and provide adequate financial and technical resources to promote them, particularly in areas in which it is possible to replace production of drugs with production of other goods. The UK government, for example, is considering a program of price support for farmers who produce cotton (or other products) instead of poppies. Other incentives—including direct subsidies and price support programs—should be also explored. Financing these incentives could have a high rate of return for donors. Donors should also consider special preferential tariff treatment for light labor-intensive manufactures from Afghanistan, including cotton textiles.

The US has committed $750 million over the next five years to help establish "reconstruction opportunity zones" in Pakistan's tribal areas, and has promised special tariff- and duty-free access to its markets for goods produced in them (Akram 2007). The United States should extend this program to Afghanistan, and other donors should follow suit. If donors provided financing, the government could provide subsidies for the production of different crops to replace poppies. Afghans could use the crops to produce textiles and food-processing industries creating numerous jobs in the process. The country could become an exporter of these and other products to industrial markets under preferential tariff arrangements.

Opening foreign markets for Afghan exports would also make the country attractive to foreign investors, who would bring technology and establish export-processing zones to use local labor and raw materials to produce higher value-added, higher-quality goods. Exports from these zones would not only have a positive impact on foreign exchange earnings but, most importantly, would create numerous jobs, as previously occurred in post-crisis countries such as Mexico, El Salvador, and Guatemala. With an appropriate regulatory and tax regime, these reconstruction zones would also create effective links to the national economy by using other domestic goods and services, thus building the national private sector, training the domestic labor force, and transferring technology and know-how. This virtuous circle could put Afghanistan onto a path of sustainable development rather than one of aid dependency, which, unfortunately, is where it is clearly heading.

10 US-led reconstruction amid US-led occupation: Iraq

Background[1]

Contrary to the previous cases, Iraq has been the site of human civilizations dating back to 4000 BC. Mesopotamia—the land between the Tigris and Euphrates rivers—became the center of the ancient Babylonian and Assyrian empires, and was conquered by both Cyrus the Great and Alexander the Great. Persian domination lasted for about twelve centuries (550 BC to AD 652). After the Arab conquest in the seventh century, Mesopotamia became known as Iraq ("the well-rooted country") for its contributions to successive civilizations, and Baghdad was the capital of the ruling caliphate. Mass Arab migration from eastern Arabia took place at this time. The Mongols cruelly pillaged the country in 1258, and from the sixteenth to eighteenth centuries, the country was the object of repeated Turkish–Persian and tribal competition.

In the nineteenth century, the Ottomans consolidated control, imposing direct rule in 1831, after overthrowing the Mamluk regime, which had achieved autonomy eighty-four years earlier. During World War I, Britain occupied most of Mesopotamia, and the League of Nations gave it a mandate over the territory. At the end of the war, the international community recognized Iraq as a kingdom.[2] In 1932, the Sunni Hashemite monarchy achieved full independence and it adopted a currency board exchange rate regime, in which the Iraqi Currency Board issued Iraqi dinars at par with the British pound, and fully backed them with British pound reserves (Hanke 2003a, 2003b).

Britain again occupied Iraq during World War II because of its early pro-Axis stance. Iraq became a charter member of the Arab League in 1945, and Iraqi troops took part in the Arab invasion of Palestine in 1948. King Faisal II was assassinated in 1958 and a military junta, led by Brigadier Abd al-Karim Qassem, reversed the monarchy's pro-Western policies, focused on the gap between rich and poor, and allied itself with Communist countries.

As Kuwait gained independence from Britain in 1961, Iraq claimed sovereignty over Kuwait. Britain responded by sending troops to Kuwait, forcing Qassem to back down. Qassem was assassinated in another coup in 1963, which brought the Baath Socialist Party to power, with the military's support. The new regime advocated secularism, pan-Arabism, and socialism, and recognized Kuwait's independence.

However, political instability and military coups continued in the 1960s. In 1968, a junta led by Maj. Gen. Ahmed Hasan al-Bakr—with Saddam Hussein (after referred to as Saddam) as his deputy—took over and used its oil revenue to become a regional military power. Saddam replaced President Bakr in 1979. Control of the Shatt-al-Arab waterway, long disputed by Iraq and Iran, provided the pretext for Iraq's invasion of Iran in late 1980. In the ensuing eight-year war, both countries are thought to have used poison gas, and roughly 1.5 million lives were lost before a UN-brokered peace agreement ended the fighting.[3]

The UN and the Gulf War

In mid-1990, after Arab leaders failed to mediate Iraq's territorial claims on Kuwait, Iraq invaded Kuwait and established a puppet government. Despite UN-imposed comprehensive sanctions as per Security Council Resolution (SCR) 661 of August 1990, Iraq refused to withdraw, and UN forces under US leadership launched the Gulf War (Operation Desert Storm), liberating Kuwait in less than a week. The Security Council created the UN Compensation Commission (UNCC) in 1991 to process claims and pay compensation for losses and damage suffered as a direct result of Iraq's unlawful invasion and occupation of Kuwait.[4]

Despite the success of Operation Desert Storm and the US-encouraged rebellions by both Shiites and Kurds that followed, Saddam Hussein proved a resilient dictator, brutally crushing both rebellions. In 1991, the UN set up a no-fly zone in northern Iraq to protect the Kurdish population; in 1992, the UN established a southern no-fly zone as a buffer between Iraq and Kuwait, as well as to protect the Shiites.[5]

In 1991, with growing concern over the humanitarian situation in Iraq, the UN proposed measures to enable Iraq to sell limited quantities of oil to meet its people's needs. The Iraqi government declined these offers (SCR 706 and SCR 712 of 1991). In April 1995, acting under Chapter VII of the UN Charter, which contemplates enforcement of Security Council resolutions, the Council adopted SCR 986 establishing the Oil-for-Food Program. Iraq would sell oil to provide financing for purchases of humanitarian goods, and various mandated UN activities, including reparations. The Security Council approved this program as a "temporary measure to provide for the humanitarian needs of the Iraqi people, until the fulfillment by Iraq of the relevant resolutions." The most important was SRC 687 of 1991, which stipulated the elimination of weapons of mass destruction—including all nuclear, chemical, biological, and ballistic arms.

The Oil-for-Food Program became operative only in mid-1996, after the UN and the Iraqi government signed a Memorandum of Understanding (MOU), and after the UN had granted Iraq the possibility of exerting much greater control over the program. As originally planned, the UN would have had full control of the program, with strong controls of both oil exports and imports of humanitarian goods. The first oil was exported in December 1996, and the first shipment of supplies arrived in Iraq in March 1997. Initially, the program capped oil exports at $2 billion every six months, with two-thirds to meet Iraq's humanitarian needs. In 1998, the Council raised the six-month cap to more than $5 billion every six months, and by December 1999 removed it altogether.[6]

Sanctions had a devastating impact on the population, and failed to modify the behavior of the ruling class as had been the explicit intent. This was because careful targeting was difficult to achieve and hence spillover effects were large. As a blunt instrument used instead of force, the broad economic sanctions imposed under Article 41 of the UN Charter inflicted incalculable human cost. What UN member states did not anticipate was that it would become so difficult to enforce them and so politically controversial to remove them when it became clear what impact they were having. As a result they remained in place for twelve years.

Owing to a large extent to the way the Oil-for-Food Program degenerated, Iraqi leaders benefited financially from the sanctions, as leaders had in Haiti and other countries where UN sanctions have been imposed. At the same time, Saddam Hussein continuously set impediments to the operations of the UN inspections team mandated by the Security Council to ascertain that Iraq had destroyed all weapons of mass destruction. After Saddam expelled the American members of the UN inspections team in November 1997, readmitted them in February 1998, and again halted inspections that August, the US and Britain launched Operation Desert Fox in December 1998, which included four days of intensive air strikes. Sustained low-level warfare with air strikes on Iraqi targets within the no-fly zones continued until March 2003.

US-led military intervention in 2003

After the 9/11 terrorist attacks in New York and Washington, D.C., President Bush included Iraq as part of an "axis of evil" and started talking about "regime change" and preparing for military intervention. The Bush administration cited several justifications for its position. Perhaps the most important was the alleged existence of weapons of mass destruction and the UN weapons inspectors' inability to carry out their investigation. Other reasons included Saddam's alleged links to international terrorism, his record of serious human rights violations, and his non-compliance with 14 Security Council Resolutions. While the Arab countries, Latin America, and many in Europe were adamantly opposed to the US position, which they made clear at the Security Council, the UK supported the US. Exactly a year after 9/11, Bush addressed the UN General Assembly to present his case for US unilateral intervention—quite distinct from the case in Afghanistan—unless the UN managed to enforce its resolutions against Iraq, particularly SCR 687.

In November 2002, the UN Security Council unanimously imposed tough new arms inspections on Iraq, with those of Iraq's military sites beginning soon after. By January 2003, however, the report of the chief weapons inspector, Hans Blix, was not encouraging, and seemed to strengthen the Bush administration's case for invading Iraq. Blix concluded, "Iraq appears not to have come to a genuine acceptance—not even today—of the disarmament that was demanded of it and which it needs to carry out to win the confidence of the world and live in peace" (Malone 2006: 197). Disregarding efforts by several permanent members of the Security Council—France, Russia, and China—to give UN inspectors more time to complete their task, Bush and Blair continued to plan for war with a "coalition of the willing." Failing to gain Security Council support, on March 17 Bush delivered an ultimatum to Saddam to leave the country within 48 hours or face war. On March 20, the war began with the launch of Operation Iraqi Freedom. The lack of a mandate by the Security Council had important consequences for the legitimacy of both the military intervention and policies designed for post-conflict reconstruction after the US officially declared on May 1st that the war was over.[7]

Despite intensive searches, the coalition forces did not find any evidence of the existence of weapons of mass destruction, eroding what little support the US government had for occupying Iraq. At the same time, violence and instability in the country required a large number of troops. The US kept roughly 140,000 American troops in Iraq in 2003, supplemented by 11,000 British and 10,000 other coalition troops. Despite efforts to decrease the number of US troops in Iraq, in early 2007 the US had to increase its forces again. After the surge, the United States had over 170,000 in October. As security improved, the year ended with 160,000 US troops, with plans to withdraw 5 brigades of about 20,000 troops by mid-2008.

The transition from US-led military intervention to US-led occupation and economic reconstruction has been widely analyzed.[8] It has also received a large amount of attention from the US and international media. The purpose here is to focus on some policy issues that did not arise in the case studies in Chapters 7–9. As always, the aim is to nurture debate, so that post-conflict reconstruction has a better chance of succeeding in the future. Hence, after a cursory discussion of political, security, social, and economic developments, I will focus on these specific issues and how they were addressed to draw lessons and best practices for future operations.

The political and security transitions amid US-led occupation[9]

Contrary to the other case studies in this book, Iraq's state did not collapse due to civil war or other internal conflict, but due to US-led military intervention with the purpose of regime change. Furthermore, rather than the burden of post-conflict reconstruction being shifted to the international community led by the UN—as in Kosovo and Afghanistan—reconstruction remained US-led, first by choice and then by default.[10]

Nevertheless, as Diamond (2005: 3) points out, the challenges were not unlike those of other post-conflict experiences. Occupying forces had to fill the vacuum left by the collapse of political authority and establish public order. There was a need to rehabilitate basic services and infrastructure and to prevent fighting among the different ethnic groups, each with its own militia. The Bush administration seem to have naively assumed that Iraqis would receive US troops as "liberators," and that power could soon be transferred to an Iraqi administration.[11] The US Department of Defense originally planned for a quick transition to an interim pro-US government led by Ahmed Chalabi and other exiles.

The Pentagon, leading the post-conflict transition, established its Office of Reconstruction and Humanitarian Assistance (ORHA) in Iraq, headed by Jay Garner, a former military man with experience in humanitarian assistance. However, ORHA failed to maintain law and order and to establish political leadership in the immediate period following the fall of Saddam's regime in early April.[12] As a result, the US government eliminated this office in mid-May as leadership for the strategy and implementation of political and economic reconstruction in Iraq started shifting towards the State Department.

Paul Bremer, a former US Ambassador linked to the State Department, rather than the Pentagon, arrived in Baghdad on May 13 and assumed his functions as head of the Coalition Provisional Authority (CPA) and US Administrator of the country. As Diamond (2005: 4) notes, he arrived with a set of bold new initiatives for a full occupation that might last two years or longer. One of the CPA's initial mistakes, however, was to fire all Baath Party officials from positions of responsibility and to disband the Iraqi army without a program to disarm, demobilize, and reintegrate (DDR) them.[13] These two measures left about 400,000–500,000 armed people unemployed, and deprived the civil service of critical technical expertise. The foolishness and shortsightedness of this policy at the time when unemployment could have verged on 60 percent cannot be justified on any grounds. The CPA partly reversed the ban in the following weeks, but considerable damage already had been done.[14]

Under pressure from the Iraqi exiles and the autonomous Kurdish regions in mid-July 2003, Bremer appointed a 25-member Iraqi Governing Council (IGC) for the occupation period and until an interim government was established. The CPA, however, kept all powers. The IGC could appoint government officials including ministers, but it played only an advisory role, prompting many Iraqis to consider it a US puppet government.

Security Council Resolution 1483 in May 2003 affirmed that the US and the UK were occupying countries. Thus, as Malone (2006: 205) notes, Iraq remained a US–UK venture, not a UN-sanctioned undertaking. Nevertheless, the resolution mandated the Secretary-General to appoint a Special Representative (SRSG). The SRSG was tasked with coordination of humanitarian assistance and aid to refugees and internally displaced persons; promotion of human rights and legal and judicial reform; and collaboration with other organizations on economic reconstruction. The resolution also contemplated that the UN "would play a vital role in ... restoration and establishment of national and local institutions for representative governance." The resolution also supported "the formation, by the people of Iraq with the help of the Authority [the CPA] and working with the Special Representative, of an Iraqi interim Administration." Although the resolution clearly gave the UN a subordinate political role, Bremer did not welcome it at all, since he saw no political role whatsoever for the UN in Iraq.[15]

The UN set up a large mission headed by Sergio Vieira de Mello, one of its top civil servants, who had a long and distinguished career in UN peace-building operations, including in Kosovo and East Timor. As SRSG, Vieira de Mello had broad contacts in Iraq, including with Grand Ayatollah Ali al-Sistani, who strongly supported wider Iraqi participation in policymaking and the formation of an interim government as soon as possible. Vieira de Mello communicated to Bremer the Ayatollah's position on this issue and appealed for an early transition to sovereignty. As Diamond (2006: 186) argues, the political and economic reconstruction of the country probably would have proceeded much more rapidly and successfully and with far less violence had the United States accepted UN appeals earlier.

In August 2003, a vicious terrorist attack on the UN headquarters killed Vieira de Mello and many of his colleagues. After another attack on the UN in September, the Secretary-General decided to reduce the UN presence to a minimum.[16]

Iraqis increasingly demanded an end to the US occupation and the restoration of national sovereignty. For different reasons, both the IGC, which resented its lack of power, and the Shiite majority, which expected strong representation in an elected government, favored the establishment of an interim government. As security conditions deteriorated, anti-American sentiments deepened, and the UN exited the country, Bremer presented a plan for the political transition called the "November 15 Agreement." This was the first time that the United States contemplated a comprehensive timetable for the end of its occupation and the transfer of political power to Iraqi interim authorities, which was set for June 2004, much earlier than originally planned.

The November 15 Agreement contemplated that, by the end of February 2004, the IGC would draft a Transitional Administrative Law (TAL), which would essentially function as an interim constitution. The TAL would structure and limit power for the roughly 18 months between the end of the occupation and the inauguration, by the end of 2005, of an elected government under a permanent constitution.[17] The Agreement also contemplated the selection of members of a provincial caucus, which in turn would elect representatives to the Transitional National Assembly (TNA), a body that would appoint a prime minister, a cabinet, and a three-member presidency council.[18] Ayatollah al-Sistani strongly opposed the caucus system and insisted that any constitution-making body had to be elected rather than appointed.

Unable to deal with al-Sistani's opposition and refusal to meet with CPA authorities, the Bush administration welcomed UN involvement for the first time. The Secretary-General appointed Lakhdar Brahimi, the veteran UN peacemaker, as special envoy in January 2004. Brahimi convinced al-Sistani of the impossibility of conducting national elections before the end of the occupation and brokered a compromise, reflected in SCR 1546 of June 8, 2004. The resolution welcomed the end of the occupation by June 30, endorsed the formation of a sovereign Interim Government, and called for democratic elections by January 2005.[19]

TRANSFER OF POWER FROM THE CPA TO AN INTERIM IRAQI GOVERNMENT

On June 28, 2004, the United States ended its political occupation of the country with the dissolution of the CPA and recognition of Iraqi sovereignty. By then, Brahimi had already announced the selection of the Interim Government. In theory, this government assumed leadership of the complex and multi-pronged transition to peace. However, it did so under taxing security conditions and in the presence of a large number of foreign forces. Thus, in practice, US influence remained strong.[20]

As Diamond (2006: 173–4) argues, by the time the CPA ended, Iraq had fallen far short of the progress on political and economic reconstruction that the Bush administration had promised. In his view, the CPA left the country in far worse shape than it need have done, diminishing Iraq's prospects for political stability and democracy, and costing many more Iraqi, American, and other lives than would have been the case had a better strategy been put in place.

In January 2005, elections to the new Transitional National Assembly (TNA) were held. Except for the so-called "Sunni Triangle," Iraqis voted to elect a legitimate and representative assembly. In early May, the Assembly swore in a new Iraqi Transitional Government (ITG) and charged it with the preparation of a permanent constitution to replace the Transitional Administrative Law (TAL). A popular referendum in October 2005 approved the draft constitution, which could be amended by the first Assembly elected under it. That election took place in December 2005, though the formation of Iraq's First Constitutional Government since the fall of Saddam Hussein took until the end of May 2006. The difficulty of agreeing on a national government was a harbinger for the future. Bringing peace, order, and reconstruction to the country proved an insurmountable challenge to Prime Minister Nuri al-Maliki's government.

At the same time, the political impasse in forming a government invigorated insurgents and militia groups. With the Sunni bombing of one of the holiest shrines in Iraq—the Askariya Shrine in Samarra, known as the Golden Dome—in February 2006, the country came close to civil war. Indeed, by mid-2006, security conditions had deteriorated so badly that many believed that the country was already in civil war. Writing in the *New York Times* in July, Galbraith (2006b) noted that "Baghdad is the front line of Iraq's Sunni-Shiite civil war. It is a tragedy for its people, most of whom do not share the sectarian hatred behind the killing. Iraqi forces cannot end the civil war because many of them are partisans of one side, and none are trusted by both communities."

The economic transition

If mistakes during the political US occupation were a large factor behind the poor security conditions that hampered economic reconstruction, mistakes in economic policymaking also failed to create conditions such that people could see any improvement or "peace dividend" in their daily lives. Good policymaking for economic reconstruction could have made a difference in the period following regime change in Iraq.

US involvement in reconstruction was more intense in Iraq than in Afghanistan, in large part because of strong opposition to the war and the general lackluster support of the international community in the post-conflict period. More importantly, the United States was, from the very beginning, determined to occupy the country and set up its own administration, as it had done in Germany and Japan after World War II. The lure of large contracts for economic reconstruction and of investments in the oil sector was perhaps not far from the minds of those planning the US occupation.[21] Naturally, Iraqis reacted negatively to what they saw as an American effort to disempower them by giving contracts to foreign contractors and taking over their oil wealth through privatization.

Given questionable American intentions and Iraqi suspicions, it is not surprising that many factors worked against a successful war-to-peace transition. Since some of these factors relate specifically to economic reconstruction, both good and bad examples need to be analyzed. A cursory analysis of the main factors that gave rise to current conditions in Iraq is nonetheless necessary before turning to the particular issues that affected economic reconstruction, some of which were critical in plunging the country into civil war.

ECONOMIC AND FINANCIAL CONDITIONS

Despite US leadership, the United Nations Development Group (UNDG) and the World Bank, with assistance from the IMF, prepared the needs assessment. The assessment covered 14 priority sectors most urgently in need of reconstruction assistance. The organizations estimated that about $36 billion was necessary in 2003–7 and $55 billion overall. The International Conference on Reconstruction took place in Madrid on October 23–4, 2003, but a year later donors had only disbursed less than 3 percent of the amounts they had pledged.[22]

Iraq is potentially a rich country,[23] with the world's fourth-largest proven oil reserves, estimated at about 115 billion barrels (about 9 percent of the total).[24] However, following three wars since 1980, pervasive state intervention, and the devastating impact of comprehensive economic sanctions imposed and maintained by the UN in 1991–2003, the Iraqi economy was in ruins. According to the US Treasury Department (Taylor 2007), GDP in purchasing power parity terms—that is, taking prices into account—fell from $128 billion in 1980 to $40 billion in 2002. Income per capita collapsed, impoverishing the Iraqi people.[25] Thus, there was a marked deterioration in Iraq's human development indicators over the past 20 years. Until the war with Iran in 1980, Iraq had been one of the more developed and prosperous countries in the region. Even after the war with Iran, Iraq ranked 76th in the 1990 UNDP Human Development Index.[26] While its economic and social indicators had been among the best in the Middle Eastern countries, it now lags behind those countries in relation to the UN Millennium Development Goals (IMF 2005a, Box 1: 6). Furthermore, given the accumulation of military debt since the 1980s, and compensation payments imposed by the UN after its invasion of Kuwait, Iraq had become one of the most highly indebted countries in the world.

In addition to poor initial conditions, including serious infrastructure problems, the hostilities, looting, and sabotage following US occupation compounded the lack of investment and war damage of the Saddam era. Despite some steps taken by the CPA, security conditions made it difficult for reconstruction of infrastructure to begin in any significant way. Throughout the summer of 2003, shortages in electricity and other services made it difficult to reactivate economic activity. It also made Iraqis frustrated and resentful. With temperatures of up to 112 °F (45 °C) this was understandable. What was surprising was that the CPA did not try to involve the Iraqis in repairing basic infrastructure, after the success they had had in repairing oil and other infrastructure while sanctions were in place.[27]

RELATIONS WITH THE IFIS

Although Iraq's arrears to the IFIs were not significant, Iraq is a highly indebted country. By the end of 2007, Iraq had signed bilateral agreements with all Paris Club members except Russia and had settled about $20 billion (close to 100 percent) of private claims through debt and cash exchange, including arbitration. However, even after the application of Paris Club debt reduction to non-Paris Club members, the debt stock at the end of 2005 was about $70 billion or 200 percent of GDP. By end-2007, Iraq had signed bilateral agreements with 9 of more than 30 non-Paris Club creditors. This represented only about $3.5 billion out of $70 billion, since the bulk of unresolved debt (more than 80 percent) is to the Gulf countries and China. The IMF (2008a: 19–20) reports that understandings with China have been reached on part of the debt but that progress with the Gulf countries and Russia has been slow. Despite substantial debt reduction from official and private creditors, the IMF reckons that further reductions are needed to ensure debt sustainability.[28]

Negotiations on debt relief were contingent on an IMF-supported economic program. In September 2004, the Executive Board approved a $435 million (25 percent of quota) Emergency Post-Conflict Assistance (EPCA) loan to Iraq. In addition to meeting some of their urgent balance of payments needs, the Iraqi authorities made commitments under this program to improve the administrative and institutional capacity to seek further financial support from the Fund in the form of an upper credit tranche facility (which involves conditionality).

The World Bank's board discussed the first *Interim Strategy Note* (ISN) in January 2004, and the second one in August 2005. Donors contributed to the Reconstruction Fund Facility for Iraq (IRFFI), which consisted of two trust funds, the World Bank Iraq Trust Fund (ITF) and the UN Iraq Trust Fund.[29] The UNDP, acting on behalf of the UN Development Group (UNDG), administers the latter, for the first time jointly coordinating planning and funding among UN agencies.

In December 2005, the IMF Board approved a 15-month stand-by arrangement (SBA) to support an economic program for the period December 2005–March 2007. Iraq was able to draw up to about $700 million, or 40 percent of quota, but the government treated this facility as precautionary, that is, it did not draw from it. In December 2007, Iraq completed the early repayment of its outstanding obligations under the EPCA of close to $500 million. Soon after the Board approved a successor SBA for about $750 million, which the government also intends to use as precautionary, to support Iraq's economic program through March 2009. Maintaining macroeconomic stability remains a key objective of the authorities' program for 2008–9.

Going over the economic program in Iraq gives a sense of déjà vu since it embodies the same "development as usual" policies that we saw in the previous case studies. For example, Deputy Managing Director Takatoshi Kato (*IMF Survey* 2006) noted that a critical component of the overall strategy was to contain expenditures within revenues and available financing. This required prioritizing expenditures for reconstruction, controlling the wage and pension bills, reducing subsidies for petroleum products and expanding the participation of the private sector in the domestic market for them, and strengthening the social safety net. As usual, the IMF ignored how politically incorrect and dangerous these policies can become in a post-conflict situation. Lifting subsidies on fuel and other products has led to violence in countries in the normal process of development and can be clearly explosive in post-conflict situations, while low wages in the public administration is a recipe for corruption. Furthermore, social safety net programs, which often discourage work, need to be replaced as soon as possible by attractive employment opportunities which tight monetary and fiscal policies often deter.

In partnership with the UN and with the support of the World Bank, in July 2006 the government launched the International Compact for Iraq (ICI) to develop, with the assistance of the international community, a medium-term framework for comprehensive political, security, and economic reform. Could this program become the reconstruction strategy that Iraq has so far clearly lacked? As this book goes to press, there is little sign of it. On the contrary, by end-2007 the country had established a macroeconomic framework that allowed it to negotiate a successor stand-by arrangement with the IMF but social and security conditions were deplorable and lack of jobs continued to be the top economic concern of the Iraqi population. At the same time, professionals and other qualified people continued to leave, depriving the country of expertise that is essential for economic reconstruction (for data see IMF 2007f).

PERFORMANCE UNDER THE IMF-SUPPORTED PROGRAMS

Many post-conflict countries that start from a low base and have a large international presence during the transition to peace grow rapidly in the initial period. This was not really the case in Iraq. After an adjustment from the post-invasion paralysis in 2003, when GDP fell by 35 percent (after having fallen by 20 percent the year before), the economy grew by close to 50 percent in 2004, largely owing to the reactivation of the oil sector, which had practically collapsed in the early part of 2003. However, largely because of stagnation in the oil sector, Iraq experienced anemic growth of less than 3.5 percent in 2005 and 2006—significantly lower than the 17 and 10 percent rates that the IMF had projected for those years.[30] In 2007 the country grew at 6 percent but this growth is projected to fall to only 1 percent in 2008 (IMF 2008, 2007e).

With Iraq having enormous needs for infrastructure investment, and a young population resulting from an annual 3 percent increase for many years, its economy and private sector must grow much faster in order to create employment for the growing labor force. Yet, despite the large expatriate presence and the high inflows of military and reconstruction aid that have helped other countries to growth fast in the first few post-conflict years, the economy grew at unacceptably low rates.

Oil production was stagnant from 2003 to 2007, fluctuating around 2 million barrels per day (mbpd). Oil exports remained at about 1.5 mbpd until 2007, although exports have increased in recent months as a result of the resumption of oil shipments through the northern pipeline to Turkey. Iraqi oil prices, however, increased by close to 90 percent from 2004 to 2007, from $32 dollars to about $60 per barrel. As a result, oil export revenue doubled in value terms from $18 billion in 2004 to over $36 billion in 2007, and international reserves grew from $8 billion in 2004 to about $27 billion in 2007. The combination of great damage to oil refineries caused by the Gulf War and lack of investment will continue to necessitate imports of refined products amounting to more than $2 billion annually.[31]

Several factors influenced the slow growth in Iraq in 2005 and 2006, not least, the ongoing insurgency and militia activity, which resulted in acute shortages of certain goods (especially gasoline and other fuel products). As a result, inflation reached 65 percent at the end of 2006 but was brought down to an estimated 5 percent in 2007 through a combination of monetary and fiscal tightening and measures to reduce fuel shortages by allowing their domestic prices to increase. Faced with a highly dollarized economy (not surprising given the domestic uncertainties), the central bank raised its interest rate and allowed the dinar to appreciate. However, tightening monetary and exchange rate policies to fight inflation favors imports, discouraging private investment in the non-oil sector and making the ambitious investment program for the oil sector—a key component of the 2007 budget—more difficult to implement.[32]

Although the government decided to postpone the increase in the reconstruction (import) levy from 5 to 10 percent until 2008, the government acceded to the IMF's pressure to eliminate subsidies for fuel products. Rather than following a gradual approach, the government opted for "shock therapy." While governments under normal conditions find it difficult to reduce subsidies for gasoline and other fuels, in Iraq, amid security problems and soaring unemployment, the government decided to raise $1 billion in 2005 by reducing the price subsidy for domestic consumption of oil derivatives (starting at the end of 2004). The reduction of such subsidies was even more drastic in 2006, and liberalization was programmed to increase further in 2007. As a result, the official price of regular gasoline increased from ID20 to ID250 per liter in 2006 and was set to increase to ID350 in 2007. The price for a 12-kg cylinder of cooking gas increased 12-fold, from ID250 to ID3,000, during this period.[33]

In addition to the sharp cut in subsidies, the 2006 budget contemplated controlling growth in current spending, in order to increase investment, particularly in the oil sector. Because of the increase in violence, the civil service's inability to implement laws, and the difficulties in importing oil-related capital inputs, only 40 percent of budgeted investment was spent (*IMF Survey* 2007), which is reflected in stagnant oil production since 2003.

Iraq's unique situation with regard to financing for reconstruction

Reconstruction in resource-rich countries is quite different and implies different priorities than in resource-poor countries. The situation in Iraq contrasts sharply with that of El Salvador, Kosovo, or Afghanistan because of the government and external accounts' dependence on oil revenues. In 2004, oil accounted for about 70 percent of Iraq's GDP and 98 percent of exports. Oil was very important to government finances as well, representing close to 90 percent of government revenue.[34] Because resource-rich countries should pay more of the cost of reconstruction, reconstruction of the oil sector had to be given high priority and a sense of urgency. Billions of dollars were necessary to reconstruct the sector, which had suffered years of sanctions and lack of investment since the early 1980s.

At the same time, the situation of Iraq was unique for many reasons. First, following military intervention, the US occupied the country, as it had done earlier in Japan and Germany. Given concerns about legitimacy and security, this precluded the option of attracting foreign direct investment to reactivate the sector. Second, the UN imposed comprehensive sanctions for 12 years, from 1991 to 2003, and created the Oil-for-Food Program in 1995. While the sanctions had a devastating effect on the population at large, Iraq started reconstruction with a food distribution system in place that fed about 60 percent of the population.[35] Third, Iraq also started reconstruction with large external assets held abroad. Security Council Resolution 1483 allowed relevant banks to deposit Iraqi funds in the US-controlled Development Fund for Iraq (DFI).[36] The DFI included funds frozen when the UN imposed sanctions (over $1 billion), and funds remaining in the Oil-for-Food Program escrow account (about $8 billion). Including oil export proceeds (over $11 billion), interest, and other small items, the DFI had funds of over $20 billion (Cooper and Jaffe 2004).

What was necessary and done well: The currency plan

In the move from war to peace, one of the critical issues that often must be dealt with is the establishment of a sound currency, which is necessary to pay civil servants and conduct monetary and exchange rate policies. Military intervention often interrupts basic economic and financial transactions. Furthermore, in post-conflict situations, currencies often have lost their value through counterfeiting and hyperinflation. This makes it imperative to replace previous currencies with a new currency—be it domestic or foreign.[37]

In either case, the introduction of new currencies (printing, importing, and shipping) creates a number of physical and logistical problems. At the same time, the large inflow of foreign currencies will tend to have an inflationary impact and cause the domestic currency to appreciate, undermining the country's competitiveness and budgetary conditions.[38] Although a new currency was introduced in both Afghanistan and Iraq, in Iraq it presented new challenges and raised new issues. In addition to the substitution of the new dinar for the old, Iraq also had to bring into the country large quantities of foreign exchange that international banks had frozen abroad owing to sanctions. This presented major challenges that perplexed many observers.

"Who in their right mind would send 360 tons of cash into a war zone?" The Chairman of the US Committee on Oversight and Government Reform,

Henry Waxman, posed this question in his opening statement in early February 2007. The question, which the media widely quoted, does indeed make the policy sound crazy.[39] However, many crazy things happen in conflict and post-conflict situations. Belisario Bentancur, a former President of Colombia, referred to the Salvadoran peace process as the transition from madness to peace.[40]

Despite its seeming madness, shipping tons of cash into a war zone is necessary in many post-conflict situations—though the scale of this was much larger in Iraq because of the country's sheer size and the frozen funds that it had abroad. I was involved in paying stipends in Kosovo. Although I was not involved in Afghanistan and Iraq, these cases seem to have avoided some of the pitfalls experienced in Kosovo. Since many countries will have to go through this type of decision as they enter the transition to peace, it is worth detailing all the issues involved.

It is important first to have some background. During the previous regime, the (old) Iraqi dinar was legal tender in the country and comprised two types of co-circulating banknotes: the Swiss dinar, issued between 1979 and 1989, and circulated only in the northern Kurdish provinces after 1989, and the Saddam dinar, issued by the Central Bank of Iraq (CBI) from 1990 onwards. In setting the stage for reconstruction, the authorities had to deal with several practical issues. First, the central bank did not fully control the printing of the Saddam dinar, which caused soaring inflation. Extensive counterfeiting obviously was not sustainable. Second, there were only two denominations of the Saddam dinar (ID250 and ID10,000 banknotes), which was not practical for transaction purposes. Third, only the Kurds used the Swiss dinar, which was clearly a divisive issue. As a result, the Iraqi government, with assistance from the CPA, USAID, and the US Department of Treasury, conducted a three-month program (between October 15, 2003 and January 15, 2004) to exchange all denominations and types of existing Iraqi banknotes for higher-quality notes with new security features. The operation involved shipping and distributing about ID6.1 trillion new dinars (roughly $400 billion), while destroying the old currency.[41]

After the military intervention and regime change operation, the United States was hardly going to allow banknotes featuring Saddam to circulate in Iraq. Even under different circumstances, reconciliation in a post-conflict situation requires eliminating all remnants of the old regime that can prove divisive and an impediment to peace consolidation. Thus, in January 2004, the central bank launched the new dinar at slightly less than ID1,500 per $1, featuring scenes from the history of the Iraqi nation. Contrary to the Saddam dinar, the new currency is much more secure, with features that make it very difficult to counterfeit. Banknotes also come in six (rather than two) denominations, which has improved the efficiency of monetary transactions. The IMF complimented the conversion to a new currency as a significant accomplishment in a very difficult security environment, which was critical in the reactivation of commercial activity.

As the detailed account of John Taylor (2006, 2007), the US Under-Secretary of the Treasury from 2001 to 2005, reveals, the US authorities had carefully planned the currency operation months before the invasion. Its purpose was to prevent financial collapse in a country where checks or electronic funds transfers were nonexistent. The plan consisted of two phases.

In the first phase, the US would pay Iraqi civil servants and pensioners in US dollars. The funds would come from $1.7 billion in frozen Iraqi assets held in the United States since the UN imposed sanctions on Iraq in 1990. On March 20, 2003, President Bush issued an executive order instructing US banks to relinquish Iraqi's frozen dollars. Of the total amount, about 240 tons in $1, $5, $10, and $20 bills were sent to Iraq in April.

Contrary to the situation in Kosovo, where there were no payroll records at the time the UN wanted to pay civil servants (mostly teachers and health workers), Taylor describes how Iraqis had painstakingly kept payroll and pension records, despite the looting of the ministries, to ensure that the right people were paid. By the end of April, Jay Garner, who was still heading the reconstruction effort, reported that the payments had lifted the mood of people in Baghdad during those first few confusing days. As Taylor also points out, the exchange of currencies averted a collapse of the financial system.

In the second phase, new Iraqi currency would be printed. Within a few months 27 planeloads (in 747 jumbo jets) of the new currency had been delivered to Iraq, from 7 printing plants around the world (Taylor 2007). While NATO troops transported the new money in Kosovo, in Iraq US armed convoys delivered the money to 240 sites around the country. From there, 25 million people acquired new dinars by exchanging their old ones. Trucks collected and shipped the old dinars to incinerators. There was wide acceptance of the new dinar, and its value has remained stable vis-à-vis the US dollar through intervention to avoid appreciation. In the process, the central bank has acquired a high volume of dollar reserves, part of which the central bank deposited in 2006 at the New York Federal Reserve Bank to earn interest.

What has gone wrong or should be done differently in the future

Despite some notable successes such as the exchange of currencies, poor choices and corruption have plagued reconstruction in Iraq. It is worth noting that, despite sharp criticism of the UN, the US government faced many of the same problems in economic reconstruction. These included a lack of clear leadership within the US government for reconstruction, messy lines of authority resulting in a lack of accountability, poor and inefficient coordination among departments and agencies, inadequate human resources, including lack of language skills, and nepotism in allocating resources.[42] If the US is to become a better partner in post-conflict reconstruction throughout the world—preferably under the leadership of the UN—its government must heed recommendations concerning how to minimize these problems in the future.

In Iraq, many decisions affected support for reconstruction—both inside and outside the country—and strengthened opposition to US policies, including by US taxpayers. Issues related to the design of reconstruction policies, the allocation of contracts and handling of technical assistance and procurement, and the restructuring of foreign debt have been at the forefront. The issue of debt restructuring, moreover, may not only have important implications for Iraq itself, but also may create a precedent with wide implications for debt arrears and debt forgiveness in future post-conflict situations. Although it will not create a precedent for all post-conflict countries, it may do so for resource-rich, highly indebted countries such as the Democratic Republic of Congo (DRC).

PRIVATIZATION: LACK OF LEGITIMACY AND PROPERTY RIGHTS

One of the tragic errors of the US-led occupation was the early indication that the US authorities intended to privatize Iraqi assets, including in the oil sector.[43] The bidding proposal for the USAID project on Economic Recovery, Reform, and Sustained Growth in Iraq of June 2003 (and running through 2006) was an early indication of the CPA's intended policy. Annex C on the Scope of Work, indicated that the contractor would initiate and complete a study of state-owned enterprises (SOEs) in Iraq (to be identified by USAID). The purpose of the study was to assess these enterprises' market value and to evaluate the potential for liquidation or dissolution of specific firms or industries for sale to strategic investors. The purpose was also to study the feasibility of "mass privatization" of SOEs (including vouchering) where strategic investment was unlikely.[44]

Annex C also specified that the contractor, with USAID approval, would begin implementing a Comprehensive Privatization Program (CPP), focusing on strategic investors or on creating and supporting the institution responsible for undertaking privatization. Furthermore, if legislative changes were required to allow for the privatization of SOEs and/or establish a privatization entity, the contractor would provide assistance in developing the required legal framework.

More astonishing, Annex C specified that the contractor would implement USAID-approved recommendations to begin supporting privatization—especially in the oil sector and supporting industries—and it set what were acknowledged to be "quite aggressive" benchmarks on which the contractor's success would be judged. These benchmarks contemplated that, within eight months, the contractor would tender materials for the electronic trading system, which would be in operation within a year. Furthermore, benchmarks did not include any safeguards in case opposition from the Iraqi interim authorities or other sources delayed the contractor's work. Instead, USAID simply assumed that it could sell Iraq's "crown jewels" without any opposition whatsoever.

Although it is not the purpose here to discuss the legitimacy of the US-led occupation of Iraq,[45] it is important to note that the legitimacy of the CPA was highly questionable. Hence, its policy of privatization was clearly in violation of Premise 3 for effective reconstruction, which states that leadership legitimacy will determine policymaking choices. Moreover, the CPA's intention to privatize Iraqi assets was not only politically naive, but was naive on purely economic grounds as well.

As I discussed in connection with privatization in Kosovo, foreign investors, in particular, look at the domestic framework for investment and property rights not only at the time of the investment, but also at what could happen to property rights and the investment framework in the future. The fact that the occupation authorities designed this framework without a broad-based discussion of the issue among Iraqis—who had been historically opposed to foreign ownership of their assets, particularly in the oil sector—was a clear indication that privatization would not succeed. National opposition would be strongest in the case of US firms.[46]

Although the US authorities soon backtracked on oil privatization, they continued with their plan to privatize most other SOEs.[47] This lack of judgment carried a high cost in terms of security, both of the Iraqi population and of the occupying forces. Even Iraqis who had welcomed Saddam's ouster became incensed by US intentions in the country.

DEBT RESTRUCTURING UNDER FIRE[48]

Saddam Hussein's government had selectively defaulted on its debt during the war with Iran in the 1980s. However, it had avoided arrears with some creditors and hence maintained access to foreign borrowing until the UN imposed comprehensive economic sanctions after its invasion of Kuwait in 1991. By the time of the US-led invasion of the country in 2003, the IMF estimated that foreign debt amounted to $125 billion, or more than 7 times GDP. Iraq's debt included liabilities to about 60 governments (including $32 billion from reparations after the Kuwait invasion), and to about 600 private entities, including investment banks, hedge funds, suppliers, construction companies, and many others.[49] The debt instruments covered a wide spectrum including bank loans, letters of credit, promissory notes, suppliers' credits, debt guarantees, and construction payables. Debt to the IFIs was small (less than $1 billion), and Iraq cleared its arrears in 2004.

In early 2006, Iraq and Paris Club members reached an agreement on debt relief. After years of UN economic sanctions and debt arrears to some countries going back more than 20 years, on July 17, 2006, Iraq made its first interest payment amounting to close to $90 million. With an acceptance rate of 100 percent—not seen since the 1985 Mexican deal—the Iraqi debt exchange became one of the most successful ever.

As Chung and Fidler pointed out, debt restructuring in Iraq was different from other cases because of heavy US pressure on creditors to negotiate favorable terms to aid the interim Iraqi government installed in 2004. Negotiations led to a division of debt into four categories, three of which had separate advisors. Citibank and JP Morgan advised on the restructuring of commercial debt; Lazard Frères on bilateral debt owed to the Paris Club; and the firm Houlihan Lokey Howard & Zukin on non-Paris Club bilateral debt, with the exception of China and Turkey. The authorities would tackle those debts, as well as debt owed to the Gulf States, the fourth category of debt, at the political level. In this case, Iraq disputed the amount claimed by Saudi Arabia, Kuwait, the United Arab Emirates, and Qatar, since the government's documentation implied much lower figures.[50]

Iraq owed more than $48 billion to 19 governments under the Paris Club of bilateral creditors. The United States wrote off its own debt—less than $5 billion—and supported Iraq's call for a 95 percent write off on other debt. The four countries with the largest claims—Japan, Russia, France, and Germany— did not want to exceed a 50 percent discount. After 10 days of tough negotiations, the Paris Club agreed to an 80 percent discount conditioned on reaching agreement for a stand-by arrangement (SBA) or other program in which the IMF imposed conditionality.[51] Debt relief would take place in three phases: an immediate 30 percent write-off after signing the agreement with the Paris Club in November 2004, another 30 percent upon agreement with the Fund on a program, and the final 20 percent upon successfully concluding the IMF program, expected by end-December 2008.[52] Iraq will have to repay the remaining 20 percent over 23 years, starting in 2011. Because interest payments accruing during the period 2005–10 will be mostly capitalized, debt service to Paris Club members will be relatively small until 2010, before increasing sharply to about 5 percent of GDP in 2011.

Beyond the amount of money involved, the debt restructuring with the Paris Club was significant because other creditors cannot benefit from better terms. Thus, the Paris Club terms also imposed a ceiling on what was offered to holders of $22 billion of commercial debt. Commercial creditors also were constrained by a 2003 UN resolution, reaffirmed a year later, which prevented them from resolving their debt claims through litigation or by attaching liens on Iraq's oil exports until the end of 2007. The terms of commercial debts varied widely. To simplify matters, the government decided that for all claims after August 6, 1990—the date of adoption of Security Council Resolution 661 forbidding most financial transactions with Iraq—every creditor would be paid the same rate: Libor plus 75 basis points (equivalent to 3/4 of 1 percent). In 2006 Iraq retired about $20 billion of commercial debt, including by issuing close to $3 billion in 22-year bonds carrying a coupon of 5.8 percent.

Restructuring of non-Paris Club debt with the Arab League has made little progress, since these countries are dissatisfied with the Paris Club terms. Some would prefer to exchange their debt instruments for newly issued government securities.[53] The IMF and the Paris Club have prepared different scenarios for Iraq's debt based on whether the third stage of restructuring with Paris Club members takes place on time, and on whether non-Paris Club members accept Paris Club terms (IMF 2007c, Appendix Table 5: 29). As mentioned earlier, some already have and a few have accepted 100 percent terms. Nevertheless, even under the best scenario Iraq will remain a heavily indebted country.

Details provided by Chung and Fidler on Iraq's debt restructuring raise many interesting issues for policymaking in post-conflict economic recon-struction. First, it is clear that the CPA made the decision to carry out debt restructuring—even if the Iraqi Government upheld it after assuming sov-ereignty in June 2004.

More worrisome, until April 2005, when Ali Allawi became Finance Min-ister, debt restructuring had proceeded on a "cash basis," which would have required $2 billion from the meager government budget, to the detriment of other national expenditure, including security and basic social services. Fortunately, this did not occur, and the deal included a debt-for-debt swap and a bond issue rather than cash disbursements. If Iraq was to restructure its debt at this time at all—which I argue below it should not have done—a debt-for-debt swap was clearly a better option than a cash-based arrangement. As Allawi argued, this would "help Iraq develop a creditor profile in international markets and debt management capabilities. It would establish a price for Iraqi debt, too."[54]

The US move also raised other issues. First, it was easy for the US to push for debt forgiveness at the Paris Club, since it held only a small share of the debt. Second, the fact that the United States promoted a cash solution to the debt problem, and that it involved US investment banks, lawyers, and accountants, was perceived as an effort to benefit US firms at the expense of Iraq. By the time the Iraqi government took power, the US had appointed not only Citibank and JP Morgan to advise on the commercial restructuring, but also Cleary Gottlieb Steen & Hamilton (CGS&H) as legal advisors, and Ernst

& Young as auditor and reconciliation agent. Chung and Fidler report that by the time the commercial restructuring was over in February 2006, the Iraqi government had paid between \$120 million and \$150 million in fees, with \$65 million going to the two investment banks.

The spirit in which the United States arranged this restructuring clearly followed a "development as usual" pattern. While the focus should have been on accelerating economic reconstruction and peace consolidation, debt restructuring was oblivious to these needs and proceeded with unrealistic and untimely objectives. Citigroup Senior Vice Chairman William Rhodes argued that this restructuring paved the way for Iraq's possible eventual re-entry into the international capital markets, while Lee Buchheit, a lawyer with CGS&H, argued that the objective was to reduce debt to the point that it would not inhibit fresh investment.

However, how realistic is the reactivation of foreign investment and reinsertion into international capital markets at a time when the country in question is on the brink of civil war? Was this expensive restructuring the best possible allocation of the authorities' energies and resources, at a time when civil unrest and sectarian violence had significantly increased, and at a time when economic reconstruction was lagging, resulting in extreme hardship for large segments of the population? Was this the best allocation of national resources when a large part of the financing needed to pay salaries, fix infrastructure, provide basic services, and train the security forces had to come from the international community, in large part financed by American taxpayers?[55] Would it have been such a hardship for creditors, who in some cases had not received any debt servicing for twenty years, to wait, say, three more years?

On the one hand, had reconstruction proceeded well, creditors could have expected much better terms. On the other, postponing the issue of debt relief for a later date would have saved efforts and resources for more pressing needs, including peace-related projects that could have facilitated reconstruction and improved its prospects for success.

"SHARING THE RICHES IN WAR": NEPOTISM, CORRUPTION, AND UNNECESSARY COSTS

Corruption, nepotism, lack of transparency, and unnecessary costs—among both the Iraqis and the US-led forces—have plagued reconstruction in Iraq. Most of the reconstruction financing went to US contractors. This was even true of Iraqi funds and was condoned by SCR 1483 of May 2003. As Malone (2006: 206) points out, the resolution authorized the use of oil-related funds deposited in the Development Fund for Iraq (DFI) for reconstruction projects. In December 2003, the US authorities announced that only contractors from coalition partners could bid for such projects (although the policy was later relaxed). As several studies have shown, the CPA could not account for as much as $9 billion of the $20 billion in the DFI.[56]

The title of a *New York Times* editorial on July 24, 2006, "Sharing the Riches in War," illustrates the widespread perception that American companies well connected to the government were benefiting greatly from economic reconstruction in Iraq. While debt restructuring clearly benefited several top US firms, Halliburton "was awarded the major contract for supplying all manner of logistics and support services to soldiers at war, from meals to morale," which "proved to be worth more than $15 billion as the company became a ubiquitous player in Iraq—and a symbol of cronyism in Washington for its old ties to Vice-President Dick Cheney." The editorial also pointed out that it took the Pentagon from the March 2002 invasion until the end of 2006 to solicit new bids from companies to share in Halliburton's business in Iraq in order to lower costs, increase accountability, and reduce operational risk.[57]

Likewise, lack of transparency, if not pure favoritism, resulted in the allocation of a large USAID project on economic governance to Baring Point (formerly KPMG) without competitive bidding.[58] After complaints from other consulting firms, USAID agreed to open the project to other pre-qualified firms. However, once the bidding process was complete, the USAID again awarded the project to Baring Point, which had previously carried out USAID projects in Kosovo and Afghanistan with little success. As other international consulting firms prepared their bids for this project, Baring Point was already in Iraq under USAID sponsorship, which gave it an unmatched advantage.

Nepotism and corruption in the allocation of reconstruction projects to large US contractors had collateral costs as well. This policy not only excluded Iraqi firms early on—and thus failed to create local employment and capacity building—but also entailed large costs associated with security for the US contractors. Thus, in addition to the security-related spending of the Iraqi government, which the US Government Accountability Office (GAO 2006, footnote 12: 14) reckons was over $5 billion in 2006, providing security to foreign contractors consumes a significant portion of reconstruction funds.[59]

Corruption in Iraq's civil service also has been widespread, further impeding reconstruction. Experts estimate that 150,000–200,000 barrels of oil per day—and perhaps as much as 500,000—were stolen in 2006 (Baker and Hamilton 2006: 23). A Commission for Public Integrity (CPI), an independent body reporting directly to the Interim National Assembly, the legislative body overseeing the country's more than thirty ministers, the prime minister, the president, and other officials, has acknowledged that some Iraqis have had to pay to get civil service jobs. For example, guards hired at the Ministry of Housing and Construction had to pay a fee of around $200. According to the UN Office for the Coordinator of Humanitarian Assistance, "Paying money to get a job is only one form of corruption and certainly not as bad as some shoddy construction and financial mismanagement, in a country where corruption has been part of the government culture for so long, and continues to be so" (UNOCHA 2004).

According to Iraqi officials, someone took $300 million in American bills from the central bank in January 2004, packed them into boxes, and quietly put them on a charter jet bound for Lebanon. The money was supposedly to be used to purchase tanks and other weapons from international arms dealers to strengthen the Iraqi Army—a deal that took place outside the American-designed financial controls intended to help Iraq pay for imported goods. Although it is not clear where the money went or how it has been used, the episode reinforced the perception among Iraqis and Western officials of endemic corruption within the Interim Iraqi Government (Filkins 2005).

Similarly, in their periodic reports measuring Iraq's reconstruction, the Center for Strategic and International Studies (CSIS) (September 2004: 37) found that one of the major challenges of institution building related to "rampant corruption in Iraq." Although the CPA attempted to address the problem by enacting anti-corruption measures, there were no enforcement mechanisms, particularly given the lack of judicial capacity. Furthermore, a culture of corruption had become so ingrained that people did not even blame the new government for it. Although ethical norms are up to nationals to decide, corruption by Western standards will be a major factor discouraging international assistance and hence slowing reconstruction.

MOVING THE COUNTRY FORWARD

In connection with the International Compact for Iraq that the government and the UN launched in mid-2006, Secretary-General Ban Ki-Moon noted that

There is no doubt that more must be done to bring a halt to the ongoing violence in Iraq, the brunt of which is being borne by innocent civilians. Beyond the terrorist attacks and sectarian violence, a humanitarian crisis is stretching the patience and ability of ordinary people to cope with everyday life. This makes it even more important to develop a framework for Iraq's normalization. Essentially, the *Compact* represents a road map for the next five years aimed at helping Iraq to achieve its long-term goals of economic prosperity, political stability, and lasting security. Much work will be needed to keep Iraq on track, but I am confident that the people and Government are up to the challenge.

Unfortunately, there is not much reason to be optimistic that the Compact will help to move economic reconstruction forward. First, a country that by many accounts is in the middle of civil war will require serious peacemaking efforts and more stable security conditions before it can make any significant progress in economic reconstruction. Second, the government needs to revise its policies for economic reconstruction to eliminate the "development as usual" bias and to follow the basic premises for effective reconstruction. Unless the government makes some basic efforts at disarming, demobilizing, and reintegrating militias and other groups involved in the violence, establishing benchmarks on "development as usual" policies will hardly help economic reconstruction in Iraq.

Lessons from Iraq

Iraq's chance for successful economic reconstruction was squandered, partly owing to policies sought by the United States and the inability of the UN to play a supportive role. Thus, the Iraqi experience offers important lessons for economic reconstruction elsewhere, particularly in the early transition from war. I will focus on five such lessons, four of which are particularly relevant to other resource-rich countries.

THE UN IS NOT WELL PLACED TO DEAL WITH RECONSTRUCTION FOLLOWING COMPREHENSIVE SANCTIONS

Although I argued that the UN, if revamped, could be the first choice to lead economic reconstruction, there are always exceptions to any rule. Iraq was clearly such an exception. Twelve years of comprehensive international sanctions had devastating effects on large segments of the population, discrediting the UN not only in Iraq, but also in world public opinion and among NGOs. It was thus naive to believe that the Iraqis would welcome the UN with open arms, or that other actors would be willing to work under UN leadership. The same was true of the United States—the world's most implacable advocate of maintaining the sanctions—and to a certain extent of the United Kingdom. As a result, a Security Council-authorized occupation may not have made much of a difference in terms of how Iraqis felt. Had the international community decided on regime change, an invasion by a "coalition of the willing" led by one of the countries that had been more in favor of removing sanctions— France, for example—probably would have had a better chance of stabilizing the political and security situation in the post-invasion period, and setting the basis for effective reconstruction.

I think many would argue—certainly, I do—that the UN should never impose comprehensive sanctions against another country as it did in Iraq. In Iraq, the UN imposed sanctions without the ability to enforce them and without a clear exit strategy. The result was a humanitarian disaster, which elicited a nationalistic response against the UN and those pushing for sanctions in the Security Council. The lesson from Iraq is clear and costly in terms of the lives lost in Baghdad and elsewhere.

ESTABLISH THE RULE OF LAW EARLY

Whoever leads the transition to peace, be it a sovereign country, the UN, or an occupying force, must establish the rule of law as soon as possible. This often requires working with existing police and military forces until an appropriate program for disarmament, demobilization, and reintegration (DDR) is in place. A favorable environment is necessary to start restoring essential services—electricity, communications, water treatment, and sewerage—and thus bring some sense of normalcy to the population.

While the international community is willing to support poor countries in rehabilitating basic services and infrastructure, resource-rich countries will have to bear more of the cost of reconstruction. Thus, it will be particularly important to rehabilitate the infrastructure required to produce and export the main commodity—be it oil and gas, diamonds, or any other resource. However, the reactivation of these sectors should not lead to the neglect of agriculture, as this may lead to food shortages. Neither should manufacturing be neglected, as this might deprive the population of needed employment. Thus, policymakers must maintain a balance to ensure sustainable growth, without which the rule of law may not last long.

FOREIGN INVESTMENT REQUIRES LEGITIMACY AND SECURE PROPERTY RIGHTS

Governments that lack legitimacy—and even more so the UN or an occupying force—should abstain from economic reforms whose sustainability investors may question. This applies to state-owned enterprises in general, and to investments in critical sectors in particular, such as oil is to Iraq. The fact that foreign investment in such sectors should not be expected does not mean that the country cannot attract foreign investment at all. In other sectors, which are not considered critical and satisfy the needs of large segments of the population, foreign investment can probably be safely promoted. For example, the only major investment during the US-led occupation in Iraq was that of PepsiCo, which invested $100 million in its old soft-drink bottling plant in Baghdad. Foreigners could also invest in "reconstruction zones," that is, export-processing zones to create labor-intensive employment. The population could look upon such zones favorably, particularly if donor countries open up their markets to goods produced in them.

DEBT RESTRUCTURING IN THE IMMEDIATE TRANSITION TO PEACE HAS POLITICAL COSTS

The US occupation authorities initiated debt restructuring in Iraq. Even if the Iraqi authorities, once in place, supported it, the decision had a political and economic cost. Despite the fact that Paris Club members will not receive much debt servicing until 2011, negotiations resulted in high fees to investment banks, law firms, and others.

The argument that countries need to restructure their debt before they can borrow in the international credit markets is not a strong one for countries in post-conflict transitions. These countries normally finance their reconstruction largely with grants and concessional lending from creditors who are interested in ensuring that the country does not revert to war. Political, not financial, arguments determine their assistance to these countries.

I always recall the response of Rimmer de Vries, the distinguished chief economist and managing director of J.P. Morgan, to the late MIT Professor Rudiger Dornbusch at a conference in New York in the early 1980s. Dornbusch vehemently advocated large debt forgiveness for Latin American countries, while Mr. de Vries listened patiently and responded: "Of course, Rudi, it is easy to give money away when it is not your money." I will not fall into the same temptation.[60]

I think, however, that given the tremendous costs of recent experiences with reconstruction—in terms of both human lives and financial resources—the international community should debate measures to improve the prospects for success in the future. For example, I believe that creditors and other actors in post-conflict reconstruction should consider the possibility of establishing an automatic grace period with respect to debt payments. This period could extend from three to five years, depending on the conditions of the country, as specified by certain clear criteria. The international community also should consider a grace period on arrears to the IFIs.[61] Such grace periods would spare countries in the early transition to peace from expenditures of scarce technical and financial resources on debt relief negotiations and debt servicing, thereby creating greater scope for quick peace-promoting and confidence-building projects.

Creditors should agree to this automatic grace period for three reasons. First, even if they enter into negotiations right away, they are unlikely to get any debt servicing for many years. Second, they most likely have committed grants or concessional loans to the reconstruction of the country, and therefore have a stake in its success. Third, and most importantly, if reconstruction succeeds, creditors will be able to negotiate better terms, enabling them to maximize their political and economic objectives simultaneously.

RESOURCE-RICH COUNTRIES NEED A FAIR ALLOCATION OF RESOURCES

The allocation of resources is a critical issue in resource-rich countries. A legal framework that contemplates a fair allocation of resources can support peace, while an unfair one is likely to derail the transition. In the case of Iraq, the constitution contemplates central government control of existing oilfields, but it is vague about who controls new discoveries and developments. This has led to problems with new contracts negotiated by the Kurdish Regional Government (KRG) with foreign oil companies, including Norwegian and Turkish groups. In June 2004, DNO, a Norwegian company, signed a production-sharing agreement with the KRG, after discovering at least 100 billion barrels of oil reserves before the national Iraqi Government was established (Ibison 2006). The national government has questioned the validity of such contracts, while the Kurds argue that the KRG's autonomy provides the legal basis for them. In mid-May 2007, DNO started pumping oil from a field in Tawke—the first time that a foreign oil company had done so since the industry's nationalization in 1972.

As the 2006 *Iraq Study Group Report* notes, Iraq needs an adequate Hydrocarbon Law that defines the rights of regional and local governments and creates a stable legal framework for investment (Baker and Hamilton 2006). However, negotiating such a law has been extremely difficult politically, particularly since the Sunni live in an oil-poor part of the country.[62] In March 2007, the Council of Ministers approved a law reaffirming that oil and gas resources belong to all the people of Iraq and establishing a revenue-sharing mechanism among regions and provinces based on population.[63] The Council of Representatives must ratify this law. At stake is whether Iraq's oil wealth will strengthen federalism or contribute to the country's disintegration. More broadly, the establishment of a fair legal framework for the use of natural resources is critical to effective reconstruction in all resource-rich countries.

Part V

A Strategy for Economic Reconstruction: Lessons, Policy Guidelines, and Best Practices

"Economics is the science of choice. . . . Economics seems to apply to every nook and cranny of human experience. . . . Economics is a way of looking at things, an ordering principle, a complete part of everything. It is a system of thought, a life game, and element of pure knowledge."

Robert A. Mundell, 1999 Nobel Laureate in Economics, in the Preface to *Man and Economics* (1968)

The objective of Part V is to facilitate the preparation of a strategy for post-conflict economic reconstruction, by including activities and policy guidelines that governments could adopt to maximize chances of success. Policymakers will be constantly opting among different economic choices and need to be well informed about such choices. Thus, the following chapters will present lessons from the case studies that are relevant to different aspects of the strategy, as well as what have been discerned to be best practices in post-conflict reconstruction. These, need not be—indeed, in most cases will not be—best practices under normal development conditions. In cases where recommendations or best practices are controversial, the idea is to bring the issues up for debate.

Once governments design their strategy, they will have to check it constantly for consistency and effectiveness during its implementation. Post-conflict situations are dynamic and often volatile; as a result, conditions may change, and frequent revisions may be required. For example, policymakers will need to revise and fine-tune their strategy if pledged aid is not readily committed and disbursed.

11 Setting the stage

Basic assumptions

In countries where reconstruction follows a peace agreement, the design of the peace agreement will be critical in its successful implementation. For this reason, careful thought and the right kind of expertise in the outset of the peace process can facilitate the elaboration of an agreement that governments can realistically implement with the assistance of the international community. The design of peace agreements and reconstruction strategies should take into account realistic prospects for international aid. Over-optimistic projections will lead to unworkable plans and will lead to expectations that governments will not be able to fulfill.

THE SIX PREMISES

Each country will end up with a different strategy, depending on factors that are peculiar to its own situation and on the level of international support that it can manage to attract.[1] Nevertheless, the six basic premises that I proposed in Chapter 4 need to guide the design of any strategy for post-conflict economic reconstruction.

Because it is a development-plus challenge (premise 1), policymaking will differ from that of normal development. It will be constrained by the need to incorporate activities and expenditure related to reconstruction and national reconciliation, in addition to those related to normal development. This will often require broad-based civil service expertise and national policies that are pragmatic and ad hoc. It will also require the IMF to be flexible in establishing monetary and fiscal targets in programs that it supports, and in designing the legal and institutional framework, to ensure that the peace process will not collapse due to lack of financing.

Because the political objective should prevail at all times in post-conflict economic reconstruction (premise 2), optimal and best-practice macroeconomic policies are not usually available, or even desirable. In addition, critical peace-related programs, such as disarmament, demobilization, and reintegration (DDR) of former combatants and confidence-building projects for national reconciliation, should take priority, including in budget allocations.

Because political legitimacy will determine policymaking choices (premise 3), interim governments—and even more so the United Nations, the United States, or any other country or entity that has assumed the prerogatives of national government in carrying out executive and legislative functions—should refrain from including in the reconstruction strategy controversial policies. Such policies would include, for example, privatization of state-owned enterprises, deregulation of key sectors, opening regulated sectors to foreign investment, or major changes in the legal and regulatory system. Furthermore, in designing their strategy, governments and the international community should be aware of the limitations that an absence of legitimacy imposes on property rights. Reconstruction strategies must take into account that uncertainty about property rights will be a serious deterrent to investment.

Because of the political and policymaking constraints, as well as the data limitations of post-conflict situations, a different yardstick is necessary to measure success (premise 4). The strategy for economic reconstruction should clearly specify the yardstick for both the overall strategy and its component programs. This will facilitate reconstruction by avoiding unrealistic expectations. At the same time, governments should develop a basic statistical system in order to facilitate policymaking, as well as to measure and record social and economic progress.

Because of the critical importance of political factors in post-conflict economic reconstruction, development institutions should not lead the effort (premise 5). Former rebel groups are frequently equal partners in peace agreements, and even after military intervention, the relationship with groups that challenge peace involves political, military, and security issues. Thus, in the presence of a peacekeeping/peacebuilding mission, the UN itself, through the Special Representative of the Secretary-General (SRSG) and the National Reconstruction Coordinator (NRC) under him that I propose to advise on economic and financial issues (see Figure 3, p. 64), should have overall responsibility for coordination within the programs and agencies of the UN system and with other actors. This will be essential to integrate effectively economic reconstruction with other aspects of peacebuilding.

The motto of post-conflict economic reconstruction should be "keep it simple and flexible" (premise 6). This is because in the post-Cold War period, countries in the process of post-conflict reconstruction have been at low levels of development. They have often experienced a brain drain and capital flight during the war. As a result, they lack basic managerial and technical capabilities, their physical infrastructure has often been destroyed, and their international reserves have been depleted.

Countries at this stage nevertheless need a framework for macroeconomic management, as well as a legal and institutional structure to create the appropriate environment for investment and trade, and, more importantly, for the effective use of aid. Under such vulnerable conditions, it is unrealistic and even counterproductive to create a sophisticated framework that requires resources that the country does not have and may not have for a long time. To establish such a framework under these conditions will probably lead to inefficiencies and even corruption.

The "11 c's"

Following the six premises is necessary but not sufficient for a post-conflict economic reconstruction strategy to be effective. Both governments and the international community that supports reconstruction must pay attention to 11 "critical c's". These include consistency of policies adopted; consensus at the national level; constructive approaches based on incentives rather than penalties; coherence among programs and projects; continuity in and conclusion of the process;[2] credibility of the organizations involved; cooperation and coordination among organizations; confidence-building measures to promote national reconciliation; and cost-effectiveness of resources (del Castillo 1995a). The case studies illustrated how failure to proceed according to the 11 c's often affected reconstruction negatively.

Other considerations

In designing a reconstruction strategy—as is the case with peace agreements or UN resolutions—those involved in the negotiations will need to weigh the pros and cons of specificity versus vagueness. The letter of the agreement and of the strategy itself can determine the ease or difficulty with which governments will be able to implement the resulting programs. The operational difficulties encountered in the implementation of the land program in El Salvador, for example, related to both the specificity and the vagueness of the Chapultepec Peace Agreement. The Bonn Agreement gave warlords standing in the new political framework of the country and legislated their unworkable relationship vis-à-vis the central government, making it difficult for the latter to administer the country.

As most post-conflict countries are sovereign countries, they must be in charge of their destiny and "own" their reconstruction strategy. Ownership means that it is up to their leaders to set the priorities and build up consensus for them. However, since most post-conflict countries are poor and possess scarce human resources, they will find it difficult to design and carry out such a strategy on their own and will need training, capacity building, and technical and financial assistance at every step.[3]

Thus, in discussing the elements that should be included in any reconstruction strategy, I assume support from the international financial institutions (IFIs), the United Nations and its other agencies and programs, bilateral and regional donors (bilateral development agencies, the European Union and others), and non-governmental organizations (NGOs). Support at every step will be necessary to strengthen the authorities' policymaking capacity and training of local civil service staff, as well as for assisting them in the design and implementation of particular policies and projects and building up required institutions. However, the involvement of the international community will vary greatly across countries. Donors are more likely to help countries in strategic geopolitical locations or in their own backyard. They are also more likely to help countries with which they have colonial, linguistic, ethnic, ideological, or other such ties.

In some countries in which there is no sovereign government, the Security Council has given the UN a major role in carrying out executive and legislative decisions in post-conflict economic reconstruction. This was the case in UN protectorates in Kosovo and East Timor. In these cases, as well as where one country assumes a major role in reconstruction through military intervention and occupation—either with the blessing of the international community (Afghanistan) or without it (Iraq)—uncertainty surrounding the sustainability of economic reform and property rights represents a serious deterrent to investment. Therefore, a quick political resolution by which a sovereign government and parliamentary body make all executive and legislative decisions is, together with an independent judiciary system, imperative for the success of economic reconstruction. By contrast, the involvement of the international community in reconstruction over a long period will create unnecessary distortions and aid dependency, as we have seen in Kosovo and Bosnia and Herzegovina in Europe, and in Mozambique and Uganda in Africa.[4]

The UN should avoid ambiguous mandates. As former SRSG in Angola Margaret J. Anstee argued, the Secretary-General should take the initiative to present a strategic, overall policy framework for peacebuilding activities to the Security Council, which then must act on it. Once the framework is in place, the Secretary-General should follow a practice of maximum delegation of responsibility to the field, that is, to its SRSG.

As I discuss the different elements that need to be included in the post-conflict economic reconstruction strategy in this and the following chapters, I will draw on lessons and best practices from past experiences. This will help policymakers and the international community in making the tough policy choices that will be necessary when designing a particular strategy for economic reconstruction.

If countries in the transition to peace decide to give more weight than they did in the past to market mechanisms to allocate resources—which is likely, given widespread disillusionment with state-led planning—they will need to adopt a number of measures. Thus, any post-conflict economic reconstruction strategy should include not only the rebuilding of physical, human, and institutional infrastructure per se, but also the stabilization and structural reform policies and the appropriate legal, regulatory, and institutional framework needed to create a market-friendly economy and reactivate broad-based economic growth. This means growth that is sustainable, creates employment, brings about poverty alleviation and greater opportunity for the majority, and protects the environment.

This type of growth, which is not always present in some of the rapidly emerging economies, is particularly important in post-conflict countries, where economic reconstruction must contribute to national reconciliation. Improvement in the fiscal situation has proved essential for governments to afford decent salaries—required to avoid corruption, which is often rampant in countries coming out of war—and be able to staff an adequate civil service to support reconstruction. But job creation and decent salaries are also important because, without them, these countries have a high probability of reverting to war.

Policymaking at both the macro and micro levels is a crucial element of any strategy for economic reconstruction. For each policy area, I will describe the instruments, organizational structures, legal and regulatory framework, and accounting and statistical systems that will be necessary to carry out the specific activities. In some areas, there will be a checklist of the relevant issues. Whenever there is a need to reconstruct institutional mechanisms or adopt new policies, the government should seize the opportunity to eliminate inefficient structures and adopt more modern technologies and best practices. However, in designing such a framework, policymakers, the IFIs and other organizations that support them, should keep in mind the simplicity and flexibility that are necessary for effective policymaking under difficult security and political conditions.

Furthermore, the institutional, legal, regulatory, and judicial systems of a country should conform to national customs and traditions. This means, for example, that if the country had or wants to have an Islamic banking system or an informal *hawala* system, the international community, as a whole, should facilitate it rather than imposing their own views. This is particularly relevant for countries at low levels of development with low absorptive capacity and scarce technical expertise, which should not seek to import and establish an overly sophisticated legal and regulatory system that will burden them and will likely lead to corruption.

While any reconstruction strategy will have to rely on an assessment of initial conditions, it will have to change as internal and external conditions vary. Thus, government policies and institutional mandates may need to change often during the transition. Similarly, UN mandates and the mandates of other institutions involved, particularly the IFIs, will need to be flexible so that they can adjust to the rapidly changing on-the-ground conditions in post-conflict situations.

The World Bank and/or UNDP should convene an international donors' conference as soon as feasible and create a trust fund for the country's reconstruction. At the beginning, this fund will have the important objective of providing budgetary support to the government. Although there may be reasons why a single fund is not optimal, in most cases a well-managed single fund would not only contribute to transparency, but would also facilitate the authorities' policy decisions on reconstruction expenditures by clarifying the availability and prospects of future aid financing.[5]

An inventory of available professionals and trained manpower—inside and outside the country—that can be used to fill critical posts in the public service and carry out reconstruction and rehabilitation programs should be established as soon as possible. Because of the large brain drain that normally occurs during the conflict, policymakers should identify talented nationals in the diaspora and persuade them to return home. This does not mean, however, that the government (or the international community) should give them unlimited control, as occurred in Iraq with very negative consequences.

Although the list of activities for economic reconstruction in countries at a similar stage of development will look remarkably similar, initial conditions—including domestic capabilities, institutional memory, and the deterioration in human and physical infrastructure that occurred during the conflict—will largely determine the appropriate policy mix. Thus, economic reconstruction should reflect national needs and priorities, and policymakers must mold it according to the particular political, security, and socio-economic conditions existing in each country.

The way I will bring the different activities into the strategy does not necessarily indicate the sequence in which they should be carried out. For example, the design of economic policies and institutions usually go hand in hand. In a number of cases, there may be some necessary precondition for an activity. For example, agricultural production can restart only on demined land and banks can be licensed only after banking laws are in place.

A number of generic principles will apply to most activities. For example, an overriding concern must be the development of national capabilities. Training and institution building must therefore be an integral part of all activities.[6] Effective market-supporting institutions are indispensable to countries' development. Policymakers should promote employment-generating activities across the board to incorporate a large number of former combatants, returnees, and other groups marginalized during the conflict, which will help to consolidate peace. Indeed, peace and development must reinforce each other to improve the often-appalling living conditions in which a large part of the population lives during the war-to-peace transitions.

A second overriding concern is to build a broad-based policy consensus. This is imperative if economic reconstruction is to succeed, if the country is to reunite, and if the economy is to regain a path of sustainable development. If policies are imposed—particularly from abroad—they are not likely to be successful or sustainable.

Finally, the reconstruction strategy must emphasize the need to improve transparency and governance throughout the public sector and to intensify the fight against corruption and nepotism. In this process, a culture of account-ability and respect for the rule of law and property rights must be established and ingrained in every activity throughout the process.

Political and security constraints

In developing a post-conflict reconstruction strategy, it is necessary that both the country itself and the international community as a whole understand the roots of the conflict, the political constraints of the war-to-peace tran-sition, and the expected political path ahead. As discussed earlier, political factors will be major determinants, as well as constraints, in designing the strategy.[7] National policymakers and those supporting them need to make a special effort at communicating political developments to all those involved throughout the different stages of the process. Only this will allow economic and financial decisions to be taken with due respect for the limitations that political factors may impose. Pursuing separate but concurrent paths for the political and economic transitions is a recipe for failure, as the early experience of El Salvador attests. Disregard for the political constraints of carrying out certain reconstruction policies in Iraq, Afghanistan, and Kosovo, for example, in turn led to serious political and security problems.

Elections are often a distraction at best and a deterrent at worst from economic reconstruction. This is why policymakers need to consider the political cycle in designing the strategy. In some countries, elections mark the end or the transformation of international support. For example, UNTAC (UN Transitional Authority in Cambodia) ended soon after the elections. So did UNTAET (UN Transitional Administration in East Timor) as the coun-try moved to independence. Elsewhere, different actors—both national and international—view elections as a "graduation ceremony," with the result that attention and determination are often diverted from pending issues on the reconstruction agenda, as was the case in El Salvador in 1994.

A post-conflict economic reconstruction strategy should include all possi-ble mechanisms to bolster security. Early deterioration in security, which often happens after a ceasefire or political settlement, accompanied by looting and other criminal activities against government offices and other property, could have tragic consequences for economic reconstruction. In Iraq, this occurred in large part because of the de-Baathification process and the dismantling of the Iraqi army following US occupation of the country. Policymakers will need to weigh the elimination of repressive military and police forces against the security vacuum that this may create. Plans for training of civilian police forces and reform of the military should take top priority, along with the financing required for such activities.

Operational, logistical, and ownership issues

ECONOMICS AND SOCIAL NEEDS ASSESSMENT

In addition to ensuring that political constraints are well-mapped and adequate security conditions are in place, governments should base any strategy for post-conflict economic reconstruction on an accurate assessment of the economic and social needs of the country. In this respect, the UN agencies, which are often the only international organizations that have maintained a presence in the country during and in the immediate aftermath of conflict, can play a critical role. So do some of the major international NGOs. The UN Development Group (UNDG) and the World Bank have new mechanisms in place—the Post-Conflict Needs Assessments (PCNA)—and can certainly contribute, as the IMF does, to this important initial phase.

Assessments will vary widely across different countries and will depend largely on pre-conflict conditions. Countries in which the IFIs and other multilateral and bilateral organizations were involved immediately before the conflict usually have a much better infrastructure (institutions and people) to conduct a quantitative and qualitative assessment of current conditions, particularly if the conflict was short-lived. On the other hand, countries coming out of prolonged conflict, particularly if comprehensive economic sanctions had been in place that precluded a relationship with multilateral, regional, or bilateral organizations, usually have few statistics and little of the infrastructure necessary for a good assessment of existing conditions. This was certainly the case in Iraq. The situation in Kosovo was more difficult because, as a province, it never maintained separate statistics. This was also true of East Timor, and a similar challenge will face the Palestinian territories when they hopefully embark on reconstruction.

Because an assessment of economic and social needs involves so many areas, best practice indicates that a group of institutions participating under the leadership of one of them can carry it out more effectively. In the case of Haiti in the early 1990s, for example, the Inter-American Development Bank (IADB) led the assessment. To indicate the importance that the international community attributed to the democratization and reconstruction of Haiti, and in an effort to induce donors to support economic reconstruction of the country, Enrique Iglesias, IADB President at the time, led the assessment mission.

A good economic and social assessment before the war-to-peace transition or at its inception will identify the critical factors to be addressed in the reconstruction strategy. It is especially important to analyze carefully the country's human and physical infrastructure, its capacity to absorb assistance, the population's entrepreneurial abilities, the availability of raw materials, access to basic services, food and agriculture conditions, possibilities of aid and other financial flows, and accessibility to markets before designing the strategy. These and many other factors will determine the type of reconstruction strategy that the country can engineer.

Bosnia and Herzegovina is a typical example of what the international community—in close collaboration with the national authorities when they are in place—must do right after a ceasefire and the establishment of a minimum of security. A small team of experts from the IMF, the World Bank, the EU, and the European Bank for Reconstruction and Development (EBRD) visited Sarajevo and Mostar in October 1995. The authorities were ready to start work on reconstruction and a series of follow-up missions were scheduled. In less than two months, the teams produced a damage assessment and an estimate of technical assistance needs, prepared the country for membership of the Bretton Woods institutions, and set the stage for the country to be the first beneficiary of the IMF's new policy on post-conflict emergency assistance (EPCA). All of this was accomplished only one week after the ratification of the Dayton Treaty.[8]

The case of Afghanistan, on the other hand, illustrates the problem with poor and untimely assessments. The assessment took place in a rush at the insistence of the Japanese who were hosting the consultative group meeting in January 2002 and could not postpone it. As a result, the cost of reconstruction was significantly underestimated. Two factors were at work. On the one hand, the government did not yet have a vision for reconstruction of the country. On the other, the conflation of humanitarian and reconstruction needs resulted in an underestimation of the latter.

COMPREHENSIVENESS, CONSISTENCY, AND STAYING THE COURSE

For the implementation of the strategy to be successful, all elements need to be present and consistently implemented. It is not enough to go halfway, which is, implementing only some of the elements well. In this regard, it is important to keep in mind Lipsey and Lancaster's (1956–7) *The General Theory of Second Best*. If some of the key elements of the strategy are missing, implementing others may not necessarily move the strategy closer to success. In Haiti, for example, although the needs assessment and early support for the country were well organized, effectively implemented, and properly financed, a well-designed overall strategy was missing, and reconstruction followed a fragmented approach. Reconstruction eventually got off track and collapsed, with serious consequences for the country's future.

Furthermore, it is important to stay the course, since post-conflict economic reconstruction may take several years. Obviously, it would be disastrous to persevere if policies are not working, as has been the case in Afghanistan and Iraq. In such cases, a review of the entire strategy should take place. But if the support of the international community is working, failing to stay the course can lead to the collapse of the peace process and a return to political and security turmoil. This is precisely what happened in Timor-Leste following the early conclusion of the UN peacebuilding operation.

SOVEREIGN DECISIONS AND "OWNERSHIP"

For an effective war-to-peace transition, in addition to commitment to enforcing the rule of law, developing a fair and effective justice system, and creating a professional civil service, sovereign countries need to take responsibility or "ownership" of reconstruction policies as a basis for their sustainability.[9] As discussed above, reconstruction cannot succeed if international organizations or donors impose their vision of reconstruction on the government. Neither can it succeed, however, if key government officials, without the support of others, or of the population at large, impose their own vision. There should be a participatory process in setting national priorities.

Ownership does not imply universal consensus. Expecting that would be a recipe for paralysis. Country ownership implies that there is sufficient political backing within the country for all the policies, programs, and projects included in the reconstruction strategy, even if donors fully finance some of these. Although the ministry of finance and the central bank will have to make many of the policy decisions with respect to economic reconstruction, line ministries, parliamentary bodies, local governments, civil society organizations, and private-sector groups need to provide broad support for them. If these groups oppose them, policies as well as programs and projects aimed at steering the economy onto a long-term development path will not have a chance to succeed.

In Afghanistan, for example, only a few government officials, backed by the IFIs and the United States, supported the basic reconstruction strategy enshrined in the National Development Framework (NDF). Such strategy consisted of having a small and effective state, with regulatory functions, where the private sector would play a key role in a market-driven economy and would be the main force in the development of the country.

After the first multiparty election in almost half a century in the Democratic Republic of Congo (DRC) and Joseph Kabila's assumption of power as an elected President in December 2006, it is up to the new leaders to design a clear strategy, establish priorities, and build up domestic support for such priorities. Nevertheless, as a poor country with scarce human resources, the

DRC will find it difficult to design and implement such a strategy on its own and will need training, capacity building, technical, and financial assistance at every step. National leaders will also need support in policy formulation, institutional development, structural and public service reform, in exploiting and managing their large mineral resources, and in other areas. At any rate, national ownership of the reconstruction strategy will remain particularly difficult in countries like the DRC, owing to the government's lack of full territorial control despite some progress. Purely military means will not suffice to reestablish the government's authority throughout the country.

The DRC authorities will need to create incentives for those areas to join in a national reconstruction effort. Given that the areas outside government control are rich in natural resources, this will require focusing on a fair allocation of resources in the legal and regulatory framework of the country. Under the new constitution, 40 percent of a province's revenue should be returned to the region, and mining companies should pay 30 percent corporate tax, a 2 percent royalty on net sales, and a 1 percent tax on exports. This, however, is no guarantee of transparency and fairness in the allocation of resources since corruption often illegally taps funds into private bank accounts. Unless resources are effectively used, the government will not have support for its policies, including the need for Gecamines, the state-owned mining company, to enter into joint ventures with foreign investors.[10]

Thus, in the current context, just as at the time of the Marshall Plan, national leaders must take the lead in the design of the reconstruction strategy, with the UN, the IFIs, and other relevant organizations confined to a supporting role. None of these organizations—and least of all an occupying force—should impose on countries policies that do not have national support. Lack of ownership in Kosovo, Afghanistan, and Iraq has been—and will continue to be—a major impediment to economic reconstruction. Moreover, and more worrisome, it has greatly contributed to increased violence and discontent in these countries. As these three cases demonstrate, ownership and stability are intimately connected. As was true during the post-1945 reconstruction of Europe, interference by one country—or by the UN and IFIs, for that matter—in the internal affairs of another creates resentment and is sure to produce a result that is exactly the opposite of what was intended (Dulles 1993: 101).

BUILDING SUPPORT FOR ECONOMIC RECONSTRUCTION

As is true of any reform, post-conflict economic reconstruction comes with costs as well as benefits. Since the costs are usually short-term and the benefits will come only after some time, policymakers need to make an effort at communicating this to the public. One of the dangers is that people build up unrealistic expectations about the short-term benefits of the war-to-peace transition, and quickly become disillusioned if those expectations are not fulfilled soon. This can seriously endanger the entire peace process by creating spoilers.

In a fiscal sense, the "peace dividend" to the government from ending the war may not be large in countries where the conflict was financed from foreign sources, and where international assistance withers in the transition to peace. Furthermore, in some post-conflict countries, reconstruction aid amounts to only a small fraction of military and security costs. As discussed earlier, the United States spent ten times more on its military operations in Afghanistan in 2003 than it did on reconstruction and humanitarian assistance there. In Iraq, only $34 billion of $310 billion the US allocated in fiscal 2003–6 supported stabilization and reconstruction efforts. However, the transition to peace is costly, owing to the need for rehabilitation of physical and social infrastructure, improvements in public security, reintegration of former combatants into productive activities, as well as other required tasks. Because peace is costly, it is particularly important to build support among donors, both at governmental and civil society levels.

Moreover, a "peace dividend" associated with better living conditions is essential if people are to believe that they have a stake in the success of the peace process. For the transition to succeed, people need to identify peace with personal benefits that outweigh the short-term costs that they inevitably will have to bear. Unless people can reasonably expect a large peace dividend as they move forward in the peace process, they will have no incentive to support reconstruction.

It is also important to build support among taxpayers in donor countries. The Marshall Plan—unquestionably the most successful reconstruction programs of all time—provides conclusive evidence of the importance of building such support for reconstruction. Taxpayers in donor countries do not always see the benefit of paying the bill for reconstruction in faraway countries. Unless they appreciate the impact that the reconstruction strategy may have in the region or internationally, their elected representatives will more likely be reluctant to allocate the necessary funds. The argument should be that reconstruction is but a pittance of the cost of military intervention and the "war against terror". An investment in successful reconstruction can save donors large amounts that would be needed for maintaining the peace through military and security mechanisms.[11]

TRANSPARENT, NON-CORRUPT PRACTICES

Transparency in post-conflict reconstruction is crucial. Reconstruction, in a broad sense, provides an opportunity to root out economic criminality—ranging from large-scale tax evasion to other illicit practices in production and trade—that existed during the conflict. In view of the comprehensive transformation of the country in the transition to peace, it represents an ideal opportunity to entrench transparent, non-corrupt practices. This is particularly true in the immediate post-conflict period, when the support of the international community is strongest.

As Tanzi (1997), has emphasized in relation to countries coming out of war or other forms of chaos, a demonstration of honesty and objectivity will be essential if good governance is to characterize economic policy in the future. As he points out, good or bad habits—and good or bad policies—developed at this time are likely to become ingrained and have lasting effects.

Economic criminality poses an especially severe obstacle to successful reconstruction because illicit but lucrative activities often provide a motivation for the continuation of conflict. As I discussed in the cases of Kosovo and Afghanistan, once the authorities allow such activities to persist during reconstruction, they become more difficult to root out, which has also been true in Angola, Sudan, Sierra Leone, the DRC, and elsewhere. This is not only because law enforcement and judiciary capacities are weak, but also because such activities may serve an economic purpose.[12]

Nowhere is transparency more important than in fiscal policy. In a transparent arrangement, a reasonable tax system with low rates will bring much-needed resources to the government. By contrast, lack of transparency and high rates makes people and business more likely to adopt avoidance strategies, and can also lead to corruption with government officials wasting scarce resources. Likewise, insufficient transparency in trade and commercial policies will lead to lower government resources in the form of tariffs and other revenue.

The belief that corruption is endemic to war-to-peace transitions is widespread but false. To be sure, people in 48 out of the 69 countries covered in Transparency International's (TI) 2005 annual *Global Corruption Barometer Survey* said that corruption had risen over the past three years. Research conducted in 2004 led TI to estimate that people paid about $1 trillion in bribes in 2003, compared with a global economy worth about $30 trillion. The TI survey showed that taking bribes was particularly prevalent in Africa, with Cameroon, Ghana, and Nigeria the worst performers. It found that households in these three countries spent more than 20 percent of their income on paying bribes.[13]

Some initiatives have been designed to diminish the level of corruption, particularly in regard to the exploitation and trade of natural resources. The Kimberley process, for example, started when Southern African diamond-producing states met in Kimberley, South Africa, in May 2000, to discuss ways to stop the trade in 'conflict diamonds' and ensure that diamond purchases were not funding violence. In December of that year, the UN General Assembly adopted a landmark resolution (A/RES/55/56) supporting the creation of an international scheme for rough diamonds. By November 2002, negotiations between governments, the international diamond industry and civil society organizations resulted in the creation of the Kimberly Process Certification Scheme (KPCS). This voluntary scheme imposes stringent requirements on participants to certify that shipments of rough diamonds are free of conflict diamonds. The KPCS entered into force in 2003, when participating countries started to implement its rules. By end 2007 it had 45 participants, which supply almost 100 percent of global production of rough diamonds.

Although corruption related to natural resources in general continues to be a serious problem, there are examples of countries that have made significant progress in increasing transparency and diminishing corruption during the war-to-peace transition. For example, as recounted by Vaishnav and Crocker (2004), widespread corruption plagued successive governments in Sierra Leone. The country's rebels, having claimed that they launched the war to end decades of government-driven exploitation of diamonds, in turn financed their fight through the same means. The international community eventually focused on what analysts called "conflict diamonds" (or "blood diamonds"). With assistance from the World Bank, the European Commission, the United Kingdom, and the UNDP, the government created a Good Governance Program with the purpose of decentralizing power and creating a more transparent and accountable government. With the help of the UK's Department for International Development (DFID), the government also set up an Anti-Corruption Commission composed of government and British officials, mandated to expose corruption (although it lacked an enforcement mechanism). More recently, in February 2006, the IFIs agreed to share information and set up a task force to create a uniform framework for preventing and combating fraud and corruption.[14]

Another interesting example is that of the Liberia Governance and Economic Management Assistance Program (GEMAP) which is a partnership between the government and the International Contact Group. The purpose of the GEMAP is to build a system of economic governance that promotes accountability, responsibility, and transparency in fiscal management so that aid and resources will be used to benefit the population at large and for consolidating peace in the country.

The belief that corruption is cultural, and that leaders cannot do anything to reduce it, is also false. A decade after the signing of the peace agreements, El Salvador is one of the less corrupt countries in Latin America. The 2006 Transparency International Corruption Perceptions Index (which gives a low ranking to countries in which the perception of corruption is small) ranks El Salvador in 57th place (of 163 countries), only three places below Costa Rica, and in fourth place in Latin America. More revealing, El Salvador compares very well in this regard with major global players in international trade and investment, ranking ahead of Brazil, China, India, and Mexico, which share 70th place, and far above Russia, which the Index ranks in 121st place.

MINIMIZING DISTORTIONS

The international community can create serious distortions in the process of supporting war-to-peace transitions. The larger the involvement of the international community in reconstruction, the larger the distortions will be. Kosovo and Bosnia and Herzegovina are clear examples of this. Since distortions by a large international presence are inevitable, it is important to understand the type of distortions that this presence creates in order to minimize them.

Perhaps the most flagrant distortion is created simply by the international community's sheer physical presence in the country. Foreign workers and their activities put pressure on prices, wages, housing, transportation, and other services. Most importantly, the foreign presence lures the best local people away from the civil service by offering better wages, generally in hard currency, and more attractive working and living conditions. This, in turn, affects the future productive capacity of the country, since skilled workers and professionals that get jobs as drivers and interpreters will soon lose their skills.

Another important distortion concerns the inflationary bias of national statistics due to the international presence. Both inflation and growth figures are inflated in many post-conflict countries. Rapid growth and inflationary pressures in turn have led to unnecessarily tight monetary and fiscal policies that, as in Kosovo, had an unfortunate recessionary impact once the international presence decreased.

Distortions also arise when the provision of aid greatly exceeds the country's capacity to absorb it. This was a problem in Haiti and other countries. With low absorptive capacity, large aid flows can overwhelm post-conflict countries, often giving rise to inefficiencies and corruption.[15] Large aid flows can also crowd out the capacity of local organizations, exacerbate social and economic disparities, facilitate the growth of organized crime, and damage certain traditional sectors of national economies (IPA 2002d).

LOCAL CAPACITY AND LOCAL INPUTS

Using local capacity is not only a way of promoting employment, but also a way to minimize the distortions created by a large international community presence in the country. Thus, as mentioned earlier, capacity building should start as soon as possible. Policymakers should make a strong effort early in the process to rely on local talent and capacities in reconstruction efforts.

Furthermore, reconstruction should use local inputs as much as possible. In Kosovo, for example, the policy of "tied aid" demanded by donors, particularly the EU, which made aid conditional on the use of their own companies and suppliers, certainly delayed and distorted economic reconstruction. The inability to finance reliance on local companies and resources was responsible for the high unemployment in the province. It also created serious delays in repairing housing and other infrastructure, owing to poor road links with Macedonia, from where most aid and input supplies were transported by truck. A large part of the building materials were available in Kosovo and employment creation for both Albanians and Serbs in the province could have facilitated reconciliation.

Countries with a lack of local capabilities will need a much longer period of support before they can become self-sufficient. At the other extreme, highly entrepreneurial countries such as Lebanon need to use their resources and inventiveness from the very beginning. Pascual and Indyk (2006) argue that Iraq is an example for Lebanon of how not to rebuild using international contractors that take months to get in place and spend perhaps a third of their budgets protecting themselves. They point out that Lebanon has excellent engineers and experience from rebuilding the country after its civil war, and maintain that Lebanese and Arab contractors who employ local workers should have priority. In their view, international donors will need to help the Lebanese government design streamlined procurement rules with external auditors, and disburse payments based on results rather than the level of effort.[16]

PACE AND SEQUENCE OF REFORM

The pace and sequence of reform during post-conflict economic reconstruction will be very much dependent on initial conditions, domestic capabilities, and the availability of foreign financing and private remittances. Particularly in countries where basic institutions stopped functioning or were extremely weak, the first step should be to prepare an accurate assessment of economic and financial conditions. For example, even if policymakers want to start providing credit to micro-enterprises immediately, this will not be possible until the monetary authorities and the basic legal framework are in place. In some contexts, such as Kosovo and East Timor, the first challenge was to restore the payments system, without which all other policies would have been ineffective.

Moreover, in cases where interim governments have been installed, both the pace and sequence of reform will reflect the authorities' lack the legitimacy to carry out certain policies. In an extreme case, like Kosovo, the transition will also reflect the territory's status as a province and as a UN protectorate, with the lack of final political status imposing further constraints on policymaking.

PROPERTY RIGHTS

Since the establishment of clear and stable property rights is a precondition for investment, policymakers need to address this issue head-on in any strategy for post-conflict economic reconstruction. The experience of several post-conflict countries has illustrated how property rights issues can be very different across countries.

In the cases of El Salvador and Guatemala, where combatants and their supporters occupied lands during many years of conflict, the issue was backward-looking. It involved establishing whether land titles existed in the past and, if so, who held them. However, once a sovereign government made a decision, property rights were likely to remain fixed into the future. Indeed, the issue was never a serious impediment to investment in these countries. Nevertheless, property rights were difficult to resolve, since decisions involved numerous parcels of land that often had a long history of occupation and land registries had to be modernized and updated. In such cases, policymakers need to look for technical and financial assistance to improve the registry so that they can resolve title claims as soon as possible.

Forward-looking property rights issues are normally paramount where a legitimate government is absent, since investors do not know what will happen when legitimate authorities assume power. These issues are more difficult to resolve and are a strong disincentive to current and future investment. This was certainly the case in Kosovo and Iraq. In these cases, in addition to inadequate security conditions, the main obstacle to investment has been the uncertainty of property rights allocated by the UN, occupation authorities, or the transitional government. This has been a major impediment to efforts to privatize state-owned enterprises or promote other large investments.

Proposals to privatize the Trepca mining complex in Kosovo, the oil sector and/or other public companies in Iraq have been naive and obviously unsuccessful. The situation was somewhat different in the case of East Timor. There, the UN mandate was short-lived and included a clear exit strategy, as the new government was set to take over at a specified time, and where major political figures played an important role during the interim UN administration. Although there were many other problems in East Timor, uncertainty over property rights was not a significant issue.

Any strategy for reconstruction in countries with unclear property rights should not include privatization of large state-owned enterprises, which is always a political issue. Although it may be possible to privatize or lease smaller and strategically unimportant companies, even this may be difficult.

To stimulate investment under such conditions, policymakers will have to make special efforts to support the reactivation of domestic micro- and small enterprises (MSEs) and develop "reconstruction zones" to attract foreign direct investment to labor-intensive processing industries for exports. Policymakers will also have to think about other innovative ways of creating employment in the short-run (options for this are discussed in Chapter 15).

NATIONAL LOGISTICS AND PLANNING

Good logistics are essential to an effective post-conflict economic reconstruction strategy. Logistics relate to almost every aspect of the reconstruction, from the movement of international experts, goods, refugees, and internally displaced people to the provision of services. Policymakers cannot afford to leave any aspect of logistics to chance, which implies that careful advance planning is essential if the reconstruction strategy is to proceed in a smooth, consistent, and effective way.

Institutional and policymaking issues

Countries in the transition from war to peace normally have weak institutions, although countries vary widely in this respect. Because of the importance of adequate institutional arrangements and strong institutions, this issue will be discussed separately in Chapter 12 where a basic institutional framework to deal with post-conflict economic reconstruction is proposed. Similarly, countries in the transition from war will most often require strong efforts at national reconciliation, including disarming, demobilization and reintegration (DDR) programs as well as basic rehabilitation of services and infrastructure. This will be the topic of Chapter 13. Also, countries in post-conflict transitions normally require a major change in macro- and microeconomic policymaking. Unless economic policymaking is effective the country will at best become aid dependent and at worst will go back to war. The latter is often associated with the failure of policymakers to create viable employment for the population at large, so that they can enjoy the peace dividend of better living conditions. Macroeconomic policymaking and its microeconomic foundations are discussed in Chapters 14 and 15.

12 Basic institutional framework

Institutional arrangements for post-conflict reconstruction

The case studies in Chapters 7–10 revealed that many of the problems in implementing effective post-conflict reconstruction have to do with poor institutional arrangements and weak institutions. A poor institutional framework is a serious constraint on economic policymaking. Although it is not possible here to describe or analyze in detail all the institutions that are necessary, I will focus on a number of institutional arrangements as well as particular institutions that are essential for effective policymaking in countries in post-conflict economic reconstruction.[1]

As is true of all difficult policies, reconstruction requires leadership and political will, in addition to efforts to promote national reconciliation. Institutional arrangements for both policy implementation and coordination among the different actors are required, and these tasks are more complex than in normal development, simply because governments have to carry out "extra activities," in the presence of a larger and more diverse group of reconstruction actors. Policymakers must therefore devote considerable thought to the design of these arrangements, as well as that of the policies themselves. No leader can be effective without appropriate institutions and coordination mechanisms to support his or her policies and programs.

Some post-conflict countries need to build institutions from scratch. Most need to modernize and adapt them. Many countries coming out of statist policies and over-regulated systems may want to move towards "market-based policymaking," and they will need institutions to support this change. This is what happened in Vietnam in the late 1980s, a decade after the end of the war, when their leaders decided to abandon their central-planning system, which had led to serious imbalances and little growth.[2] Although most of the institutions that policymakers have to consider in designing their reconstruction strategy are also present in countries undergoing the normal process of development, some are specific to post-conflict economic reconstruction. Policymakers will have to eliminate these institutions as soon as the country has completed the implementation of peace-related programs and moves onto a path of normal development.

In developing institutions for economic reconstruction, a sequencing problem will arise with those related to ensuring the rule of law. Unless the rule-of-law institutions and the economic and commercial legislation, as well as other legal, regulatory, and administrative frameworks, are in place and enforced, economic institutions will be weak and inoperative. Adequate security and the enforcement of contracts are crucial for investment, the operation of the banking system, and other reconstruction-related activities. However, the establishment of institutions that ensure and administer the rule of law takes time, and thus will usually take place simultaneously with the building of institutions for reconstruction. Both processes must start as soon as is feasible.

The authorities will need to staff the new institutions with capable professionals. Given the human resource gap and the low absorptive capacity existing in most countries in the transition to peace, heavy doses of training and capacity building are required as these institutions grow and modernize. The authorities should identify and lure nationals working abroad to return to the country, by offering them key technical posts in the civil service. In order to ensure policy consistency in all sectors and across sectors, the ministries and the central bank require technical capacity and resources for data collection and analysis, budgeting and tax collection, risk analysis, and financial programming.[3] Principles of transparency, accountability, meritocracy, and equal rights for women and minorities need to guide the labor recruitment and promotion polices for all government institutions.

Ministries will need to build a working relationship with members of parliament. This is important since parliament, or an equivalent legislative body, will need to approve the institutional, legal, and regulatory framework, as well as many policies for economic reconstruction.[4] However, because of the polarization that often exists in post-conflict situations, the relationship between the executive branch and the legislative body may be tense. In this regard, the closer the relationship with legislators—and the sooner policies are discussed with them—the greater the chance that these policies will be enacted.

THE CABINET

Given that the government must provide a number of services during post-conflict reconstruction, ministries have to be set up with enough resources and capabilities to carry them out. The government should also play an important role in establishing the legal and administrative framework. For this purpose, it will require legal expertise and additional resources. Because of the human resources gap that characterizes most post-conflict situations, policymakers designing the reconstruction strategy need to streamline and integrate ministries to improve effectiveness.

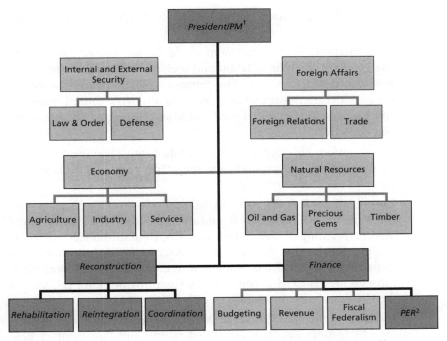

Figure 5. Proposed central government Cabinet organizational chart for effective economic reconstruction

Notes: 1. President or Prime Minister, depending on country; 2. Post-Conflict Economic Reconstruction Office.

Although policymakers can choose among many possibilities for the number and functions of the different ministries, a minimalist framework for effective post-conflict reconstruction could include six ministries (Figure 5). In designing this framework, I had in mind the Democratic Republic of Congo (DRC)—which in addition to diamonds and gold has some of the world's largest unexploited reserves of copper, rich deposits of cobalt, nickel, iron ore, and bauxite and hence requires a separate ministry to deal with natural resources. Countries which are not rich in natural resources but rely heavily on agriculture or industry could eliminate this ministry and divide the Economy Ministry to suit their needs. All countries that need to bring reconstruction on track would benefit from better institutional arrangements.

Thus, the Cabinet of a resource rich country could have the following structure (Figure 5):

- A Ministry of Internal and External Security to reestablish law and order, as well as organizing the country's defenses against external threats.
- A Ministry of Foreign Affairs to reestablish essential diplomatic, trade, investment, and strategic relations with other countries.

- A Ministry of Reconstruction, which would be divided into three Departments:
    - Rehabilitation. This Department could be subdivided further and charged with the rehabilitation and regulation of (i) basic socioeconomic infrastructure, including primary education and basic health; (ii) essential transport (roads, ports, and airports), communications, and logistics; (iii) essential public utilities (electricity, potable water, and sanitation).
    - Reintegration. This Department would deal with all political and technical aspects related to short- and long-term programs for reintegration and national reconciliation.
    - Coordination. This Department would deal with coordination with the Ministry of Finance to ensure that all substantive and technical aspects regarding reconstruction are reflected in the budget, according to the priorities that the Ministry determines for each of them. This Department would also coordinate with the international community through the National Reconstruction Coordinator Office (NRCO) of the UN Peacebuilding Mission (see Figure 3, p. 64).
- A Ministry of Finance. This could be divided initially into four Departments: Budgeting; Revenue; Fiscal Federalism; and Post-Conflict Economic Reconstruction (PER).
- A Ministry of the Economy. Different countries would need different Departments, depending on the importance of agriculture, industry, services, and mining or other natural resources.
- A Ministry of Natural Resources. In countries where natural resources (oil and gas, diamonds, timber, or others) are a significant part of the country's production, employment, and trade, policymakers should create a separate ministry.

While the Ministry for Reconstruction would focus on the technical aspects and establish the political priorities for the different programs and projects, the Post-Conflict Economic Reconstruction (PER) Department at the Ministry of Finance would focus on the financial aspects of reconstruction. The PER Department would have two main tasks. First, in consultation with the Ministry of Reconstruction and the UN NRCO, the PER Department would decide on the reconstruction expenditures to be included in the regular budget (recording the recurrent expenditure of the government, including wages, salaries, and pensions). Second, it would prepare the reconstruction budget in consultation with the Ministry for Reconstruction, the UN NRCO, and all donors.[5] The centralization of the preparation of the regular budget as well as the reconstruction budget in the PER Department would ensure proper financing for the government's priorities. It would also eliminate the common practice of having several donors' budgets, without any control by the government.

Centralizing relations with donors in the PER Department would also help centralize data and information, thereby helping to avoid situations in which donors work at cross-purposes and even undermine the new government, as they did in Afghanistan. In the process of preparing the reconstruction budget, the PER Department would also have the leading role in fund-raising, and would be responsible for following up with donors to ensure that they eventually disburse their pledges.

By having all information related to needs, donors' financial assistance, and other capital flows, including from remittances, the PER Department would be able to prepare the regular and reconstruction budgets in the most effective way. Eventually, it would be the responsibility of the PER Department to consolidate the two budgets, as the country moves onto a path of normal development and the PER Department withers.

Ministers should make every effort to ensure that their ministries' staffs are as small, well trained, and capable as possible, and that the ministries' organizational structure is as efficient and effective as is feasible. It is in the area of capacity building and training that the international community can and should play a critical role in supporting institutional effectiveness.

In normal situations, economists do not consider the central bank to be part of the government (although it is a government institution and is part of the public sector). Hence the central bank governor or president is not a member of the Cabinet, despite the fact that in some countries the central bank depends on the Ministry of Finance. In post-conflict situations, because of the need to integrate political and economic issues and ensure their financing, it is highly recommended that the governor or president of the central bank participate in Cabinet meetings, even if not officially part of it. The central government will also have to coordinate policies with the rest of the public sector, including the local governments, the state-owned enterprises, and the public banks.

The Ministry of Finance (MoF)

The Ministry of Finance in any country has a mandate, among other functions, to carry out fiscal policy. Thus, the MoF must make critical decisions concerning new taxes and rates, tax collection and administration, as well as maximum levels of expenditure given financial constraints (which include expected tax collection, inflows of aid, and the amount of annual debt that the country is willing to assume). The MoF negotiates expenditure with the line ministries (the other five spending ministries) after they present their spending needs for the year. This is a highly political process, all the more so during reconstruction. At this time, the MoF may have the additional burden of dealing with two separate budgets—the regular budget and the reconstruction budget, financed with earmarked funds from international donors.

During the budget process, the MoF must ensure that no peace-related program or project that is critical for the consolidation of peace goes unfunded. In this regard, it has to work very closely with the country's political leadership as well as with the Ministry for Reconstruction and the Special Representative of the Secretary-General (SRSG) and its National Reconstruction Coordinator (NRC) to assess the importance and needs of such programs. The selection of the Minister of Finance should be a key decision of new governments, and should be based on an assessment of his or her political, technical, and managerial skills. A technocrat will not do.

The Ministry for Reconstruction

Although I have placed the Reconstruction Czar—in charge of all political and technical decisions regarding reconstruction—in the position of Minister for Reconstruction, a good alternative would be to locate the Czar in the Office of the President. Because of the importance of political factors in the decision-making process, proximity to the President could be an advantage. In large countries such as the DRC the Reconstruction Czar's team may have too many members to locate it in the President's Office. Hence, it would make sense to have it in a separate ministry. Wherever he or she is located, the Reconstruction Czar should take important decisions on the strategy or any aspect of its implementation only after consultation with the President and the Minister of Finance. He should also consult with other reconstruction actors, including the donor countries and others, providing technical assistance and other inputs into the process. Effective reconstruction requires not only a good strategy, but also financing for priority programs and projects.

The Ministry of Natural Resources (MNR)

The MNR plays a critical and complex role in economic reconstruction, for it must deal with the political implications that natural resources may have had during the conflict, to ensure that those affected by peace receive some kind of compensation for giving up the spoils of war. Indeed, peace agreements often create carrot-and-stick mechanisms related to natural resources, which the MNR will have to respect and enforce.[6] Groups that believe that the allocation of vast natural resources is not fair will not support the consolidation of peace. As Polgreen and Dugger (2006) put it,

From Angola to Nigeria, Gabon to Sudan, riches from oil have often ended up in the pockets of the ruling elite, inciting conflict over the spoils. In Congo, the off-again-on-again fight over a very similar issue, that vast country's mineral riches, has killed four million people, more than any conflict since World War II. Most died of disease and hunger as wars over diamond and copper mines raged.

In countries where one or more natural resources play a critical role in government revenue and exports, the MNR, aside from ensuring that those who benefited from the spoils of war have an economic or political stake in the transition to peace, may face four challenges. First, as many of these countries start the peace transition, war-torn infrastructure, lack of investment, and inadequate technology will impair their capacity to exploit their resources, while financing provided by the IFIs is often inadequate.[7] At the same time, investment by the private sector may create a dilemma for policymakers, similar to the one that countries face with regard to privatization, discussed in Chapter 14. Countries can give large incentives to the private sector to invest early in the war-to-peace transition, and thus help in the reactivation of the economy. They can also wait until reconstruction has progressed, and the economy has been reactivated, in an effort to obtain a better deal from private investors. In many cases, however, countries will not be able to muddle through until the second alternative is feasible, and thus they are forced to part with their resource assets at bargain prices.

In the DRC, for example, this meant that, in exchange for investment to upgrade the capacity of the country's diamond production, the government had to agree to future commodity-supply contracts, at prices well below market, for many years to come. The UN and others have denounced these contracts as unfair. However, only risk-prone investors would invest early in the peace transition. This is because of the high probability that new governments will reverse former contracts. To invest under such conditions of risk investors obviously expect a commensurate return.[8]

More and more governments are renegotiating resource contracts with private investors entered into by previous governments—the equivalent in a way of debt restructuring. This is true not only in post-conflict situations, but also in countries undergoing normal development, such as Bolivia and Venezuela. One of the functions of the MNR should be to reevaluate contracts signed by previous governments to assess their fairness and renegotiate those that are unfair, which may well be the case with some diamond contracts in the DRC.

Second, infrastructure linked to richly endowed resources is often at risk of attacks. Thus, the provision of security for such infrastructure is important and often expensive. AFP reported that Iraq's oil ministry had losses of more than $6.3 billion from a total of 186 attacks by rebels on various oil installations in 2005.

Third, countries that rely heavily on exports of one or two commodities are vulnerable to "Dutch disease," that is, they are likely to have appreciating real exchange rates that distort the price of non-tradable goods and services, while undermining export competitiveness. Pressure for a real appreciation of the domestic currency early in the transition also stems from large inflows of aid and other financial resources as happened in El Salvador. Since real appreciation undermines export competitiveness, the MNR must coordinate with the MoF and the central bank to minimize this effect.

Finally, economies that are heavily dependent on production and exports of one or two commodities are highly susceptible to changes in international demand and prices. Thus, a "resource or stabilization fund" for these commodities is the most effective way for the government, which accumulates funds during booms and draws on them during recessions, to attenuate pro-cyclical fiscal policy. While the rules governing such funds will have to depend on the needs and characteristics of the country, they also play an important role in allocating resources between present and future generations, as discussed below in more detail.

One of the immediate problems of the MNR in post-conflict situations will be to find ways to finance infrastructure needed to exploit natural resources and reactivate the economy, which in turn would help finance reconstruction. This has been the case in countries such as the DRC, Angola, Chad, Iraq, and many others, where security and other concerns often impede private-sector investment. In many cases, a private–public partnership (PPP), perhaps with the support of an IFI, is a way to reduce political and economic risk (see Chapter 13). Investors and the IFIs are often reluctant to participate in these investments, however, because of corruption and other non-transparent practices in host countries. As a result, the IFIs are increasingly asking governments for a commitment to spend oil and other revenues from royalties and dividends transparently, with a strong focus on poverty alleviation and the attainment of the Millennium Development Goals (MDGs). For example, with the support of the World Bank and financing by a consortium led by ExxonMobil, Chad recently constructed a $4.1 billion pipeline—one of Africa's largest investments—to export oil through neighboring Cameroon. For this, Chad had to adopt a law committing the government to use oil revenue to support social spending.[9]

Angola is another example in which natural resources played a key role in the war. According to Global Witness, $8.5 billion of public money went unaccounted for between 1997 and 2001. Transparency International ranks Angola among the ten most corrupt countries. More recently, Angola and the IMF have failed to reach agreement on a program to support economic reconstruction because of the Fund's misgivings about how the country accounts for its resource-related revenue. The Paris Club of sovereign creditors had put pressure on Angola to enter into an IMF-supported program in order to reschedule its debts of about $1.5 billion to $1.8 billion. On a positive note, Angola has announced that it is planning to adhere to mechanisms, such as the UK's Extractive Industries Transparency Initiative (EITI), to improve the transparency of government revenues (Reed 2005). During its reconstruction, it is critical that Angola manages its oil and diamond reserves in a sound and non-corrupt manner and that proceeds from these resources be effectively used for the creation of dynamism and inclusion in the country.

These examples illustrate the economic issues related to the so-called "resource curse," which refers to the fact that many countries that are rich in national resources mismanage them to such an extent that they derive little economic benefit.[10] The way countries manage natural resources will be critical for post-conflict economic reconstruction, and the MNR has a key role to play. Policymakers in richly endowed countries should not forget that the international community expects them to bear more of the reconstruction bill than poor countries, and that only a good strategy and good policies can enable them to do so.

If done within the multilateral political and economic framework discussed earlier for post-conflict countries, and if included as part of the strategy for economic reconstruction, the exploitation of natural resources could be more transparent than has been the case within a strictly bilateral framework. This could prevent both foreign firms from taking advantage of vulnerable countries and corrupt government officials from doing the same.

THE CENTRAL BANK

In industrial countries, as well as in the majority of emerging markets, many experts, including former governors of central banks, argue that the fundamental function of the monetary authority is to promote and maintain price stability. Even in cases in which price stability is not the only—or even the most important—objective of economic policymaking, both theory and practice provide support for the view that the central bank should focus its operational activities on the fight against inflation and the long-term preservation of gains in this area. Empirical evidence indicates that the instruments within reach of the central bank—that is, the instruments related to monetary policy—are particularly effective in eliminating inflationary pressures. At the same time, there are clear indications that such instruments are not the best to achieve other policy objectives—such as growth, full employment, or greater income equality. On the contrary, the use of monetary policy for such objectives may have perverse consequences.[11]

Empirical evidence shows, moreover, that the fight against inflation requires the adoption of a long-term framework. This, in turn, requires insulating the central bank, as the institution that is mainly responsible for ensuring price stability, from the daily political, social, or sectoral pressures to which it might be exposed, by guaranteeing its institutional independence. Such independence entails—among other things—protecting the central bank and its officials from the effects of changes in the domestic political environment.

As Blejer and I argued (Blejer and del Castillo 2000b), it was not, as many argue, the centers of power of the industrial world nor the neo-liberal beliefs prevailing at the international financial institutions (IFIs) that determined best practices in this area. Instead, they reflected the decisive influence that international capital markets have in the allocation of resources and in penalizing countries that have higher rates of inflation. Countries that lack at least de facto if not *de jure* central bank independence, and that are non-compliant with the objective of price stability and other rules of the game, risk being bypassed by the large international flows of private capital that characterize today's increasingly globalized world.

This is not at all the case for countries in post-conflict situations. Countries in the war-to-peace transition have no possibility whatsoever of tapping the international capital markets. They are dependent on official financing flows, mostly in the form of grants and concessional loans. Hence, the discipline of the capital markets is not something that should concern them in the initial period.

On the contrary, during post-conflict economic reconstruction, the objectives of the central bank have to expand, diminishing the importance of price stability, or subordinating it to different types of political and business-cycle needs. Although best practice in the long run should be the objective of price stability, in the short run this objective might be affected by immediate and critical financing needs of reconstruction-related projects. Such financing needs may arise from the reluctance of donors to fund projects that are often critical in a successful transition to peace. In such cases, central banks, in conjunction with the President and the Ministers of Reconstruction and Finance, should seriously consider domestic financing, even if it carries a short-term inflationary cost. Problems with financing reconciliation programs, including employment creation in Kosovo, the arms-for-land program in El Salvador, and much-needed confidence-building measures in East Timor, Afghanistan, Iraq, the Democratic Republic of Congo (DRC), and elsewhere, have endangered a fragile peace in many of these countries.

Countries in the process of reconstruction differ greatly, both in the institutional capacity of their central banks and in how war affected their payments and banking systems. In general, countries undergoing reconstruction will need to strengthen and modernize the central bank and build up an efficient and solid banking system by improving its regulatory and supervision powers. In some cases, as it was in Afghanistan, countries may also need to move to a two-tier banking system, where the central bank stops performing commercial functions and focuses on monetary policy and its regulatory and supervision policies. Although countries could establish a Banking Superintendence during reconstruction, it may be better to locate regulatory and supervisory powers, in addition to monetary policy functions, within the central bank. This would allow the head of the central bank to coordinate with the Ministers of Reconstruction and Finance, the President, and other political actors in incorporating political considerations as needed, so that monetary and exchange rate policies could be fully attuned to the demands and constraints of the war-to-peace transition.

Some have likened the financial sector to the blood of the human body that permeates the economic system throughout. Stiglitz (1998) likens the financial system to the brain of the economy. At any rate, both analogies are good to illustrate the fact that a well-functioning financial sector is necessary to ensure the efficient allocation of scarce capital. In post-conflict transitions, too, a sound financial system is a requisite for effective intermediation and effective monetary policy. However, the formal financial system often consists only of banks, which are frequently state-owned. In the immediate post-conflict period, therefore, the authorities need to assess and audit existing banks. Given that reform of the banking system is essential for improving the mobilization and allocation of savings, the authorities should close banks deemed to be insolvent and beyond recovery, and must develop a plan for the revival of other banks. The need to finance micro- and small-sized enterprises (MSEs) is large, requiring the establishment of microfinance institutions if they do not exist. Banking regulation and on-site supervision needs to be improved. The central bank must eventually build the capability for surveillance of the financial system and enforcement of prudential rules, which will become stricter and in greater accordance with international standards as the system develops.[12]

In countries such as the DRC and Afghanistan, where a large part of the territory remains outside the control of the national authorities, a major challenge in the monetary and banking area will be to extend the payments and credit system to areas of the country that will gradually come under the authorities' control. This will create a great demand for external financial and technical assistance.

RESOURCE FUND: ALLOCATING RESOURCES BETWEEN CURRENT AND FUTURE GENERATIONS

In addition to the basic institutions for economic policymaking, governments will have to establish a number of institutional arrangements to deal with specific issues. For instance, commodity-producing countries often create resource funds and other savings schemes. These have become best practice as a countercyclical policy in normal development, following the practice in industrial countries.

Although it is best practice to save for a rainy day, in post-conflict transitions it pours everyday and what is best practice under normal development may be a wasted opportunity during the post-conflict transition. In fact, it should be an issue for debate among policymakers designing the strategy for reconstruction whether resource-related income should be saved in a fund for a financial return or whether it should be invested in human and physical infrastructure to improve the future productive capacity of the country and improve the welfare of the population at the same time. The latter—if effectively and transparently invested—would probably have a higher rate of return than the former. Most importantly, by raising the "peace dividend," it will likely lower the high risk that a country in the transition to peace otherwise has to revert to war.

What, in my view, policymakers should not even consider is to replicate institutional arrangements that originate in a completely different environment. What may be best practice for a developed country such as Norway, with an aging population at the top of the Human Development Index, will certainly not be best practice for a developing country like Timor-Leste, which has the fastest population growth in the world, one of the lowest per capita income levels, seriously damaged infrastructure, and is at the bottom of the Human Development Index (HDI). A different institutional arrangement for its oil and gas revenue could have accelerated reconstruction and prevented the renewed violence that broke out in 2006, after the UN had already filed the country as a success story.

Rather than using a large proportion of the increasing oil and gas revenue starting in 2004 for reconstruction purposes—including investment in human and physical infrastructure—Timor-Leste, with IMF support, created a Norwegian-style petroleum fund. According to the IMF, the key element of this fund is a savings rule that permits the country to use only interest income for development purposes. The World Bank strongly supported this policy, as José Ramos-Horta, then Foreign Minister and since 2007 President, noted in a speech to the 60th General Assembly.

In the Bank's view, the country has adopted a state-of-the-art legal framework for on- and offshore petroleum production and taxation and a draft savings policy and associated Petroleum Fund Act consistent with the *Extractive Industries Transparency* principles even before EIT existed.... True to stated principles, the government has adhered to a provisional savings policy for petroleum revenues ahead of the adoption of the permanent savings policy.[13]

This policy, in conjunction with a policy of zero domestic or foreign borrowing, has unnecessarily constrained economic reconstruction. Under normal conditions, poor countries should get grants rather than loans, since they will have difficulties repaying loans. The situation of resource-rich countries is different. As mentioned earlier, on one hand, donors are less likely to be generous and, on the other, borrowing may be necessary for investment in infrastructure and resource development that is likely to have a high rate of return, which would allow the country to develop and service its debt in the future. Furthermore, by investing their oil and gas proceeds in human and physical infrastructure the country would have facilitated the transition to peace.

Thus, it seems to me that, in following optimal economic policies and best practices, the government of Timor-Leste—with the advice and blessing of the Bretton Woods institutions—was more royalist than the king. In fact, I would argue that the petroleum fund went beyond even "development as usual" practices. The Asian Development Bank (ADB 2006: 246) showed more sense, noting, "it is unclear that the current policy on drawdown is the best approach, given the early stage of the economy's development . . . [and the fact that] new discoveries of energy in the future . . . may well mean that future generations are much better off than the current generation."

The ADB also notes that government policy makes it possible to use more revenue for development and for social support in the short and medium term, because the parliament can authorize spending from the petroleum fund in a particular year that exceeds the limit. The government will serve its people well by disregarding the Bretton Woods institutions' advice and accelerating the use of petroleum and gas revenue for economic reconstruction. In Timor-Leste, the rehabilitation of basic infrastructure and services, the creation of jobs for the 30 percent of the labor force that is unemployed, and the development of the agricultural sector, which currently accounts for 75 percent of employment, should have top priority. There, as in any other post-conflict situation, the objective of peace should prevail at all times, and peace will be ephemeral unless economic reconstruction takes place within a framework of political inclusion and national reconciliation. Because post-conflict economic reconstruction is a development-plus challenge, business-as-usual policies, best practices, and institutional arrangements in pursuit of purely economic objectives can have tragic consequences.

INSTITUTIONS FOR THE TRANSITION TO NORMAL DEVELOPMENT

The experiences of El Salvador and Timor-Leste brought to light the importance of exit policies for the transition from reconstruction to normal development. The international community and national authorities need to plan and coordinate the exit strategy well. These cases also highlighted two issues that countries must negotiate to ensure the proper institutional arrangements for the new transition.

First, the government should ensure that the UN (or any other organization involved) creates the necessary institutional arrangements to carry out any unfinished business related to the implementation of the peace agreements. Governments should not assume that development institutions will deal with them appropriately on their own. As the UN peacebuilding mission winds down, the UN Development Group (UNDG) National Coordinator should become both the UNDP Resident Representative and UNDG National Coordinator (see Figure 3, p. 64). The experience that he or she would bring to the job would ensure support for the sustainability of the peace process, while at the same time facilitating a smooth transition to the "development as usual" functions of the UN system. Countries at low levels of development that have had comprehensive support from the international community for some period of time should not be deprived of such support drastically and abruptly, as happened in Timor-Leste. Diminution of international support should be gradual and well monitored to ensure that it is not proceeding too fast. The inadequate institutional framework to deal with "unfinished business" related to peace-related programs was a critical factor in making some of them unsustainable.

Second, the transition to normal development is the time when national authorities, supported by the development institutions, will have to design their strategy to alleviate poverty and achieve the MDGs. Although institutions dealing specifically with reconstruction should disappear, reformed national institutions will be stronger and will be able to assume their full responsibilities in the development of the country.

Summary of institutional arrangements for effective reconstruction

Effective post-conflict economic reconstruction will require a new institutional framework within the countries involved and also within the UN. I have argued that if the UN were reformed, strengthened, and adequately staffed, it would be the best organization to lead reconstruction.

For this, the UN institutional arrangements—required at headquarters and at the peacebuilding mission in the field—need to be revised to ensure the organization's technical capacity to carry out its mandate in this area. Since the UN will need the strong support of the IFIs, the UN programs and agencies, non-governmental organizations (NGOs), and other donors, the institutional arrangements also reflect the need for effective coordination and collaboration. For this, the UN institutional arrangements-required at headquarters and at the peacebuilding mission in the field-need to be revised to ensure the organization's technical capacity to carry out its mandate in this area. Since the UN will need the strong support of the IFIs, the UN programs and agencies,

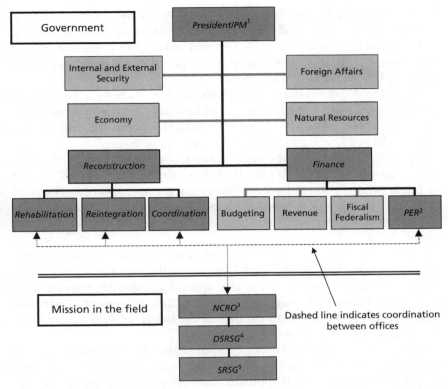

Figure 6. Proposed coordination links between the Government and the UN Peacebuilding Mission in the Country

Notes: 1. President or Prime minister, depending on country. 2. Post-Conflict Economic Reconstruction Department; 3. National Reconstruction Coordinator Office; 4. Deputy Special Representative of the Secretary-General for Economics and Finance; 5. Special Representative of the Secretary-General.

nongovernmental organizations (NGOs), and other donors, the institutional arrangements also reflect the need for effective coordination and collaboration. My proposal for an institutional framework for effective reconstruction is shown in Figures 2–6.

Figure 2 (p. 63) indicates the need for a Post-Conflict Reconstruction Unit (PCRU) in the UN Secretariat to provide leadership, support, and operational guidelines to the mission in the field. Due to the political nature of reconstruction, the PCRU would be located in DPA, with strong links to the DPKO and the DESA, with each of these departments having a Post-Conflict Reconstruction Coordinator (PCRC) that would facilitate coordination among them.

Figure 3 shows the National Reconstruction Coordinator Office (NRCO) in the UN peacebuilding (or integrated) mission in the field, as counterpart to PCRU, and with overall operational responsibility for economic reconstruction. The National Reconstruction Coordinator (NRC) would be either under a Deputy Special Representative of the Secretary-General (DSRSG) for Economics and Finance or directly under the SRSG, depending on the size of the mission. The NRCO would include four units, each headed by a Policy and Strategy Coordinator, an Aid Coordinator, an IFIs Coordinator, and a UNDG National Coordinator.

Figure 4 (p. 65) shows the proposed links through which the UN Secretariat and the peacebuilding mission in the field should communicate and coordinate in matters related to post-conflict economic reconstruction: directly between the PCRU at headquarters and the NCRO in the field.

Figure 5 (p. 241) shows the institutional arrangements to deal effectively with reconstruction at the country level. The Cabinet, headed by a President or Prime Minister, would have a Ministry for Reconstruction, in charge of all political and technical decisions regarding reconstruction, and a Minister of Finance, who would address all financing issues related to reconstruction, including aid.

Finally, Figure 6 shows the proposed links for effective coordination between the government and the UN peacebuilding mission. Coordination between the government and the international community is essential to ensure that international support strengthens the government rather than bypass it. It is also essential to ensure that the impact of scarce resources is maximized rather than wasted.

Unless a clear institutional structure is put in place for the channels through which the UN and the rest of the international community will support the government, a piecemeal approach, conflicting interests, duplication and waste, and other inefficiencies will remain the rule rather than the exception.

13 National reconciliation efforts

Disarmament, demobilization, and reintegration

FROM EMERGENCY TO NORMAL DEVELOPMENT

National reconciliation efforts include the disarmament, demobilization, and reintegration (DDR) of former combatants and other groups affected by the war as well as the rehabilitation of basic services and infrastructure. Governments need to carry out these efforts continuously and implacably, from the early emergency phase to the end of post-conflict economic reconstruction, when the country moves back onto a normal development path. This is what clearly makes reconstruction during the war-to-peace transition a development-plus challenge.

As discussed in the case studies, peace agreements, UN resolutions, and statements by high-level officials of occupying countries often build up expectations about what peace will bring to the population at large, which are often unrealistic and difficult to satisfy. Unfulfilled expectations of disgruntled groups can seriously endanger an entire peace process. For this reason, planning and financing of peace-related programs, as well as synchronization among the different programs, and continued support until their completion are important to make these programs effective and sustainable. This is why the design of the reconstruction strategy is so important.

Many countries in post-conflict situations need to deal with large numbers of returning refugees and internally displaced persons. Plans for reintegration of all these people into society and the economy need to be in place. In many cases, the speed with which the new authorities and the international community have to deal with the issue of returnees has taken the authorities by surprise. This was certainly the case in Kosovo. This is why it is so important to incorporate this issue in the strategy for economic reconstruction.[1]

One of the dangers of economic reconstruction is that many of the emergency programs that are started at the time war ends are allowed to wither over time, mainly because of lack of financing, technical assistance, or interest from the national authorities or the donor community and multilateral and bilateral organizations that support reconstruction.

Humanitarian aid will increase the consumption possibilities of vulnerable groups during the emergency phase and should be welcome. However, policymakers need to be aware that humanitarian assistance will not create investment and employment in the country. Hence, reconstruction aid should start as soon as possible so that rehabilitation of infrastructure and other investment will promote employment creation, increase productivity, and avoid long-term aid dependency. This, of course, will only happen if governments utilize reconstruction aid largely to contract local companies and employ nationals. Good aid utilization will facilitate the move from short-term emergency programs to longer-term reintegration programs that are sustainable over time and that facilitate the transition from post-conflict economic reconstruction to normal development.

One of the conditions for successful reconstruction of a country is the DDR of former combatants, including all militia groups. This involves their cantonment, the storage, custody, and disposal of their arms, and the provision of short-term emergency programs to satisfy their immediate needs in terms of food, documentation, housing, tools, and training. In addition to former combatants, emergency and longer-term reintegration programs will also need to include returnees, internally displaced persons, and other groups marginalized during the years of conflict.

Disarmament and demobilization of former combatants is critical since these groups are those more used to violence and therefore more likely to resort to banditry or to take up arms if promises to them are not kept. Post-Sandinista Nicaragua in the early 1990s and Angola a few years later were relevant in this regard. The recent experience of Lebanon is painfully conclusive in that countries that do not succeed at disarming their militia groups are likely to go back to war. In Lebanon, failure to disarm and demobilize Hezbollah largely reversed the gains from fifteen years of economic reconstruction after the civil war in the 1980s.[2]

In designing the strategy for DDR it should be kept in mind that, as Salomons (2005: 19–20) points out, disarming represents the decisive moment for any peacebuilding process. When combatants have to give up their arms, they face a point of no return. They, and their leaders, must have faith in a future where the advantages of peace for better living conditions outweigh those of war. As Salomon also notes, supporting a demilitarization process is not just a technical military issue. It is a complex operation, which has political, security, humanitarian, and economic dimensions. It requires the resolve and perseverance of the national leaders and the international community to carry it out effectively.

Because disarmament is a point of no return, former combatants are likely to cheat and keep some of their arsenals outside the verification process, and this is likely to put severe pressure on the peace process, as it did with the missiles that the Salvadoran FMLN kept in Nicaragua. Thus, the UN (or any other organization doing the verification) needs to have adequate resources to ensure proper disarmament. Spear (2002: 157), for example, attributes the large cheating by UNITA in the implementation of the Bicesse Accords in Angola to UN logistical and technical problems which allowed UNITA to return to war in a relatively stronger position.

No peace process has ever succeeded without the reintegration of former combatants, as well as other groups affected by the conflict, taking place in an effective manner. This is because effective reintegration promotes security by limiting the incentives to these groups to act as spoilers. Reintegration, however, is the longest and one of the most expensive reconstruction activities. As the IPA (2002d) notes, reintegration is typically neglected, as major donors shy away from open-ended commitments to the costly social and economic programs that are often essential for sustainable peace. Donors should consider that, without effective reintegration, their military and security expenditure to keep the peace may be significantly higher.

The UNDP and several of the UN agencies support UN efforts at DDR of former combatants and other groups. This process is critical in supporting national reconciliation and the promotion of peace. In December 2006, the UN launched new Integrated Disarmament, Demobilization, and Reintegration Standards, acknowledging the difficulty of transforming individuals scarred by conflict into productive members of their societies. In order to facilitate the transition, the Standards call for measures to provide psychosocial counseling, job training, educational opportunities, and mechanisms to promote reconciliation in the communities to which those individuals return.[3]

Short-term emergency and training programs

Governments need to establish short-term emergency programs as soon as possible with the assistance of the international community. Humanitarian assistance should target the former combatants, groups displaced by the conflict, and returning refugees, as well as other victims of the conflict. Refugee repatriation and the relocation of displaced populations are critical in peace consolidation. Any strategy for post-conflict reconstruction needs to include plans and sources of finance for this process.

The government—or the international community in cases where the government is still not in place or too weak—need to provide relief and humanitarian assistance in the immediate post-conflict period. This includes basic food and health services, temporary housing, potable water and sanitation, logistics, and other basic services to vulnerable groups. They also need to provide psychological, social, and medical support programs for people emotionally affected by the conflict, including women, children, and people with physical disabilities.[4]

As the war winds down, it is necessary to rush relief supplies to points where people need them the most. For this, it is essential to start the planning and logistics as soon as feasible. As I argued earlier, emergency programs do create serious distortions and need to wither as soon as feasible. Thus, for the emergency phase to be successful, relief workers would ideally leave the country after the crisis is over, having built up basic local initiatives and capabilities that would allow local people to carry out the next stages of rehabilitation and reconstruction. This will not happen in countries at a very low level of development, where capabilities are limited and there is a huge resource gap. In those countries, the international community should be prepared to be fully involved in the country long after the emergency phase is over. Nevertheless, emergency programs should be restricted to as short a period as possible.

Despite the urgency of establishing a number of programs immediately, these need nevertheless to have a medium-term framework from the very beginning. Thus, emergency programs should be as much as possible a first step in long-term reintegration of targeted groups. A good strategy and advance planning are necessary for such programs since otherwise, the urgency of establishing them for humanitarian reasons, and to ensure the ceasefire, often operates against their longer-term relevance and program sustainability. This is particularly true of programs in education, skill- and job-training, and other capacity building activities that cannot be restricted to the emergency phase only.[5]

Lessons from Mozambique, El Salvador, Guatemala, and many other countries are conclusive in this respect: short-term reintegration programs served an important purpose in providing demobilizing soldiers with a means of survival and an alternative to banditry that indeed helped maintain the ceasefire. However, these short-term programs lacked planning, coordination, and synchronization with demobilization dates. As a result, people used short-term programs for economic gain rather than as a first step in the process of developing a viable, longer-term professional occupation. For example, many of the beneficiaries of the land program in El Salvador had not participated in training programs in agricultural production, while many that had were not entitled to the land program. This made longer-term reconstruction particularly challenging and expensive and failed to ensure its sustainability.

Medium- and long-term reintegration programs

Building on the short-term emergency and training programs, medium- and long-term programs should aim at ensuring proper reintegration of former combatants, their supporters, returnees, and other such groups into society. Policymakers should design this strategy carefully and as well-integrated as possible to the emergency one. It is important that the strategy have enough financial and technical support at each stage, to make reintegration sustainable over time, since it has proved a *sine qua non* for peace consolidation. If the strategy fails, former combatants and other groups that were closely involved with the war may go back to arms in order to secure their livelihoods. Even if this does not derail the peace process, it will be responsible for the great public insecurity that has characterized many post-conflict situations from El Salvador to Afghanistan.

If policymakers want a consistent and effective strategy for reintegration, they will need to have an overall integrated strategy to ensure good planning of the various programs. Having the whole picture would allow policymakers to react to rapidly changing circumstances. This is clearly preferable to having donors or different local and international organizations carry out and finance programs separately. This would be a problem for effective policymaking.

There can be different avenues for reintegration. Reintegration often takes place through the agricultural sector, micro-enterprises, fellowships for technical and university training, and even through the incorporation of former combatants into new police forces, the national army, or political parties. Reintegration programs for the disabled are particularly important. These involve not only short-run emergency medical rehabilitation (including the provision of artificial limbs, hearing aids, wheelchairs, and specialized vehicles) but also programs to reintegrate as many as possible into the productive life of the country, with long-term financial support for those who are not able to support themselves because of their physical or psychological disabilities.

Reintegration programs also have to address the needs of other vulnerable groups, including children, women, and the elderly. Child soldiers and other children suffering from the devastating impact of war or other disasters require a wide variety of special services relating to health, education, training, and rehabilitation. Policies should foster the reinstitution of family life, after years of conflict during which families often drift apart. Particular attention is necessary to women who need to redefine their positions in society. Women are often empowered by the war and see their roles and responsibilities redefined at the time of peace. In such circumstances, women are especially vulnerable and require support in terms of social services, access to credit, training, education, and technical assistance. Returnees and displaced people also have particular needs that governments need to contemplate in designing the reintegration programs. For example, children may not have attended school while they were refugees or internally displaced. In addition, it is common that somebody else may have taken over their family house while they were away.

It is important to analyze carefully the viability of implementation and the financing implications of different options before deciding on a particular channel for reintegration. Policymakers also need to look at reintegration programs in an integrated manner. The Salvadoran land-for-arms program is illustrative, not only of how the lack of integration can affect reintegration, but also of the need to explore different avenues. The lesson was that providing credit for the purchase of land was not sufficient. Unless governments and the international community provide training, technical assistance, and credit for both housing and agricultural production that is well coordinated, reintegration will not succeed or be sustainable. The lack of integration of these programs drove many recipients of the arms-for-land program away from their land and greatly increased urban insecurity. In retrospect, given Salvadoran entrepreneurial abilities and land shortages, other avenues of reintegration could have been perhaps more effective.[6]

Reintegration is the most complex, challenging, expensive, and longer-term activity relating to post-conflict reconstruction and the one in which the political and economic objectives of reconstruction are so intertwined for national reconciliation. The success of reintegration programs is often dependent on economic recovery and foreign financing. Reintegration becomes particularly difficult in stagnant economies and in countries undergoing necessary but rigorous economic stabilization and structural reforms programs. This is so because the financial implications of peace-related programs are often in conflict with the objectives of economic stabilization. For this reason, the design and implementation of stabilization programs require flexibility and pragmatism. Successful reintegration is often dependent on governments making difficult political and financial decisions to solve critical problems relating to property rights, lack of credit, housing, and technical assistance.

For reintegration programs to serve their purpose, people need to perceive them as fair. Both in Nicaragua and in Angola, reintegration programs contemplated better treatment of Contra guerrillas and former UNITA combatants than government troops. This obviously created serious resentment. Thus, reintegration programs failed to be peace-supporting, as they should be.[7]

In Sierra Leone, considered a basket case before May 2000, post-conflict economic reconstruction is proceeding reasonably well with the strong support of the international community, in part because of the strong effort at DDR of the various groups. Although now the big challenge is creating sustainable employment for the population at large, particularly the young one, DDR programs had an important impact in stabilizing security conditions.[8] The success of post-conflict economic reconstruction in countries such as El Salvador, Mozambique, and Uganda, for example, is also associated with the priority they gave to DDR. By contrast, in Kosovo, a large part of the Kosovo Liberation Army (KLA) remained united and under the same leadership, which is a potential source for trouble.

It is for all these compelling reasons that any strategy for post-conflict economic reconstruction should include a well-designed, consistent, fair, and well-financed DDR program. The success of reconstruction will depend on the dedication and continuity with which governments implement this program over time. The UN, its agencies, the World Bank, and other humanitarian and development organizations should work together with bilateral development agencies and NGOs in supporting governments and financing their DDR strategies.

PRIVATE-SECTOR INVOLVEMENT

In developing a post-conflict reconstruction strategy, it is important to keep in mind that support for micro- and small-sized enterprises (MSEs) should be a priority of any government in post-conflict situations. The creation of private-sector jobs is essential for effective long-term reintegration since most countries start from a very weak fiscal situation that does not allow them to create public-sector jobs, which donors are reluctant to finance.

One of the main challenges for countries in post-conflict situations—not unlike those in post-financial or natural disaster crises—is how to pass from emergency programs, which often enjoy strong financial and technical support, to the post-emergency phase in which external support will drop sharply to more normal levels. During the latter, employment and services created cannot become recurrent expenditures of the government, simply because there will not be financing for budgetary support of the magnitude available during the emergency. That is why the establishment of long-term reintegration programs is so challenging. Although these programs will need financial support from the reconstruction aid budget, they will eventually have to become self-sustaining. Furthermore, the challenge of involving the private sector in these post-emergency situations should not be underestimated and policymakers need to address it head-on. MSEs can be an important source of employment and the creation of employment is a *sine qua non* for national reconciliation and peace consolidation.

The private sector should be involved early on in the transition but security and political considerations often make it practically impossible. Furthermore, the government needs to create an adequate—and as simple and flexible as possible—macroeconomic framework, as well as an institutional, legal, and regulatory one, that would support the private sector to develop competitiveness in certain areas, so that they will be able to create jobs and exports. The macroeconomic and microeconomic framework needed to support the private sector will be discussed in more detail in Chapters 14 and 15.

OTHER ISSUES RELEVANT TO THE DESIGN OF A REINTEGRATION STRATEGY

In designing specific projects, national policymakers and those supporting them should keep in mind a number of factors that can affect the transition to peace, as well as those that affect the chances of moving the country onto a path of normal development. The strategy for reconstruction should balance these two factors, which may work in different directions.

In 1947 Dulles (1993) argued that it would be a waste of money merely to feed the Europeans for a year or two and not give them the tools, fertilizer, and fuel without which they would have little chance of righting their own (post-war) economies. He believed that what they did in the first year of the Plan was going to be decisive. The same applies to present day experiences, and policymakers should design specific projects with this in mind.

Food aid

Countries in the war-to-peace transition are likely to rely on food aid for some time. The UN, mainly through the World Food Program (WFP), has significant experience in providing it. Food aid is particularly important to countries that have lost their capacity to produce or acquire food because of war or natural disaster, or to those in which war has uprooted, internally displaced, or forced to seek refuge elsewhere a significant proportion of the population.

However, food aid, as all types of aid, can create dependence and distortions and policymakers need to analyze them carefully as the transition proceeds. To avoid such dependency, policymakers need to plan for the phasing out of food aid. By affecting local prices, aid often interferes with or distorts domestic food production. The transition from food aid to reliance on domestic production must be encouraged through the provision of essential inputs such as seeds, fertilizers, and pesticides. Donors can initially provide these goods in kind or can provide budgetary support to the government so that it can subsidize them.[9] Technical assistance and credit are essential elements in this transition. The UN system—mainly through the Food and Agriculture Organization (FAO) and the International Fund for Agricultural Development (IFAD)— with NGOs and bilateral donors can play an important role in providing or facilitating both.

Fuel

Fuel is a basic humanitarian necessity. Although there are no special UN agencies that can provide such a service, the UN Joint Logistics Centre (UNJLC), an interagency mechanism led by the World Food Program, supports humanitarian actors in this area. Various aspects, from the production of crude, to the transportation through oil pipes, to the refinery of gasoline, to the distribution and allocation, are often the target of sabotage attacks that can be a serious deterrent to humanitarian assistance and economic reconstruction. The local and foreign population will use fuel for various activities including cooking, the distribution of food, running a heating system, in all types of production and transportation, and many others.

Fuel demand will increase in post-conflict situations, not only because of the reactivation of growth but also in relation to the expatriate civilian and military presence in the country. This is what happened in large operations such as those in Kosovo and during the occupation of Iraq. As they plan the strategy, policymakers need to make a careful and realistic assessment of the needs.

Policymakers need also to be concerned about increasing supply. Just as with food, the issue of fuel has both humanitarian and reconstruction objectives that often conflict with each other. On the one hand, subsidies to oil and oil products, which often mitigate the hardship of post-conflict situations, will create distortions by delaying and discouraging production and refining of oil products. The phasing out of subsidies will be politically difficult, and should be done gradually and at the right time, so as not to have a large humanitarian impact on the population at large, which could backfire politically.

Conflict causes environmental damage, often through deforestation or through attacks on refineries, power plants, or other such infrastructure. Thus, after an assessment of initial conditions, those drawing up the strategy for reconstruction will need to contemplate plans for reversing or cleaning up of environmental damage. The United Nations Environmental Programme (UNEP) is the UN body on which to rely both for assessments as well as for support in dealing with the problem. For example, when Israeli air raids hit the Jiyyeh thermal power plant south of Beirut in the July 2006 conflict in Lebanon, an estimated 10,000 to 30,000 tonnes of fuel oil spilt into the Mediterranean Sea. UNEP sent a team of international experts to deal with this problem as well as to assess pollution risks to drinking water, sewage treatment, and hospital facility sites.[10]

Demining

The removal of mines is frequently a prerequisite for many reintegration activities. It is a very costly operation and it can involve environmental considerations, since it is often necessary to burn large stretches of forest or fields to remove mines. Mines are not only a danger to the population, but can also seriously impede agricultural production and endanger cattle.

According to the Humanitarian Demining Program Office of the US Army, the challenge of demining is related to the fact that those that use landmines bury them at different depths, in different soils, and in different terrains. In addition, there are over 600 types, models, and varieties. These are composed of different materials, contain different explosives, different components, and sometimes unique anti-tampering or triggering devices.[11]

Demining primarily includes the detection, clearance, and neutralization of mines. Other activities necessary to support demining include increasing mine awareness in the population and advising governments accordingly, and training soldiers, former combatants, and others in mine removal. There are few alternatives for demining. El Salvador, for example, used private companies that relied on former combatants (from both the military and the guerrilla groups) for guidance in locating the mines. In Nicaragua, on the other hand, demining took place under the auspices of the Organization of American States (OAS). The UN Mine Action Services (UNMAS) has field programs in Afghanistan, Democratic Republic of Congo (DRC), Burundi, Ethiopia, and elsewhere, where it works with governments, NGOs, commercial companies, and donors.[12]

DESIGNING THE REINTEGRATION STRATEGY

Since the Salvadoran experience with reintegration is by most accounts one of the most successful in the post-Cold War period, three lessons from this experience are worth considering in designing the strategy for reintegration.

Target the "right" avenue

The need to target the right avenue for reintegration is imperative given the scarce resources—both human and financial—in post-conflict situations. Targeting land was the wrong decision given the scarcity of land; the difficulties in financing land purchases (because of donor restrictions); the existing tenure and property rights problems and the likelihood that they would give rise to a variety of legal difficulties in transferring land. Furthermore, in spite of their rural origin, many former combatants were not naturally inclined toward farming. Given the renowned inventiveness and entrepreneurial capacity of the Salvadoran people, programs for MSEs should have been much larger. In developing the reconstruction strategy, policymakers will need to analyze carefully the factors—both positive and negative—that can have an impact on the different options. They should consider both the viability of implementation and the financing implications of different options before deciding on a particular channel for reintegration.

"Preferential" treatment becomes more difficult as time goes by

In designing the strategy, policymakers should remember that it is more politically expedient to target groups directly affected by the war for preferential treatment right after the ceasefire agreement than at any later point in time. As the economic reintegration process proceeds, it often becomes more difficult to justify adopting preferential treatment for these groups, when there are others in similar conditions of poverty and need, violating thus the "equity principle" of development.

It is important for governments to understand so and realize that it is politically better to comply with peace agreements as soon as possible. It is also important for targeted groups to realize that, as time goes by, they are likely to receive less rather than more. Moreover, leaders who negotiated peace will change and their successors may not be as committed to the peace process as those that were involved in the negotiations.

In El Salvador, President Cristiani signed the peace agreements and was committed to their implementation. President Calderón Sol, though openly supportive of the peace agreements, made social development the top priority in his agenda; as such, it was more difficult for him to discriminate among groups, particularly since poverty was widespread. Because of this, remaining problems of implementing the land and other reintegration programs, including human settlements, in El Salvador became more difficult to solve with time. The policy of the FMLN of postponing certain decisions with the expectation that further efforts at negotiation would yield better results was—in retrospect—misguided.

Integrate programs to ensure success and viability

In designing the reintegration strategy, policymakers need to integrate programs if they want the strategy to be successful and sustainable. Providing credit for reintegration through the purchase of land or the establishment of MSEs is not sufficient. Unless governments and the international community that supports them provide well-coordinated training, technical assistance, and credit, reintegration will not succeed or be sustainable. Medium-term programs in El Salvador proved to be inadequate in terms of their scope and breadth. Most beneficiaries of the arms-for-land program lacked agricultural experience and were entitled to very small plots. The agricultural credit and technical assistance available only allowed beneficiaries to produce basic grains for subsistence, which was clearly insufficient to allow them to repay their debts. In addition to the fact that many lacked houses, this led them to abandon the land.

Thus, policymakers need to complement medium-term reintegration programs with adequate credit and technical assistance facilities to ensure their success and long-term viability. Unless production becomes profitable, those who received loans for reintegration projects might end up worse off than they were before: in the past they did not have an asset (for example, land, truck, house, or micro-enterprise) but they had no debts; after reintegration programs are finalized they will have an asset but they will also be indebted. Unless they service their debt, they will soon be ineligible for any further credit, making future production difficult. The international community should play a crucial role in providing adequate credit and particularly technical assistance in support of medium-term programs.

Rehabilitation of basic services and infrastructure

It is vital that in the early transition from war there be a rapid improvement in the wellbeing of the population through the restoration of basic services and infrastructure. Signing of a peace agreement or other settlement to the conflict should not only bring the prospect of a ceasefire, elections, or freedom of the press, but should bring also a quick improvement in the living conditions of the population. Infrastructure is also critical in reactivating economic activity. Almost every productive sector needs transport, energy, and water and sewerage to function, and thus, infrastructure destruction in these areas is a serious threat to growth reactivation in the early stages of the transition.[13]

Policymakers should look at the rehabilitation of infrastructure and basic services as a source of short-term employment for local firms and workers. Both by its potential to improve living conditions and by creating employment, rehabilitation of infrastructure and services will help to consolidate peace. On the other hand, if electricity, fuel, water, communications, and other basic services and infrastructure do not improve, or if foreign contractors get a large proportion of the jobs created as in Iraq, the population will resent it and the security situation will deteriorate.

Rehabilitation and reintegration of former combatants, returnees, and other war-affected groups are intricately linked and both essential to peace consolidation. The provision of basic infrastructure will facilitate the reactivation of productive activities in the private sector. This in turn will promote longer-term employment, which will facilitate reintegration.

Short-run rehabilitation will often take place across a wide variety of areas. Short-term rehabilitation includes the restoration of power generation and other basic infrastructure such as the repair of roads, bridges, and railroads; the improvement of housing[14] and infrastructure for education and health services (schools, health clinics, hospitals); the collection of garbage and the provision of safe water and adequate sanitation to the largest number of people possible. The last three programs should jointly be geared towards reducing the burden on overextended health services, as wars, sanctions, and other disasters often cause epidemics and diseases as well as physical and psychological disabilities that require specific drugs, nutrition, and medical treatment.

Short-run rehabilitation in these areas is often a prerequisite for the resumption of productive activities. In the early phase, many post-conflict countries' best chance to resume productive activities is through the reactivation of agricultural production. The rehabilitation of roads, bridges, and railroads will support it. The rehabilitation of the infrastructure for exports, which will also include airports and ports, is important so that the countries can increase their export capacity and access to foreign exchange as soon as possible.

At the same time, policymakers should look at rehabilitation programs as a way of creating employment for the local population. Rehabilitation should encompass labor-intensive community projects that can utilize former combatants as they disarm and demobilize until they can find longer-term productive jobs in the private sector. These programs can be important in helping to maintain a ceasefire and avoiding the high delinquency rate that can result if former combatants are idle right after demobilization. In putting together former combatants, ethnic groups or other enemies, quick-impact and rehabilitation projects are often confidence building and contribute to national reconciliation.

Quick-impact and longer-term rehabilitation programs should minimize the use of foreign contractors. As discussed earlier, the presence of a large number of foreign workers creates a number of distortions by increasing the demand for housing and services, as well as by the higher cost of security to protect such workers. This results in an ineffective use of aid resources and a diminished capacity to create local employment. In cases where rehabilitation necessarily requires foreign expertise, there should be quotas for expatriates, say 25 percent of the total workers employed. At the same time, this would contribute to capacity building of the local labor force. The experiences of Iraq and Afghanistan, as well as those of Kosovo and Timor-Leste, are illustrative of the distortions created by the large presence of the international community, and the need to utilize aid flows to improve productive employment of the local population. These experiences are also illustrative of how lack of progress in these areas is likely to be a great obstacle to national reconciliation and to worsen security conditions.

In the area of rehabilitation of infrastructure, the UN system has a strong institutional capacity to help countries, mainly through the UNDP, ILO, WHO, UNICEF, DHA, UNHCR, FAO, and UNESCO (see List of Abbreviations). If well coordinated and financed, and in collaboration with the World Bank, the regional development banks, bilateral donors, and NGOs, the UN agencies can play a major assistance role in this area. Whenever financing is available, countries can also resort to private companies—both local and foreign—to solve their immediate and longer-term rehabilitation needs.

During the war, countries' infrastructure suffers to very different degrees. In addition, many countries have also suffered from the lack of investment, even before the war. This was certainly the case with Kosovo, Afghanistan, and Iraq. Deterioration may also occur in the immediate transition from war. In Iraq, for example, although damage to infrastructure was limited during the

US military intervention itself, looting, insurgent attacks, and sabotage have been recurrent since, and have undermined efforts to rebuild the economy. Although export revenues have been larger than anticipated due to the high price of oil, attacks on oil pipelines and other infrastructure have prevented Iraq from reaching targeted export volumes.

The reactivation of productive activities should by no means be restricted to the increase in exports, to the detriment of more labor-intensive domestic production. All countries in reconstruction, however, have to reactivate exports, since this will eventually have to become their main source of foreign exchange, as aid withers after a few years in the transition. This is particularly imperative in resource-rich countries that have to foot a larger part of their reconstruction bill. For this reason, the rehabilitation of infrastructure related to the export sector may be even more urgent in these countries.

DIFFERENT ACTORS IN REHABILITATION OF INFRASTRUCTURE

The role of the government

National governments (including the central government, local governments, and state-owned enterprises, SOEs) can finance infrastructure utilizing public sector resources (including the central government budget and those of local governments and SOEs). Governments of countries in post-conflict situations, however, are generally not in a position to finance infrastructure from their own resources, at least in the immediate transition to peace. This is true in general, even in resource-rich countries. Those governments will need to rehabilitate the infrastructure related to the natural resources that are abundant in their countries, together with the transportation, storage, ports, and airports needed for the country to export. Only then, will governments have resources to invest in other things.

Governments, however, have a critical role to play at this early stage. First, security is a prerequisite for the rehabilitation of infrastructure. Rehabilitation in insecure areas will be difficult, as has been amply demonstrated in the recent experience with reconstruction in Afghanistan and Iraq. Second, governments will need to set up the basic institutional, legal, administrative, and regulatory framework for infrastructure. Donors will not be willing to finance, nor investors be willing to invest, without such a framework.

The role of donors

Because of the weak fiscal situation of countries coming out of war, and the fact that reactivation of the economy is dependent on basic infrastructure, rehabilitation is one of the areas which donors are more likely to support during reconstruction. Assistance is normally of two types. As part of their humanitarian assistance, donors either finance or repair basic infrastructure and services. Expatriate experts often get involved in short-term rehabilitation. This does not create local employment and, at the same time, the international presence creates distortions. For both reasons, this has to be only a short-term phenomenon. Longer-term, donors should target reconstruction funds and technical assistance to improve the infrastructure the country needs, to provide basic services to the population at large, and to restore production and trade.

Public–private partnerships

As it was clear from the case studies, financing—from both the government and donors—is often inadequate for the large investment needs of countries in post-conflict situations. Thus, governments have to explore different alternatives to finance public sector infrastructure. Under normal conditions, private investors finance infrastructure, through either equity or debt issuing. In post-conflict situations, however, private investors hardly ever get involved, unless it is in partnership or with guarantees from the government or donors. In between the options of fully publicly financed infrastructure and fully privately financed ones, there is a variety of mixed public–private partnerships (PPPs). PPPs include a number of innovative financing techniques, which are partly off-budget, that is, that do not affect the public sector finances.[15] PPPs tend to reduce the fiscal implications of the investment or at least defer its impact, which is something that post-conflict governments could welcome. Although PPPs may not really be an option for the early transition, governments should definitely explore and debate them, particularly for the time when donors' financing starts dropping. Financing normally peaks two to three years after the end of the war and falls sharply thereafter.

Each country will have different needs and constraints, and both the international financial institutions (IFIs) and many of the bilateral ones will advise them to privatize their SOEs. For this reason, policymakers need to investigate and analyze innovative practices used by other countries—successfully and otherwise—in financing infrastructure in the critical sectors, particularly transportation and energy sectors which require large investments. These include different types of public sector concessions to the private sector, including leasing, which do not necessarily require the sale of public assets. Other options include asset-backed securitization, where short-term financing has claims on long-term resources such as exports, or mechanisms to postpone the fiscal cost of the investment, as Mexico used following its 1994 financial crisis. There are many other options, including schemes through which the IFIs, including the regional development banks, provide guarantees and assume some of the longer-term risks of investing in public infrastructure.[16]

As discussed in relation to the case studies, privatization may not be a viable or recommended option for post-conflict countries, either because of the political implications of selling "the crown jewels" or because of lack of legitimacy in the existing political framework that creates uncertainty about property rights that would discourage potential investors. Other options may be politically and economically preferable and governments should consider all the options.

Rules for national reconciliation

Despite some inter-state wars, most conflicts in the post-Cold War period took place within nations. This means that after the war was over, people had to continue living with each other. This is why national reconciliation is so important following intra-state wars. The activities I have been discussing, both in the area of reintegration of former combatants and other war-affected groups, as well as in the rehabilitation of services and infrastructure are critical in national reconciliation. Most countries that have gone back to war did so because they failed to carry out these activities in a methodical, consistent, effective, fair, and sustainable way.

The political transition is important to national reconciliation but there are also practical conditions that need to be satisfied. The large number of returnees, displaced people, former combatants (including child soldiers), and other groups affected by the war need houses to come back to. In their houses, they need food, water, and electricity. They also need jobs that allow them to reintegrate into the productive activities of the country and they need transport to get there. All these things are necessary but, in post-conflict situations, they may not be sufficient.

As Ambassador Mota Sardenberg of Brazil pointed out in an *Open Debate on Post-Conflict National Reconciliation: The Role of the UN*,[17] reconciliation efforts are compromised when the legacy of past violence is left unaddressed. To build long-lasting peace, national reconciliation is the most effective way for divided societies to confront threats to their stability, and to promote durable peace as well as viable democratic institutions and practices.

One thing the UN cannot do—or anybody else for that matter—is to impose reconciliation.[18] The different parties to the conflict need to be ready to reconcile. Where that is the case, governments in post-conflict situations have a critical role to play: reconciliation requires that governments respect the diversity of their people and rule by taking into account the needs and rights of all rather than particular groups. It also requires that governments build up the institutional framework to ensure that future grievances—rather than resulting in conflict as in the past—are addressed through peaceful means and that impunity be no longer tolerated. Such a framework often includes the creation of civil society organizations, a national ombudsman, a human rights prosecutor, and a Commission on the Truth. The latter would examine the most notorious cases of violence and human rights violations. This is important as a catharsis but also to draw recommendations to ensure that such actions will not happen again.

The catharsis of past atrocities is necessary but not sufficient. In many cases people demand and are entitled to compensation. In all cases, governments will need to attend to the needs of those most affected by the conflict and should be concerned about the future distributional impact of their policies. Poverty and social needs are high during post-conflict reconstruction. Thus, to give preferential treatment to some groups to the exclusion of others will often violate the ethics principle of normal development, where you attend to all those in need equally. Governments in post-conflict transitions need to be prepared to violate this principle in the short-run for the purpose of national reconciliation, and the sooner they do it in the transition, the better.

14 Macroeconomic policymaking

Before I discuss policymaking in the macroeconomic area, it is important to keep in mind that the ongoing economic policy debate at a specific time has affected economic reconstruction in countries coming out of war, from the Marshall Plan to the post-Cold War experiences. This debate has naturally influenced the way sovereign governments and the international community plan for reconstruction and has been a major determinant of the international assistance and the conditionality imposed by donors. Policymakers need to be aware of the general policy debate in setting their own strategy for economic reconstruction. They also need to consider the particular policy constraints in countries in a post-conflict situation. Together these factors will determine government choices for policymaking in the macroeconomic and microeconomic areas, the institutional arrangements the country needs to support it, the policy mix they will favor, and the particular role for the state and the markets in economic reconstruction.

The economic policy debate

A CONSTANTLY SHIFTING DEBATE

Following the Great Depression of the 1930s, economists and policymakers profusely debated the role of the state in economic growth. As Stern (1997: 143) points out, in the Keynesian era, a consensus on "big government" emerged in economic policymaking in industrial countries, and was extended to the developing countries. On the macroeconomic front, by focusing on fiscal policy, the government would control aggregate demand, to secure full employment and inflation, although the latter was not the primary goal. The balance of payments was a constraint that policymakers could handle, if necessary, through exchange rate devaluation and controls. On the microeconomic front, governments had sole responsibility for infrastructure—that is both important and a natural monopoly. Government also had the responsibility for promoting or protecting strategic sectors and correcting or regulating market failures such as the establishment or abuse of monopoly power.

The government had social responsibilities as well, particularly over income distribution. In this regard, the government was the provider of social security in the form of pensions, unemployment insurance, health, and a safety net for the most vulnerable groups outside the social security system. In industrial countries, fulfilling these responsibilities resulted in high expenditures and high taxes. In developing countries, the responsibilities of the government were even larger because the market was too weak and inefficient to channel investment and output in critical areas. These countries often failed to raise the taxes they needed to finance a large government and ended up highly indebted, both to domestic and foreign creditors.

Stern attributed the weakening in this consensus to the oil shocks of the 1970s. The two oil price shocks of 1973 and 1979 provided evidence of the inappropriateness of addressing supply shocks with demand tools. Stagflation in industrial countries undermined confidence in the unemployment– inflation tradeoff and the focus of the debate shifted towards understanding how to fight inflation and structural unemployment.

In 2006, the Nobel Committee granted the Economics Prize to Edmund S. Phelps, in recognition of work done mostly in the 1970s analyzing the relationship between inflation and unemployment, and the impact of expectations. Since the latter change over time, so does the relationship between inflation and unemployment. Stiglitz (2006b), a Nobel Laureate himself and Phelps's colleague at Columbia University, pointed out that Phelps's analysis has led some policymakers to conclude that they cannot lower the natural rate of unemployment (consistent with stable inflation) without ever-increasing inflation. The policy implication of such a conclusion is to focus on price stability by targeting the rate of unemployment that is consistent with zero inflation growth. As Phelps has shown, the problem with this conclusion is that such a rate of unemployment changes, since governments are able to implement a number of structural reforms to bring it down. The other policy implication, as Stiglitz also noted, is that adopted by most central bankers, namely to make low inflation the central bank's only objective. This may have a negative impact on investment, growth, and employment and it can inhibit policy measures for "social inclusion" (another of Phelps's important contributions, as discussed in Chapter 15).

In the 1970s and 1980s, the Union of Socialist Soviet Republics (USSR) and many developing countries followed statist economic policies in which the state participated heavily in the economy, not only as regulator but also in production and trade. At the end of the 1980s, with the fall of the Berlin Wall, the pendulum tilted away from state participation and over-regulated economies. These had a mixed record at best and resulted in inefficient and bloated bureaucracies and industries, which were uncompetitive internationally and had a negative impact on national budgets. In this process of critical evaluation, the pendulum rapidly shifted towards the other end: a liberal and lightly regulated trade and investment framework with a small government where pro-market policies guided economic policymaking. The "neo-liberal" or "Washington-consensus" was the model of liberalization, privatization, private-sector led investment, and sound monetary and fiscal policies of the 1990s. The US Treasury, the IMF, and the World Bank adhered to this model and were among its strongest supporters.

Interestingly, although many argue that this model was "imposed" by the international financial institutions (IFIs) on developing and transition economies, Vietnam adopted it independently of these institutions since the IFIs did not get involved in the country until 1993. After failed attempts at economic reconstruction through central planning following the end of the war in 1975, Vietnam followed a piecemeal approach to socialist reforms starting in 1986. This included an effort to reactivate agriculture but neglected to address the strong distortions in the economy. As the economy continued with large disequilibria (high inflation, low growth and large fiscal and external deficits), and as aid from the Soviet Union and preferential trade agreements with the Council of Mutual Economic Assistance (CMEA) area collapsed with the fall of the Berlin Wall, Vietnam adopted "Doi Moi" (renovation) reforms in 1989. These included bold and comprehensive land reform, price liberalization, tax reform, public enterprise restructuring, modernization of the financial sector, and freer trade.

By 1991, the *World Development Report* of the World Bank already noted the gradual formation of a consensus in favor of a "market-friendly" approach to development. Despite such a consensus, there were, nevertheless, great controversies—both at the academic and policymaking levels. These focused on the policies to be adopted (fixed versus flexible exchange rates, the fiscal–monetary mix) and over the trade and investment strategies to be used (the degree of government intervention, the advantages of liberalization versus managed trade, the role of foreign investment, the need for privatization and deregulation). There was controversy as well over the nature of the necessary institutional frameworks (legal, judicial, fiscal) and over the breadth, speed and sequence of the necessary reforms. The broad consensus of the 1990s started to wither, however, as expected results did not always materialize, and income disparities increased. It has suffered a serious backlash since then.[1]

Over-reliance on market forces and a diminished role for the state in the provision of services had worsened income distribution and resulted in social hardship for a large part of the population in many countries. This was most notorious in countries in transition from the former socialist soviet republics and those experiencing financial crises in emerging parts of the world. The latter often took place in economies that had relied more heavily on dollar-denominated market instruments in international capital markets to finance their public-sector borrowing requirements. As risk factors shifted against these countries, leading to a quick reversal of capital flows, governments found it difficult to finance the social and physical infrastructure and other basic needs of the population. In both cases and with few exceptions, widespread privatization of state-owned enterprises had taken place, often leading to corruption, high-cost services, high unemployment, and other inefficiencies.[2]

Only seven years later, a "Post-Washington Consensus" had emerged at the World Bank, led by Chief Economist Joseph Stiglitz. Stiglitz (1998) argued that making markets work required more than low inflation. It required a sound financial system,[3] an adequate regulatory and competitive framework and policies to facilitate the transfer of technology, transparency, and other factors neglected by the Washington Consensus. It also required broadening the concept of development to include other goals, like sustainable development, egalitarian development, and democratic development—a vision that Boutros-Ghali (1995b) had advanced in his *An Agenda for Development*.

Elections at the turn of the new century were indicative of how the pendulum had shifted, this time towards a more central position, rather than the two previous extremes of "Statism" and "The Washington Consensus", with a marked preference for strong government in only some areas of the economy.[4] Although preferences have shifted towards a more active government, there is no longer a debate, however, on the importance of good macroeconomic management and the need for solid micro-foundations to support it, and create an environment conducive to investment and growth. Fiscal and monetary orthodoxy has largely prevailed among the newly elected leaders.

Because of this shift in the pendulum, the debate on whether the state should provide basic infrastructure and services, particularly to the most vulnerable sectors of the population, has a heavy tilt in favor of it. This often means other trade-offs, such as, for example, higher taxes on those in higher-income brackets. A country that wants to have the resources to provide basic infrastructure and services needs to have a solid fiscal system. Fiscal imbalances and a large public debt will force the government to allocate a large part of the budget to financing the deficit and servicing the debt. A good fiscal position, on the other hand, will allow the country to allocate financial and other resources to improving human capital and ensuring high living standards for the population.

A LACK OF DEBATE ON POST-CONFLICT ECONOMIC RECONSTRUCTION

Although academics, policymakers, and other practitioners have discussed economic policy issues ad nauseam, policy issues specifically relating to economic reconstruction still lack a broad-based and open international debate.

In the absence of such debate, reconstruction issues continue to be treated as "development as usual." Among the issues that need to be debated is the appropriateness for countries coming out of war to solve their arrears with the international financial institutions (IFIs), and restructure their debt with other creditors early on in the transition to peace. Debate needs also to take place with respect to the allocation of resources between present and future generations and the creation of resource funds; on the necessity of developing sophisticated institutional frameworks; on the need for independent central banks; and on the need to consolidate the financial accounts in a single national budget under government control. Other issues for debate include the choice of monetary and exchange rate policies and the choice of currency. The list should also include the tax and customs systems. The debate on these issues will differ from the debate on the same issues in countries in the normal process of development, simply because of the political and security constraints that characterize the transition to peace, and the necessity to carry out a number of extra activities for national reconciliation, which have real and financial consequences. Most importantly, policymaking in post-conflict transitions takes place under the great uncertainty and risk caused by an estimated fifty–fifty chance that the country will revert to war.

THE CHOICE BETWEEN THE MARKET AND THE STATE

As Robert Mundell (1968a: 63–5) points out,

A market is a mysterious thing. . . . There are many types of markets. . . . All markets have two sides, buyers and sellers. The buyers take goods off the market, the sellers put goods on the market. But every buyer is at the same time a seller, since his demand for a good is made effective by his offer of something else in exchange for it. By the same token, every seller is at the same time a buyer, since his offer of something to the market implies the demand for something in exchange. . . . In barter markets, where there is no common thing used as money, sellers have to spend a great deal of time looking for profitable exchanges. But this system of trade, which takes great skill, is a primitive one . . . and an inefficient way of matching demands and supplies; . . . Market price is determined by demand and supply. . . . Market equilibrium is established when demand equals supply; the price prevailing at this time is the equilibrium price. The equilibrium price is the price at which markets clear.

Efficient markets, however, are not a feature of post-conflict countries. This is because of the price and quantity distortions created by government controls, other interventions, and different market failures. Market failure refers to the inefficiencies created by the wrong product mix (too much of some good and too little of others); exchange inefficiencies (exchange could make everyone better off by allocating goods to those who would value them the most); and production inefficiencies (where the economy is producing below potential) (Stiglitz 1997: 64–6). Under such conditions, the choice between the market and the state becomes more difficult. Pointing to the market failures—particularly in developing countries—Stiglitz (2006: xiv) argued that "whenever information is imperfect, in particular when there are information asymmetries—where some individuals know something that others do not (in other words, *always*)—the reason that the invisible hand seems invisible is that it is not there. Without appropriate government regulation and intervention, markets do not lead to economic efficiency." Earlier, Stiglitz (1998) had argued that the issue was not whether the government should get involved but how. Thus, there are strong arguments for complementarity, rather than substitution, between government intervention and the markets. The appropriate level of intervention is something that governments will have to decide before designing the strategy for reconstruction.[5]

Governments can adopt many alternative policies and types of institutional framework. Even so, reform can go badly unless policymakers design policies that are consistent and well implemented. This is true in post-conflict situations and it is true even under normal development. Take the example of privatization. Chile, an early privatizer, went through two clear stages of privatization: the first one in 1974–9, was badly conceived and implemented, and had dire economic and social effects; in the later one in 1985–7, lessons had been learned, a number of things had been done differently, and the institutional framework had improved, with privatization yielding good results (del Castillo 1995b). Hence, we cannot say that privatization—or any other economic policy for that matter—is necessarily good or bad: much depends on how it is designed and under what conditions it is carried out. It depends as well on the government's ability to provide the right institutional framework and its political will to enforce the legal and regulatory system.

Furthermore, the sequence can be important. For example, it is necessary to have a legitimate government before adopting privatization. Otherwise, property rights uncertainty will make investment too risky and unattractive, as I discussed in the case studies on Kosovo and Iraq. In addition, policymakers should not adopt privatization and liberalization before they have established the rule of law institutions—including an appropriate regulatory system. This principle assumes that appropriate rule of law policies and institutions—covering contracts, bankruptcy, corporate governance, and competition—are necessary to minimize abuses.[6] If large private groups and strong politicians are able to transform public monopolies into private monopolies, the impact on the economy could be just as bad as it was in the presence of inefficient public monopolies before the privatization.

To improve the impact of privatization on income distribution, some Eastern European countries designed a system of vouchering among workers to give them a stake in the economy. According to Stiglitz (2001), this system, which dispersed shares widely in equity markets, required strong protection for investors to succeed. In his view, the Czech Republic, which pioneered this method, lacked such protection, with the result that a few people became wealthy and everyone else felt cheated. The same happened in other countries.

If governments in post-conflict countries decide to carry out privatization of their state-owned enterprises, they need to consider lessons from the experience of other countries to try to minimize all the problems associated with privatization. Furthermore, they should keep in mind that privatization is not always necessary, even for countries that want the market to play a larger role.[7]

With regard to economic policymaking, post-conflict countries—as well as those coming out of serious financial crises or natural disasters—have less flexibility, a sense of urgency and forgiveness for distortions, and large aid flows and intrusive involvement of the international community, that are largely lacking in the normal development process. Crises normally lead to emergencies that require short-run solutions to satisfy humanitarian needs and require giving preference to some groups to the detriment of others. Short-term solutions are not necessarily best if the objective is medium- and long-term sustainability. From an economic point of view, the specific challenge of reconstruction is to set the bases for a move from these inevitable and distortionary short-term measures, into longer-term policies that can eventually lead to fair and sustainable development, as well as fiscal and external sustainability. In this regard, it is relevant to remember Henry Hazlitt, the renowned US journalist who wrote *Economics in One Lesson* (Hazlitt 1946).[8] There he argued that the art of economics consists in looking not merely at the immediate but at the longer-term effects of any act or policy; it consists in tracing the consequences of that policy not merely for one group but for all groups. This is certainly the development maxim, but to get there, governments in post-conflict situations will have to break it by adopting distortionary short-term programs and giving preference to conflict-prone groups, to the exclusion of others. Without this, peace will not progress and there is a strong chance that the country will revert to war.

THE ECONOMIC POLICY MIX

The case studies in this book provide enough empirical evidence that policy choices are more restricted in countries coming out of conflict, who must reconcile the conflicting demands of peace and development. One of the critical decisions in any reconstruction strategy is the type of economy that policymakers want to build up. Without a "country vision" to guide policymaking—both in the macro- and microeconomic areas—and a clear strategy, government policies with regard to investment, production, and trade will be highly discretional and will lack cohesion, consistency, and transparency.

Despite a country vision and national ownership of the specific policy mix, policy formulation and macroeconomic management in post-conflict situations will be always constrained by donors' preferences. Preferences lead donors to finance one program and not others, or one group to the exclusion of another, although the rejected programs or groups may be critical in the peace process. Donors may also impose financing restrictions such as earmarking for specific types of programs or contracting their own companies and natural resources. This may create serious constraints on the implementation of the reconstruction strategy and policymakers will have to make contingency plans for it, including the use of inflationary finance in extreme cases.

In designing their own reconstruction strategy, policymakers should bear in mind that most donors would agree with Hazlitt that unsound fiscal and economic policies or widespread corruption in the government could make any outside help futile (Dulles 1993). In the current policy-mix debate, people rarely question any longer the need to have fiscal, monetary, and exchange rate stability as the medium- and long-term objective of economic reconstruction. Macroeconomic stability, however, is a necessary but not a sufficient condition for investment and growth. An appropriate business climate to ensure international competitiveness is important in establishing the right policy mix, particularly in countries undergoing post-conflict economic reconstruction.

In the short run, policy efforts should focus on providing the necessary infrastructure and basic services. Financial assistance from international organizations, bilateral donors, and NGOs to do so is essential since government resources—both human and financial—are likely to be scarce in post-conflict transitions. Furthermore, owing to the high risk of these transitions, private-sector involvement will not be readily forthcoming. As reconstruction proceeds, and country and other risks diminish, the government should consider public–private partnerships (PPPs) to improve the infrastructure of the country, particularly as it relates to investment and trade (discussed in Chapter 13).

With more restricted policy choices and with a high degree of polarization that makes consensus more difficult to achieve, two elements are critical in the formulation of the policy mix in post-conflict economic reconstruction. Although they are related, it is important to discuss them separately. First, governments will need to make an effort at communication to explain in plain language the policies they want to adopt and why. This is important because of the need to avoid unrealistic expectations. Governments can do this by conducting public information campaigns to inform the population at large of the expected medium- and long-term benefits of the proposed policies, as well as the short-term costs that these may imply. Unless people understand this, they will have unrealistic expectations of what peace will bring. Unless people can weigh the expected personal benefits favorably vis-à-vis the costs, they will not be willing to bear such costs. Second, policymakers need to make a special effort also to build up consensus for their policies, among civil society groups, despite the difficulties in doing so. Unless policymakers manage to build a broad-based consensus on different policies, these are not likely to be successful or sustainable. Allowing unrealistic expectations and lack of consensus on policymaking to persist will endanger reconstruction.

Macroeconomic management[9]

THE NEED FOR A MINIMALIST FRAMEWORK

In 1994, Secretary-General Boutros-Ghali created the High Level Group on Development Strategy and Management of the Market Economy, chaired by Amartya Sen and Joseph Stiglitz, before both became Nobel Laureates. A year before, the Secretary-General had asked the Fund to prepare a basic framework for economic policymaking in countries coming out of conflict, taking into account the fragile state of these countries and the need to avoid their reverting to war. In representation of the UN Secretary-General's Office, I participated in a number of meetings with the monetary/exchange and fiscal groups, led by V. Sundararajan and Ved Ghandi, respectively, to discuss the experience and constraints of particular countries, including El Salvador, Cambodia, Mozambique, Haiti, and others, and to draw lessons. One thing that came out of those discussions was the need for a "minimalist" approach that would not put unnecessary pressure on the scarce technical, administrative, and managerial capacity of post-conflict countries.

The Fund prepared two excellent papers on the architecture of minimalist monetary/exchange rate and of fiscal policies for post-chaos/post-conflict situations (IMF 1995c, 1995d).[10] These papers discussed the "nuts and bolts" of macroeconomic management and institutional development and should be obligatory reading for policymakers, practitioners, and others involved in post-conflict economic reconstruction. Despite the fact that Vito Tanzi, the head of the Fiscal Department at the Fund, presented these papers at the Third Meeting of the High Level Group, the editors had the poor judgment (and the "development as usual" frame of mind) not to include them among the published papers and proceedings of these meetings.[11] The Fund has never published them either (perhaps because they produced them for the UN), but they should update them as necessary and publish them, so that they are easily available to all those dealing with the macroeconomic management aspects of reconstruction.

The two papers provide a checklist of institutions, policies, and instruments for each policy, and the key strategic policy choices in each area. The authors wisely followed the motto "keep it simple" (Premise 6) in enumerating the many activities that countries in these situations need to carry out in the respective areas. This is what a country like Afghanistan would have needed. It is clear that countries coming out of chaos or conflict do not need the sophisticated framework that the IMF and US Treasury recommended and Afghanistan adopted. The two IMF papers should also be obligatory reading for the institution's own staff. I found it surprising, to say the least, that these papers were not included in the bibliography of some of the later IMF work in this area.[12] The minimalist framework proposed by these papers would have better served countries like Afghanistan and Timor-Leste than the framework they ended up with.

It is not possible here to make a thorough and rigorous analysis of macro-economic issues in post-conflict economic reconstruction. Rather than presenting a detailed and comprehensive technical discussion, as the IMF papers do, I will present here a more general analysis of the issues that policymakers need to consider in designing the strategy for reconstruction. I will also identify policy options and dilemmas, which governments will face in such an endeavor. In each case, I will refer to specific countries to illustrate different options based on good and bad experiences.

When I was at the Fund in the late 1990s, I wrote a paper on El Salvador, which was published a few years later in *World Development* (del Castillo 2001a). I argued that assistance to post-conflict countries required the rethinking of analytical and operational issues to frame them in a multi-disciplinary strategy in which "first-best policies based on purely economic profit-maximizing criteria are often not appropriate or even recommended."[13] Many of my colleagues viewed this as "heresy" at the time. Nevertheless, over the years, as the IMF gained experience in post-conflict countries, the organization has come to accept this in some cases. Gupta *et al.* (2005), for example, mention that tax policy in post-conflict situations may require adopting policies that are not "first best" from an efficiency point of view (such as export taxes). In the discussion at the Board on rebuilding fiscal institutions in post-conflict countries, directors agreed that "first-best policies" may not be immediately appropriate, but that policies which are not optimal should be phased out as soon as feasible.[14]

MONETARY AND EXCHANGE RATE POLICIES[15]

Countries coming out of war often have to overcome the vicious circle of high inflation (or even hyperinflation) and currency depreciation that is the legacy of war. In this area, several key strategic issues need to be resolved expeditiously to facilitate the rebuilding of the monetary and exchange rate systems. These countries also need to improve the statistics in these areas since they are necessary for effective policymaking.

Although most countries would have probably maintained basic institutions, systems, and markets throughout the war and need only to modernize them, a few will have to start from scratch. While the former was true of El Salvador, Guatemala, and Mozambique, in Kosovo and East Timor the system of payments and banking had collapsed because of the conflict. In all cases, the monetary authorities will need to establish a basic system for exchange, internal and external payments, and the provision of credit, particularly for micro- and small-sized enterprises (MSEs). This may take some time and policymakers will often need to adopt temporary solutions to deal with urgent payment needs.[16]

In all countries, the authorities will have to make choices with regard to the currency and the exchange rate system. This will determine their role in monetary policy.[17] In any case, both the authorities and the institutions will have to build up credibility. To carry out effective monetary and exchange rate policies, the authorities will have to give priority to rebuilding or modernizing the central bank, the payments and banking system, and the foreign exchange market. They will also have to give priority to improving policy formulation and implementation, banking supervision, public debt management, and the accounting and information systems. Establishing reliable statistics is also important as a guiding mechanism for policymaking.

Inflation hawks argue that monetary policy should aim for price stability in the context of a floating exchange rate system. In their view, responsibility for conducting monetary policy should lie exclusively with the central bank,[18] which may or may not share responsibility on exchange rate policy with the Ministry of Finance. In Chapter 12, I argued that central banks should not have the power to act independently of the government in setting monetary and exchange rate policies in post-conflict reconstruction where the political objective should predominate. Thus, policymakers adopting monetary policy in such situations may consider broader objectives—including growth and employment and most importantly, the financing of peace-related projects in cases where foreign financing is lagging. Without the possibility of financing critical projects, the whole peace process may collapse. Thus, deficit financing should increase policymakers' options in particular cases in the transition from war. Nevertheless, despite the required flexibility that may lead to some temporary deviations from its basic objective, monetary policy should aim for price stability in the medium- and long-run. If central banks do not achieve relatively low levels of inflation, it will create uncertainty, discourage private savings and investment, and hurt the most vulnerable sectors of society.[19]

Flexible versus fixed exchange rates

It is common that countries coming out of war face high inflation, a depreciating currency, and scarce international reserves as they start their transition to peace. For this reason, in designing a reconstruction strategy, currency stability should be a key objective. As the transition to peace progresses, appreciation normally occurs because of large volumes of foreign exchange due to aid, the large number of expatriates in the country, and remittances from the diaspora (nationals of the country living abroad). Although this usually helps to bring inflation down, if the national currency appreciates in real terms (that is, an appreciation larger than the increase in prices), it will worsen the international competitiveness of the country's exports and facilitate its imports, worsening the external balance (or current account of the balance of payments).

Odd situations often happen with the exchange rate in war and post-conflict situations where aid and the international presence are large. For example, in Somalia in the early 1990s, at a time when there was no central government and no central bank, the national currency started appreciating. The reluctance of Somalis to accept dollars was, in part, due to the lack of tradition of using foreign currencies, as many countries do. But, the reluctance to use the dollar was also a political reaction against the UN and the US presence in the country, a presence that Somalis in general did not welcome. Thus, while the inflows of dollars and other hard currencies increased, the supply of national currency remained unchanged. This led to the bizarre situation in which the national currency appreciated in a failed state. The Somali experience also illustrated the fact that introducing foreign currencies to replace the national currency may be politically or culturally unfeasible in some post-conflict countries.

The choice of the exchange rate system is important. Under normal development, the debate on the exchange rate system is ongoing and always changing. Fixed exchange rates were popular in the hard fight against inflation that marked the 1980s and 1990s in many emerging markets. Countries in Latin America, Israel, and Turkey adopted a fixed exchange rate system. Fixed exchange rates used as the economies' anchor succeeded in taming inflation and even in smothering hyperinflation.[20] Even countries with moderate inflation adopted this system. Following the Asian financial crises in the late 1990s, and its global repercussions which included the subsequent collapse of pegged exchange rates in Russia and Brazil, debate raged about how to secure macroeconomic stability. The alternatives seemingly boiled down to two: a rigorously fixed exchange rate ("hard peg" in the sense that it is difficult legally to break it) that served as an anchor, or, a freely floating exchange rate, with the central bank targeting a low level of inflation and then doing all it could to hit that target.[21]

These two alternatives have been the choice of many countries in post-conflict situations. Countries often end the war or other conflict with high rates of inflation and with their monetary authorities having low credibility. This has often led them to adopt a hard peg or simply legally to adopt the currency of another country. This *de jure* "dollarization" can become the central feature of the stabilization policy. Countries have used different currencies to "dollarize". While Kosovo, where the Deutsche Mark was de facto used, adopted this currency and then moved to the euro, East-Timor preferred the dollar, which was more used in trade and as storage of value.

If the country decides to adopt a fixed exchange rate system, another option is possible. For example, Iraq could have opted for a currency board (as it had after independence in 1932 and as Bosnia and Herzegovina established in the mid-1990s) to fix to a stable currency.[22] In Iraq, to fix to the dollar would have been a political mistake. The fix to the euro at a time the currency was appreciating vis-à-vis the dollar could also have posed a problem, since a large part of Iraq's trade is in dollars. Frankel (2003) has argued that one possibility would have been to fix the dinar to the price of oil. However, while this would have facilitated the recovery and expansion of the oil sector, it could have discouraged production of other tradeable goods, by shifting the burden of price uncertainty to them. He proposed pegging the dinar to a basket that includes two currencies and the price of oil. For simplicity, the central bank could define the value of the dinar as one-third the value of the dollar, plus one-third the value of the euro, plus one-hundredth of a barrel of oil.

However, countries often need a new national currency to act as a symbol of the new political reality. In some cases, as the central government regains control of the country, it needs to get rid of currencies that have coexisted in different parts of the country. This was the case with the Swiss dinar, used in the autonomous region of Kurdistan. Thus, Iraq adopted a new dinar as a symbol of the new country, replacing both the Swiss dinar and the Saddam dinar used in the rest of the country. Similarly, Afghanistan adopted the new Afghani to replace the old one. Both countries have managed to keep their currencies rather stable, despite not having yet built up credibility with respect to their policies and institutions. As I mentioned earlier, a lot has to do with the large inflows of capital into these economies.

In a few countries, the monetary authorities had been implementing strong macroeconomic policies even while they negotiated peace. This had built up their credibility and they opted for a flexible exchange rate system, eliminating the multiple exchange rates of the past. This was the case in El Salvador, for example. As external aid and remittances increased significantly in the post-peace agreement period, the colón started a strong appreciation and the central bank intervened (purchased dollars) heavily to avoid a large loss in external competitiveness. The system became a de facto if not *de jure* peg to the dollar. To avoid the inflationary impact of this policy, the central bank had to issue bonds in domestic currency. The central bank kept the receipts from bond sales in a special account, which it could not use, thus "sterilizing" the inflationary impact of the original increase in the money supply. Although the inflationary impact was controlled, the interest paid on these bonds was costly and created a large quasi-fiscal deficit for the central bank.

Although I am presenting all these options, I am not promoting any. As Jacob Frenkel, a former Chief Economist of the IMF and Governor of the Bank of Israel, has often posited, it is irrelevant whether to fix or float, if the right conditions are present for each regime. Policymakers will have to decide whether conditions are present for the type of exchange rate they want to adopt, given the political and economic constraints that each country will face. This is indeed a tough choice and governments need to weigh carefully all the pros and cons before deciding.[23]

FISCAL POLICY[24]

A sound fiscal policy is essential in post-conflict situations, not only for macroeconomic stability but also for ensuring assistance from donors. External assistance will be dependent on both fiscal discipline and transparency.

The fiscal framework for supporting post-conflict economic reconstruction will consist of a budget and public expenditure management structure (the treasury); appropriate revenue policies and revenue administration; and a coherent coordinating framework for fiscal federalism to allocate the expenditure and revenue responsibilities of the central government vis-à-vis the provinces, particularly in large countries. It will also need to include a mechanism to coordinate aid with donors to ensure that aid supports government priorities, rather than acting independently of them.

In the initial transition to peace, donors often establish a separate system of aid management outside the national budget, to include both humanitarian and reconstruction assistance, with the idea of integrating it later into the fiscal structure of the country. In this case, the national budget will be restricted to recurrent expenditure (wages and salaries mostly). This has been necessary in some cases because of the difficulties and timeframe required to prepare the national budget and certain donor restrictions on financing recurrent expenditures. Although the reasons for this happening are valid, the countries should establish a consolidated government budget, including recurrent expenditure, humanitarian assistance, and capital investment as soon as feasible.

As I discussed in the case of Afghanistan, a donors-supported budget, financed through trust funds, is likely to promote activities that are on the donors' agenda but do not necessarily have priority in the government's reconstruction strategy. More problematically, such an arrangement might undermine the government and even question its legitimacy, since it does not facilitate the financing necessary for the government to carry out its basic functions. Furthermore, it is likely to favor foreign contractors to the detriment of local employment.

Because of the urgency of humanitarian activities in the early transition, a trust fund will be required as soon as feasible in the transition. Preferably, there should be only one trust fund for this purpose. The creation of several trust funds is likely to be a source of confusion and lack of transparency.

Ideally, the government, as the elected representative of the people in post-conflict situations, should be able to set up a consolidated national budget with all revenue and all expenditure, including those related to economic reconstruction, even if financed through foreign assistance. The national budget should thus include and prioritize all revenue (including grants) and all expenditure (including investment) in the country, making it the centerpiece of the government's reconstruction strategy. In cases where the government has weak implementation capacity for delivering services and rehabilitating infrastructure, it can consider "outsourcing" to national companies a large part of the tasks, strengthening the private sector in the country in the process. It is important in post-conflict situations that the legal framework for procurement be in place and modernized to make it transparent and competitive.

Policymakers often will have to create temporary budgets for three or six months. This is because of the difficulties in elaborating a longer-term budget in such dynamic situations and the uncertainty about donors' pledges. Budget priorities will have to shift as the transition proceeds. The authorities often have to establish temporary budgets to ensure payment of wages and salaries to civil service staff, and other education and health workers, and to cover basic security. A major shift to pro-poor, infrastructure, and service supporting spending should take place as soon as governments can lower security related expenditure.

Fiscal federalism

In normal development situations, federalism includes a number of fiscal issues, particularly in relation to the allocation of revenue and expenditure responsibilities of central and local governments. Revenue and expenditure responsibilities should move together. If provinces have their own revenue, they also need to have spending responsibilities in education, health, or other specific services. In addition, post-conflict transitions often involve the drafting of new constitutions in which issues relating to fiscal federalism might be included.[25]

As happens with peace agreements, the difficulty of interpreting the constitution will depend of the clarity and specificity with which experts draft it. Because many of the issues included may have to be tested, this is another operational difficulty in the post-conflict transition. As the case study on Iraq in Chapter 10 revealed, issues in the allocation of existing and new oil fields become a political issue in post-conflict situations, often difficult to deal with. To be peace supporting, legislation on the exploitation of natural resources will have to be well specified and fair, and enjoy wide support. Adequate regulation, enforcement mechanisms, and an efficient judiciary will need to be in place. The issue of allocation of resources—particularly in resource-rich countries—may well present one of the most difficult political and economic decisions policymakers will have to make as they design and implement the strategy for economic reconstruction. If the different stakeholders do not perceive the framework as fair, there will be pressures to go back to conflict and the country may even break up, as some experts warn may happen to Iraq.

REAL SECTOR POLICIES

Real sector policies relate to decisions by firms, households, and the government to save and invest. Countries record the annual (or quarterly) production of all goods and services of these three sectors, as well as the trade (export and import) transactions of the country with the rest of the world in their National Income Accounts (NIA). Both the analysis of events and the design of appropriate economic policies require accurate economic information and statistics, available in a systematic and timely fashion. In post-conflict situations, the quality of the NIA recording production and trade of all goods and services in the economy is often poor, and in need of major improvement. Better estimations of price indices and the exchange rate are also critical in improving the national accounts.

In addition to the shortage of technical capabilities necessary for the compilation and analysis of data, one of the major distortions in the NIA in war economies has to do with the fact that a large part of the activities that take place internally and externally relate to illegal transactions (contraband, narcotics, black markets, and so on). The NIA do not record such transactions. An improvement in the fiscal and monetary policies discussed earlier will help to improve the NIA by improving public sector data, monetary data, and customs data (covering exports and imports). To improve data collection, reporting, and analysis, governments can request technical assistance from the IMF and the World Bank, as well as from other institutions. Because of the importance of good data for effective policymaking, training and capacity building in this area should start as soon as feasible in the transition to peace.

Real sector policies focus on the strategy to promote savings and investment—domestic and foreign—both of which are usually low in post-conflict countries. Given political and economic constraints in the early transition, domestic investors producing on a small scale for the domestic market will probably be the most important factor in growth reactivation. Other factors will include the local expenditure of the expatriates in the country, as well as other activities facilitated by foreign assistance. Since the institutional framework for creating micro-lending banks will take some time, governments will need to provide some credit and facilitate technical assistance, particularly for MSEs. As the economy recovers and reform of the banking system proceeds, the challenge will be to attract capital that left the country as capital flight and maintain domestic savings in the country through an efficient banking system.

EXTERNAL SECTOR POLICIES

Policies with respect to the external position of the country, both with regard to flows recorded in the balance of payments, and stocks of external debt, are critical in post-conflict countries. The balance of payments records the yearly exchange in goods, services, and assets between the national economy and the rest of the world. In this sense, it is the mirror image of what happens in the local economy. The balance of payments is divided into the current account and the capital and financial accounts. The current account is the sum of the trade balance (exports minus imports of goods and services), plus factor income (interest payments, dividends, royalties, and fees), plus personal transfers (remittances). The capital account consists mainly of official transfers (grants), which are often large in post-conflict countries. The financial account consists of debt-generating flows (loans and portfolio debt) and equity-generating flows (foreign direct investment and portfolio investment). Portfolio flows and foreign direct investment are often low or non-existent in post-conflict countries.

If the economy is internationally competitive in trade and investment, the balance of payments will record a surplus, that is, a capital inflow into the national economy. This is because foreigners will be buying its exports and investing in the local economy, more than its citizens will import from and invest abroad. This is not the case in post-conflict economies. Rather than resulting from high international competitiveness, capital inflows into post-conflict countries are the result of aid. Although a large part of the aid to these countries comes in the form of grants (and hence without a quid pro quo), countries in post-conflict situations also borrow abroad. These flows allow countries to import large amounts for humanitarian and reconstruction purposes, often exhibiting large trade deficits.

While grants are recorded in the capital account as "official transfers," remittances are included as "personal transfers" in the current account. These two types of transfer are in principle differentiated on the basis of whether they are used for consumption (current account) or investment purposes (capital account). This is not clear-cut: part of the remittances is often used to build housing (investment), and humanitarian aid is largely used for consumption.

In designing the strategy for economic reconstruction, policymakers will have to make critical decisions with respect to arrears on foreign debt and debt restructuring. Most importantly, they will have to decide on how to solve arrears with the international financial institutions (IFIs) since these institutions will not be able to play an active role in the country unless this is done. They will also have to make a decision on how to restructure their foreign debt to other creditors.

15 Microeconomic policymaking

Microeconomic foundations

In designing the strategy for post-conflict economic reconstruction, policy-makers will need to keep in mind that good macroeconomic management is necessary but not sufficient for the reactivation of investment, trade, and employment. Thus, they will also need to adopt a number of measures to improve the domestic business climate so that markets and industries can perform better.

Distortions in economies undergoing post-conflict transitions are significant, as discussed in the case studies in Chapters 7–10. Governments will have to address these distortions to improve the productivity and international competitiveness of the country and the private firms in it. Without this the country will find it difficult to reintegrate into the international trade and investment system. Policymakers need to improve the business climate keeping in mind the political and security constraints under which they operate. For example, reducing subsidies for food and fuel that are distorting domestic prices and hence production may be a desirable reform, but if carried out too drastically or at the wrong time, it may have an adverse political, social, and security impact—as happened in Iraq, for example—that may jeopardize the transition to peace.

Countries can create a virtuous circle of sustainable growth only through increased investment, and post-conflict countries are no different from other developing countries in this regard. Higher investment is necessary but not sufficient to increase the value-added of exports, which in many post-conflict countries consist principally of raw materials that create little employment. Countries need also to improve productivity and competitiveness through better technology and innovation at the level of the firm. For this to take place, the government needs to create an appropriate business climate, as discussed below. This is difficult in countries at very low levels of human development. Contrary to what many policymakers believe, international competitiveness cannot be achieved solely by relying on a more competitive real exchange rate (depreciation of the national currency above its rate of inflation).

BUSINESS CLIMATE

The business climate includes all those factors that the government controls and that, by affecting returns and risk for the private sector, influence decisions about whether to invest. The business climate of a country thus includes a wide range of macroeconomic and microeconomic factors, as well as social conditions. The World Bank defines a good business climate as one that provides firms with an adequate legal, regulatory, and institutional framework, promotes competitiveness, strengthens governance, minimizes bureaucratic inefficiencies, and facilitates access to basic infrastructure, human capital, technology, and financial services.

Improving the business climate in post-conflict situations is important, but doing so takes time. International indices, including the World Bank's Doing Business Project, the World Economic Forum's Global Competitiveness Index, and others, rank countries in post-conflict situations at the bottom in this area. In addition to macroeconomic mismanagement, some of the features that are common to most post-conflict situations and that are a strong deterrent to investment include

- Lack of "country vision" to lead public policies;
- Discretionary public policies that often lead to uncertainty, corruption, and discrimination;
- Rules of the game that are unclear, nontransparent, and change frequently;
- High government bureaucracy (red tape);
- Impunity of the civil service in its treatment of clients;
- Unfair and illegal competition (informal markets, smuggling);
- Lack of protection for intellectual property (patents and trademarks);
- Deficiencies in physical infrastructure (roads, airports, ports, bridges, etc.);
- Uncompetitive quality, price, and availability of public services (electricity, fuel, communications) due to public monopolies;
- Low investment in technology and innovation;
- Large gaps in human infrastructure (education, health, housing);
- Education systems not adapted to the needs of firms;
- Unproductive labor forces due to failures in education, brain drain, high emigration;
- Inflexible labor markets that make it prohibitively expensive to recruit young and inexperienced people;
- Weak judicial systems that fail to enforce contracts.

Strong leadership, a country vision, and lack of widespread corruption will facilitate and make policymaking more effective. It will also make possible strong support from donors. In Rwanda, for example, despite the difficulties of escaping the legacy of the genocide, the government has developed an ambitious strategy for the densely populated and green country known as the "Land of the Thousand Hills." The goal is to become a regional hub for communications and computing. To achieve this, fiber-optic cable is being laid throughout the country, and the country may soon have the most advanced broadband wireless Internet network on the continent. The challenge is great in a country with scarce skilled labor and shortages of energy supply, where only 5 percent of the population was connected to electricity, which has the highest cost in the region. The government is also planning to add value to their production of coffee and tea, their main commodity export, and is committed to finding new trade routes through regional integration for this land-locked country (Whitelaw 2007; England 2006a; White 2006a).

Policymakers need to keep in mind that the more clear, simple, transparent, trustworthy, and stable the institutions, laws, regulations, and other government procedures are, the larger will be the incentive for firms to invest and grow in the country. If the business climate does not improve as the transition to peace proceeds, foreign investors will not invest in the domestic market, and capital flight by domestic firms and individuals will continue.

FOUR TYPES OF INVESTMENT

It is important to distinguish between four types of investment in an economy: domestic investment for the domestic market (DD), domestic investment for the foreign market (DF), foreign investment for the domestic market (FD), and foreign investment for the foreign market (FF).

Foreign investment for the domestic market (FD) is not likely to be significant in post-conflict countries in the short run. First, even if the domestic market is large in terms of people, it will be low in terms of purchasing power and thus not attractive to foreign investors. Of course, there will be exceptions, as the reopening of the Pepsi plant in Iraq indicates. Second, investment in the domestic market will normally require strong improvement in the domestic business climate—which is often a strong deterrent to investment by both foreign and domestic firms.

Privatization of state-owned enterprises or opening up of critical sectors to private investors, both domestic and foreign (DD, FD), is always a political decision and a path that only governments with some legitimacy can pursue. Interim governments—and even more so countries under UN or US protectorates—are better off avoiding it. This is not only because of the likely political backlash it may cause, but also because uncertainty about property rights will discourage potential investors. Furthermore, governments may want to delay a decision to open up critical sectors or privatize assets until conditions are right. By then, the government probably will have had sufficient time to stabilize the economy and create the appropriate legal, institutional, and regulatory framework necessary. As the government advances in these areas, the attraction and value of national assets will increase.

However, in resource-rich countries, which have to bear a larger part of the reconstruction bill, policymakers may want to accelerate the exploitation and export process. In some cases, they can safely assume that foreign investors will be willing to invest (FD, FF), even if the risk is high. Greed often prevails over caution when prices are right, as they were in the oil market in 2007. In any case, oil companies are normally the most willing to accept high risk, probably because of their experience in operating in high-risk conditions in places like Colombia, Nigeria, Chad, and many other countries around the world. As we have seen in Iraq, however, the absence of a legitimate government, uncertainty about property rights, and a lack of security can make it difficult to attract foreign investors under any circumstances.

Five-pronged employment promotion strategy

The inadequate business climate prevailing in post-conflict countries will discourage investment and employment. Given that reform in this area takes time, governments will need to think about reactivating investment and employment through innovative mechanisms that are not directly dependent on an improvement in the business climate. In order to establish the virtuous circle of employment and growth, increased domestic productivity and international competitiveness, governments should promote these mechanisms with the assistance of the donor community, unless the country is resource-rich and can finance it themselves, as is the case in Angola, for example. Aid channeled this way will create national capabilities and livelihoods and will avoid creating the aid dependencies that donors have created in many countries.

With this in mind, governments in post-conflict countries could consider a five-pronged strategy aimed at creating both dynamism with social inclusion, through the short-run reactivation of investment and trade. Such a strategy, which would have to be adapted to local circumstances, could focus on the provision, promotion, or creation of (type of investment shown in brackets)

- Subsidies to domestic enterprises, financed through aid, to hire and train targeted groups, and produce for domestic and foreign markets (DD, DF);
- Subsidies or price support to agricultural production for the domestic and foreign markets (DD, DF);

- Special "reconstruction zones" for domestic and foreign firms to produce exclusively for exports (DF, FF);

- Investment by micro- and small-sized enterprises (MSEs) for the domestic markets (DD);

- Investment in infrastructure, by both national and international companies (DD, FD).

PROVIDING SUBSIDIES TO DOMESTIC ENTERPRISES TO HIRE AND TRAIN TARGETED GROUPS (DD, DF)

Although I cannot provide in this chapter a detailed analysis of Phelps's major study *Rewarding Work* (1997) or his more recent work (2003, 2006), suffice it to say here that he presents a strong case for how work is a key component of a normal life. In his view (Phelps 1997: 11–13)

Work is at the center of a normal life. Most people who have experienced a job cannot get along without its important rewards.... Our jobs become a central part of who we are.... The lack or loss of a job may be dangerous to your health.

In the Introduction to *Designing Inclusion* (Phelps 2003: 1), he posited that

People want the dignity brought by self-support and the autonomy brought by having a substantial income of their own to meet their special needs. Earning one's own way—making enough to support one's self at a decent level by society's standards and to be a part of community life—is hugely important for people's self respect. For these reasons, the *availability* and the quality of a country's jobs as well as the wages employers can afford to pay, hence the *productivity* of work, are among life's "primary goods" in John Rawls' terminology. It is no wonder, then, that people want to be included. The recognition of inclusion, by the way, is not new to economics, which has long prized low unemployment, high job satisfaction and high productivity.

With regard to the appropriate policy response to the lack of inclusion, and in particular the role of government, Phelps notes that (2003: 6)

A basic question here is whether the deficiency of inclusion among the less advantaged is, to any degree, a problem for society to address through the state. In the view of some observers, low inclusion, however regrettable, is not a phenomenon appropriate for social intervention—not something to be corrected through collective action by the state.

The reply to that position, a reply dating back to the eighteenth century Enlightenment, is that a democratic country's formal economy is a project for citizens' mutual gain, so the accessibility of this project and the satisfactoriness of the terms it offers participants are a legitimate object of social policy.

Although Phelps's work has focused on how to restore participation and social inclusion in the industrial world, the need to restore a normal life to people through gainful employment is a *sine qua non* for post-conflict countries. Efforts at inclusion will fail, however, in stagnant economies. Thus, in countries coming out of war, efforts at improving the dynamism of the economy and those at social inclusion should go hand in hand, which makes it particularly challenging (del Castillo and Phelps 2007).

Making the labor market flexible, as many suggest, will not by itself improve dynamism and inclusion, particularly in the midst of political, social, and institutional vulnerabilities, as well as the damage to human and physical infrastructure that are the legacy of conflict. Income support and other welfare programs adopted during the transition to peace, unless restricted to the very short run and emergency phase, will aggravate the unemployment and exclusion problem by reducing incentives to work and creating a culture of dependency (ibid.).

In Iraq, for example, Crane (2007) reports that the employees of state-owned enterprises still receive paychecks, although about a third of these enterprises were destroyed. Not surprisingly, many have shown no interest in going back to work. His conclusion that the fundamental problem in Iraq is not jobs and that foreign assistance will be best spent in improving the police, the prisons, and the courts is misplaced.[1] Improvement in those areas can help deal with the insecurity problem but will certainly not eliminate a major root cause of conflict. The sectarian groups in Iraq and in other places would have much less of a reason to resort to violence if they could make a decent living for their families and be productive members of a society in which the means of production—including key natural resources—were fairly distributed among the different groups and regions.

But fast growth is no guarantee of inclusion in post-conflict countries. Angola's recent macroeconomic performance has been good. The IMF shows that output growth has been robust since 2001 both in the oil and non-oil sectors (diamonds, manufacturing, construction, processing, and services). GDP growth averaged 20 percent in 2005–7. Although poverty figures are disputed, the Catholic University of Angola reckons that two in three Angolans still live on $2 or less a day. In its 2007/8 report which uses data for 2005, the UNDP Human Development Index ranks Angola in 162nd place out of 177 countries, with a life expectancy at birth of 42 years, and a combined enrolment ratio for primary, secondary, and tertiary education half that in Rwanda, a poor country in comparison with Angola. In a December 2006 poll by a pro-democracy group and the USAID, six out of ten Angolans said their economic situation was no better then than five years before (LaFraniere 2007). This dismal social situation amid fast economic growth is directly related to corruption and lack of job opportunities for the large majority of the population.

As Conte (1997) noted, Phelps reminds us that work builds character, gives us a sense of place, employs our mental faculties, and establishes a nearly inseparable link to family and community life. No matter how routine or how boring, work is far better than the alternative of idleness. Furthermore, high unemployment, particularly among young people, leads to crime and drug abuse and to increased spending on preventing both, as well as in the administration of justice. Post-conflict countries from El Salvador to Afghanistan provide strong empirical evidence of the danger of unemployment and its heavy impact on crime and public insecurity. This is another reason why everyone should participate in (personally and financially) rewarding work in post-conflict situations.

According to Phelps, inclusion will not be forthcoming unless governments adopt sound policies. In his view, a flexible labor market like that in the United States, as many propose for Europe, will not by itself promote inclusion. In fact, social exclusion has been growing in the United States. Specifically, he recommends the adoption of an employer subsidy program that would lower the cost of hiring unskilled workers to a minimum and hence make it more attractive for firms to hire them, with on-the-job training making it attractive to workers and to society as a whole.

Having been concerned about the social impact of stabilization in developing and post-crisis countries throughout my professional life, I have naturally been attracted to Phelps's proposal. However, I have also been aware that most of these countries suffer from weak fiscal positions, rendering the provision of subsidies infeasible in most cases. Having worked in conflict and post-conflict situations for almost two decades, and after conducting new research for this book, I am convinced that aid policies are in disarray, and that donors must reorient them if they really want to support post-conflict reconstruction effectively. In particular, a large part of donors' support is channeled through projects that they carry out, independently of the government or national priorities, and involving their own experts and firms. The population at large in post-conflict countries resents this. Nowhere has this become clearer than in Afghanistan.

This is why Phelps and I have proposed—and I put it up here for debate— that donors could use aid more effectively and in support of national-led reconstruction if they channeled aid through national budgets for specific purposes. This could, among other things, allow governments to subsidize domestic firms to hire unskilled workers in post-conflict countries. Given lower labor costs, national entrepreneurs could decide to invest under the conditions of uncertainty and high risk that characterize these countries. The advantages in terms of employment creation, reintegration of former combatants into productive activities, savings from safety-net programs, and improved public security would be many. At the same time, aid of this type would provide political support for the authorities, since the population would be grateful to a government that promotes active policies for employment creation.

More importantly, from an economic point of view, this policy would have neither the fiscal cost associated with government-financed subsidies nor the cost in terms of distortions caused by the difficulties in cutting subsidies once the government has offered them. We have argued that grant-supported subsidies would remain in place for a finite period, and would gradually be phased out once the aid program ends. Furthermore, such subsidies would help reactivate the private sector, which is essential as large-scale post-conflict aid withers to the low levels that are common under conditions of normal development (del Castillo and Phelps 2007).

PROVIDING SUBSIDIES OR PRICE SUPPORT TO AGRICULTURAL PRODUCTION (DD, DF)

Reactivation of labor-intensive agriculture should be a priority in most post-conflict countries as a source of employment for groups affected by the war as well as for other workers in the community. This, however, has not proved easy. Food aid often distorts prices. The infrastructure is lacking or in disrepair, which makes it difficult to take the produce to the market. Demining is often a precondition for sowing. Furthermore, the trend is for young people to move to the urban areas and away from the rural ones. Even if credit is available, which is often not the case, farmers are reluctant to get indebted to purchase fertilizer and seeds and acquire basic skills under conditions of high uncertainty.

Larger production of vegetables, fruits, grains, and animals could lower domestic food prices in the urban areas. If in large supply, these products could find foreign markets, or be processed domestically, to increase their value-added. However, the reactivation of agriculture is not likely to take place unless subsidies or price support programs are put in place. The same arguments used above apply here: donors should make aid available for these programs since the fiscal situation of these countries would not allow it. In addition to price subsidies, donors should finance improvements in basic infrastructure, and provide technical assistance and capacity building for primary production, higher-value processing, and marketing. Donors should also open up their markets for products produced in post-conflict countries.

Both the United States and the European Union assist their farmers through loan and price support programs and other incentives.[2] Now, countries like Malawi have defied the advice of donors and the IFIs and started to subsidize fertilizer and seeds with spectacular results (Dugger 2007b). If donors want to improve the effectiveness of the aid they provide to countries coming out of war, they should channel reconstruction aid through the national budget. Only aid would enable those governments to provide subsidies or other incentives to agricultural producers. This would be particularly effective in countries, such as Afghanistan, where it could provide farmers with an alternative to drug production. While the UK government is at present considering price support for Afghan farmers, other donors should do the same (Phelps and del Castillo 2008).

PROMOTING INVESTMENT BY MSEs FOR THE DOMESTIC MARKET (DD)

An unattractive business climate affects the activities of the micro- and small-sized enterprises (MSEs) as well. Furthermore, many of these enterprises operate in the informal market. One possibility that policymakers could debate is whether the government—with financial and technical support from the international community—can develop an "emergency program" to reactivate these enterprises in areas such as light manufacturing (textiles, leather, clothing) or in agricultural production (meat or fish processing, dairy products, frozen vegetables, fragrances). Governments would use this program largely for the reintegration of former combatants and other war-affected persons. However, eligible candidates would also include other MSEs that want to reactivate old businesses or start new ones. MSEs are labor-intensive and hence potentially an important source of employment in post-conflict situations. Thus, this program would constitute a good use of aid for economic as well as political, social, and security reasons. A framework for the quick reactivation of enterprises of this type should include

- A simple legal form and procedure for opening and registering MSEs;
- A simple tax form and a very low tax rate (say, 5 percent) which would facilitate the creation of a culture of tax payment, not common among MSEs, especially in post-conflict situations;
- A single "window" in the government for dealing with MSEs;
- Effective training, capacity building, and support for MSEs in various fields;
- Intensive training in information technology, management, and basic finance;
- Creation of "reconstruction parks" where MSEs would share necessary infrastructure and benefit from externalities;
- Initial grant financing for start-up MSEs.

PROMOTING SPECIAL "RECONSTRUCTION ZONES" TO PRODUCE EXCLUSIVELY FOR EXPORTS (DF, FF)

"Reconstruction zones"—or "free-trade zones" as they are called under normal development conditions—include assembly plants (*maquila*-type operations) that use mostly foreign inputs, processing plants that use local inputs, and other outsourcing-related activities.[3] The *maquila* involves mostly the temporary admission of imported inputs. Local workers assemble them and re-export the final product tax-free, normally to the United States or to other mature economies. This type of investment was an important source of Mexico's reactivation after the 1994 crisis, and countries such as El Salvador and Guatemala used *maquila* during their own post-conflict reconstruction. Processing plants that use domestic commodities to supply world markets also have great potential in countries with abundant natural resources and agricultural sectors and low value-added in their traditional exports. Foreign direct investment in *maquila*, processing plants, and other outsourcing service activities in Costa Rica, for example, or in Ireland in the 1980s, transformed these countries by increasing their exports' value-added and increasing their international competitiveness. In countries at a higher level of development— from Dubai to Singapore to Uruguay—these zones include mostly services (software, biotechnology, finance).

The World Trade Organization (WTO) is, however, in the process of phasing out the tax preferences under which the free-trade zones operate in commodities. Thus, countries such as Costa Rica, El Salvador, Guatemala, and Mexico will have to increase gradually the taxation of firms that operate in these zones until they reach a level comparable to the taxes they impose on firms in the national economy, thus eroding their competitive edge. What Ireland did a few years ago, in order to comply with European Union requirements similar to those of the WTO, was to decrease the domestic tax rate radically, thereby maintaining the free-trade zones' competitiveness. However, this is impossible in many developing and post-crises countries, given their serious fiscal constraints.

Although there are a priori a number of difficulties with respect to the establishment of "reconstruction zones"—policymakers should nonetheless explore possibilities for the export-oriented production of goods and the provision of low-skilled services from these zones. These possibilities could be attractive if

- The WTO approves a "special status" for "reconstruction zones" in post-conflict/post-crisis countries and donors give preference in their own markets to goods originating from such zones (in this donors could play a constructive role);

- Governments create the appropriate legal and regulatory framework for these zones, including requirements for links to the rest of the national economy;
- Governments promote their "reconstruction zones" aggressively.

One of the advantages of this type of operation is that it is rather self-contained. Indeed, these zones are possible in some areas, even if the rest of the country is in turmoil and outside the control of the authorities. With the assistance of donors, governments could establish the basic infrastructure, while foreign or domestic investors producing in the zones could finance the assembly plants. For example, in a study that I conducted on the Democratic Republic of Congo (DRC) for the Organization for Economic Cooperation and Development (OECD) Development Centre (del Castillo 2003a: 24), I argued that

Foreign investors...could set up *maquila* for exports. This, for example, could be possible in the Bas-Congo area on the Atlantic Ocean where security conditions are acceptable, infrastructure is adequate and labor supply is abundant or could be brought from other areas of the country. *Maquila* operations producing low-tech products, mostly clothing, leather products, and other goods produced with intensive use of low-skilled labor, could be an important source of employment creation and raise disposable income in the country.

Empirical evidence on this type of operation is conclusive about the importance it can have in generating employment, both direct and indirect, with the use of national goods and services as inputs. At the same time, production in such zones would facilitate the training and capacity building of the local labor force, particularly if investors are top firms in their respective fields. Empirical evidence also shows that this type of investment can help improve corporate and safety practices for suppliers of local inputs. Some of these effects occur through osmosis. Others occur simply because investors in the zones impose on their local providers standards for quality, labor, and safety practices, and environmental protection. In addition, investors in the zones can create links to local technical schools and universities by helping them develop courses and training that are more attuned to firms' labor demand. Investors can also offer internships to students, contributing to technology transfer.[4]

With the preferential access that Kosovo has to EU markets and with its huge number of unemployed young people, its lack of intense "reconstruction zones" production has certainly been a missed opportunity. Serious development of this option would not only have drawn on the large and growing work force, thus improving the standard of living of those employed, but also would have had an impact on the wide balance-of-payments deficit by increasing exports. More importantly, it could have offered possibilities to Kosovars—of both Albanian and Serbian origin, as well as other minorities—to work together, which could have contributed to national reconciliation and improved security.

PROMOTING INVESTMENT IN INFRASTRUCTURE (DD, FD)

The four previous proposals to increase investment and employment require that there be better infrastructure. Chapter 13 addressed this issue. Suffice it to say here that investment in infrastructure is not only important to the production and trade of all goods and services, but it should also be seen as a source of employment and an important factor in national reconciliation. Governments should consider using both domestic companies and foreign companies, depending on the political and security situation, the relative strength of the companies, the needs of the country, and the constraints related to donors' financing. Governments can impose quotas to ensure an appropriate number of jobs for local workers. In sectors in which the government wants to keep control, it could consider public–private partnerships (PPPs) to build, operate, manage, and finance certain infrastructure projects.

Concluding remarks: Putting reconstruction on track

Countries coming out of war or chaos confront a multi-pronged transition. Crime and violence must surrender to public security; lawlessness and political exclusion must give way to the rule of law and participatory government; ethnic, religious, or class confrontation must give in to national reconciliation; and war-ravaged economies must reconstruct and become functioning economies that enable ordinary people to earn a decent and licit living. The fact that economic reconstruction takes place amid this multi-pronged transition makes it fundamentally different from "development as usual." The fact that without the creation of dynamism and social inclusion in the economy the path to peace will be elusive makes reconstruction particularly challenging. The fact that countries in the transition to peace have roughly a fifty–fifty chance of reverting to war makes reconstruction a high risk–high reward investment for the international community and the respective countries.

Case studies presented in Chapters 7–10, as well as others discussed in the literature provide ample evidence that economic reconstruction is a critical aspect of the war-to-peace transition. However, the development as usual approach, the failure to develop a realistic comprehensive strategy for reconstruction in most countries, the lack of effective aid and technical assistance mechanisms, and the inexistence of appropriate and specific institutional arrangements to deal with reconstruction at the international and national levels have failed to help countries to stand on their own feet in the transition to peace. Without a change of course, countries will not be able to create the productive investment and the sustainable employment that is necessary to improve their livelihoods, sustain the peace, and avoid aid dependency. It is thus imperative that national governments and the international community that supports them rethink and debate the way in which they carry out post-conflict reconstruction.

Reconstruction has proved particularly difficult in the post-Cold War context. Although often with regional implications, reconstruction has taken place in countries coming out of civil war or other internal chaos—requiring special efforts at national reconciliation so that the warring groups can live together in peace. At the same time, reconstruction has taken place in countries at low levels of development—often failed states, breakaway provinces, and countries at the lowest levels of human development which lack basic resources and capabilities, require large amounts of humanitarian assistance, and call for special efforts to lure spoilers away from the illicit and profitable war economy into the peace process.

Contrary to what happened in the post-world war periods, post-conflict economic reconstruction in the new context has failed to generate a rigorous theoretical and practical debate about how to design an overall strategy for effective reconstruction, and to articulate what are the best policy options and practices for different situations, what are the pros and cons of different programs, how to address the different trade-offs and sequences involved in the process, and how to deal with the economic and financial consequences of the transition to peace.

In the absence of such debate, post-conflict economic reconstruction has been approached—both by national governments and by the international community that supports transitions to peace—as if it were development as usual. Empirical evidence in the case studies shows that reconstruction is fundamentally different from normal development. Although it is true that these countries face the development challenges that other countries do, such as alleviating poverty and complying with the Millennium Development Goals (MDGs), these are long-term propositions. In the short run, the challenge of economic reconstruction is primarily to contribute to national reconciliation and the consolidation of peace. Unless this succeeds, peace is not going to be long-lasting. This is why the cost of failure is high indeed.

In fact, economic reconstruction is a development-plus challenge: in addition to the normal challenge of development faced by post-conflict countries in the post-Cold War period, those countries also need to carry out critical peace-related programs which are clearly distinct from development ones and have important financial and technical implications. These include the disarmament, demobilization, and reintegration (DDR) of former combatants; the return of refugees and internally displaced groups and their reintegration into productive activities; the rehabilitation of basic services and infrastructure destroyed during the conflict; and the clearance of mines, without which it is often impossible to restart agricultural production.

Post-conflict countries need to carry out all these activities among the uncertainties, risks, constraints, and expenditure imposed by the political, social, and security transitions that take place simultaneously. In addition to economic reconstruction, countries need to advance political reform; reform the armed forces; create and train civilian police forces; establish an adequate institutional framework to create trust and respect for human rights, to facilitate the resolution of disputes and be able to address future grievances through peaceful means; and to deal with the psychological trauma of the war. All these activities are critical to the peace process and have serious financial implications. Without them, efforts at reconstruction will be futile.

Because the main short-term challenge of economic reconstruction is national reconciliation, the objective of peace should prevail at all times over that of development—if the two ever clash, as they often do. This is why optimal and best-practice macroeconomic policies are not usually possible or even desirable at this time, even though they should be the objective for the longer term. Policies such as the independence of the central bank and the no-overdraft rule for budget financing adopted in some countries—a desirable policy framework under normal conditions—has proved too restrictive and inflexible in the post-conflict context. Sophisticated macro- and microeconomic frameworks established in some countries have proved too complex for governments lacking technical, administrative, and managerial capacities, and have led to lack of transparency and even corruption.

Reconstruction requires an alternative, simpler and more flexible set of policies and practices. Furthermore, the extra activities which countries in post-conflict situations need to carry out need to be given priority in budget allocations, even if macroeconomic stabilization is somewhat delayed in the process. Failure to give such priority has proved a major factor in countries' relapse into war.

With regard to economic policymaking, post-conflict countries—as well as those coming out of serious financial crises or natural disasters—have less flexibility, a sense of urgency and forgiveness for distortions, and large aid flows and intrusive involvement of the international community, that are largely lacking in the normal development process. Crises lead to emergencies that require short-run solutions to satisfy humanitarian needs. These solutions are inevitable but often create distortions and are not necessarily the best ones if the objective is medium- and long-term sustainability, as it is under normal development. These crises generate at the same time an interest and concern from the international community that leads to spikes in aid and an intensive and often intrusive political involvement which post-crisis countries find difficult to deal with. Under normal development such involvement would be considered interference in national affairs. Crises also require giving preference to some groups to the detriment of others, breaking the "equity principle" of normal development where those in need should be treated equally. To give preference to groups affected by the crisis is imperative in the short run to ensure that spoilers and others that had benefited from the illicit war economy get a stake in the peace process and are willing to support it.

During post-conflict reconstruction, economic policymaking is also constrained by the legitimacy of the government or other policymaking body. A weak interim government—and even more so the UN, the United States, or any other country or organization that temporarily assumes executive and/or legislative functions in the country—should avoid adopting controversial policies that may create a political backlash. Such policies include, for example, privatization of state-owned enterprises, deregulation of key sectors, opening up regulated sectors to foreign investment, or major changes in the legal and regulatory system. Similarly, reconstruction efforts should take into account the fact that lack of legitimacy creates uncertainty over property rights and is a strong deterrent to investment.

Thus, although reconstruction policies should set the bases for an eventual move to normal development, it should be accepted by all that economic policymaking in post-conflict situations and under normal development differ greatly. Because of the political, security, and policymaking constraints, as well as data limitations, a different yardstick should be used to measure success in economic reconstruction—both for the overall strategy and for its component programs. These should not be measured by purely economic or financial profit maximizing criteria but by whether they contributed or not to reconciliation and peace consolidation. At the same time, governments should develop a basic statistical framework to facilitate policymaking and to measure and record social and economic progress.

With more restricted policy choices and with a high degree of polarization that makes consensus more difficult to achieve in post-conflict situations, three elements are critical in effective policymaking. Although these elements are related they have different policy implications. First, an immediate "peace dividend" is essential if people are to believe that they have a stake in the success of the peace process and should support it. In this regard, quick-impact projects should take place immediately in the transition to peace to improve basic services and to provide other humanitarian assistance to save lives and improve livelihoods. At the same time, humanitarian assistance, which increases consumption rather than investment, needs to wither as soon as possible to avoid aid dependencies.

Second, for the peace dividend to be sustained, reconstruction aid needs to start promptly and concurrently with humanitarian aid so that countries can create employment, investment, and growth. Humanitarian aid and reconstruction aid should not be conflated—as is often the case—including by the UN in its institutional arrangements in the field, where it has humanitarian coordinators leading reconstruction activities. Their impact on the economy is quite distinct and they should be carried out by different people and organizations with specific expertise and know-how. Humanitarian aid, although essential as a palliative to crises since it increases the consumption possibilities of those affected by the crises, does not improve the productive capacity of the country. On the other hand, reconstruction aid, if well invested to strengthen the government, to create a good business climate to support private initiative and to replace illegal production, will allow countries to avoid aid dependencies and help them to move into sustainable development. The Marshall Plan, by all accounts the most effective reconstruction plan ever, was based on a clear distinction between the two, in terms not only of expertise but also of financing. While financing for humanitarian assistance was on a grants basis, there was some quid pro quo for reconstruction assistance so that national governments would assume responsibility for it.

Third, policymakers need to make a special effort also to build up consensus for their policies—not only within the government but also among civil society groups—despite the difficulties in doing so as a result of the polarization created by war. In this regard, governments will need to make an effort at communication to explain in plain language the reconstruction strategy that they want to adopt and why. Governments can do this by conducting information campaigns to inform the public of the expected medium- and long-term benefits of the proposed policies, as well as the short-term costs that these may imply. Unless government officials and people in general can weigh the expected personal benefits favorably vis-à-vis the costs, they may not be willing to bear such costs. This will also avoid building up unrealistic expectations of what peace can bring. Unfulfilled expectations of disgruntled groups can seriously endanger a war-to-peace transition.

Unless policymakers manage to build a broad-based consensus on different policies, these are not likely to be successful or sustainable. A building up of unrealistic expectations, lack of consensus on policymaking, a slow move from humanitarian to reconstruction aid, and an inadequate macro- and microeconomic framework for post-conflict countries have been important factors in recent failures with reconstruction.

Because of the critical importance of political and security issues in post-conflict situations, leadership of operations in the field should be done at the political level, rather than by the UNDP or another development organization. The UN, through the Special Representative of the Secretary-General (SRSG) in the field could be the best placed to do this except that the UN has proved incapable of doing it effectively. This is partly due to the lack of adequate institutional arrangements, and partly because of lack of qualified experts and internal training programs to create the necessary team to deal with post-conflict economic reconstruction.

Although the UNDP and other development and financial institutions need to play a critical technical role in post-conflict economic reconstruction, their mandate is to collaborate with governments and ensure their ownership in national programs. Thus, former rebel groups which are frequently equal partners in peace agreements or other political solutions see these organizations with misgivings since they do not feel treated by them in an equal manner to governments. Only the UN can play an impartial political role and balance the various factors and trade-offs necessary to carry out the multi-pronged transition. The UN needs—and recent reforms have not provided—the right institutional arrangements, expertise, and talent to be able to play an effective role in economic reconstruction. The institutional arrangements that I propose (see Figures 2–6), if complemented with good leadership and adequate technical resources, would give the UN the capacity to lead and coordinate economic reconstruction effectively, not only with the development and financial institutions, but also with national governments.

At the same time, both the case studies and the analysis of donors' support for economic reconstruction in Chapters 5 and 6 provide convincing evidence that aid policies are in disarray. Although the arguments are too many to enumerate here, it is clear that donors need to reorient their policies if they want to support economic reconstruction in an effective way. Unless they do so, rather than contributing to the multi-pronged transition to peace they have often become an obstacle to it. Several factors could improve the effectiveness of aid in post-conflict situations.

First, there is a need for greater flexibility in the payment of debt arrears and more aid on concessional terms from the international financial institutions and other donors. Financing reconstruction could be a good investment for the international community. Leaving aside the human cost, the cost of financing reconstruction has proved to be a pittance compared to what it would cost the international community in military and peacekeeping operations should the country relapse into conflict.

Second, donors' policies requiring that the government build up policy credibility before they get access to certain financing often threatens the early transition to peace. Although it is imperative to make strong efforts at building the policy implementation capacity of national governments and at improving economic governance, aid in the immediate transition to peace is necessary to carry out the critical peace-related activities without which the process will not prosper. Delaying aid until such time that the government has a better managerial and absorptive capacity can have tragic consequences.

Third, although donors have been more willing to provide budgetary support than they were in the early post-Cold War period, in more recent operations, aid has been increasingly channeled to projects that donors carry out independently of the national government, and that involve their own contractors and experts. This policy needs to be reevaluated. This weakens the government, is resented by the local population, and creates aid dependency. On the contrary, budgetary support for specific expenditures including subsidies and price support programs could reactivate the agricultural sector and other labor-intensive activities in post-conflict countries. If at the same time donors provided know-how, other technical support and credit, as well as access to their markets under preferential tariff treatment for exports from "reconstruction zones" in post-conflict countries, this would greatly contribute to reconstruction and national reconciliation. Lack of viable employment has been a major feature of all post-conflict economies and one of the main deterrents to the consolidation of peace.

An emphasis on the role and responsibility of the international community in supporting economic reconstruction, should not, however, detract from the responsibility of governments and other domestic actors to use aid effectively.

The case studies also provide convincing evidence that governments in post-conflict countries often lack the responsibility, transparency, and accountability for dealing with aid and reconstruction issues. For effective reconstruction, governments must follow sound economic policies and provide an appropriate legal, fiscal, judicial, and institutional framework essential to fostering domestic savings and attracting private capital inflows as soon as possible. Although such a framework will take time to develop—because of the restrictions of the multi-pronged transition—without it, a country will be unable permanently to reintegrate large numbers of people into productive activities, let alone move onto a normal development path, regardless of how much foreign money is poured into its economy.

An improvement in economic governance in the post-conflict transition is imperative if aid is to be sustained. Unless taxpayers in donor countries support international assistance to countries in the post-conflict transition, and can appreciate the impact that the reconstruction strategy is having in those countries, as well as in the region or internationally, their political leaders will not allocate the necessary resources. Without proper financing, technical assistance, and strengthening of national governments' capabilities, the chances of effective reconstruction are indeed slim.

Governments need to have a comprehensive strategy for economic reconstruction. Piecemeal approaches have not worked. The objective of this book has also been to facilitate the preparation of such a strategy by describing activities and policy guidelines that governments could adopt to maximize their chances of success. Policymakers will be constantly opting among different economic choices and need to be informed about such choices. Thus, in Chapters 11–15 I have presented lessons from recent experiences that are relevant to different aspects of the strategy, as well as what have been discerned to be best practices in post-conflict reconstruction. In most cases, these have not necessarily proved to be the best practices under normal development.

I hope I have provided enough substance and empirical evidence to convince the reader that the status quo is not sustainable with regard to post-conflict economic reconstruction and that major changes are necessary in this area for peace to have a chance. Because of the great variety of stakeholders and their often conflicting goals during reconstruction, many of the premises, lessons, best practices, and policy guidelines are likely to be controversial since changing the status quo has never proved easy. My purpose, however, will be fulfilled if I can help to stimulate, and perhaps contribute constructively to, the type of fruitful public debate about reconstruction that followed the publication of *The Marshall Plan*, and that has been so notoriously lacking in the post-Cold War period.

☐ NOTES

Introduction: Reconstruction off track

1. It was called East Timor before it became an independent country in 2002. Throughout the text the two names are used, depending on whether it refers to the period before or after independence.
2. Although the International Monetary Fund (IMF) and the World Bank are part of the UN system, for purposes of the analysis, and because of their specific role in financing, I include them among the international financial institutions (IFIs) or refer to them as the Bretton Woods institutions.
3. "Aid" refers to official assistance that provides some relief to the receiving country, and includes both "grants" (assistance without a quid pro quo) and "concessional loans" (loans at interest rates below commercial or market terms). See Chapter 6.

1 Features of recent transitions

1. To avoid repetition, this book often uses "war-to-peace transitions," "peace transitions," "transitions to peace," or simply "transitions" interchangeably.
2. Debt forgiveness is often referred to by its technical name, "debt condonation."
3. Stanley and Holiday (2002) argued that, "The government and the URNG (*Unidad Revolucionaria Nacional Guatemalteca*) transformed a negotiated surrender into an internationally supported peace process. The Guatemalan parties sold the international community an image of a war-weary country seeking to excise the roots of conflict through political and social transformation. The accords promised major political, institutional, social, and economic reforms aimed at democratization and greater equity." The authors also argued that the UN's inability to verify compliance with the accords reflected the absence of Security Council clout, while other international actors like the United States lacked leverage because of Guatemala's limited wartime dependence on international assistance.
4. The $ sign indicates US dollars throughout the book.
5. See Giersch *et al.* (1993: 15–16). In the case of West Germany, the ratio was only 1.4 percent, well below the average of 2.1 percent for all countries. By the time the ERP started in June 1947, the US had already provided about $9 billion in aid to Europe since the end of the war. For analyses of the Marshall Plan, see Dulles (1993), Schain (2001), De Long and Eichengreen (1993), and Hogan (1987).
6. Staines (2004: 5) notes that after the end of the Cold War, donor practices shifted away from support for countries in conflict towards post-conflict assistance. As will be discussed in the case studies, this shift in donors' practices sometimes facilitated UN-brokered peace negotiations.
7. See, for example, the 1992 and 1996 peace agreements for El Salvador (UN 1992a, DPI/1208-92614) and Guatemala (MINUGUA, 1997).

8. While 13 operations were established during the first 40 years of UN peacekeeping from 1948 to 1988, 36 new operations were launched in the following decade. At its peak in 1993, the total deployment of UN military and civilian personnel reached more than 80,000, and represented 77 countries. In March 2008, there were more than 100,000 personnel including uniformed personnel (70,000 troops, 11,000 police, 2,500 observers) and civilians (5,000 international, and 11,500 local recruits) in 18 missions (See UN web site).

9. See de Soto and del Castillo (1994). At the time, we both were at the Office of the Secretary-General, de Soto as Assistant Secretary-General and special political advisor to the Secretary-General and I as Senior Officer in charge of economic matters and post-conflict reconstruction.

10. I refer to these later as "UN protectorates". Jenkins (2006) refers to them as "neotrustee-ship." In his view these are arrangements whereby multilateral institutions temporarily govern states that have collapsed in spasms of misrule and violent conflict.

11. I refer to this in the text as "US-led occupation."

12. For a detailed analysis of the security transition, see, for example, Call and Stanley (2002), Feil (2004), and Salomons (2005).

13. Rubin *et al.* (2003: 18) refer to this two-way causality between security and reconstruction as a "virtuous circle" and Weinbaum (2006: 139) refers to it as "two sides of the same coin."

14. Orr (2004: 58) posits that the extent to which a coherent, legitimate government exists or can be created is arguably the most important factor in determining the success or failure of the post-conflict transition. Dobbins *et al.* (2003: xix) argue that democratization is the core objective of nation-building operations. In a study of 14 peacebuilding operations launched between 1989 and 1999, Paris (2004: 5) posits that underlying the design and practice of these operations was the hope and expectation that democratization would shift societal conflicts away from the battlefield and into the peaceful arena of electoral politics.

15. Failed states and breakaway provinces will be analyzed in the case studies of Kosovo and Afghanistan (Chapters 8 and 9).

16. For more details on the political transition, see, for example, Doyle (2002), Lyons (2002), and Dobbins *et al.* (2003, 2005).

17. For more details on the social transitions see, for example, Prendergast and Plumb (2002) and Spear (2002).

18. As Woodward (2002: 183) pointed out in 2002, there had not been any systematic analysis of the contribution of economic factors to the success or failure in the implementation of peace agreements. Her 2002 piece on economic priorities made a significant contribution but very little has happened since. Much more is needed in terms of analysis and debate.

19. Stabilization and liberalization carried out by post-conflict economies have been criticized by several authors (for example, Paris, 2004), without a proper analysis of the consistency and comprehensiveness with which this strategy has been applied to see whether the prob-lem was with the strategy itself, or rather, with the way it was implemented. Indeed, in my view, the problem is not with the strategy per se, but its application. Some of the policies were inconsistent and critical reforms were missing. As I will discuss in Chapter 13, policy inconsistencies and incomplete reforms were often the cause of financial crises in the 1980s and 1990s as well. See also Dobbins *et al.* (2003, 2005).

20. See, for example, work by the IMF and World Bank on Kosovo, Timor-Leste, and the DRC.

2 **Debate on the economic consequences of peacetime**

1. Reparations also took place following earlier wars. For example, Devereux and Smith (2005) noted that during the 1871–3 Franco-Prussian War, France transferred to Germany an amount equal to 22 percent of GDP each year for a period of three years.

2. The famous debate between Keynes and Bertil Ohlin on the economic consequences of peace in 1929 is documented in the *Economic Journal*. See Keynes (1919, 1929a, 1929b, 1929c) and Ohlin (1929a, 1929b). For the theoretical underpinnings of the transfer problem, see Mundell (1968b: 17–26), and Mundell (1991: 3–7).

3. The US Secretary of State, George Marshall, revealed the details of the plan for the reconstruction of Europe in a speech at Harvard University on June 5, 1947. At the time, many thought that the post-conflict reconstruction of Europe had come to a halt, and that democracy and stability in Western Europe were once again under siege. Marshall addressed this issue and spoke of the need to "break the vicious circle" (Schain, 2001: 4). The Marshall Plan marked the end of isolationism and the beginning of what Henry Luce, the influential American publisher, called the "American Century" (Hogan 1987: 1).

4. In fact, a survey of the American Institute for Public Opinion showed that no more than 45 percent of the public supported the Marshall Plan.

5. According to Dulles (1993: 69), "the sum is vast. This is not even debatable. But it is certainly pertinent to remind those who are impressed ... that the sum is also less than the cost of three months of war, when at the peak of our military expenditure, we were spending at the rate of $80 billion a year." In December 1947, President Truman pointed out that the Plan's cost represented a pittance compared with the cost to the US of World War II, and less than 3 percent of the national income. Nevertheless, the sum was "decried as being almost twice the annual appropriation for national defense, as amounting to about half of the annual government budget, or as constituting a 'gift' to Europe of approximately $120 from every person in the United States." The US would provide aid mostly in the form of agricultural products, fuel, commodities, machinery, and other capital goods, but not in money terms. American supply of such goods was limited, and this limited available aid.

6. For an analysis of the factors that make countries vulnerable to armed conflict, see, for example, International Peace Academy (IPA 2002d), and Collier and Sambanis (2005). According to the World Bank (2002), all but 7 of the 110 conflicts recorded between 1989 and 2000 were civil wars. An accepted definition of civil war, though by no means the only one, is that the conflict is between a government and an identifiable rebel group and generates at least 1,000 dead on both sides.

7. Development theory and practice have undergone major changes in the post-World War II period, particularly with respect to the role of aid. See, for example, Burnside and Dollar (2000), who found that aid is effective only if domestic policies are adequate and consistent. This has often created problems for aid delivery to post-conflict countries, which have not yet built up policy credibility. See also, Bourguignon and Sundberg (2007).

8. This point was strongly made in de Soto and del Castillo (1994).

3 **Definitions and characteristics**

1. For simplicity, I often refer to it as "economic reconstruction" or simply "reconstruction."

2. Development is thus broadly defined to include fundamental human rights, environmental concerns, and justice. See Boutros-Ghali (1995b).

3. See UN (2005c: 31). See also IPA (2002d) and Paris (2004). Collier (2001) estimated a slightly lower probability of relapse into conflict (about 44 percent).

4. Thus, the term "post-conflict development," coined by Junne and Verkoren (2005), is unfortunate, for it elides the striking differences and distinctive policy implications relating to post-conflict reconstruction and normal development.

5. See also UN (1995b) and del Castillo (2001a: 1900).

6. In a letter of August 10, 1995, to Anstee, the Secretary-General particularly noted "the finding of the Colloquium that the mission involved in post-conflict peacebuilding, while using a variety of tools, is essentially political, and is thus fundamentally different in nature from normal relief or development activities." The Secretary-General also "notes the suggestion that appropriate systems and procedures need to be set up at Headquarters to ensure that these responsibilities are discharged on my behalf, and particularly the idea that 'a specific Department should act as a focal point, and marshall all the necessary staff and other elements needed on an ad hoc basis whenever circumstances demanded, and that this might be the Department of Political Affairs.'"

7. Others also eventually recognized the differences between reconstruction and normal development. See, for example, Orr (2004a: 21).

8. In the case study of Kosovo, for example, I illustrate this point by making reference to how short-term programs to winterize destroyed houses were a waste in terms of the future housing development of the province. Perlez (2006) discusses how houses built by Save the Children after the tsunami were so quickly and badly built that they only served a short-run purpose.

9. Demekas *et al.* (2002b: 3) point out that post-conflict aid can reach extraordinarily high levels, both in per capita terms and relative to the size of the recipient economy immediately after the conflict ends, but typically declines very rapidly. In Rwanda in 1994, aid reached 95 percent of GDP, but declined to under 20 percent within five years. In Bosnia and Herzegovina in 1994, aid reached 75 percent of GDP, but fell to less than 25 percent by 1999. By contrast, aid during normal development fluctuates much less and remains at much lower levels. For example, according to World Bank data, official development assistance (ODA) to the group of low-income countries in 1995–2000 ranged from 2.5 to 3 percent of gross national income (GNI).

10. Funds are "pledged" at donors' meetings or bilaterally. Funds for which agreements have been signed become "committed" funds. Once the funds are deposited into the accounts of the recipient country, they become "disbursed" funds.

11. Contagion refers to the impact on a country's financial system from policies or events in another country.

12. After the personal involvement of President Bush, the US government agreed to a bridging loan until a large package was negotiated with the IMF, the Inter-American Development Bank (IADB), and the World Bank. The overall IMF package was unprecedented for the institution, and, given Argentina's default at the end of 2001, it was clearly targeted at avoiding another "default precedent" for Brazil, and preventing contagion to other emerging markets. Uruguay's rescue package represented 23 percent of its GDP in 2002, whereas the much talked about $30 billion assistance package to Brazil in 2002 amounted to only 5 percent of GDP. As a result of the crisis, in just 15 months beginning in February 2002, Uruguay went from "investment grade" ratings from the three major rating agencies (Moody's, Standard and Poor's, and Fitch), to the largest ever IMF package for any country (del Castillo 2004).

13. In Uruguay, for example, the leftist government coalition that assumed power in March 2005 had to adopt a 1-year Emergency Social Program (extended for another year) costing roughly 1 percent of GDP. Despite an astonishing public-sector external debt level of more than 100 percent of GDP, the IFIs supported and facilitated its financing.

14. When fiscal deficits cannot be financed through bond issues, they usually lead to monetization (money creation). If the central bank creates money to finance the government deficit, this is likely to generate inflation (unless the demand for money is increasing).

15. The "Washington Consensus" is a term coined by John Williamson in the late 1980s to describe a set of policies recommended by the IFIs to Latin American and other emerging countries that had suffered serious financial crises. These countries needed to reactivate their economies by creating a policy and institutional environment conducive to private-sector activity. Since the crisis in Argentina at the beginning of this century, the terms "Washington consensus" and "neo-liberalism" have increasingly been used pejoratively to describe policies that restrict the state role in the economy. See Chapter 14.

16. Failure in these situations can be explained by the "Theory of the Second Best" developed by Lipsky and Lancaster in the mid-1950s, who argue that adopting some policies but not others that are equally necessary will not necessarily move the economy closer towards the desired state.

17. See Chapter 10 for an analysis of debt restructuring in Iraq.

18. Referring to the latter, a 1996 study by the Center for Preventive Action at the Council on Foreign Relations stated that, "History will judge us harshly if we do not build on the achievement of Dayton to establish a comprehensive peace in the Balkans" (p. 3). Because the two sides were too far apart in Kosovo to reach agreement on the final status, they urged pursuit of "an interim settlement that would defuse tension." Such a proposal, if implemented, would have avoided the human tragedy and physical devastation that ensued in 1998–99. However, it could not be pursued, mostly for the reasons discussed above.

4 Basic premises for policymaking

1. Following Bildt (2004a), I use the term "state-building" rather than "nation-building" because "the task is not about 'building nations' but building states, very often in areas where several nations and nationalities have to coexist within one framework. State-building as we see it in the real world from Bosnia and Herzegovina in the north-east to Basra in the south-east, is often about transcending nations and overcoming nationalism. Much the same applies in Afghanistan and certainly in the problem areas of Africa." Furthermore, as Bildt points out, the term "nation-building" was invented "to discredit such efforts rather than give guidance about their nature." Although de Soto and I have used the term "nation-building" in the past, I find Bildt's arguments compelling against its use now.

2. In addition to the economic and financial implications of disarmament, demobilization, and reintegration, this process involves many other issues that need to be well integrated. See, for example, Berdal (1996), Ball (2001), and Spear (2002). The issue of disarmament, demobilization and reintegration will be discussed in detail in relation to the case of El Salvador (Chapter 7).

3. The different reconstruction actors are discussed in detail in Chapter 5.

4. On El Salvador, see de Soto and del Castillo (1994) and Goulding (2002); on Angola, see Goulding (2002) and Anstee (2003); on Cambodia, see Doyle *et al.* (1997) and Doyle (2001). On Nicaragua, see Overseas Development Council (1995); on Guatemala, see Stanley and Holiday (2002); on Kosovo, see Chapter 8.

5. The discussions took place with members of the Office of the UN Secretary-General. World Bank policy changed in fundamental ways after James Wolfensohn took over in 1995. The Bank became closely involved in supporting post-conflict economic recon-struction, including reintegration efforts, although even a year earlier, in 1994, the Bank had begun work on reintegration in Uganda.

6. The UN has four programs (UNDP, UNFPA, WFP, and UNICEF) and several agencies. The most relevant to post-conflict economic reconstruction are UNHCR, FAO, IFAD, WFP, WHO, UNICEF, and ILO. Although the Bretton Woods institutions—the IMF and the World Bank—are, strictly speaking, also UN agencies, I include them sepa-rately because of their particular status as IFIs. In addition to these institutions, the IFIs include the regional development banks, of which the four most important are the African Development Bank (AfDB), the Asian Development Bank (ADB), the European Bank for Reconstruction and Development (EBRD), and the Inter-American Develop-ment Bank (IADB). The major bilateral development agencies include: USAID, DFID (UK), CIDA (Canada), SIDA (Sweden), and AFD (France). See List of Abbreviations, pp. xvii–xxi.

7. See del Castillo (1995a: 31).

8. In matters of "peace and security," the Secretary-General is assisted principally by the Under-Secretary-Generals of the departments of Peacekeeping Operations (DPKO), Polit-ical Affairs (DPA), Humanitarian Affairs (DHA), and Legal Affairs (DLA).

9. The IMF recognized such leadership in post-conflict situations early on. See Camdessus (1993). O'Donnell (2005: 6) contrasts the UN's broad mandate with the restricted man-date of the World Bank. She notes that the Bank needs to avoid involvement in political affairs, particularly concerning elections, disarmament, and other sensitive issues. She argues that the impartiality and legitimacy of the UN in post-conflict reconstruction is equivalent to that of peacekeepers, whose strongest "weapon" is drawn from the fact that they have a Security Council mandate and represent the international community as a whole.

10. As with every rule, there might be exceptions. The most notorious relates to Iraq. Because of comprehensive sanctions imposed by the UN for 12 years in Iraq, which had a dev-astating impact on the population at large, it was hardly reasonable to expect that Iraqis would view the UN as impartial. In other cases where the UN has imposed sanctions, UN leadership in post-conflict reconstruction may be questioned as well.

11. This is an important difference with humanitarian agencies. While the development agencies have a mandate to collaborate with governments, humanitarian agencies must keep a distance from the political process to ensure that assistance is provided to those most in need, irrespective of political considerations.

12. Murphy (2006) cites the UNDP's impartiality on several occasions. But it is difficult to believe that an organization with a clear mandate to collaborate with the government can be perceived as impartial by groups that have been fighting the government for many years, as was the case in El Salvador and Guatemala, for example. Unfortunately, Murphy's history of the UNDP is short on any serious evaluation of the organization's role in post-conflict reconstruction.

13. As a World Bank case study on El Salvador (2000: 39, 65) notes, the primary relationship of the Bank is with the government. This was necessarily so because of the Bank's Articles of Agreement, which specify that it can negotiate loans only with a member government (or an enterprise or other government when a member government provides a satisfactory, full guarantee of the loan). In principle, a dialogue with former guerrilla groups could take place only with the government's consent. As the country director for El Salvador pointed out, however, it was first essential to gain the trust of the government in power in the early 1990s, so that the Bank could "afford" to talk to opposition groups. O'Donnell (2005: 7) quotes a World Bank official, according to whom "our long-term client is the local institutions."

14. Under-Secretary of the Treasury, John Taylor (2007: 48) described the "distressing lack of urgency" he perceived in meeting with Asian Development Bank (ADB) staff on the building of a new road from Kandahar to the border with Pakistan at Spin Boldek. He conveyed the sense of urgency of such projects as follows: "This isn't business as usual; we're fighting a war, a war on terror, and if you don't get moving like development banks never have before, we could lose that war. Afghanistan's political situation is delicate; if it went back to the wrong people it could again become a training ground for terrorists."

15. The division of labor between DPA and DPKO should be clearly delineated, since there is a continuing unresolved debate about the respective mandates, with DPKO invariably arguing that it is also a political department. See Chapter 5, note 17 for a discussion of Goulding's proposal to merge the two departments.

5 The multilateral framework for international assistance

1. For the complete Organization Chart of the UN System, including the six organs (the Security Council, the General Assembly, the Trusteeship Council, the International Court of Justice, and the UN Secretariat), all the programs and agencies, and the Secretariat Departments, see UN web site. For the development organizations and the international financial institutions (IFIs) see Chapter 4, note 6. Bilateral and regional donors are important sources of finance and technical assistance, particularly in countries in their respective backyards, or areas of influence/preference (e.g. Japan in Cambodia, Australia in Timor-Leste, the United States in Haiti, the EU in Bosnia and Herzegovina and Kosovo, the Asian Development Bank (ADB) in Afghanistan, and the World Bank in Liberia). Some foreign and local NGOs are important sources of humanitarian assistance. See, for example, Abiew and Keating (2004) and O'Brien (2004) for the role of NGOs. For a broader discussion of humanitarianism see, for example, Donini *et al.* (2004), Fisher (2007), and Barnett and Weiss (2008).

2. See Meyer and Califano (2006) and Turner (2006b). As Turner notes, an internal review of the UN peacekeeping operations found "substantial evidence of abuse" in procurement operations, leading to "financial losses and significant inaccuracies in planning assumptions." Issues relating to UN staff have been a serious problem as well in the capacity of the organization to deal effectively with the problems the organization faces. In *The Best Intentions*, Traub (2006: 139), for example, mentions how US Ambassador Richard Holbrooke frequently assailed the institution, "observing in almost every speech that the UN employed far more people in its public information department than it did in peacekeeping—meaning that the UN was more preoccupied with bureaucratic

self-preservation than with effective action." For a vivid and disheartening description of poor management and the lack of accountability at the highest level of the UN led by Kofi Annan, see Traub (2006: 294, 415).

3. The latter applies also to the UN Secretary-General's association, through his membership in the Middle East Quartet, with a policy toward the democratically elected government of the Palestinian Authority that is widely seen by Palestinians and people in the Arab world as collective punishment for the way they voted in those elections. The bombings of the UN offices in Baghdad in August 2003 and in Algiers in December 2007 point to the need for the UN to maintain a steady, even-handed approach so as not to be seen as a puppet of policies of dubious legitimacy. The UN's role in Iraq raises additional questions about whether the UN can be an effective player in an environment in which it is so closely associated by many groups as part of the occupation. These and other factors have led to the marginalization of the UN in some cases. As pointed out by the UN envoy to Sudan at the time, Jan Pronk (2006), the Sudanese government withdrew its support in March 2006 for a UN peacekeeping force to replace African Union troops in the Darfur region, portraying the UN's entry as a precursor to a Western takeover of the country. Cousens (2002: 544) noted that in Bosnia and Herzegovina, for example, the Organization for Security and Cooperation in Europe (OSCE) rather than the UN was asked to supervise elections, despite its lack of experience in doing so, because the UN had been largely discredited by its peacekeeping performance during the war. Sexual exploitation and abuse by peacekeepers, most flagrantly in the Democratic Republic of Congo (DRC), has not helped either.

4. For a detailed discussion of how the UN is financed, see Laurenti (2004). While the UN's regular budget and peacekeeping costs are financed through mandatory contributions by member states, the agencies and programs are financed primarily through voluntary contributions. In the earlier period of UN peacekeeping operations, when these operations were a rare occurrence, the Secretary-General was dependent on the regular budget to establish the mission. The large cost of the Congo operation in the 1960s started the practice of assessed contributions where the permanent members of the Security Council paid a larger share. By the late 1990s, a new practice of using trust funds with voluntary financing made it possible to establish operations in a shorter period of time. This was, for example, the case in East Timor.

5. CEPAL is the Spanish acronym for the UN Economic Commission for Latin America and the Caribbean (ECLAC), one of the five UN Regional Commissions.

6. DPA's main role is in peacemaking. DPKO plans, directs, and supports peacekeeping and peacebuilding operations, often with support from DPA. Peacebuilding operations of a basically political (rather than military and security) nature are under DPA's direction. See also Chapter 4, note 15.

7. Furthermore, neither the DPA nor the DPKO has acquired adequate expertise of their own on economic and social issues, and the DESA continues to be marginalized from the UN's political work. A cursory look at the DESA's Divisions and Offices, as well as their research and activities listed in their web site, demonstrates that the DESA follows a "development as usual" approach. DESA's involvement would require a mandate from the Secretary-General.

8. At the time, DESA was called Economic and Social Information and Policy Analysis (DESIPA) and was headed by Jean-Claude Milleron. DPA was headed by Marrack Goulding.

NOTES **319**

9. Until 1992, the Director-General for International Economic Development and Cooperation was the number-two person at the UN. The Director-General was in charge of coordinating all economic functions of the organization. When Boutros-Ghali took over as Secretary-General, he eliminated the Director-General's Office and merged the departments dealing with economic and social issues and technical assistance and moved the Centre on Transnational Corporations dealing with foreign direct investment to Geneva to be part of the UNCTAD. As part of this restructuring, I was transferred into his cabinet, to become the first economist in the Secretary-General's Office. In the process, he left out of the reorganization the three most capable and effective assistant secretary-generals in the economic area: Enrique ter Horst, Goran Ohlin, and Peter Hansen. In my years at the Secretary-General's Office, I could not find anybody claiming authorship of this policy, which proved disastrous. It greatly diminished the UN Secretariat's capacity not only to deal with economic and social issues, but also to support economic reconstruction efforts throughout the world.

10. The DESA's first attempt to deal with more political issues took place in November 2004, when Under-Secretary General José Antonio Ocampo convened a one-day Expert Group Meeting on Conflict Prevention, Peacebuilding, and Development. As I argued earlier, although they are closely interconnected and often require comparable expertise and operational tools, conflict prevention, peacebuilding, and development are clearly distinct issues. To lump them together, following the approach of the Brahimi and the Millenium reports, detracts from their important differences, and the constraints under which each should operate to be truly effective. After this, some timid efforts were also made to involve the DESA in activities with the peacekeeping department.

11. The SMG was a committee of senior heads of departments. The Policy Committee included the Secretary-General, the Deputy Secretary-General, and the eight under-secretary-generals heads of areas.

12. Of 200 people interviewed by the group preparing the report, members of the World Bank staff were included, but no one from the IMF was. The report mentioned the "hybrid of political and development activities targeted at the sources of conflict," and argued that the Executive Committee on Peace and Security (ECPS), chaired by the head of the DPA, was the ideal forum for the formulation of peacebuilding strategies. The ECPS is one of four committees created by the Secretary-General in 1997 as high-level bodies for interagency and interdepartmental coordination. The other three are the Executive Committees of Economic and Social Affairs, Development Cooperation, and Humanitarian Affairs.

13. Soon after the *Brahimi Report*, the focus of UN reform fully shifted toward "normal development." As with previous Secretary-Generals, Kofi Annan found it difficult to keep a balance between the UN's work in the areas of peace, security, and development. Such a balance is necessary to serve both the interests of the industrial countries, which tend to focus more on peace and security, and those of the developing countries, which have a higher stake in development. This was reflected in the reform agenda. The Millennium Summit took place in September 2000 to advance the process of UN reform and in light of the differential impact that globalization in the world economy was having on the UN membership. In preparation for the Summit, the Secretary-General presented a report entitled *We the Peoples: The Role of the United Nations in the 21st Century* (UN 2000a). Although this report discussed matters of peace and security, its focus was the ambitious development targets that it included. The Millennium Declaration adopted, with some changes, the Millennium Development Goals (MDGs). Except for a single mention of

post-conflict reconstruction, the Millennium Declaration is a typical "development as usual" document. It is thus hard to believe that institutional and other mechanisms created to promote the MDGs would necessarily be adequate for post-conflict reconstruction.

14. For details on the functions of these bodies, see UN web site.

15. Such an organizational structure can succeed in integrating the political and economic structures of the transition to peace only if the ERSG or SRSG, in addition to having political or diplomatic credentials, has the background or relevant experience to lead the economic team. This is not often the case since secretary-generals normally fill these posts with people who have political and diplomatic skills but are often uninterested in or ignorant of economic and financial matters. Thus, putting the UNDG or UNCT under them directly is a recipe for "development as usual" led by the UNDP. My proposed structure, by ensuring the integration of political and economic matters would have a much larger chance of success (see Figure 2–4).

16. For details, see note 9 above.

17. Although it is well beyond the topic of this book, my proposal would be more effective had Marrack Goulding's proposal to merge DPA and DPKO been accepted. Goulding, who had been both Under-Secretary-General for peacekeeping operations and for political affairs—recommended that an enlarged political department be created, with DPKO becoming an operational arm as an office for peacekeeping operations. As the situation stands, DPKO also considers itself a political department and it is a source of confusion that most missions in the field are under DPKO (including some political ones) but some are under DPA. See also caplan (2005: 234).

18. Although some missions have two Deputies, they do not necessarily follow this model. For example, the United Nations Assistance Mission for Iraq (UNAMI), a DPA field mission, has two Deputies, one for Political Affairs, Electoral Assistance, and Constitutional Support and the other for Humanitarian Coordination (see UN web site). The lack of capacity to deal with reconstruction issues per se—in contrast to humanitarian ones—is most surprising in light of its Security Council mandate. According to its mandate, UNAMI should advise, support, and assist in the implementation of the International Compact with Iraq, including coordination with donors and international financial institutions. Its mandate includes also the coordination and implementation of programs to improve Iraq's capacity to provide essential services for its people, and continuing active donor coordination of critical reconstruction and assistance programs through the International Reconstruction Fund Facility for Iraq (IRFFI).

19. The UNDG, created in 1997, is composed of UN programs and agencies as well as some parts of the Secretariat (DESA, DPI, UNOPS), the five regional commissions, and UNCTAD. In addition there are some observers, including the World Bank and OCHA. The Secretary-General created the UNDG in 1997 to improve the UN's effectiveness in development at the country level. The Group is chaired by the UNDP's Administrator on behalf of the Secretary-General and has focused on achieving the Millenium Development Goals (MDGs). The aid coordinator would also coordinate with NGOs since donors often channel aid through NGOs. See List of Abbreviations pp. xvii–xxi.

20. Although the need for centralization would seem obvious, as Woodward (2002: 200) noted, most peace missions either have no database of donors and projects or multiple databases, each with different assumptions and criteria for recording the data. It is no

exaggeration to argue that aid coordination has been, and remains, one of the most chaotic aspects of reconstruction.

21. The UN has never been good at preserving institutional memory in the economic area. For example, when Sidney Dell, one of the most distinguished UN economists, died, his family tried to give his papers to the UN. The UN refused them on the grounds that the library had no space. Thus, his papers were archived in a university library, far away from UN headquarters in New York. When I was offered a job at the IMF, I had to take all my files after I tried unsuccessfully to leave them at the UN. The Office of the Secretary-General argued that they, or the DPA had the originals, and the DESA refused them flatly. Since I was the only person dealing with post-conflict economic reconstruction in the Secretary-General's office, there were many documents, particularly the more technical ones, of which only I kept copies. On a more positive note, this gave me an incentive to write this book and helped me to document it.

22. This is, for example, what the World Bank did when war broke out in El Salvador in 1980. However, although the country was still at war in 1986, when an earthquake devastated the capital, the Bank renewed its engagement. When a new government took over in June 1989, normal relations were reestablished with both the World Bank and IMF, even before the peace agreement was signed. Both the World Bank and the Fund severed relations with Iraq in 1980, when the war with Iran started. Relations were not reestablished in the 1990s because of comprehensive UN sanctions, and were only renewed in 2003, after the US-led occupation.

23. Informal programs that do not involve any financing from the Fund are referred to as "shadow programs" or "staff-monitored programs" and often take place before clearance of arrears. For example, when the peace process in Angola was experiencing serious difficulties in the mid-1990s, the country had a staff-monitored stabilization program involving policy dialogue and capacity building.

24. For a discussion on the role of the IFIs in capacity building in Africa, see Nsouli (2002).

25. The report found that some of the best examples of cooperation between the Bretton Woods institutions occur when both institutions have essentially been mandated, often by their shareholders, to pursue joint products. In the absence of such mandates, the report notes good examples of the staff of the two organizations working together. The report emphasizes, however, the need to ensure that good collaboration does not depend on the personalities and initiative of individuals involved but on a more systematic and institutionalized system (p. 25).

26. Notwithstanding the broad division of labor between the Fund and the Bank, there are areas of overlapping responsibility between them. They relate mainly to financial market issues, public sector reform, and issues of transparency, governance, corruption and legislative reform, trade policy, and debt management. The Fund, the Bank, and the UNDP often collaborate in rebuilding capacity in different areas.

27. For a detailed legal and institutional analysis of these arguments, see Boon (2007: 521–2).

28. At this time, the President of the World Bank argued that while the Bank's Articles of Agreement prohibit the organization from intervening in the domestic political affairs of member states, the new post-conflict framework contemplated that the Bank had to ensure that the activities it supports "do no harm" and avoid aggravating existing inequities in fragile situations. This justified their involvement in activities that were clearly political in nature. See also Boon (2007).

29. See World Bank (1998a). In 2001, the Post-Conflict Unit became the Conflict Prevention and Reconstruction Unit (CPRU). According to Boyce (2004), however, the fact that the CPRU remained in the Bank's Social Development Department limited its role in operational policy making. Other organizations also created special arrangements to deal with crises and post-conflict countries. The UNDP, for example, created an Emergency Response Division in 1995. In 2001, this Division was elevated to become the Bureau for Crisis Prevention and Recovery (BCPR) with funding from extra-budgetary resources. The OECD and bilateral development institutions have also created specific arrangements for peacebuilding activities. See, for example, Orr (2004c: 28–30); Tschirgi (2004: 5–9), and Boyce (2004).

30. The Watching Briefs monitor country developments in cases where regular Bank assistance is no longer possible because of the conflict, with the aim of being able to provide assistance as soon as conditions allow it. A Transitional Support Strategy is a short- to medium-term plan that is prepared for countries where the Country Assistance Strategy (CAS) is no longer possible because of the conflict or for countries just emerging from conflict.

31. Boyce (2004) relates this decision to the 9/11 terrorist attacks, arguing that they were a wakeup call to staff about what they were doing and what they could have done differently in Afghanistan. This led the Bank's staff to question the "selectivity policy" of the late 1990s, according to which resources were targeted at countries with "good policies" in the belief that this would improve the effectiveness of aid. A new Unit in the Bank's Operational Policy and Country Services was created to manage LICUS, in contrast to the CPRU, which had a limited operational policymaking role. In my view, by addressing the issues of post-conflict countries and other low-income countries together, the LICUS office reinforces the "development as usual" approach which I argue has been an impediment to effective post-conflict reconstruction. Furthermore, having two units, rather than centralizing all matters dealing with post-conflict countries, may also lead to duplication of efforts and, even worse, inefficiencies and fragmentation. The reason for the persistence of two offices may be the difficulty that bureaucracies have in eliminating offices once they have been established.

32. El Salvador and Guatemala in the early 1990s had an average per capita income of over $1,000, thus exceeding the threshold for concessional terms to support post-conflict reconstruction, although both countries' income distribution was extremely skewed, with a large part of the population living in abject poverty.

33. My experience at the UN and the Fund, and later in Kosovo, made me appreciate the cultural differences between these two organizations. While UN lawyers always immediately told us what we could not do every time we had to consult with them, IMF lawyers were more inclined to find a way to do something that needed to be done. For example, given the political restrictions on the Bank's activities, it created a Trust Fund for financing the establishment and training of a civilian police force in Afghanistan where actual appraisal and supervision of the project was handed over to UNDP, with the Bank retaining management of the Fund.

34. Following an agreement between the Bank and the UNDP, countries are precluded from having both a consultative group meeting and a roundtable process concurrently.

35. Bosnia and Herzegovina became the first beneficiary, receiving $45 million.

36. For example, $130 million of a $151 million loan that the Federal Republic of Yugoslavia (FRY) received at the end of 2000 was used to repay bridge loans taken to pay arrears to the

Fund. Repayment took place amid what the IMF itself described as disastrous conditions: "Ten years of regional conflicts, international isolation, and economic mismanagement have left a dire legacy in the FRY. Output, which has only partly recovered from the economic devastation caused by the Kosovo war, stands at about 40 percent of its 1989 level. Unemployment amounts to one half of the labor force. The country's infrastructure is in disrepair following years of inadequate investment and the damage inflicted during the Kosovo war. About 900,000 refugees and internally displaced persons live in FRY under difficult conditions. Serious energy shortages are being somewhat alleviated with humanitarian assistance. The macroeconomic situation is very fragile, and with declining output, the ratio of external debt to GDP has risen to about 140 percent in the absence of debt servicing." The loan was approved soon after the FRY fulfilled the necessary conditions to succeed to the former Socialist Federal Republic of Yugoslavia's membership of the IMF (see IMF web site).

37. This is a quote from the July 2004 statement by Anne Krueger (First Deputy Managing Director of the IMF) concerning an EPCA loan to the Central African Republic (IMF web site).

38. Rwanda's civil war, for example, ended in July 1994, but a $12 million loan under the EPCA was approved only in April 1997 (another $8 million was approved in December 1997). In the interim, the Fund provided technical assistance to the National Bank of Rwanda and the macroeconomic situation improved under a staff-monitored program in 1996. In 1997, the IMF hoped that a transitional phase would lead to a program supported by a loan under the Enhanced Structural Adjustment Facility (ESAF), through which the IMF provides financial assistance on concessional terms to low-income countries. According to a press release that the IMF issued in April 1997, "the authorities' medium-term strategy seeks to promote economic and social reintegration of over 2 million former refugees, foster economic and financial recovery, and pave the way for sustained growth and development." Reintegration should have had top priority in the immediate transition to peace, and the fact that Rwanda was still in that process three years after the end of the civil war was not a good signal of how reintegration was proceeding or how the IMF was assisting it. In other cases, the time gap with regard to EPCA was shorter. For example, an EPCA loan to the Republic of Congo was approved in July 1998, less than one year after the civil war ended in October 1997, and another to Sierra Leone was approved in November 1998, eight months after the end of the military government.

39. The interest rate on loans to such countries was subsidized down to 0.5 percent per year, with the interest subsidies financed by grants contributed by bilateral donors. The ESAF became the PRGF in 1991, and was redefined to increase countries' "ownership" of the poverty-alleviation program through broad-based and participatory processes. At the same time, with the participation of civil society and development partners, the Bank and the Fund launched the *Poverty Reduction Strategy Paper* (PRSP) for low-income countries. In November 2001 the Poverty Reduction Strategies Trust Fund (PRSTF) was established as a multi-donor trust fund to finance capacity-building activities in low-income countries that are undertaking poverty reduction strategies. Weak country capacity was perceived to be a major constraint to effective preparation and implementation of poverty reduction strategies. The PRSP became a key input for the HIPC Initiative, launched by the IMF and the World Bank in 1996 to eliminate unsustainable debt in the world's poorest, most heavily indebted countries.

40. IDA countries receive interest-free loans (with a service charge of 0.75 percent of funds paid out) with payback periods of 40 years.

41. No post-conflict country has yet borrowed more than 25 percent of quota. In 2004–5, only three countries borrowed under this facility: Iraq ($435 million, or 25 percent of quota), the Central African Republic ($8 million, or 10 percent of quota), and Haiti ($16 million, or 12.5 percent of quota). At the end of 2006, after a decade in its existence, only 12 countries had received EPCA (on 19 different occasions). In January 2007, following a major donor conference that yielded pledges of close to $8 billion, EPCA negotiations started with the Lebanese authorities to support efforts to deal with the country's massive debt, rebuild infrastructure destroyed during the previous summer's month-long war between Israel and Hezbollah, and reform the economy. In April 2007, the IMF Board approved an EPCA of 25 percent of quota amounting to about $80 million, to support the five-year reform program presented by the authorities at the Paris III conference in January. In August, the Board approved an EPCA of about $60 million for the Ivory Coast. In 2007, the Central African Republic and Haiti repaid their EPCA loans earlier than scheduled.

42. A Trust Fund is a separate accounting entity with a designated trust manager that receives and manages donor funds for a broad thematic purpose (such as budgetary support) rather than for a specific project. Funding comes mainly from bilateral sources but World Bank trust funds also include net income from the Bank's capital.

43. Emergency funding was used to finance critical imports for agriculture, power, and transport; lines of credit for small- and medium-sized enterprises; support for the functioning of key government institutions; and an Emergency Social Fund to provide minimal levels of cash assistance to the poorest households, and for water supplies and war victims' rehabilitation.

44. Contrary to UN practice up to that time, which discouraged UN officials from publishing articles—least of all of a critical nature—under their own names, Boutros-Ghali encouraged us to write about the problems in El Salvador. We succeeded in stimulating debate at the main organizations' highest levels, including the Secretary-General of the UN, the Managing Director of the Fund, and the President of the World Bank. Furthermore, even we were surprised by the extent to which scholars and practitioners alike agreed with our warning concerning the danger of implementing UN-sponsored peace agreements, while independently carrying out "business as usual" economic programs supported by the IFIs. Our warning of the problem continued to be cited even many years after. Orr (2001: 167–8), for example, pointed out that, "As chief architects of the accords and the land transfer program respectively, de Soto and del Castillo were concerned that the stringent fiscal policies of the government demanded by the multilateral lending agencies were hampering the development of the new National Civilian Police and the land transfer program—central elements of the UN's peacebuilding strategy."

45. Stanley and Holiday (2002) acknowledge that "coordination within the (all inclusive) UN system was exceptional in Guatemala, reflecting lessons learned in El Salvador. The Bretton Woods institutions participated during the negotiations phase, and have been supportive of the peace process and its financial requirements."

46. O'Donnell (2005) concurs with this assessment. With respect to the UN and the World Bank in particular, she notes that "in general, communication between the two organizations appears to have improved somewhat since 1994, when de Soto and del Castillo described post-conflict assistance as two doctors operating on a patient with a curtain down the middle." She notes, for example, that Bank staff contributes to economic and social sections of reports of the Secretary-General to the Security Council. In turn, Bank staff defer to the UN on political issues such as elections.

47. See, for example, the letter from Boutros-Ghali to Camdessus at the Fund (and a matching one to the Bank) of March 18, 1996. The Secretary-General recalls their meetings in July 1995 in Wyoming, where they agreed to enhance cooperation between their organizations in post-conflict situations, and holds out Angola as a test case to identify ways of enhancing coordination in such circumstances. A letter from Camdessus to Annan on September 21, 1997, and Annan's reply of October 23, 1997, indicate that collaboration also existed in the case of Guatemala. The spirit and tone of these letters contrasts with that of the Secretary-General to World Bank President James Wolfensohn on December 22, 1995, raising concerns about the implementation of the peace accords in El Salvador, and particularly with previous letters, for example, those of July 13, 1992, to the heads of the two institutions.

48. The Enclosure to the Secretary-General's letter of March 18, 1996, to the Managing Director of the IMF and the President of the World Bank notes the lessons learned from El Salvador, particularly with respect to the need to collaborate and coordinate the peace program with the economic and financial program of the country, supported by the Bretton Woods institutions.

49. For details see Chapter 7.

50. Ten years later and five days before leaving the institution, his perspective on building peace had mellowed in light of the little success there had been in winning the peace. He welcomed the Peacebuilding Commission and the opportunity to participate with the Security Council in matters concerning peace and security.

51. For problems of interagency coordination within the UN, see Flournoy (2004).

52. For an interesting discussion of the distortions created by the large UN presence in East Timor, see Pires and Francino (2007).

53. Developing countries, led by the Group of 77, rejected the proposal for integrated offices, largely because they believed that the Secretary-General was trying to make development ancillary to peace. At a less altruistic level, the proposal was resisted by the sectoral ministries at the national level, which benefited from the direct relationship that their ministries had with the different UN agencies. The existing system gave the ministry of agriculture, for example, a direct relationship with the representatives of the WFP and the FAO. Ministers were in general more inclined to preserve these personal connections than to improve the overall use and efficiency of scarce resources. The proposal was also resisted by the agencies themselves, which lobbied governments against it.

54. For more details, see note 18 above.

6 Issues for debate on international assistance

1. Cited by De Long and Eichengreen (1993: 189).

2. Just as there is a need to revise the mechanism to improve multilateral aid, the same is true with bilateral aid. For example, Dugger (2007a) reports how the Millennium Challenge Corporation, a federal US agency set up with bipartisan support, that has approved close to $5 billion for projects in 15 countries for 2007, has only spent $155 million by the end of the year. This is making it vulnerable to a Congressional budget slash in 2008. European Union aid also needs to be revised. In addition to many constraints and inefficiencies identified in relation to specific cases, Barber (2007) describes how funds earmarked for agriculture end up in the coffers of golf and riding clubs and railway companies. In fact,

the European Court of Auditors reckoned that 12 percent, or close to $4 billion, of regional aid programs had been incorrectly spent.

3. The media has reported that US military expenditure in Iraq was $800 million to $1,000 million a week following occupation of the country.

4. Multilateral and bilateral donors spent about $106 billion in aid to developing countries in 2005. See Bourguignon and Sundberg (2007: 56).

5. The cost of collapsed peace agreements is often high in terms of lives as well (Angola and Rwanda in the 1990s are but two examples). It is also costly in terms of economic reconstruction. The setback to Lebanon in infrastructure damage caused by the recent conflict is estimated at close to $3 billion. In addition, output loss is estimated at an additional $2 billion. See *IMF Survey* (January 29, 2007: 19).

6. The accounting for such a quid pro quo relationship would involve the donor country budgeting as an expense the cost of aid (given in cash or goods) in terms of its own currency. The compensating item on the other side of the balance sheet would be the local currency proceeds from the sale of the goods (Dulles, 1993: 83).

7. Collier and Hoeffler (2002: 3) show that historically the actual donor response to post-conflict situations has not been poverty-efficient. This is not surprising, since poverty reduction per se should not be an objective of reconstruction aid, which should be targeted at national reconciliation and an effective transition to peace, with the aim of putting the country on a normal development path, where the objective of aid shifts toward poverty alleviation. As discussed in the case studies, many analysts conflate this distinction, resulting in unrealistic expectations concerning how much can be accomplished in the transition from war to peace. More interestingly, Collier and Hoeffler also report some evidence that aid in post-conflict situations is considerably more effective in augmenting growth than in normal development.

8. The authors discuss the literature on the impact of aid on growth under normal development and conclude that it does not provide a framework to analyze the impact of post-conflict aid.

9. See, for example, Collier and Hoeffler (2002) and World Bank (2003b). These studies find that for aid to be more effective it should gradually rise in the first 3–5 years as the capacity of the country to absorb it grows, and taper to normal development levels by the end of the first post-conflict decade. This is not at all the observed pattern so far.

10. As Stedman (2002: 2) notes, far from being a time of conflict reduction, the period immediately following the signing of peace agreements is fraught with risk, uncertainty, and vulnerability for the warring parties and the civilians caught between them.

11. El Salvador, for example, eventually gave up benefits under US Government PL480 because it was decided that the long-term benefit of basic grain production was more important for the country than the short-term assistance provided under this program.

12. In December 1947, President Truman's report to Congress indicated that whether aid would be in the form of grants or loans would depend on the capacity of each country to pay and the effect of debt accumulation on its recovery. In deciding how much aid should be allocated, the Marshall Plan was also noteworthy in that it contemplated that countries should be rewarded for sound fiscal and economic policies.

13. In nominal terms, the Marshall Plan was significant. The Plan's $13 billion in 1948–52 represents roughly $100 billion in inflation-adjusted 2003 dollars. See Orr (2004a: 17).

14. See, for example, Stiglitz (2002 and 2006b).

15. In the case study of El Salvador in Chapter 7, I will show that the government did, in fact, pursue these policies with a significant degree of success. Indeed, tax revenue increased by close to 60 percent during the first six years of the economic program, to 12 percent of GDP in 1995, from 7.6 percent of GDP in 1989. See also del Castillo (2001a).

16. The same is true of the IMF.

17. Cited by Boyce (2004: 2), from the case study of El Salvador (World Bank, 1998c: 51).

18. For a discussion of problems related to peace implementation in Guatemala, see Stanley and Holiday (2002), pp. 421–62. The authors note (p. 430) that donors generously pledged $1.9 billion when the peace accords were negotiated. Although they do not quote a figure, they give the impression, not surprisingly, that much less was disbursed.

19. The Secretary-General in his reports to the Security Council regularly reports compliance with peace agreements. However, the staff of the Bretton Woods institutions does not normally read these reports.

20. The Paris Club is an informal group of bilateral creditors that provide official (government-to-government) debt. The Club's role is to find coordinated and sustainable solutions to the payment difficulties experienced by debtor nations. By agreeing to the rescheduling of debts due to them, the Paris Club provides a country with debt relief through a postponement and, in the case of concessional rescheduling, a reduction in debt service obligations.

21. Only Iraq and Albania had standing stand-by programs in early 2007.

22. As the situation stands, however, the chances of the IMF getting more heavily involved in post-conflict reconstruction are not great. As *Finance & Development*, a quarterly publication of the IMF, revealed in its September 2004 issue devoted to development and aid, at the time of the IMF's 60th birthday, post-conflict economic reconstruction is not in the minds of the organization's staff. It is significant to note that the only reference to "conflict" in one of the ten articles referred to "civil conflict" resulting from banking crises in Latin America. The word "reconstruction" was nowhere to be found.

23. A final agreement, however, has not been reached as of May 2008.

24. This means that countries stop being current on their obligations by not serving their debt.

25. Liberia, for example, was in continuous arrears to the Fund for twenty years starting in 1984. The Executive Board suspended the country's rights in 2003 because of lack of cooperation in solving the arrears problem. Cambodia was in arrears to the Fund for fifteen years from the end of 1978 to the end of 1993 and also had its rights suspended.

26. In Angola, for example, the IMF 2007 Article IV report estimates that the government will collect revenue amounting to 35 percent of GDP (27 percent of which was oil related) while grants represented only 0.1 percent of GDP. By early 2007, Angola had paid the bulk ($2.3 billion) of its principal and interest arrears to Paris Club creditors and is planning to get current on other arrears amounting to $50 million. The question to be debated is whether this is an optimum use of resources, or would the country have been better off by accelerating reconstruction in the short run through inclusive growth, employment creation, and investment in infrastructure?

27. Gardiner and Miles (2003) raised the moral dilemma of whether the citizens of a liberated country should be burdened with the debts of a brutal dictatorship. They quote Wolfowitz, US Deputy Secretary of Defense at the time, arguing that much of the money borrowed by the Iraqi regime had been used to buy weapons, to build palaces, and to build

instruments of oppression. Boyce (2004) recommends that, building on precedents in international law, the international financial institutions should establish a body to assess the possible scope and complications of initiatives to erase odious debts inherited by post-conflict governments. In addition to Iraq, other countries also built up a large volume of odious debt. Ndikumana and Boyce (1998), for example, document how the DRC had to devote 25 percent of its government revenues in 2004 to servicing the $12 billion debt inherited from the Mobuto era. The concept of "odious debt" has been discussed more in the framework of post-conflict situations rather than in the framework of financial crises. Although large amounts of debt that accumulated in most Latin American countries during the military dictatorships of the 1970s and 1980s fell under the concept of odious debt, condonation did not get much support although most countries did restructure their debt at more convenient terms.

28. A "haircut" refers to the reduction of the stock of debt resulting from debt restructuring. The most notorious contrast to this behavior was that of its neighbor, Uruguay. Uruguay restructured its debt with private creditors without a haircut, after a sharp financial crisis, devaluation and recession that made the debt to GDP ratio jump over 110 percent. Without a haircut, and despite the largest IMF-support program as a percentage of GDP ever, Uruguay has had a debt burden that makes it very difficult to grow at rates that would allow a reversal of the sharp social deterioration that was the consequence of the crisis.

29. Fayolle (2006: 37) addressed the folly of the system by wondering how to explain to countries that "they are eligible for the cancellation of all their multilateral debts but that their arrears in repaying these very debts prevent them from the opportunity to get on track through an IMF-supported program and qualify for the HIPC." Building up the track record for eligibility to HIPC Initiative takes time. In Afghanistan, discussions on this issue started in early 2007, six years into the war-to-peace transition. In 2008, the Ministry of Finance will submit to the Board of Directors of the World Bank and IMF the First ANDS (Afghanistan National Development Strategy) Report (March 2008–March 2009) to enable Afghanistan to reach a completion point for debt relief under the HIPC Initiative (IMF, 2008).

7 UN-led reconstruction following UN-led negotiations: El Salvador

1. Despite the fact that they do not record drug production, official statistics would capture increased consumption as farmers and dealers spend on goods and services. This, of course, leads to data problems, which are limited by the fact that the bulk of the drug revenue remains abroad.

2. This case study relies heavily on published articles by Alvaro de Soto and me (1994, 1995), by me (1995a, 1997, 2001a), and by de Soto recounting his experience as mediator of the peace agreements (1999).

3. All institutional reports in this chapter are listed under "Country Reports: El Salvador" in the Bibliography.

4. Torres-Rivas (1997) believes that this estimate by the Central American University of 100,000 deaths is more accurate than the often-cited figure of 75,000.

5. See, for example, Orr (2001: 153) and Call (2002: 383).

6. In the 1999 HDI, El Salvador was in 107th place. Since this index was prepared with 1997 data, it illustrates that the improvement was minor from the end of the war to the end of

the implementation of the peace agreements, at least in relative comparison with the pace of some other developing countries.

7. For an analysis of the very complex land tenure problems in El Salvador, see del Castillo (1997). During the war, land tenure problems worsened; many rural properties were abandoned and settled by displaced persons who supported the FMLN.

8. I estimate national savings in the conventional way, as the difference between domestic investment and the current account deficit (as a proxy for foreign savings).

9. As Torres-Rivas (1997: 215) notes, the Salvadoran conflict was the longest formal, high-intensity civil war in Latin America, though Colombia has experienced the longest period of violence and civil strife.

10. Economic data are from the Government of El Salvador and the IMF. Social data are from published sources from the World Bank, UNDP, IADB, and CEPAL (the Spanish acronym for the UN Economic Commission for Latin America and the Caribbean).

11. Current transfers are mostly private transfers from remittances of workers abroad that residents use for consumption purposes. The current account excluding transfers thus shows the external position of Salvadorans in El Salvador vis-à-vis the rest of the world, without the assistance of Salvadorans abroad. Official transfers (grants) are mostly used for investment purposes (rather than consumption) and are included in the capital account of the balance of payments.

12. For the plan's details, see Liévano de Marques (1996).

13. A $51 million SBA was approved. Shortly after the completion of the mid-term review in February 1991, the World Bank approved the first structural adjustment loan (SAL-I) for $75 million, as well as a Social Sector Rehabilitation Project worth $26 million. Thus, the IMF arrangement and the World Bank loans were negotiated long before the Peace Agreement was signed (this is quite common; in Bosnia and Herzegovina, for example, negotiations on an economic program started while the Dayton Peace Agreement was still being negotiated). During economic reconstruction (1992–7), El Salvador treated this and subsequent SBAs as precautionary and made no purchases under them (e.g. El Salvador did not borrow from the Fund). As I will discuss later, this was because El Salvador's per capita income of around $1,100 did not entitle it to concessional financing from the IFIs.

14. For an inside account of the negotiation of the different agreements, see de Soto (1999). For an analysis of the negotiations and the series of accords, see Sullivan (1994), Doyle et al. (1997), Pérez de Cuéllar (1997), Call (2002), Goulding (2004), Antonini (2004), and Negroponte (2006).

15. Recalling the mediation process in El Salvador, de Soto (1999: 362) notes that "the FMLN handling of economic and social questions as the last substantive issue was particularly revealing, given that the root cause of much of the unrest that had led to the insurgency was grinding poverty and marginalization in a densely populated country with an acute shortage of land. Confronting brutal armed forces repression was a pressing need, but the military apparatus was at its origin and ultimately only a tool for keeping discontent about the root causes under control. The FMLN, whether because of factional divergences, lack of expertise, or a sober appraisal of political realities, left the examination of these root causes for a later stage; it was only in the last six months of the negotiation that the FMLN began to articulate its ideas, studiously refraining from any revolutionary proposal. It did not try to tamper with the economic model that Cristiani's administration was promoting, which included economic stabilization and structural reform. Instead, it substantially lowered its sights, and the economic and social question metamorphosed at

the eleventh hour into a hastily crafted arrangement on reintegration of combatants and their supporters." Without having participated at this stage of the negotiation, it seems to me that, as argued later, the other side of the coin was that the UN mediator did not have technical support on economic and social issues and hence could not make relevant proposals in this area of the negotiation, as he did successfully in other areas.

16. This is how the Secretary-General described the process in the speech delivered at the signature of the Chapultepec Peace Agreement. Karl (1992) later used the term "negotiated revolution" as the title of her *Foreign Affairs* article.

17. There is another sense of the term "peace dividend," in addition to its fiscal meaning. Woodward (2002: 186) argues that a palpable sentiment that the benefits from the peace agreements will outweigh the costs, and that they will be equitably divided, is required for people to support the peace process. In this sense, the peace dividend was unquestionably present in El Salvador.

18. During the implementation of the peace agreements there were 300 NGOs in El Salvador. Although a few of these were professional and effective, many created serious problems for the government and inefficiencies for the process. The role of the UNDP and the World Bank in El Salvador has been analyzed by the respective organizations. A UNDP Evaluation Office report (UNDP 2000) on the organization's role in post-conflict situations concluded about the quality of early interventions that "UNDP country offices found themselves unprepared when pushed towards post-conflict situations by donors and pulled towards reintegration activities by the organization's broadening understanding of its mandate. As such, they found themselves ill-equipped for the task at hand. Their meagre staff lacked experience within the context." A case study on El Salvador prepared by the Operations Evaluation Department (OED) of the World Bank (1998) (reproduced in World Bank 2000) also makes clear that, while it later participated in critical peace-related projects such as reintegration of former combatants in Africa, the World Bank did not get involved in supporting these programs in El Salvador. As the study reports, World Bank financing through SAL-I and later SAL-II (1993) was for "typical development projects," rather than "peace-related" projects. In the Bank's view, an approach narrowly targeted on ex-combatants, as opposed to an area or countrywide approach, could create resentment among local populations. On the basis of this belief, it is not clear how the Bank justified its involvement in reintegration assistance in Africa, starting with programs in Uganda in 1994 and Angola in 1995. At the same time, the study argues that, although not explicitly stated in the document, the basic rationale for SAL-II was to provide fiscal flexibility to the government to help it meet the unprecedented fiscal demands of the peace agreements.

19. For data on the 1989–97 period, see del Castillo (2001a, Tables 1–4).

20. The NFPS includes the central government, local governments, and publicly owned enterprises, and excludes the financial public sector (the central bank and other publicly owned banks).

21. Not many analysts appreciated how difficult it was to rally international support for these projects, which were critical to the peace process. Secretary-General Boutros-Ghali was a relentless troop recruiter and fundraiser. He never missed an opportunity to ask world leaders for contributions to UN peacekeepers, police force trainers, and other human resources needed in the peacekeeping operations and to lobby the IFIs for more flexible policies. He was shameless about raising funds as well, making his case in settings both obvious and remote. In his briefing notes for his trip to Japan, funding for El Salvador

and Nicaragua had some priority, and I was told that he made a strong plea. This was not always known or even appreciated by the authorities of the countries involved. For example, Mirna Liévano de Marques (1996), who was Minister of Planning and led economic reconstruction, fails to acknowledge the Secretary-General's role in facilitating financing. President Cristiani, however, recognized the Secretary-General's efforts in finding ways to finance critical peace-related programs. In fact, in a letter of August 18, 1992, he thanked the Secretary-General profusely for his efforts at lobbying the IMF and the World Bank to make their programs more flexible for this purpose.

22. Article IV consultations take place with member states on a 12–18-month cycle. The SDR is an international reserve asset, created by the IMF in 1969 to supplement the existing official reserves of member countries, which serves as the unit of account of the IMF and some other international organizations. SDRs are allocated to member countries in proportion to their IMF quotas, with their value based on a basket of key international currencies. At end 1991, 1SDR = US$1.43.

23. The OED case study (World Bank 1998b) notes that the Bank, along with USAID and the UNDP "helped the government prepare a detailed NRP in parallel with the peace negotiations in late 1991 and early 1992," in preparation for the second consultative group meeting in March 1992. At the same time, the NRP was negotiated as part of the economic and social chapter of the Chapultepec Agreement (Chapter V). The agreements specified that the government would submit to the FMLN, within 30 days of the signature of the Agreement, the NRP which it had drawn up within the parameters specified in Chapter V. According to the Agreement, the government had to take into account the recommendations and suggestions of the FMLN and other sectors of national life, thereby ensuring that the Plan would reflect the country's collective wishes. The fact that institutions such as the World Bank and the UNDP, as part of their mandate to collaborate with the authorities on development issues, advised the government in the preparation of the NRP was the reason why the FMLN—like other groups in similar situations—did not view them as impartial actors in the peace process.

24. See also Goulding (2002: 240–4).

25. During this consultative group meeting, the World Bank rightly argued that a full assessment of the macroeconomic impact of the NRP over the coming years could not be conducted until the parameters of the NRP, particularly the land program, were more clearly defined. This was done through the October 13, 1992, agreement. Although the OED study (World Bank 1998b) concludes that the most important role the Bank played in El Salvador post-conflict transition was to call the consultative group meetings, the fact that both the Bank and the UNDP channeled resources into their own "development as usual" projects made financing of peace-related programs more difficult.

26. See press conference of the Secretary-General at the Economic Commission for Asia and the Pacific (ESCAP) of April 1993 and his report to the Security Council of May 21, 1993 (UN S/25812).

27. Even after postponing lower priority projects, NRP expenditures in 1993 were 35 percent higher than in 1992 and represented about 7.3 percent of central government expenditures. About 40 percent of these expenditures were financed through grants and about 30 percent by long-term loans from official creditors.

28. In a late 1993 meeting between UN, IMF, and World Bank officials, the UN expressed concern about the lack of financing for the land program and the establishment of the PNC. Fear was also expressed that the security situation would deteriorate if reintegration

of ex-combatants could not take place within a reasonable amount of time. The Fund noted that, despite the program's fiscal targets, there were no limits on subcategories of expenditure financed by domestic resources. It was up to the government to prioritize its expenditure program—something many analysts have simply ignored—not only in the case of El Salvador, but in criticizing IMF conditionality around the world.

29. In fact, government efforts to increase taxation succeeded in raising tax revenue from 7.6 percent of GDP in 1989 to 12 percent in 1995, although it fell to 11 percent in 1996–7. This was quite an achievement, despite being criticized by several analysts. See, for example, Wood and Segovia (1995), Boyce *et al.* (1995), and Boyce (2002, 2004). Guatemala was not nearly as successful in raising tax revenue, despite the fact that an increase to 12 percent of GDP was an explicit conditionality of the UN-brokered peace agreements.

30. Citing data from IMF staff and economic development reports on El Salvador, Boyce (1995) notes lack of progress in decreasing military expenditure. He fails to distinguish, however, between "defense" expenditure and "police" expenditure, which the IMF data classify together as "military" expenditure, an important distinction since 1992 when the repressive and militarized police forces of the past were dissolved. Police expenditure (an expenditure thus related to the peace accords) increased by 1 percent of GDP in 1993–7, while defense (military proper) expenditure fell from 1.5 percent of GDP to 0.9 percent in the same period. Furthermore, in 1990–5 the fall in military expenditure in El Salvador from 3.1 percent of GDP to 1 percent (del Castillo, 2001, Table 2) was larger than in other countries with IMF-supported programs. Program countries (defined as those with at least one program in 1991–5) reduced their military spending from 5 percent of GDP to 2 percent in 1990–5. This represented a larger decrease than for all developing countries, and allowed these countries to increase social spending in the face of cuts in total expenditure. For more details, see the open letter of the Managing Director of the IMF to the Executive Director of UNICEF of December 1996. This letter was the IMF's reply to criticism by UNICEF of how Fund conditionality was threatening social spending in El Salvador. Paris (2001: 770) attributes the sharp increase in criminal violence in post-conflict countries to the effect of economic liberalization linked to IFI-imposed policies.

31. As described by Goulding, (2002: 243), "del Castillo and I went to *Perquín* to see what a *tenedor* looked like, a *'tenedor'* being a person illegally working land that belongs to someone else. *Perquín* is a mountain village in a *zona conflictiva* which had been an FMLN stronghold during the war and the clandestine site of the *Radio Venceremos*. The *tenedor* we met was a woman living with a man, an aunt, a grandmother, seven children, two pigs and two chickens in a house which they had reconstructed from a bombed ruin, with just over two hectares of maize and beans. We also met a group of recently demobilized FMLN combatants who had occupied a couple of hectares of vacant land and were clearing it to plant maize. They did not know, and cared less, who the owner was."

32. For a more detailed analysis of land problems and the arms-for-land program, see del Castillo (1997).

33. Most countries in the war-to-peace transition have significantly lower per capita income levels. For example, Liberia's income per capita at the time of its peace transition was about $120, with an estimated 80 percent of the labor force unemployed.

34. This program was part of the 1992 Peace Agreement and was included as Section 3 (Lands within Conflict Zones) in Part V on Economic and Social Questions (UN 1992a: 77–86).

35. Wilkins (1997: 275) argues that the term "conflict zones" was never defined, making it unclear which parcels of land qualified. This, however, was never a problem. The FMLN

provided an inventory of occupied lands, which were considered to be in "conflict zones." Since land sales were voluntary under the Chapultepec Agreement, there was never any question of the FMLN claiming lands other than those that they occupied during the war.

36. An important lesson from the Salvadoran experience is that careful thought and the right kind of expertise on both sides of the negotiation are needed to facilitate the elaboration of peace agreements that can be realistically implemented. In cases where peace does not follow a peace agreement, the same considerations should apply to the elaboration of the post-conflict economic reconstruction strategy. For a detailed analysis of the many problems resulting from the design of peace agreements and lessons for the future, see del Castillo (1997: 357–65).

37. In addition to his impeccable logic, I was always awed by the consistency with which UN Under-Secretary-General for Political Affairs Marrack Goulding recorded his diplomatic efforts in detailed notes, which he revised and then summarized at the start of any future meeting, giving consistency and continuity to the process. With regard to the consultations leading to the October 13 Land Agreement, he recalled that "the first two meetings, with the government and then with the FMLN, were preliminary sparring. We were looking for common ground. The government was concerned about the resource constraints: there was neither enough land nor enough money to meet the demands of the FMLN. The latter insisted that they had always made clear that "reintegration" of their combatants meant giving them land; if these promises were not kept, then the FMLN were relieved of their commitments. Del Castillo and I shared the government's concerns about resources; the FMLN's demands amounted to more than a quarter of the country's arable land and pasture. Riza [the Special Representative at the time] and his team were more inclined to sympathize with the FMLN." For details on how the land negotiations interacted with the demobilization of the FMLN and other aspects of the peace agreements, see Goulding (2002: 239–46).

38. See UN (May 1993, S/25812 Add. 2) for the full text of the agreement.

39. As recounted by Goulding (2002: 244–5), "On 30 October I was back in San Salvador, accompanied this time by de Soto and del Castillo. The FMLN's third demobilization took place that day and ONUSAL reported that for the first time real fighters had been demobilized and real weapons handed over. The principal issue discussed was *depuración*. Cristiani was in agony over his obligation to remove 103 officers from the armed forces within a few weeks." But things were never easy in El Salvador. With Goulding leaving the country for Luanda as a result of the resumption of civil war in Angola, "de Soto stayed on for another five days and achieved an agreement of some complexity, which Boutros-Ghali reported to the Security Council in necessarily opaque terms, given the secrecy surrounding the identity of the *depurables*." This was indeed another major triumph for the peace process. McCormick (1997) notes that the Clinton administration applied additional pressure by freezing $11 million in military aid until the recommendations of the Ad Hoc Commission were met.

40. As a result, the "price risk" that the government had assumed did not materialize *ex post*. When I discussed options with some of my economist friends outside the UN, there was general agreement that prices would skyrocket as soon as the program was adopted. Thus, our scheme for delaying relocation until the end—a requirement that both the FMLN and the government tried at various points to circumvent—succeeded in avoiding large increases in the price of land. On the other hand, the "foreign exchange risk," which seemed high *ex ante*, did not materialize *ex post*, either. Hence, my insistence that credit

ceilings be imposed either in dollar terms or in terms of plot size—which was strongly resisted by President Cristiani who wanted to set credit limits in colones—was misplaced, since there was no gain from it. I underestimated the impact that large inflows of aid and remittances—largely resulting from the overall success of El Salvador's war-to-peace transition—had on the colón, effectively insulating it from any loss in purchasing power. In fact, the Central Bank had to intervene heavily in the foreign exchange market to keep the colón's US dollar price fixed at 8.8 colones, and thus avoid the loss of competitiveness that a larger real appreciation of the currency would have implied.

41. 1 mz (*manzana*) is equivalent to 0.7 hectares. The assumption of $600 per mz for an average type of land created serious confusion. Landowners and the press accused the UN, the government, and sometimes both of "fixing the price of land." This clearly was not the case. We used this price purely for calculations purposes and reflected the average price at which comparable occupied land had been sold through the Lands Bank up to August 31, 1992.

42. This clearly illustrates the need for feasibility studies during peace negotiations to ensure that specific peace-related programs are implementable, and that financing is possible, lest potential beneficiaries develop unrealistic expectations.

43. Parties' informal agreements, which departed from formal agreements, made UN verification even more difficult. For example, departures from the October 13 program, agreed to informally by the two parties, often rendered ineffective ONUSAL's insistence on compliance with the letter and the spirit of the formal peace agreement. This was the case with the credit ceiling specified in the land certificates, in clear violation of the October 13 agreement. Letters to ONUSAL in December 1992 and February 1993 informed the UN of such agreements. Other informal agreements resulted from tripartite meetings between the government, the FMLN, and ONUSAL.

44. For a full analysis of the implementation of this program, see the *Reports of the Secretary-General on the United Nations Observer Mission in El Salvador* to the Security Council (UN 1992–5) and *The Situation in Central America: Report of the Secretary General* (UN 1995–2000). See also ECLAC (1993), de Soto and del Castillo (1995), and del Castillo (1997).

45. For a contrarian position, see de Soto and del Castillo (1995).

46. In my view, the reason why close advisers found it hard to be loyal to Boutros-Ghali—despite his sagacity, intellect, and much admired energy—was that even when he consulted with them, he often adopted the opposite position without any explanation. I am sure that de Soto and Goulding will remember a chartered plane trip to El Salvador, during which we briefed the Secretary-General on the problems and significant delays with regard to the land program, the "special regime" for rural human settlements, the National Civil Police, and other lagging programs. We all agreed that it would be premature for him to say that El Salvador was a "success story." Both de Soto and Goulding strongly argued that doing so would take pressure off the government and the FMLN to implement remaining commitments. As soon as we arrived in San Salvador, Boutros-Ghali held a press conference, which he began by proclaiming that "El Salvador is a success story."

47. For the problems that this created for peacebuilding, see Doyle *et al.* (1997) and Doyle (2001).

48. In his report to the Security Council of March 24, 1995 (UN S/1995/220), the Secretary-General acknowledged that "a strong case could have been made for maintaining ONUSAL after 30 April 1995....A recommendation to that effect was given serious

consideration but I refrained from making it in the light of the clear indications from members of the Council that the time had come to bring ONUSAL to a close." The parties had given assurances to the Council that substantial progress in the implementation of the agreements would take place before April 30, 1995. On the basis of this, the Secretary-General noted that "The modest proposal that I made for the size of the post-ONUSAL team was predicated on this premise, which regrettably has not materialized." Although the Secretary-General's conclusion that subsequent delays and new difficulties would warrant a somewhat larger team proved correct, nothing was done to remedy this need.

49. For the details of UN financing, including peacekeeping operations, see Laurenti (2004).

50. Letter of Ambassador Ricardo Castaneda to the Secretary-General of August 28, 1995. See also, replies of the Chief of Staff of September 5 and of the UNDP of September 1 of the same year. Ambassador Castaneda was a strong supporter of the peace process and worked closely with the UN in its implementation.

51. A major reason for this was the lack of continuity in the UN presence. In the future, this could be avoided by adopting my proposal in Chapter 5 regarding the organizational structure of peacebuilding missions (see Figure 3, p. 64). As the peacebuilding mission winds down, the UNDG coordinator in the National Reconstruction Coordinator Office (NRCO) would lead UN "normal development" activities in the country as UNDP Resident Representative and Coordinator of the UN System. Having been part of the peacebuilding mission, this person would be ready to assume some of the "unfinished business" of peace-related programs and be more aware of the need to ensure their sustainability. In El Salvador, the UNDP was not given the right resources and capabilities to ensure its ability to monitor the completion of the remaining peace-related programs and make them sustainable.

52. This was an increase from the 74 percent and 25 percent, respectively, reported in the Secretary-General's October 1995 report (UN A/50/517). In his April 1996 report (UN A/50/935), the Secretary-General reported that titles had been issued to 93 percent of the potential beneficiaries, with 50 percent of the titles registered.

53. The "human settlements" were communities in the war zone in the departments of Chalatenango and Morazán.

54. In his report to the General Assembly of October 2000 (UN A/55/465), Secretary-General Annan noted that in 1997 and 1998 a small support unit housed within the UNDP in San Salvador tracked compliance with outstanding provisions of the accords, while responsibilities for verification and good offices remained with UN Headquarters.

55. Despite tremendous difficulties, by end-1997, the government had achieved the simplification of the tax structure, creating a system based on a few broad-based taxes, and the restructuring and re-privatization of the financial sector. The latter included the liberalization of interest rates, the elimination of credit controls, the revision of the legal framework encompassing new laws for the central bank, banks, and financial institutions, and the creation of a new charter for the superintendence of financial institutions. The government also accelerated trade reform, including simplification and sharp reduction of tariff levels and elimination of non-tariff barriers, and achieved significant advances in the modernization of the public sector. For a list of the key structural reforms in 1992–2004, see IMF (2005d, Table 11: 36) and IADB (2005, Table AI-3, Annex I: 2).

56. With respect to natural disasters, a frequent phenomenon in El Salvador, the IADB (2005) noted that the entire territory is at risk or at very high risk of seismic events. They reckon that "Earthquakes such as those that struck the country in 2001 (which occur, on average,

once every 15 or 20 years) generated $1.6 billion in costs and entailed additional public expenditures of at least $700 million."

57. For the growth and development challenges to El Salvador, see various Staff Reports (IMF several years), including the last one in the bibliography (IMF 2005d). See also IADB (2005) and World Bank (2004a).

58. Paris (2002, 2004), for example, unrealistically believes that the post-conflict transition should solve a country's development problems. In fact, what a successful post-conflict transition should be expected to do is to set the country onto a path of normal development, unburdened by the overwhelming task and the financial cost of national reconciliation and peacebuilding activities. As Downs and Stedman (2002: 49) point out, by assuming that a successful transition from war to peace should also resolve the challenges of poverty, "Paris holds evaluation hostage to an unreasonable standard of success."

59. See National Human Development Report (2005). The UNDP has prepared four such reports, the last one, in 2005, focusing on the impact of migration and remittances on the Salvadoran economy.

60. The fact that the mediator of the peace agreement was not involved in the peacebuilding mission was a smart move. It left room for the mediator to maintain pressure for the peace agreement's implementation over the years. Acknowledging that de Soto's role as a mediator was well documented, Jones (2002: 98) also noted that his future role was just as important. From his position in Boutros-Ghali's cabinet, and then as Assistant Secretary-General of the DPA, "the continuous engagement by a key personality appears to have made an important contribution to the successful implementation of the accords." Stanley and Holiday (2002: 443) argue—and I agree with them—that appointing the mediator as SRSG in Guatemala was a mistake. In their view, Jean Arnault had too strong a personal stake in defending the peace accords, and was reluctant to acknowledge and criticize the government's failures to fulfill its commitments. Thus, the effectiveness of the UN in facilitating the implementation of the agreements was much diminished. Nevertheless, this factor was perhaps secondary to the lack of Security Council clout in Guatemala, the overambitious nature of the peace agreements and the weakness of the General Assembly in pushing for their implementation.

61. I always remember the puzzled expressions on the faces of my new colleagues at the IMF Western Hemisphere Department the day I joined the Fund and told them that I was coming from the UN Secretariat. After seeing a few such faces, I started telling them that I also taught at Columbia University in the hope of getting some sign of recognition. While a few economists had moved to the Fund from the UN Economic Commissions, I was the first ever to join from the UN Secretariat.

62. In addition to the human rights division, which had been created earlier, at the time ONUSAL was established it also had military and police divisions. An electoral division was added at the request of the government in 1993.

63. Interestingly, a look at the UN Human Resources web site many years later (on September 21, 2006) reveals nineteen job categories for UN peacekeeping operations, none of which is for economic affairs (although there is one for social affairs). This shows how little importance the political side of the UN attaches to economic issues in peacebuilding activities. Furthermore, the political and the economic and social sides of the UN Secretariat barely talked to each other, apparently because peacemakers and economists do not speak the same language, and so find it difficult to communicate (del Castillo: 1995a). Former National Security Advisor Anthony Lake argues that the difficulty in addressing

political-economic issues in the transition to peace is related to the difficulty associated with thinking across disciplinary boundaries. In his words, "Mention the deleterious political effects of a sound economic policy at a meeting of economic planners, and watch their fingers drum impatiently on a table. Talk about the economic details at a conference of diplomats working on a political settlement and watch their eyes glaze . . . But economists, diplomats, and political leaders must think in each other's terms, or reconstruction will fail." (Blair *et al.* 2005: 205–6).

64. The shortage of UN professional staff dedicated to reconstruction issues is clear from Goulding (2002: 241–3). At the time, he was trying to break the impasse created by the FMLN's refusal to demobilize further, and likened the experience to being a squash ball smashed against the wall by two angry players alternately. "On the land issue, my instructions were to put forward a proposal which, if accepted, would make it possible to begin the transfer of land to ex-combatants on both sides. I was accompanied by Graciana del Castillo, an economist from the Secretary-General's office . . . Del Castillo fought gallantly but she was the only economist in my team and I wished that I had brought more. After our return to New York, Graciana del Castillo worked quickly to produce a detailed proposal on land which Boutros-Ghali would send personally to the two sides. This he did on 13 October. Within a few days both had accepted it, to my surprise and relief. Most of the credit for this success was due to del Castillo who drafted a professional, coherent and well-balanced program of action." Although I appreciate the credit Goulding gives to me, it is proof of the inadequacy of UN staff, both at UN headquarters and at ONUSAL, and the ad hoc nature of mechanisms dealing with economic reconstruction. It is also proof of difficulties in working together with the Bretton Woods institutions and even with the FAO. When the peace process was close to the precipice, the Secretary-General did ask the heads of the IMF and World Bank for their assistance "on a matter of great concern and urgency" (letter of September 14, 1992). He also sought the assistance of FAO. None of the three organizations wanted to put anything in writing. I have already discussed the position of the World Bank on the land program. The IMF and the FAO visited the country on regular trips they had planned earlier. All we could get out of them was their opinion that there was not enough financing or land for this program. So much we knew, but the issue was how to get both. Because the Secretary-General acknowledged their advice in his report to the Security Council, some analysts have noted that a group of "agrarian specialists" evaluated the situation (Boyce *et al.* 1995: 53, and Rosa and Foley 2000: 142). The latter also incorrectly noted that it was ONUSAL which offered the proposal to the parties.

65. The OED *Case Study on El Salvador* (2000) argues that the land program was a political program, and that the Bank's mandate restricted lending for political purposes. Nevertheless, the Bank could have provided technical assistance that would have facilitated the land program, ensured its sustainability, and improved public security by keeping beneficiaries on their land. In fact, the Bank eventually supported land registration with good results. As the OED report also points out, no Bank project focused exclusively on the former conflict zones. In fact, they followed a "development as usual" approach, with the structural adjustment loans (SAL-I and SAL-II) that provided support to the government's 1989–94 program focusing on taxation, privatization, trade, the financial sector, social sectors, and poverty alleviation. Other economic sector projects in the Bank's portfolio fell into three groups: energy, agriculture, and competitiveness and public sector modernization. It is interesting to note that the OED study concluded nevertheless that several high-quality Bank lending operations and non-lending services made significant contributions

to post-conflict reconstruction. To reach this conclusion, the OED interviewed a large number of World Bank and government officials, UN agencies, and NGOs, but failed to interview the UN or any of the former FMLN commanders. In 1995, oblivious to the difficulties with the land program and the PNC that threatened the full implementation of the peace accords, the World Bank prepared a business as usual study on how El Salvador should meet the challenge of globalization and learn from the experience of successful East Asian tigers. See Grandolini (1996).

66. For a description of what this really entails and why it is so important to any organization or national civil service, see Solimano (2006, 2008).

67. As Zhang (2006) points out, "In fact, some middle- or higher-level officials in the UN human resources management possess an inadequate level of education or training. This represents a major resistance to management reform and has a negative impact on recruiting young, qualified professionals." Sidney Dell told me years ago about how he was unable to recruit Richard N. Cooper, owing to UN personnel problems in recognizing his academic credentials and arguing he did not have the required years of experience for the post. Today, Cooper is a renowned Professor of International Economics at Harvard. This, and many other cases over the years of which I am aware, are an indication of the lack of ability of the department of human resources at the UN to detect talent in the economic area.

68. By contrast, Stanley and Holiday (2002: 432) argue that the difficulties of implementing the accords in Guatemala had to do with the fact that they were unusually sweeping in their identification of key national issues, but provided few specific measures to facilitate their implementation.

69. This was more the case in Guatemala, where the accords contemplated major economic and social reform for the population at large, whereas in El Salvador the peace agreements included only those directly involved in the conflict. Nevertheless, some programs in El Salvador did create expectations that could not possibly be satisfied with available resources.

70. The security situation in El Salvador has seriously deteriorated more recently, owing to the criminal activities of gangs (the so-called *maras*). Many of the people involved belonged to gangs in Los Angeles and other US cities, and returned to El Salvador following the adoption of US legislation in April 1997 that calls for the deportation of illegal immigrants. The shortsightedness of the United States, given its large investment in the peace process, has had critical consequences for the country. For a detailed and frightening account, see Thomson (2006).

8 UN-led reconstruction following NATO-led military intervention: Kosovo

1. Unless otherwise specified, data are from the IMF. Institutional reports on Kosovo are listed in the Bibliography as "Country Reports: Kosovo."

2. Marshall Josip Broz Tito established the SFRY, consisting of Serbia, Montenegro, Croatia, Bosnia and Herzegovina, Macedonia, and Slovenia.

3. For the details, see Heinbecker (2004), who discusses the similarities in the way the Security Council handled Kosovo in 1999 and Iraq in 2003, where the reasons for military intervention were quite different: basically humanitarian concerns in the former case and regime change in the latter. See also Caplon (2005), and Fisher (2007: 105, 117),

who argues that NATO's operation in Kosovo, which was not a UN operation, was by far the most successful humanitarian intervention to prevent the ethnic cleansing of K-Albanians.

4. With the creation of the Federal Republic of Yugoslavia (FRY) in 1992, which included Serbia and Montenegro, Milosovic became President of the FRY. Croatia, Bosnia and Herzegovina, the Former Yugoslav Republic of Macedonia, and Slovenia became independent states.

5. Despite its iconic significance to K-Serbs and K-Albanians, the Trepca complex, by all accounts, lost money under Yugoslav socialism.

6. As in other socialist countries, official statistics in the SFRY measured total output in the form of "social product" or "gross material product," roughly corresponding to GDP. However, the allocation of that output to the different provinces, one of which was Kosovo, is unknown. Thus, it is hard to compare Kosovo's performance during reconstruction with that in the pre-conflict period. For data on the pre-conflict situation, see European Commission/World Bank (2005) and World Bank (2005c).

7. See Yanis (2003), as cited by Ballentine and Nitzschke (IPA 2003: 9).

8. The Contact Group included the United States, the United Kingdom, France, Germany, Italy, and Russia.

9. Daalder and O'Hanlon (1999) note that NATO went to war in March 1999 by attacking a sovereign country, not to uphold the inherent right of individual or collective self-defense. Neither did NATO go to war with explicit authorization from the UN Security Council or justify its action under the 1948 Genocide Convention. In their view, however, these facts do not mean that the alliance's action was illegitimate. The Security Council had identified the crisis in Kosovo as a threat to international peace and security in 1998. NATO did not request the Council's authorization to use force because Russia (quietly supported by China) indicated that it would veto it. Woodward (2007a: 7) also argues that the NATO operation against Serbia was defined in terms of K-Albanian human rights and legitimated as humanitarian intervention despite the refusal of the Security Council to authorize force.

10. The Group of Eight included members of the Contact Group plus Canada and Japan.

11. For a variety of views and a more detailed description of political and security developments in Kosovo, including issues relating to final status, see Woodward (2007a, 2007b, 1999, 1998), Shawcross (2000), Dobbins *et al.* (2003), US Congressional Research Service (2003), and Crocker (2004c). For historical background, see West (1941) and Malcolm (1999).

12. Daalder and O'Hanlon note that the UN responsibility in Kosovo is akin to a 1920s League of Nations mandate for a protectorate, and exceeds anything the organization has done before. Woodward (1999) points out that the UN mandate in Kosovo contrasted with other UN transitional administrations such as those in Eastern Slavonia (Croatia) and East Timor (Indonesia). In those cases, while international intervention was considered necessary to protect human and minority rights during the political transition, the political status of the territory was settled (reintegration into Croatia in the first case and independence in the second). She points out that the international presence in Kosovo has temporarily deprived a country of the right to rule over part of its territory and population. In Namibia, which was under the protection of the UN Trusteeship Council, the UN peacekeeping operation acted as the sovereign authority until elections established a legitimate government (Traub 2006: 22–3). See also Caplan (2005).

13. The mandate given to the UN in East Timor a few months later was very similar to that of Kosovo, although the political path to nationhood in East Timor was clear from the beginning.

14. Humanitarian assistance (Pillar I) was led by the UN High Commissioner for Refugees (UNHCR); civil administration (Pillar II) by the UN itself; democratization and institution building (Pillar III) by the Organization for Security and Cooperation in Europe (OSCE); and economic reconstruction (Pillar IV) by the European Union. Enforcement (authorized by the Security Council under Chapter VII of the Charter) was delegated to KFOR, a NATO-led force whose mandate was to maintain law and order until the UNMIK police force could take over, and to support civilian operations (particularly humanitarian and reconstruction activities) in close cooperation with UNMIK. Thus, NATO was the only organization not subordinated to the UN. By mid-2000, the Kosovo Police Service (KPS), created and trained by the UN had close to 1,000 officers. As it should be, once the emergency was over, the humanitarian pillar was closed and Pillar I became the security pillar—"Police, Courts, and Prisons," also led by the UN itself.

15. Some analysts have described UNMIK's lack of resources at an early stage as "scandalous" (Crocker 2004c: 194–7).

16. For a general discussion of institution building in Kosovo, see Herrero (2005).

17. The OSCE (Press Release of November 19, 2001 in OSCE web site), reports that turnout in the election was 63 percent of the 1.25 million people that were eligible to vote. The turnout among K-Albanians was 65 per cent while that of the K-Serbs was 46 percent. The newly formed K-Serb party won about 11 percent of the vote.

18. The three parties were the Democratic League of Kosovo (LDK), the Democratic Party of Kosovo (PDK; ex-KLA), and the Alliance for the Future of Kosovo (AAK; also ex-KLA).

19. The standards included functioning democratic institutions; the rule of law; freedom of movement; refugee return and reintegration; economic reforms; enforcement of property rights; dialogue with Belgrade; and establishment of the Kosovo Protection Corps (KPC).

20. This was not an easy meeting, as Kosovo's Prime Minister, Agim Ceku, a former KLA commander, is considered a war criminal in Serbia, while Ceku's own father was among the many K-Albanian civilians killed by Serbian forces. In the case of El Salvador, talks had taken place mostly through the UN mediator, rather than face-to-face. Throughout the 22-month negotiations, there had been, however, formal sessions of face-to-face meetings in the presence of the UN mediator.

21. For more details, see Wagstyl and MacDonald (2008); Bilefsky (2008a, 2008b); *The Economist* (April 12, 2008); and Woodward (2007a, 2007b). *The Economist* reports that Kosovo's Parliament adopted a new constitution in April and that by then only 18 of 27 EU members (and only 36 countries of the world) had recognized the new state.

22. Prior to Kosovo, the UN's only recent experience in civil administration as such was running Cambodia's central bank. Sergio de Mello, the Under-Secretary for Humanitarian Affairs who had been appointed as SRSG on an interim basis at the time UNMIK was established, argued that Kosovo was probably the greatest challenge the UN had faced since the launch of peacekeeping operations in the late 1940s. In his view, the UN had never assumed such a broad, far-reaching, and important executive task anywhere, including Cambodia, where he had worked.

23. By end-2002, the International Crisis Group estimated that about 130,000 Serbs and 100,000 other minorities were living in Kosovo (Dobbins *et al.* 2003: 113).

24. While Kosovo could not borrow from the IFIs, the FRY also could not borrow at the time, because it was not a member of the institutions. In fact, the FRY did not become a member of the Bretton Woods institutions and solve its arrear problems until the end of 2000. On the other hand, both the IMF and the World Bank provided policy advice and financial support to neighboring countries, including the Former Yugoslav Republic of Macedonia, Bosnia and Herzegovina, Bulgaria, Croatia, and to a lesser extent Romania, which were affected in many ways by the Kosovo crisis. Among the wide-ranging implications of the Kosovo war were inflows of large numbers of refugees and disruption of trade and tourism in neighboring countries. In December 2005, Kosovo signed a Letter of Intent and a Memorandum of Economic and Financial Policies, for policy dialogue but without financing. This was not renewed following its expiration at the end of 2007, since agreement could not be reached, in part because of uncertainty due to coming elections. In May 2005, the European Investment Bank (EIB), the EU's long-term financing institution, became the first IFI to agree to lend to Kosovo despite its unresolved legal status.

25. Sergio de Mello may well have been the best-qualified person to serve as SRSG in Kosovo and lead UNMIK. He was one of the few high UN officials at the time who could comfortably manage the link between the political and economic aspects of reconstruction and be an effective interlocutor to UN officials as well as the IFIs. However, the EU, which was to play a large role in financing, insisted on the appointment of one of its own officials.

26. See European Commission/World Bank, "Kosovo: Donors Pledge $1 billion in support of the reconstruction and recovery programme" (World Bank web site). As is often the case, only a small portion of those pledges had been disbursed a year later.

27. The dedication of the expatriate staff was reflected in the harsh conditions in which they lived, often bathing with a gallon of cold water, collected during the few hours that it was available. While this was not a significant hardship during the hot summer days, the temperature in the winter could drop to as low as $-25\,°C$ in the mountains.

28. All figures have been converted into dollars using IMF data (average rates for flows and end-of-period rates for stocks).

29. According to the ICRC (2000: 9), a cluster bomb is a metal canister that is dropped from an aircraft where the canister opens and ejects many dozens or hundreds of bomblets into the air. These bomblets are supposed to explode upon impact with the ground but many fail to do so, leaving a serious hazard to civilians after the end of hostilities since they can easily detonate upon contact. The ICRC study concluded that "cluster bomblets are, along with anti-personnel mines, the leading cause of mine/UXO-related injury or death in Kosovo. Cluster bomblets and antipersonnel mines accounted for 73 percent of the 280 incidents individually recorded by the ICRC between June 1st, 1999 to May 31st, 2000, with each type of ordnance responsible for 102 deaths or injuries or just over 36 percent each. In addition, as compared to those killed or injured by anti-personnel mines, those injured or killed by cluster bomblets were 4.9 times as likely to be under age 14."

30. According to Crocker (2004c: 200), the failure of KFOR troops to stop ethnic violence in the first months after the war signaled that K-Albanian violence was somehow acceptable, causing lasting problems for establishing the rule of law, promoting respect for human rights, and fostering reconciliation among K-Albanians and Kosovo's minority populations. This was certainly a major problem in the implementation of post-conflict economic reconstruction in Kosovo, and the situation has not improved much since. Bugajski (2003) claimed that the problem of criminalization and the lack of the rule of

law have become endemic in Kosovo. This has undermined the emergence of a democratic and law-abiding society. As an example, he cited the murder in September 2002 of Rexhep Luci, a respected K-Albanian architect who wrote the Pristina city urban plan and was Director of the Department of Planning, Reconstruction, and Development. Luci was killed for enforcing rules against illegal construction.

31. Dobbins *et al.* (2003: 121) attributed UNMIK's slowness in establishing a presence in Kosovo to the fact that, unlike NATO, the UN could not draw on standing units to supply the necessary manpower. Staff needed to be identified and hired one by one, a process that required months to complete. As I will discuss in reference to Afghanistan and Iraq, the US government faced similar staffing problems in both cases.

32. Despite the tremendous task at hand, the customs system miraculously started on time, owing to the professional and efficient direction of a young, dynamic team of EU experts who offered operational advice and worked closely with Gerard Fisher, an invaluable UN official with a distinguished career in post-conflict reconstruction, who became the first Director of Customs. All customs officials had to be recruited and trained in modern techniques and procedures, since Kosovo had been part of the anachronistic FRY customs system. Nevertheless, UN procurement as well as financing difficulties delayed revenue collection unnecessarily. Taxes were levied on all goods except those from the FRY, which were not considered imports. In June, the Economic and Social Council introduced a two-tier tariff system that subjected capital goods and certain production inputs to a 0 percent tariff (Ministry of Trade and Industry/UNMIK 2004: 5). For this and other policy measures adopted by the SRSG through Regulations, see UN web site.

33. The CFA ceased to exist when budget responsibilities and other economic policymaking were transferred to the PISG (see UNMIK Regulation 2001/19). Budget and tax responsibilities became the sole responsibility of the Ministry of Economy and Finance (MEF).

34. Unfortunately, this policy, as well as others adopted by UNMIK, often following EU recommendations, became divisive rather than contributing to national reconciliation since it clearly favored K-Albanians.

35. Some senior US officials opposed the use of KFOR forces for "nation-building" activities such as this, but it was part of KFOR's mandate to maintain law and order and support reconstruction in the early period.

36. Some analysts, nevertheless, have shown surprise that foreign direct investment inflows have been minimal, and that privatization has not proceeded as quickly as the United States, UNMIK, and others envisioned. See, for example, Crocker (2004c: 197).

37. In September 2000, an acid spill resulting from the rupture of a tank at the complex's battery factory formed a stream that reached the Ibar River. See News Reports at UN web site.

38. See Hedges (1998). Residents of Svecan, particularly women, reacted to the closure of the plant by throwing stones at members of KFOR and UNMIK. See also Flounders (2000).

39. Still another tender offer was published in *The Economist* in September 2006.

40. For some of the Serbian views on this matter, see Bozinovich (2005).

41. The KLA "Prime Minister" Hachim Thaci signed the "Undertaking of Demilitarization and Transformation" jointly with KFOR Commander Lieutenant General Mike Jackson on June 21, 1999. However, as Feil (2004: 50) argues, a viable and seamless DDR strategy must dismantle command and control structures, relocate soldiers to communities, limit

the circulation and possession of weapons and small arms, and establish programs for the productive reintegration of former combatants.

42. See various UNMIK Press Releases in UN web site. See also Dobbins *et al.* (2003: 118–19) and Crocker (2004c). As Crocker (2004c: 200–1) points out, owing to the close ties that NATO and the US in particular had developed with the KLA before and during the 1999 bombing campaign, KFOR was reluctant to tackle the security issue with the KLA and accepted its demands that 50 percent of KPC officers be former KLA members. UNMIK and KFOR were accepting the KPC as a compromise between KFOR's need to demobilize the KLA and the KLA's determination to maintain a standing force that could eventually become the national army of an independent Kosovo. The KLA supposedly completed its demobilization in September 1999. However, a few months later there were credible reports that armed groups, believed to be offshoots of the dismantled KLA, were attacking targets inside Serbia, apparently trying to unite the largely Albanian population in the Presevo Valley (southeast of the capital, Pristina). Solomons (2005: 32) refers to the KPC as "a state within the state that may devour the society that built it." O'Neill (2002: 117) notes that, according to UN officials, the idea of turning the KLA into some kind of benign civil emergency corps came from NATO.

43. On the issue of reintegration, see del Castillo (1995a, 1997, 2001), Crocker (2004c), and Solomons (2005).

44. Financing needs for such jobs exceeded the FY-2000 budget of $18 million to cover wage payments. Many of these people could have been productively employed in the agricultural sector. Kosovo relies heavily on imports of food products, many of which could be produced domestically.

45. See reports of the Secretary-General on the UN Interim Administration Mission in Kosovo, UNMIK press releases, the *Kosovo Status Report* (2000), and *UNMIK at Nine Months* (2000). See also IMF and World Bank reports.

46. In general, parallel security and administrative structures dissolved rapidly after January 2000. See UN, *Report of the Secretary-General* (2000).

47. According to Special Representative Bernard Kouchner (2004: 137), it was thanks to the Archbishop of Kosovo, Monseigneur Artemje, that the interim administration could mix K-Albanians and K-Serbs. Kouchner recounts that Serb extremists severely criticized Artemje for his action, and thus Serb participation remained largely marginal.

48. The EU was the largest donor in Kosovo, accounting for about 40 percent of the total, while the United States accounted for about 15 percent (see Crocker 2004c: 198). It appears that EU financing is included under "international organizations" on the ground that the EU was one of the four pillars of UNMIK. The Ministry of Finance and Economy estimated that cash remittances represented roughly half of GDP in 2000, or close to $700 million.

49. Later, other projects, such as the Village Employment and Rehabilitation Program in Mitrovica, were fully financed by the EU.

50. The IMF estimated per capita GDP to be in the $650–850 range in 2000, significantly below that of Albania or Bosnia, where it was about $1,000. GDP per capita rose in dollar terms to about $1,400 in 2003–7, in part as a result of the depreciation of the dollar. See ESPIG (2004) and IMF (2005e, Table 5: 11–12; Aide-Memoires) for more details.

51. Traub (2006: 117) notes that the nation-building effort in Kosovo proved far slower and more frustrating than anyone had imagined at the time.

52. According to Blair *et al.* (2005: 226–38), UNMIK was successful in its early relief effort but had much less success in rehabilitating basic services. In their view this was partly due to the approach of the international community to focus resources on "long-term construction of the private sector," to the detriment of immediate reconstruction of basic services that were provided by the publicly owned enterprises, such as Kosovo's power company. Thus, UNMIK focused on creating a long-term economic framework to enable the move from socialism into a market economy, to the neglect of other aspects that could have improved national reconciliation and the consolidation of peace.

53. Figures of 50 percent unemployment are frequently reported, in part because of the difficulty of estimating the situation in the informal sector.

54. See ESPIG (2004: 6). Although Kosovo is well endowed with lignite to produce power, even for export, poor electricity service is a major constraint on economic activity (UNMIK 2005: 8–17, and World Bank 2004: iii). However, as with deposits of lead, zinc, nickel, magnesium, and other natural resources, investment has been restricted by uncertainty regarding property rights and the existing institutional and legal frameworks. Contrary to other countries in reconstruction, financing does not seem to be a main constraint to investment. Commercial banks have abundant funds, part of which they invest abroad. Furthermore, Kosovo is among the top ten countries with respect to the inflow of remittances per capita, but most of this money finances consumption rather than investment (UNMIK 2005: 11).

55. Inward FDI amounted to only $42 million in 2004, and was projected to reach a similar level in 2005–6 (IMF 2005e, Table 5: 11–12).

56. Of course, under "normal development" it could make sense to have a budget surplus, particularly considering that, if "final status" means recognized independence, Kosovo will probably have to start servicing its share of the former Yugoslavia's external debt and will gradually have to assume the cost of maintaining infrastructure that has so far been donor-financed.

57. High-level UNMIK officials had misgivings about privatization in 2004. One even suggested that privatization be placed on hold until final status was resolved, "given the legal uncertainties and the proclivity of prominent Kosovars to align themselves with criminal figures" (Higgins 2004). By 2006, only about $250 million had been obtained through privatization.

58. Gerard Fischer argues that many of the problems UNMIK has had over the years largely relate to the lack of effective counterparts among the mostly K-Albanian authorities in Kosovo. This might well be the case in the later period, but it was certainly not a factor in the difficulties that the UN had in setting up UNMIK and in its early period of operation.

59. This would have obviated the need for an Economic Policy Adviser to the SRSG, a post I was invited by the Head of DPKO to fill as UNMIK was set up. In September 1999, I recommended the abolition of the post to make it clear that the Head of Pillar IV was the economic policy adviser to the SRSG.

60. This situation was similar to that existing in Boutros-Ghali's office, where advisers to the Secretary-General often performed functions, including those related to economic reconstruction, that normally would have been performed by the respective functional departments. (See Chapter 7 on El Salvador).

61. For example, in an August 1999 visit by Claire Short, UK Secretary of State for International Development, Pillar IV and the Economic Policy Adviser to the SRSG, the post that I occupied at the time, were not invited. This omission was due to inexperienced staff in

the Office of the SRSG, who, in setting the SRSG's agenda, were oblivious to the fact that Short's office played a key role in financial assistance and assumed that Secretary Short's visit was "political."

62. In 2000, the EU granted preferences to countries in the region (Albania, Bosnia and Herzegovina, Croatia, the former Yugoslav Republic of Macedonia, Montenegro, and Serbia including Kosovo), allowing most of their exports to enter the Union free of duties and any quantitative limits. The only exceptions included wine and certain fisheries products, sugar, baby beef, and textile products originating in the customs territories of Montenegro and Kosovo. These preferences, which were originally adopted in 2000 for a period until the end of 2005, were extended until the year 2010.

9 UN-led reconstruction following US-led military intervention: Afghanistan

1. Unless otherwise specified, data are from the IMF. Institutional reports on Afghanistan are listed in the Bibliography as "Country Reports: Afghanistan". For data on the informal market, see Goodson (2006: 154).

2. Ghani *et al.* discuss how, between the communist coup of 1978 and the collapse of the Taliban in December 2001, Afghanistan had been the scene of a brutal Soviet invasion, 10-year occupation, civil war, and proxy regional war. They mention how the cost of destroyed infrastructure and the opportunity cost of lost production during this period had been estimated by the World Bank at $290 billion.

3. Vaishnav (2004: 251) notes that US reluctance to support the expansion of the ISAF allowed spoilers to disrupt reconstruction in areas outside Kabul. Over time, this eroded initial goodwill toward the American presence and degraded popular support for the government. The Security Council charged the ISAF with helping the government to build a civilian police and new military forces. NATO assumed permanent command of the ISAF in August 2003, in what became the Alliance's first deployment outside Europe. According to NATO's Secretary-General, this was "the most complex and perhaps the most challenging mission that NATO has ever taken on." This is partly because of the operation's emphasis on reconstruction (Dombey *et al.* 2006). In October 2003, SCR 1510 lifted the ISAF's restriction on operating outside Kabul.

4. For the state of the Afghan infrastructure, see ADB web site.

5. See, for example, Rubin (2007a, as well as previous work listed in the bibliography), Dobbins *et al.* (2003a), Donini *et al.* (2004), Vaishnav (2004), Oliker *et al.* (2003), Montgomery and Rondinelli (2004) Donini (2006), Taylor (2007a) and Rotburg (2007).

6. As Hamre and Sullivan (2002: 89) point out, in failed states or countries devastated by war, the short-to-medium-run objective should be "to create a minimally capable state, not to build up a nation or address all the root causes that imperil peace."

7. The mujahedin had US support at the time they organized a "jihad" against the Soviet occupation. The Soviets had sent their military to Afghanistan in December 1979 to bring a communist government of their liking to power, replacing the leaders who had staged a coup in April 1978 (Rubin 2007a: 4).

8. Haneef Atmar, Minister of Rural Rehabilitation and Development, was the other strong supporter of the NDF within the government. Nevertheless, he pointed out that there was no significant consensus among Afghans in favor of the vision presented in the NDF. See Leader and Atmar (2004: 169).

9. In its "Doing Business" index of 175 countries, the World Bank ranks Afghanistan in 174th place with respect to "getting credit," 173rd place in "protecting the investment," 165th place in "enforcing contracts." These rankings are indicative of the problems to be faced in reactivating the private sector. (See World Bank Doing Business web site). The US Commercial Service (2006) prepared a study on the difficulties and opportunities of doing business in Afghanistan. Continued lack of electricity, for example, is a serious impediment to private-sector development, as are corruption, an unclear legal framework, and land tenure problems.

10. For an articulate and valid criticism of this document, see Novib-Oxfam Netherlands (2004). According to the authors, "the model presented in the SAF of a light enabling state, an active private sector and community driven development denies the reality of Afghanistan's current context. It is inconsistent with the historical experience of state building both of the West and the recent past in the Near East. It also ignores the reality of a highly uneven playing field in the world economy and fails to address the fundamentals of social justice and existing inequalities... there should be a heavier state playing a more interventionist role economically and politically, both domestically and internationally."

11. The I-ANDS and the Compact can be found at the government's web site. For a detailed analysis, see IMF (2006d).

12. Since the late 1990s, sixteen donors had formed the Afghanistan Support Group (ASG).

13. The Northern Alliance was a multiethnic group of mujahedin fighters that had fought the Taliban since the mid-1990s and had controlled the area north of the Kukcha river in Badakhshan. The United States, Japan, Saudi Arabia, and the EU co-chaired the ARSG. The ATA chaired the IG with the ADB, the World Bank, UNDP, and the Islamic Development Bank (IsDB) as vice-chairs. For a description of the numerous past and present arrangements for aid assistance and coordination see, for example, Brynen (2005).

14. Rubin attributes to Richard Haass this term, which was coined at a meeting in the State Department in September 2001. See also Ignatieff (2002) and Vaishnav (2004).

15. For the philosophical and practical dilemmas faced by NGOs and other humanitarian agencies in the transition to peace in Afghanistan, see O'Brien (2004), Jones (2004), and Costy (2004).

16. As with other military operations, the war in Afghanistan had disruptive repercussions on neighboring countries. While the war in Kosovo caused neighboring countries to suffer trade disruption and require balance of payments support from the IMF, in Afghanistan the assistance was related more to war aims than to economic hardship. In this regard, the Treasury prepared a financial plan for assistance to the "frontline states." Taylor (2007a: 31–2) described these as countries that could help the US in the "war on terror" by providing intelligence, allowing overflights, enhancing border control, or permitting the US to establish anti-terrorist bases of operations. There were 13 such states, including Pakistan, Uzbekistan, Kyrgyzstan, and Tajikistan. The package was particularly large for Pakistan, where a combination of debt relief, World Bank grants, and direct support from USAID, linked to a reform program to improve budgetary transparency and spending controls, resulted in increased economic growth from 2 percent in 2001 to 5 percent in 2005.

17. I would question Taylor's (2007a: 33) assertion that "the needs assessment is where most of the economic analysis—both microeconomic and macroeconomic—of postwar reconstruction would take place.... You had to show the donors what their contribution would be used for and that it would be used wisely in order to get them to contribute."

If this were the case, the institutions carrying out the assessment would determine the priorities. With a sovereign government in place, this is not acceptable or even recommended. It should be the sovereign government that designs its post-conflict economic reconstruction strategy, determines priorities—as the Afghan authorities did in their NDF—and carries out reconstruction according to its own vision. The needs assessment should provide an analysis of initial conditions and an evaluation of immediate needs. In no way should it set the priorities for reconstruction.

18. Three zeros were dropped from the currency; thus, 1,000 Afghani became 1 new Afghani. The currency exchange started in October 2002 and lasted until the end of January 2003, after which the Afghani stopped being legal tender. For a thorough discussion of the issues involving the choice of currency, the currency exchange, and the selection of the currency regime, including arguments in favor of a fixed or flexible exchange rate, see IMF (2003e).

19. Taylor (2007a: 53–9) describes efforts to bring Ismail Khan, the powerful warlord of Herat into the national government. This eventually happened in December 2004, when Khan finally accepted the position of energy minister and gave up his militia, whose members were recruited into the Afghan National Army.

20. See IMF Country Reports on Afghanistan listed in the Bibliography (various years). See also Bennett (2005).

21. The *hawala* is an informal system, widely used in the Middle East, Africa, and Asia, for transferring money, including remittances, based on performance and honor. People in Afghanistan's rural areas rely heavily on it. The system operates via a network of *hawala* brokers, or *hawaladars*. A customer approaches a broker in one city and gives a sum of money to be transferred to a recipient in another, often foreign, city. The *hawala* broker contacts a colleague in the recipient's city, gives instructions for the delivery of the funds (minus a small commission), and promises to settle the debt at a later date. All this takes place without promissory instruments. Because terrorists and drug dealers often use the *hawala* to transfer funds, Afghanistan's central bank introduced legal provisions in September 2004 to regulate and supervise their activities. For an analysis of the financial system at the end of 2001 and on the reforms adopted to modernize the system, see IMF (2003e).

22. Indeed, the central bank moved from one extreme to the other: from the previous practice of unlimited overdraft financing, which had resulted in high inflation and a sizeable depreciation of the exchange rate, to "adopting a simple and straightforward rule ... that would signal an unambiguous commitment to fiscal discipline." (IMF 2003e: 103).

23. Likewise, the US Treasury Department's "development as usual" approach to Afghanistan is obvious from a report by Larry Seale in June 2002. Seale argues that, despite a number of features to establish strict budgetary discipline, there were pressures on the government to accommodate various political interests, including payments to several provincial governors to support celebrations of the overthrow of the Soviet Army (Taylor 2007a: 42). These and other expenditures—which may seem unreasonable during normal development—are often critical for the government to consolidate its position and its legitimacy. In Mozambique, for example, Afonso Dhlakama, the rebel leader, wanted to keep his troops in the bush rather than demobilize, since force was his only bargaining chip as he entered into a peace agreement with the government in the early 1990s. To compensate for the many nonmilitary advantages of incumbency that the government had, Dhlakama insisted on acquiring financing for his political campaign. To his credit, Aldo Ajello, the head of the UN mission at the time, managed to convince donors to create a UN Trust

Fund and raised $18 million. Financing a rebel group was highly unconventional at the time, and even heresy for many, but it was a major positive factor in the consolidation of peace in Mozambique. See Ajello and Wittmann, 2004.

24. See IMF Country Reports on Afghanistan in the Bibliography. See also Bennett (2005). See IMF web site for quotes.

25. Afghanistan completed a Staff Monitored Program (SMP) in 2006 and started a formal program supported by a three-year Poverty Reduction and Growth Facility (PRGF) amounting to roughly $120 million. In December 2003, the IMF concluded Article IV consultations with the government for the first time in 12 years.

26. The Afghan solar year and fiscal year start March 21st and ends March 20th of the following year.

27. See also UNODC (2007a, 2007b), Rubin (2007a: 10; and 2004), Rohde (2006), Afghanistan (2005), Care and CIC (2003: 2), and IMF Country Reports (various years).

28. See IMF (2005f, Box 1) for a detailed explanation of the various budget concepts, and IMF (2005g, Table II.1: 20) for data. These reports clearly indicate the lack of transparency in the way donors finance Afghanistan.

29. I am fully aware that this is a chicken and egg problem. Had the government operated in a more efficient, transparent, and non-corrupt manner, donors would probably have been more likely to channel funds through the government budget and with less conditionality. Solving this problem therefore requires working at both ends: improving the fiscal framework of the government while ensuring that donors are more flexible and do not tie most aid to the use of their own resources.

30. For details and different views, see, for example, Care and CIC (2003), Costy (2004), Stockton (2004), Oliker et al. (2003), Vaishnav (2004), and Rubin (2006).

31. To qualify, countries need to establish a track record under programs supported by the IMF and the International Development Association (IDA), the concessional lending facility of the World Bank.

32. Although figures differ according to different sources and may not be accurate, they are nevertheless indicative of social conditions in the country. Life expectancy at birth is 44 years, one in four children dies before the age of five, one in 12 women dies in childbirth, fewer than four million people have access to water, and the population growth rate, at 3 percent, is one of the fastest in the world (ADB 2002: 5; Taylor 2007a: 38). Afghanistan ranked 169th out of 174 countries in the *Human Development Index* in 1996. In the past few years, Afghanistan has not been included in the index. Had it been included, its ranking probably would have worsened.

33. The term "seamless transition" used by Taylor (2007a: 138–9) is unfortunate, since "transition" implies sequence or passage from one state to another. Both humanitarian and reconstruction activities should take place simultaneously to be sustainable. What Taylor refers to as "transition" is, in fact, two "simultaneous actions." For example, returning refugees and demobilizing soldiers should be given food to eat, but at the same time they need to be given seeds, fertilizer, and technical training for planting. This is why short-term demobilization and reintegration programs need to be well planned and synchronized to be sustainable.

34. Data on estimates of reconstruction, pledges, and disbursements vary widely among different organizations and analysts. Furthermore, it is not always clear whether they are referring to reconstruction only or it also includes humanitarian assistance. This is a clear

example of the need for the UNDP and/or the World Bank to coordinate and centralize this type of data. It would be very useful for the recipient countries to know how much money is coming into the country and for what purpose. Without these data, effective policymaking is difficult to achieve.

35. Using a population figure of 22 million (before the return of refugees), the IMF (2003f: 16–17) estimated that from January 2002 to March 2003, per capita assistance was $67, while in Bosnia it reached $256 in 1999–2001. In terms of GDP, however, the assistance was comparable, at about 40 percent, although significantly lower than in Rwanda and Timor-Leste, where it reached about 60 percent. According to Thier (2004: 41), Afghanistan would be getting only about one-eighth of the funding Bosnians received on a per capita annual basis in the first three years of reconstruction (1996–9). Other studies have found large disparities as well (Dobbins *et al.* 2003; Rubin *et al.* 2004: 8–12). Although the estimates differ greatly, they are nevertheless indicative of the much larger volume of resources allocated to reconstruction not only in Europe, but even in Haiti and Rwanda.

36. Care and CIC also note that, at $10–12 billion a year to support Operation Enduring Freedom, the United States was spending about three times what the government was requesting for annual reconstruction funding (Care and CIC 2004: 139).

37. Although growth in 2002–6 averaged 15 percent, by 2006 the rate had slowed to 9 percent. Although these rates may seem high, it is important to bear in mind that economic growth started from a very low base in 1999–2001. Thus, the international presence created a bubble, which—like financial or real estate bubbles—is not likely to be sustainable. This has been the case with other post-conflict experiences.

38. For example, in the NDS (2005: 27) the government argues that the international community has imported models of security forces that impose costs that Afghanistan may not be able to sustain.

39. One obvious reason for resentment relates to pay. Rubin *et al.* (2004: 14–15) mention that an educated Afghan employed by an NGO receives a monthly salary of $200–300. A non-Afghan employee doing the same job for the same NGO receives $100 per hour. Although some experts question this figure, arguing that it is the level paid by private security contractors rather than NGOs, it nevertheless reveals the large gap between local and expatriate salaries.

40. Professor Nadiri, on leave from New York University, is presently in Kabul in charge of the I-ANDS.

41. See Rubin *et al.* (2004: 6–8) for an analysis of these scenarios. Ghani had previously been the head of the AACA.

10 US-led reconstruction amid US-led occupation: Iraq

1. For details see Encyclopedia Britannica, Wikipedia, Allawi (2007), Dodge (2003), and Tripp (2002). For an interesting account on how the past would affect reconstruction, see Braude (2003). All institutional reports in this chapter are listed under "Country Reports: Iraq" in the Bibliography.

2. According to Ignatieff, Iraq was an imperial fiction, cobbled together at the Versailles Peace Conference in 1919 by the French and the British and held together by force and violence since independence.

3. For details on the war, see Pérez de Cuéllar (1997: 131–80), chapter 7. For the use of chemical weapons by the two countries, see p. 168.

4. The term "compensation" is comparable to "reparations," the term used in the periods following the two world wars, so I use them interchangeably. For an authoritative and detailed account of the UN Security Council's role in Iraq during and after the Gulf War, see Malone (2006). See also Pérez de Cuéllar (1997), chapter 10.

5. As Malone (2006: 75 and chapter 4) noted, fearing for Iraq's cohesion after the Gulf War, Saddam Hussein turned to internal rebellions. Thousands of Kurds and Shiite were killed indiscriminately and many more were internally displaced.

6. For the details of everything that went wrong with this program and the involvement of UN staff as well as companies and officials of member states, including the permanent members of the Security Council, see Meyer and Califano (2006), which summarizes the findings of the Reports of the Independent Inquiry Committee chaired by Paul A. Volcker.

7. As Secretary-General Annan posited at a press conference in Tokyo in May 2006, "the Security Council acted and performed its duty. The Security Council did not endorse the war. The United States could not get the support of the Council to go to war. . . . The US did put together a coalition of the willing and went to war. . . . When an action is supported by the Council and the United Nations, the peoples and countries of the world are much more likely to accept it as legitimate. When governments move outside the Council or act without Council approval or outside the Charter, or do things that are not in conformity with the Charter, there is a perceived lack of legitimacy and things become quite difficult . . . when it comes to collective security, that must be taken by the Security Council."

8. See, for example, Baker and Hamilton (2006), Bremer (2006), Diamond (2005, 2006), Dobbins *et al.* (2003, 2005), and Crocker (2004a, 2004b, 2004c). Several authors have noted the lack of planning and the improvization of the US-led occupation of Iraq. See, for example, Fallows (2004), Crocker (2004a), and Rieff (2003).

9. For more details on the political and security transitions see, Baker and Hamilton (2006) and Diamond (2005, 2006).

10. As Dobbins *et al.* (2003: 169) have pointed out, the prewar splits at the Security Council made it much more difficult for the United States to adopt the burden-sharing model of Bosnia, Haiti, Kosovo, and Afghanistan.

11. The fact that K-Albanians had perceived US troops as liberators probably was a factor in the Bush administration's reckoning. However, the situation in Iraq was radically different following the unilateral decision to invade the country, particularly owing to the US position with regard to sanctions. Any initial goodwill also soon disappeared as it became clear that there was no clear exit strategy for US troops, and that their number was inadequate to ensure security. For the inadequacy of US troops and an analysis of the different insurgent and militia groups that posed a mounting threat, see Diamond (2006: 174–5) and Baker and Hamilton (2006: 3–21).

12. This was partly due to the failure of the US government to consult with the UN agencies and NGOs that had been in Iraq before the invasion. Had they done so, they probably would have been more aware of the political and economic realities in the country. The ORHA–CPA staff language gap was another factor that acted as a barrier to understanding. Baker and Hamilton (2006) note that only 33 of 1,000 people in the US Embassy in Iraq in 2006 were Arabic speakers, only 6 of whom were fluent.

13. Crocker (2004b: 272–3) argues that DDR typically is an "orphan" issue within the US government that is not housed in any particular agency, with the result that programs are neither coordinated nor cohesive. In his view, the government had no plans for DDR, particularly reintegration, even well into the reconstruction effort.

14. This figure was reported by Crocker (2006: 279) and was often mentioned in the media. Even if inaccurate, there is not much question that unemployment was extremely high. This is not surprising, as GDP had fallen by 20 percent in 2002 and by a further 35 percent in 2003.

15. For an interesting discussion of how the UN had become subordinate to the CPA through SCR 1483, see Malone (2006: 205–8). In August 2003, the Security Council (SRC 1500) established the UNAMI (UN Assistance Mission for Iraq), just five days before the terrorist attack on UN headquarters.

16. The UN also overestimated Iraqis' goodwill toward an organization that had maintained comprehensive sanctions against them for twelve years. As a result, the poorly protected UN mission became the target of terrorist attacks.

17. The TAL stated that all CPA laws, regulations, and orders would remain in place after the transfer of sovereignty unless duly enacted legislation rescinded or amended them. As per the mandate given by SCR 1546, the interim government could not take such a decision, because it would affect the country beyond the interim period (Crocker, 2004a: 85).

18. For an analysis of the power that this indirect selection process would give to the CPA, see Diamond (2005: 5).

19. The "occupation"—the period in which the US government took all executive and legislative decisions—lasted until the Interim Government was appointed and assumed national sovereignty. US troops remained in the country afterwards, but "at the request of the authorities." Therefore, the occupation ended at the time of the CPA's departure, after which the United States opened an embassy.

20. For a description of how security evolved throughout this period and how it affected reconstruction, see CSIS reports (various issues) listed in the Bibliography.

21. The CPA's 2003 reconstruction plan assumed that creating or restoring essential services for the Iraqi people took precedence over economic growth and job creation (US Government Accountability Office (GAO), 2006: 12). Because the task of reconstruction was given to foreign contractors rather than to Iraqis, Iraqis eventually had neither: security problems delayed reconstruction and no employment was generated. Baker and Hamilton (2006: 7) report that 5,000 foreign contractors were in Iraq in 2006.

22. For details on the multi-agency assessment of the situation in the immediate transition following military intervention, see UNDG and World Bank (2003) and IMF (2003g). See also IMF (2004g: 19). Baker and Hamilton point out that, despite non-US pledges of $13.5 billion, only $4 billion had been disbursed by mid-2006, which they attribute to donors' lack of confidence in the process.

23. As I argued earlier, donors expect resource-rich countries to foot a larger share of their reconstruction costs. However, it is not uncommon that policymakers, even those closely involved, have been entirely wrong about what countries can contribute in post-conflict situations. Deputy Defense Secretary Paul Wolfowitz infamously told Congress in March 2003 that "We're dealing with a country that can really finance its own reconstruction, and relatively soon." A month later, Defense Secretary Donald Rumsfeld added, "I don't know that there is much reconstruction to do" (Allawi 2007; Naim 2007).

24. New studies have shown the potential existence of additional reserves amounting to 100 billion barrels in the western desert highlands. If experts confirm this, Iraq would move to second place. Of the 78 oilfields that the government has identified as commercial exploitable, only 27 are currently in operation. A further 25 could begin producing soon, and 26 are not yet developed. For details on potential reserves, see Crooks (2007). For data on proven reserves, see Energy Information Administration (2006, Table 3).

25. The IMF (2003g: 6) estimates that GDP per capita had dropped from over $3,600 in the early 1980s to as low as $200 in the 1990s, to recover to $770 in 2001. Given the absence of reliable statistics, estimates must be taken with caution.

26. Given the poor statistics throughout this period, the figures are only indicative and are used solely for analyzing the deterioration of economic and social conditions. Both the IMF and the US Treasury Department state that Iraq's ranking had dropped to 126th (or 127th) place 10 years later (IMF 2005h: 5; Taylor 2003). However, the UNDP stopped including Iraq in the published Human Development Index; hence it is not clear where the data come from.

27. In the early 1990s, discussions with European and American oil experts took place at the UN Director-General's office, first on how much Iraq could contribute to the compensation fund, and later in relation to the Oil-for-Food Program. I remember well how surprised the experts had been to see the rapid recovery of the oil sector after the Gulf War. The degree of "cannibalization"—using parts from old machinery and infrastructure to repair oil facilities—and the inventiveness that the Iraqis had used to bring the sector back to production impressed everyone in the oil market.

28. As a result of the first two stages of the Paris Club debt rescheduling, as well as rescheduling of some of the non-Paris Club debt and most of the private sector claims, external debt has fallen to about $100 billion at end-2007 (about 162 percent of GDP). The IMF argues that the third tranche of Paris Club debt rescheduling (worth 20 percent in NPV terms) and progress with restructuring non-Paris Club debt are needed for sustainability. The former is expected after completion of the final review of the stand-by arrangement (SBA). This would bring the debt down to about $35 billion (slightly less than 50 percent of GDP) by end-2008 and secure debt sustainability over the medium term.

29. Between March and December 2004, the Bank approved and launched nine emergency projects for close to $400 million, thereby committing nearly all donor deposits in the Iraq Trust Fund. For more information on World Bank activities in Iraq, see the *Second Interim Strategy Note* (World Bank, 2005c).

30. Similarly, the World Bank in its *Second Interim Strategy Note* had very optimistic projections for these years: 17 percent growth for 2006 and a gradual decline to 7 percent by 2010. See World Bank (2005c and its web site).

31. Iraq's oil production peaked in 1979 at 3.5 mbpd. Since then, the highest level, 2.6 mbpd, was recorded in 2000 (Dobbins *et al.* 2003: 193). The US Government Accounting Office (GAO) Report (2006: 14) noted that the CPA overestimated the oil sector's capacity to contribute to reconstruction by assuming production would grow to 2.8 million–3.0 million barrels per day, an increase of one-third over 2002 levels, which never materialized. For an analysis of the oil sector in 2003, see IMF (2004g, Box 2: 8). For recent data see IMF (2008b).

32. The central bank raised its interest rate to 16 percent at the end of 2006 and to 20 percent in January 2007, from 8 percent at the beginning of 2006.

33. In addition to subsidizing sales from domestic production, the government imported petroleum products (amounting to $3.2 billion in 2004) for sale domestically at subsidized prices. The IMF estimated that this resulted in a loss of budget revenues of nearly $8 billion, or roughly 30 percent of 2004 GDP (see IMF 2005h, Box 2: 11). For prices, see data submitted by the government (IMF 2007f, Table 3). By March 2007, regular and premium gasoline prices were comparable with the averages for the region but those for diesel exceeded regional averages.

34. See IMF (2007e, several tables) and Baker and Hamilton (2006: 22–3).

35. The Global Policy Forum compiled a thorough list of publications and documents related to sanctions, including their humanitarian impact on the civilian population of Iraq (see their web site). Although the food distribution in place was beneficial in the early stages of the transition, the government had to replace it as soon as possible since it had the same impact as other humanitarian aid discussed earlier: it created disincentives to the reactivation of agriculture and distorted prices.

36. The Central Bank of Iraq holds the DFI and the International Advisory and Monitoring Board (IAMB) supervises it. Representatives of the UN, IMF, the Arab Fund for Social and Economic Development, and the World Bank are members of the IAMB. The resolution contemplated that the CPA, in consultation with the Iraqi Interim Administration, would authorize the disbursement of DFI funds.

37. Iraq could have opted for a currency board, as it had in the 1930s or as Bosnia adopted in the mid-1990s. It also could have pegged the ID to a stable currency or dollarize the economy *de jure*. However, to peg the ID to the dollar would have been a political mistake, and to peg it to the euro at a time when the euro was appreciating against the dollar would have been also problematic. For the advantages that a fixed rather than a flexible exchange rate would have provided Iraq, see Dobbins *et al.* (2003: 207–8). Chapter 14 discusses options for exchange rate arrangements.

38. Such inflows may result from aid, as in Afghanistan; repatriation of funds from abroad, as in Iraq; large inflows of remittances, as in Kosovo and El Salvador; a large expatriate presence, as in Kosovo; or from a combination of these factors.

39. See, for example, Kirchgaessner (2007).

40. President Bentancur was a member of the Truth Commission in El Salvador in the early 1990s. The Report of this Commission was entitled *From Madness to Hope: The 12-Year War in El Salvador*.

41. For more details, see IMF (2004g, Box 1: 7) and Taylor (2006, chapter 8; 2007).

42. See, for example, Dobbins *et al.* (2003, 2005) and Baker and Hamilton (2006).

43. An editorial in the *Financial Times* of September 24, entitled "Iraq as laboratory: Privatization talk lacks a sense of reality," is revealing. The editorial pointed out that the hyper-free market blueprint signed into law by Paul Bremer, including low tariffs, low taxes, and a wide-open door for foreign investors seeking to privatize assets, was likely "to stoke further the rising anger of many Iraqis at the occupation authorities' failure to get a grip on the country."

44. In a vouchering scheme, employees receive a stake in the privatized SOE.

45. Several books and articles discuss the issue of legitimacy. See, for example, Malone (2006), Slaughter (2004), and Crocker (2004a: 84–6).

46. As Crocker (2004a: 74) notes, the status of CPA legal reforms was uncertain after June 28, while the CPA's pursuit of its economic program with minimal Iraqi input called into

question its sustainability after a legitimate government took over. See also Dobbins *et al.* (2003: 210) on the inadvisability of privatization.

47. Because of the policy reversal, many analysts do not seem aware of the earlier stance. See, for example, Klein (2007). Analysts are more familiar with the infamous CPA Order 39 of September 19, 2003, according to which, "Foreign investment may take place with respect to all economic sectors in Iraq, except that foreign direct and indirect ownership of the natural resources sector involving primary extraction and initial processing remains prohibited. In addition, this Order does not apply to banks and insurance companies." Thus, Order 39 allowed 100 percent ownership of SOEs except in oil, banks, and insurance companies.

48. I have borrowed the title of this section from Chung and Fidler (2006), who conducted a thorough and detailed analysis of the restructuring from which I draw extensively in this section, unless otherwise indicated. Their work, which managed to piece together, for the first time, the practical details of this complex restructuring, should interest policymakers involved in future debt deals. For analysis and data on foreign debt, debt restructuring, and debt sustainability, see also IMF (various Country Reports listed in the Bibliography). For an inside account, see Allawi (2007).

49. In 2004, Gulf War reparations consumed about 5 percent of oil revenue (Crocker 2004a: 83).

50. Data varied somewhat according to different sources. See, for example, Chung & Fidler (2006), CRS Report for Congress (2006) and Allawi (2007).

51. Critics of the debt restructuring, including Jubilee Iraq, a donor-funded NGO, argued that it came with dangerous strings attached, including greater access for foreign investors to critical sectors. See, for example, Dominick (2004) and Jubilee Iraq at its web site.

52. Because of the decrease in debt and the large increase in GDP, the total debt fell to $114 billion in 2004, representing about 450 percent of GDP.

53. See IMF (2007f: 8).

54. It was impractical, however, to offer bonds to small creditors. Thus, the government paid small claims of less than $35 million in cash, at a discount of 90 percent.

55. According to the US Government Accountability Office (GAO), the US government allocated about $311 billion in fiscal 2003–6 to support US stabilization and reconstruction efforts in Iraq, including over $34 billion for reconstruction assistance alone. Moreover, the administration requested about an additional $51 billion to support US stabilization and reconstruction operations in Iraq and Afghanistan in fiscal year 2007 (see GAO web site). *The Iraqi Study Group Report* (Baker and Hamilton 2006: 9, 32, and 38) reckoned that by mid-2006, the US was spending $6–8 billion a month. From the time of the invasion to mid-2006 the US had spent $400 billion, with the bill possibly growing to $2 trillion once the cost of caring for veterans and replacing lost equipment was added. Since they do not explain how they arrived at this figure, they probably took it from Stiglitz (2006c). In addition to budgetary costs, Stiglitz, working with Linda Bilmes, included in the calculations the cost of dead soldiers and severely wounded veterans (lost earnings, lifetime disability payments, and health costs), equipment, recruitment bonuses, and interest on financing costs to arrive at an estimate of total cost ranging from $1 trillion to $2 trillion up to end 2005. As hinted in the title of their recent book (Stiglitz and Bilmes 2008), after five years of war, the cost to the US government has reached $3 trillion. In their view, three major factors are behind these ballooning costs. First, the rising cost of personnel, mainly as a result of a considerable rise in cost per troop; second, much higher

cost of fuel (from $25 to $100); and third and most importantly, the need to replace used equipment and weaponry as the stock of military equipment wears out.

56. In addition to the DFI, the CPA had at its disposal millions of dollar in cash, rugs, jewels, and other objects seized by US soldiers from Baathist properties, as well as an $18.6 billion allocation from the US Congress (Catan *et al.* 2004). For the details on the lack of transparency, missing money, incompetence, and other such issues related to CPA activities, see Malone (2006: 205–6), and Cooper and Jaffe (2004).

57. Other foreign contractors often mentioned in connection with reconstruction problems include Bechtel and Kellogg, Brown, and Root (KBR), a subsidiary of Halliburton. For additional evidence of nepotism, corruption, and unnecessary costs of US-led reconstruction, see Glanz (2006a, 2006c, 2006e, 2006g, 2006h), Brinkley (2006), Negus (2006a), Shumway (2005), and Pelhalm *et al.* (2004).

58. For details, see Horowitz (2003).

59. Diamond (2006: 177) points out that by early 2004 it was simply not safe for foreign officials and contractors to move around Iraq without an armored car and a well-armed security escort—expensive precautions that often were insufficient. Crocker (2004a: 82) notes that the CPA initially allocated 10 percent of the $18.6 billion appropriated by Congress for Iraq's reconstruction for security expenses related to protection of foreign contractors, but that actual costs pushed spending to 20–25 percent. Crocker also notes that corruption in Iraq is rampant and ingrained, in part as a vestige of the thriving black market during sanctions. The CSIS (December 2004: 1) reports estimates of security costs ranging from 15 to 50 percent of total contract costs. In analyzing how funds are spent, the report also accounts for the "numerous cases of rampant corruption and fraud in Iraq, poor oversight of US spending, and waste or mismanagement by contractors that have been documented in several US government and international audits as well as press reports." The report does not assign a percentage to the amount lost to corruption, however, and questions the 30 percent figure attributed to Transparency International.

60. Many analysts have advocated debt cancellation in Iraq on the theory of "odious debt." See, for example, Gardiner and Miles (2003), Wall Street Journal Online Editorial (2003), and Jubilee Iraq at their web site.

61. This proposal may not be that radical. In fact, in 2003 David Mulford, former Under-Secretary of the US Treasury and then International Chairman of Credit Suisse First Boston, proposed an interest-free three-year moratorium on Iraqi debt payments. See Mulford and Monderer (2003).

62. The Kurds aim to control Kirkuk and the fields around it, which account for about 10 percent of proven reserves. Article 140 of the Iraqi Constitution approved by the Shiite and Kurds, calls for a reversal of the "Arabization" policy that Saddam Hussein implemented in Kirkuk. This has allowed thousands of Kurds to return to the city and its surroundings. A census and referendum will take place sometime in 2007 to determine whether or not Kirkuk will be assimilated into the semi-autonomous Kurdish region (Senanayake, 2006). About 60–70 percent of proven reserves are in areas that the Shiites control. Sunni controlled central Iraq is the poorest region in terms of oil.

63. For details on the draft law, see Khalilzad (2007). Khalilzad suggests that the chances of ratification of the draft law are high, but Iraqi officials are much less optimistic. For an analysis of why oil companies may dream of entering Iraq, see Hoyos and Khalaf (2007). For production-sharing agreements that the Kurdistan government has signed

with foreign oil companies and that the central government does not want to recognize, see Blas (2007) and Negus (2006b, 2006c).

11 Setting the stage

1. Hamre and Sullivan (2002: 92) note that a coherent strategy is indeed absolutely necessary. As they point out, this is because all necessary tasks—humanitarian, military, political, social, and economic—are interconnected and hence need to be pursued all at once. If financing for one is lacking, all of the others may turn out to be in vain.

2. This implies staying the course with the right policies throughout economic reconstruction or modifying such policies if they are not working.

3. In the restricted sense used here, "capacity building" refers to efforts by international and bilateral organizations, as well as NGOs, to increase the human capacity of governments, both at the central and local levels, by educating and providing practical training to civil servants and other nationals involved in the reconstruction process. The objective is to improve their performance and enable them to carry out basic activities in a broad range of areas.

4. For a discussion of Bosnia and Herzegovina, see Hurtić et al. (2000). For Mozambique see Addison and de Sousa (1999). For Uganda, see Ndikumana and Nannyonjo (2007).

5. Along the same lines, Pascual and Indyk (2006) have argued recently that Lebanon should establish an international fund with procedures for fast, audited disbursements. They argue, and I fully agree, that it is important that there be only one trust fund, with a single set of rules for all donors. Otherwise, policymakers would need to spend more time on the bureaucracy of spending than on restoring economic activity.

6. The IFIs (particularly the IMF and the World Bank) and bilateral donors usually play an important role in capacity building in a wide range of economic and financial areas. They should do so at the invitation of national governments, keeping national priorities and preferences in mind, without trying to impose their own beliefs.

7. As the Steering Committee of the Joint Evaluation of Emergency Assistance to Rwanda revealed in 1996, the lack of in-depth knowledge of the historical, political, social, and economic context of the crisis undermined the effectiveness of international intervention (World Bank, 1998a).

8. See IMF (2005a) for more details. See also Hurtić et al. (2000).

9. The same is true of development in general.

10. For an interesting discussion on these issues, including the interest of foreign investors in the DRC's large copper and cobalt deposits, see England (2006c, 2006e). See also Bream (2007); Stearns and Wrong (2006); Gettleman (2006); Polgreen (2006); Mahtani (2006a); and del Castillo (2003b). For a discussion of the UN-backed certification scheme known as the Kimberly Process, see Wallis (2003a).

11. The Comptroller General of the United States testified to the Senate on March 11, 2008 that Congress appropriated nearly $700 billion for the global "war against terror" in Iraq and Afghanistan. According to GAO, this amount covers military operations, base security, reconstruction, foreign aid, embassy costs, and veterans' health care for the three operations initiated since the 9/11 attacks: Operation Enduring Freedom (OEF) in Afghanistan and other counter terror operations; Operation Noble Eagle (ONE),

providing enhanced security at military bases; and Operation Iraqi Freedom (OIF). The majority of this amount was used for military operations in support of Operation Iraqi Freedom, including the cost of equipping, maintaining, and supporting deployed forces. About $45 billion was provided for reconstruction efforts, including rebuilding Iraq's oil and electricity sectors, improving its security forces, and enhancing Iraq's capacity to govern. As I mentioned in Chapter 10, this total relates to budgetary expenditures. If other related future costs are included, Stiglitz and Bilmes (2008) estimate that the total may reach $3 trillion. (See chapter 10, footnote 55 for details).

12. The African Union estimated that corruption costs Africa about $148 billion per year, or roughly 25 percent of Africa's official GDP (Quote from President Obasanjo of Nigeria addressing the Extractive Industries Transparency Initiative (EITI) in Abuja and reported by the BBC website (see IMF, *Today's Morning Press*, the summary of daily news emailed to IMF staff, February 17, 2006)). As the International Peace Academy (IPA, 2002e) points out, in practice, making a functional distinction between legal and illegal commerce can be difficult, as informal markets and clandestine trade may serve vital economic needs—albeit often alongside other clearly criminal activities.

13. See IMF, *Today's Morning Press*, February 21, 2006 and Transparency International web site.

14. For an interesting account of mining, conflict, and corruption in Sierra Leone, see Polgreen (2007).

15. Transparency International's 2006 Corruption Perceptions Index places Haiti with the worst ranking among 163 countries.

16. See Schimmelpfennig (2007) and England (2006b) for the cost and other issues involved in Lebanon's reconstruction.

12 Basic institutional framework

1. As discussed in Chapter 5, the UN also lacks institutional arrangements of its own to support countries with economic reconstruction in an effective way. If the chances of successful reconstruction are to increase significantly, the recommendations that I made there (Figures 2–4), together with my proposal here (Figures 5–6), should be a subject of debate among the different actors. Without the right institutional arrangements, policy-makers will implement policies piecemeal, without consistency, integration, or support, and most probably lacking the necessary financing for priority programs.

2. For some of the issues involved in the transformation of Vietnam into a market economy in the late 1980s, see Lipworth and Spitäller (1993). Although Vietnam was still in the post-conflict reconstruction phase, many of the problems that it faced in this transforma-tion were similar to those of the Eastern European countries as they moved toward market economies in the early 1990s (see Blejer and Škreb 1997, 1999a, 1999c). In other respects, Vietnam was more like China than other post-conflict countries, insofar as the economic transition took place independently of—rather than in conjunction with—the political transition.

3. Financial programming is the mechanism for ensuring consistency across the four sectors in an economy: the real sector, the activities of which are recorded by the national income statistics; the fiscal sector, which is covered by the government's fiscal statistics; the monetary sector, recorded in the consolidated financial system accounts (including

the central bank, commercial banks, and other financial institutions); and the external sector recorded in the balance of payments statistics.

4. In some cases, governments have special powers to adopt legislation by decree. This was also the case in UN protectorates in Kosovo and East Timor, where the UN exercised all executive and legislative decisions.

5. This assumes that there will initially be two budgets: the "regular budget" (recording all recurrent expenditure of the government, such as wages, salaries, and pensions) and a "reconstruction budget" for humanitarian and reconstruction expenditure, financed by donors, but prepared by the Ministry of Finance, in consultation with donors. It is theoretically possible, but it has not happened in practice, to have a single national budget from the outset. The important point, as mentioned earlier, is that the government consolidates the two budgets as soon as possible, most probably as the country begins its transition to normal development.

6. The Paris Peace Agreement, for example, contemplated economic rehabilitation programs only for those groups that would collaborate with the peace process in Cambodia. By isolating certain factions from financing, the agreement was supposed to create incentives to cooperation in the peace process. This, however, did not work, because factions that opposed the peace process easily found alternative sources of financing through illegal sales of gems and logs (Doyle 2002: 82). In the case of Angola, the willingness of UNITA's Jonas Savimbi to respect the ceasefires might have been quite different if he had received the right incentives to stop fighting. Giving up war, diamonds, and power at the same time was not an attractive prospect, which may well explain UNITA's preference in 1992 for a return to civil war over participation in the run-off election.

7. As the minister of finance of Angola told the *Financial Times* in 2004, the $200 million offered by the World Bank was his "cash budget for a week" (Reed 2005).

8. See, for example, the three reports of the United Nations Panel of Experts on the Illegal Exploitation of Natural Resources and Other Forms of Wealth in the Democratic Republic of the Congo (DRC). See also Wallis (2003).

9. If Chad amended the law to allow for more recurrent expenditure or to decrease the transparency of government spending, this would create problems with the World Bank (Mahtani 2005). Despite the law, revenue of about $400 million since mid-2004 "has been seriously marred by mismanagement, graft, and, most recently, the government's decision that a hefty share can be used to fight a rebellion." The World Bank has suspended project loans to Chad, which is an indication of a "good practice model" gone sour. Chad is seeking alternative sources of financing, such as China, which is already a dominant investor in neighboring Sudan (White 2006b).

10. For a discussion of specific cases and comparison between countries that have been cursed and others that have been blessed, see Humphreys *et al.* (2007); Stiglitz (2006a, 2004a); Moody-Stuart (2004); and Ross (2003).

11. See, for example, Frenkel (1999b) and Blejer and del Castillo (2000b). Others oppose the independence of the central bank, particularly the need to target zero or very low inflation. See, for example, Stiglitz (2003a, 2005a).

12. For details, see Hilbers *et al.* (2000). For issues and problems related to the provision of microfinance in Cambodia, see Williams *et al.* (2001). The auditing and assessment of the banking system normally takes place within the framework of CAMELS (capital, assets, management, earnings, liquidity, sensitivity to market risk).

13. See speech at the UN web site. Ramos-Horta refers to a document of the World Bank (2005b).

13 **National reconciliation efforts**

1. The issue of refugees and displaced persons is critical to any country in the transition to peace. For details on this issue see, for example, Adelman (2002). If the transition goes sour, as has happened in Afghanistan and particularly in Iraq, there will be a new wave of refugees and displaced populations. In Iraq, it is estimated that by 2007 the security situation had uprooted about 4 million people, of which close to 2 million had no place to go outside Iraq since neighboring countries were already flooded with refugees (see *Financial Times* 2007b and Rosen 2007).

2. Spear (2002: 141) posits that, although disarmament and demobilization are normally bundled together, the latter is more important in ensuring a successful transition to peace. This is why the lack of demobilization of the Kosovo Liberation Army (KLA) is so worrisome, as discussed in the case study. She also argues strongly that the international community should not expect or encourage disarmament to follow a standard model. National policymakers should decide on how to do it according to the norms of the specific society. For more details on the issues involved in these activities, see also Berdal (1996).

3. UNDP (2006) provides the details of the organization's work in this area, as well as lessons learnt and guidance for DDR programs. See also Rubin (2003). For a review of the Standards see UN web site.

4. For more details on the specific activities related to relief and humanitarian assistance, see United Nations (1996a).

5. For an analysis of the many challenges related to education in post-conflict situations, see World Bank (2005a).

6. Spears (2002: 145) argues that the more modern the economy, the more complex will be the reintegration process. This makes sense because a large part of those that need reintegration might have done nothing else in their lives but fight and hence would find it more difficult to acquire the skills needed by a modern economy. My experience with the land program in El Salvador and with other reintegration programs makes me believe that there are often other factors working the other way. For example, the obstacles to the land program in El Salvador were such in terms of land scarcity, property rights problems, and others that it would have been better to reintegrate former combatants through higher skilled activities in manufacturing or services, despite the training and capacity building efforts that this would have required.

7. See Berdal (1996: 15) and Spear (2002: 152).

8. For details on Sierra Leone, see Vaishnav and Crocker (2004).

9. For the interesting experience of Malawi with subsidization of fertilizer and seeds, see Dugger (2007b).

10. See UNEP's web site.

11. For details, see Humanitarian Demining web site.

12. For information on UN activities in demining see UN web site.

13. For a detail of the different infrastructure sectors and a more technical analysis, see Brown (2005). For problems in rehabilitating infrastructure in post-conflict countries in Africa, see Hoeffler (1999).

14. Housing is "private" infrastructure and not usually included with public infrastructure. In post-conflict situations, however, the distinction is not important since donors also largely finance housing rehabilitation.

15. Many of these off-budget schemes imply, nevertheless, "contingent liabilities" for the government in the sense that they may trigger a financial obligation for the government under specified circumstances. Contingent liabilities can be "explicit" if a contract or law stipulates payment commitments, as in the case of government guarantees, or they can be "implicit," if no such legal obligation exists. In the latter case, the government may need to cover for the liabilities despite the lack of guarantee, to avoid, for example, the collapse of the banking system or the default of local governments.

16. For a detailed analysis of the different options in relation to particular case studies in different parts of the world, see del Castillo and Frank (2003).

17. See speech of January 24, 2004 at UN web site.

18. The Secretary-General (2001: 11) recognizes this in relation to the exit strategy for peace-keeping operations. Noting that "reconciliation cannot be imposed," he argued that a peacekeeping operation is the wrong instrument if the parties are bent on war.

14 **Macroeconomic policymaking**

1. In many cases, the poor results had to do with flagrantly inconsistent policies rather than with the application of a specific model. Perhaps the most notorious criticism of the Washington Consensus comes from President Chávez of Venezuela, who likes to talk about the savage "neo-liberalism" that ruined Argentina. Argentina, however, had avoided liberalizing the labor market, which was inconsistent with its fixed exchange rate system: if prices cannot adjust, wages should. Otherwise, the situation would be unsustainable, as indeed it was.

2. This, by no means, implies that there were no inefficiencies and corruption in state-owned enterprises. However, privatization policies in the 1990s often led to a few people amassing huge fortunes in a short period. At the same time, these policies created high unemployment and hardship for the large majority of those that previously had relied on public employment and high social protection.

3. Most countries in post-conflict transitions have an undeveloped financial market. Most rely on the banking system to allocate resources from savers to borrowers. Many governments control interest rates and use credit allocation of state-owned banks for political objectives. For case studies on different aspects of financial liberalization across the world, see Caprio *et al.* (2001); Blejer and Škreb (1999); Frenkel (1999); and Stiglitz (1998).

4. The elections of leaders in several emerging countries, particularly in Latin America, that come from a strong socialist tradition reflect this preference. This has been the case in Venezuela, Brazil, Argentina, Uruguay, Bolivia, and Ecuador, economies coming out of sharp economic and financial crises. It has also been true in Chile, a country that has followed successful market-based reform for several decades and that has managed to bring more people out of poverty more rapidly than any other country in the world, but with income disparities increasing in the process.

5. The choice between the market and the state is not something peculiar to countries in post-conflict situations. In 1848 John Stuart Mill in his *Principles of Political Economy* wrote: "One of the most disputed questions both in political science and in practical statesmanship at this particular period relates to the proper limits of the functions and agency of governments." Cited by Guitián (1997: 27). See also Buiter *et al.* (1997).

6. As Hoff and Stiglitz (2002: 8) have pointed out, Russia initiated mass privatization before institutions to support the rule of law were in place. They reported a qualitative difference

between Russia and most other developed, capitalist societies: there were few rules for corporate governance, and no rules to make management teams contestable. Furthermore, in Russia the president could rule by decree. In 1995–6, Russia adopted laws to protect shareholders' rights. Despite regular free elections since 1993, enforcement of these rules was very weak. The authors recount how the transfer of state property to private agents took place amid the stripping of Russia's assets. Depending on the measure used, capital flight averaged between $15 billion and $20 billion per year during 1995–2001, equivalent to 5 percent or more of GDP.

7. There exist many policy alternatives, as the experiences of Costa Rica and Uruguay, two middle-income countries with strong social protection and among the best income distributions in Latin America, indicate.

8. As the President of the Federal Reserve of Dallas Bob McTeer (Dallas Federal Reserve 2006) wrote Hazlitt was the 20th century's most famous economic journalist. In McTeer's view, "understanding economic theory is hard. Most people don't read economics directly, but absorb what they know through the popular press. For this reason, journalists have always played a key role in educating their readers on complex topics." McTeer considers that Hazlitt was such a journalist.

9. For a theoretical and practical analysis of macroeconomic management, including sources of economic growth, appropriate monetary, exchange, and fiscal policies for redressing domestic and external imbalances; exchange rate determination, and the effects of IMF-supported programs, see Khan *et al.* (2002). For an interesting and practical review of a large number of macro- and micro-economic issues relating to globalization, many of which are immediately, or will soon become, relevant to countries in post-conflict reconstruction, see Schriffin and Bisat (2004).

10. In the bibliography these are also listed under Sundararajan *et al.* (1995) and Ghandi *et al.* (1995) since references also appear under their respective names in the literature. For IMF work on monetary, exchange, and fiscal policies in post-conflict countries see also IMF web site.

11. See Sabot and Székely (1997). The Third meeting of the Group, sponsored by the United Nations University and World Institute for Development Economics Research (WIDER), took place in Helsinki in July 1995. The head of DESA, Jean Claude Milleron, provided Secretariat support for the High Level Group. The fact that these valuable papers were not included in the edited volumes of the three meetings of the group provides support for my argument in Chapter 5, that he was not at all interested in post-conflict reconstruction, which he saw as a political, rather than an economic, issue.

12. See, for example, IMF (2004c). See also Gupta *et al.* (2005).

13. This was not a new argument for me. In 1995 I wrote that in post-conflict situations countries had to "settle for less than optimal policies in their economic reform efforts so as to accommodate the additional financial burden of reconstruction and peace consolidation" (del Castillo 1995a).

14. See IMF, Public Information Notice (PIN) No. 05/45 of March 29, 2005.

15. For details on a minimalist monetary and exchange rate framework needed for post-conflict reconstruction, see IMF (1995c) or Sundararajan *et al.* (1995). For more on these issues and a discussion of particular case studies see also IMF (2004a, 2004b).

16. For details see IMF (1995a, 1995b). See also Lönnberg (2002). Apart from his proposal for using best practices for designing central banks (based on independence from government authorities) with which I disagree, he presents the operational framework for restoring

and transforming payments and banking systems, based on the Fund's experience in Kosovo and East Timor, which is useful for practitioners.

17. In theory, if policymakers decide to adopt a fixed (anchor) exchange rate, they will give up the option of utilizing monetary policy (rather than fiscal policy) to stimulate the economy since it is outside their control. Under fixed exchange rates, the authorities can only control credit, and the supply of money will adjust to the demand for it through the balance of payments, that is, through imports or exports of capital. In practice, this is not the case in post-conflict situations where there are all types of distortions that interfere with capital flows.

18. As discussed in the case of Afghanistan, countries may also have to move to a two-tier banking system, where the central bank stops performing commercial functions and focuses on monetary policy. In Afghanistan, for example, the central bank performed deposit and credit operations that in a two-tier banking system are the prerogative of commercial banks.

19. Although there is conclusive empirical evidence of the economic and social costs associated with high inflation, research has not been able to prove convincingly that very low levels of inflation make a significant improvement in growth prospects. For evidence, see for example, Tanzi (1997b); Stiglitz (2005a, 2003a, 1998). Shooting for very low levels of inflation in post-conflict situations could deprive governments of critical financing without improving growth significantly.

20. This is because monetary policy is geared towards maintaining the peg, and cannot be used for expansionary purposes unless the authorities are willing to break the peg.

21. With the fall in inflation in the late 1990s, however, policymakers sought greater discretion in managing their exchange rates and moved toward intermediate systems, including pegged but adjustable rates, exchange rate bands, crawling pegs, and pre-announced rates ("soft pegs"). That trend was set back by the financial panics of the new millennium and exchange rate regimes, previously seen as extreme policy choices, acquired new prominence. Thus, the debate shifted towards two preferable alternatives: governments can either guarantee a fixed exchange rate through some type of institutional mechanism or adopt a free floating system where they abstain from intervening in foreign exchange markets to defend the currency. At an operational level, however, few countries float freely. Most continue to intervene in the foreign exchange market. For a more detailed discussion of the options debate, see Fisher (2001) and Blejer and del Castillo (2000a).

22. For an analysis of currency boards see Hanke (2002, 2003a, 2003b). For a detailed analysis of the case of Bosnia and Herzegovina, see Coats (1999). Woodward (2002) points out how policy choices which governments make in the area of stabilization are very important and can have huge political consequences—both positive and negative—for the quality and sustainability of the peace process.

23. There is an important literature dealing with the conditions for adopting one exchange rate or another. For analysis on dollarization, see for example, Berg and Borensztein (2000a, 2000b); and Sahay and Végh (1995). For a case study on the pros and cons of dollarizing in Liberia, see Honda and Schumacher (2006).

24. For details on a minimalist fiscal framework needed for post-conflict reconstruction, see IMF (1995d) or Ghandi et al. (1995). See also IMF (2004c, 2004d) for more on these issues and a discussion of particular case studies.

25. For a discussion of these issues, see Tanzi (2000).

15 **Microeconomic policymaking**

1. Indeed, I agree with Crane (2007) that "suicide bombers and death squads are not seeking shorter working hours, higher salaries, or better pension plans." But the transition from war creates high expectations for better living conditions and when people do not find a job, those expectations are immediately dashed. Disgruntled members of society are much more likely to engage in "political, sectarian and personal" struggles, which he argues are the root causes of the current conflict in Iraq.

2. These are often justified as answers to specific problems. For example, the subsidies to biofuels are justified as a response to energy insecurity and climate change (Wolf 2007).

3. Outsourcing has grown rapidly in the last decade, and takes place at very different levels of expertise and technology. Only a decade ago, for example, pistachio production in Italy had an outsourced component. Companies shipped closed nuts to China, where workers cracked them open by hand. The Chinese exported them back to Italy, where they were packed and sold (Hill 2006). Although many post-conflict countries should aim at higher levels of value-added than pistachio opening, countries can attract low-skilled and low-investment processes as long as their labor force is competitive.

4. See, for example, del Castillo (2003c) and del Castillo and García (2006). Although I am convinced that countries can use these zones effectively under different situations, I emphasize that their success will be highly dependent on the right legal framework, as well as on an effective promotion policy to attract only "desirable" investors. In this context, desirable investors are those that, in addition to generating employment, contribute to technology transfer, build the capacity of the local labor force, respect the environment, and exercise good corporate governance.

☐ BIBLIOGRAPHY

Books and journal articles

Abiew, Francis K., and Tom Keating, 2004, "Defining a role for civil society: Humanitarian NGOs and peacebuilding operations," in Keating and Knight (eds), ch. 5: 93–118.

Acevedo, Carlos, Deborah Barry, and Herman Rosa, 1995, "El Salvador's agricultural sector: Macroeconomic policy, agrarian change and the environment," *World Development*, 23/12: 2153–72.

Addison, Tony (ed.), 2003, *From Conflict to Recovery in Africa* (UK: Oxford University Press).

—— 2000, "Aid and conflict," in Finn Tarp (ed.), *Foreign Aid and Development: Lessons Learnt and Directions for the Future* (London and New York: Routledge).

—— Abdur R. Chowdhury, and S. Mansoob Murshed, "Financing reconstruction," in Junne and Verkoren (eds), ch. 12: 211–22.

—— and Clara de Sousa, 1999, "Mozambique: Economic reform and reconstruction," in Mark McGillivray and Oliver Morrissey (eds), *Evaluating Economic Liberalization* (UK: Macmillan), vol. 4: 163–85.

—— and Mark McGillivray, 2004, "Aid to conflict-affected countries: Lessons for donors," *Conflict, Security and Development*, 4/3 (December).

Adelman, Howard, 2002, "Refugee repatriation," in Stedman *et al.*, ch. 10: 237–72.

Ajello, Aldo, and Patrick Wittmann, 2004, "Mozambique," in Malone (ed.), ch. 29: 437–50.

Allawi, All A., 2007, *The Occupation of Iraq: Winning the War, Losing the Peace* (New Haven and London: Yale University Press).

Anstee, Margaret Joan, 2003, *Never Learn to Type: A Woman at the United Nations* (UK: John Wiley and Sons, Ltd.).

Antonini, Blanca, 2004, "El Salvador," in Malone (ed.), ch. 28: 423–37.

Azini, Nassrine, Matt Fuller, and Hiroko Nakayama (eds), 2003, *Post-Conflict Reconstruction in Japan, Republic of Korea, Vietnam, Cambodia, East Timor and Afghanistan* (Proceedings of an International Conference in Hiroshima in November 2002, sponsored by UN, UNITAR, and the Hiroshima Prefectural Government).

Baker, James A., and Lee H. Hamilton, 2006, *The Iraq Study Group Report* (New York: Vintage Books).

Ball, Nicole, 2001, "The challenge of rebuilding war-torn societies," in Crocker *et al.* (eds), ch. 42: 719–36.

—— and Tammy Halevy, 1996, *Making Peace Work: The Role of the International Development Community* (Washington, D.C.: Overseas Development Council).

Ballentine, Karen, and Jake Sherman (eds), 2003, *The Political Economy of Armed Conflict: Beyond Greed and Grievance* (Boulder: Lynne Rienner Publishers).

Bannon, Ian, and Paul Collier (eds), 2003, *Natural Resources and Violent Conflict* (Washington, D.C.: The World Bank).

Barkin, J. Samuel, 2006, *International Organization: Theories and Institutions* (New York: Palgrave Macmillan).

Barnett, Michael, and Thomas G. Weiss, 2008, "Humanitarianism: A Brief History of the Present," in Barnett and Weiss (eds), *Humanitarianism in Question: Politics, Power, Ethics* (Ithaca, N.Y.: Cornell University Press), ch. 1: 1–48.

Bennett, A. (ed.), 2005, *Reconstructing Afghanistan* (Washington, D.C.: IMF).

Berg, Andrew, and Eduardo Borenzstein, 2000a, "The dollarization debate," *Finance & Development*, 37/1 (March).

Biddle, Stephen, 2006, "Seeing Baghdad, thinking Saigon," *Foreign Affairs* (March/April).

—— Larry Diamond, James Dobbins, Chaim Kaufmann, and Leslie Gelb, 2006, "Iraq: A Round-table," *Foreign Affairs* (July/August).

Blair, Stephanie A., Dana Eyre, Bernard Salomé, and James Wasserstrom, 2005, "Forging a viable peace: Developing a legitimate political economy," in Jock Covey *et al.* (eds), ch. 8: 205–44.

Blejer, Mario I., and Graciana del Castillo, 2001a, "Contagion: From higher risk to risk aversion and the danger of protectionism," in F. Rivera-Batiz and A. Lukauskas (eds), *The Political Economy of the East Asian Crisis: Tigers in Distress* (Edward Elgar Publishers), ch. 8: 227–48.

—— —— 1998, "Déjà vu all over again? The Mexican crisis and the stabilization of Uruguay in the 1970s," *World Development*, 26/3 (March): 449–64 (translated into Russian as IMF Working Paper, WP/96/80, July 1996).

—— and Marko Škreb, 1999a, *Financial Sector Transformation: Lessons from Economies in Transition* (New York: Cambridge University Press).

—— —— 1999b, "Financial reforms and economic transitions: An overview of the major issues," in Blejer and Škreb (eds), "Introduction," 1–18.

—— —— 1999c, *Central Banking, Monetary Policies, and the Implications for Transition Economies* (Norwell, Mass.: Kluwer Academic Publishers Group).

—— —— 1997, *Macroeconomic Stabilization in Transition Economies* (UK: Cambridge University Press).

—— and Teresa Ter-Minassian, 1997, *Macroeconomic Dimensions of Public Finance: Essays in Honour of Vito Tanzi* (London: Routledge).

Boon, Kristen E., 2007, "Open for business: International financial institutions, post-conflict economic reform and the rule of law," *Journal of International Law and Politics*, 39/3 (Spring): 513–81.

Bourguignon, Francois, and Mark Sundberg, 2007, "Aid can work," *Finance & Development* (March).

Boutros-Ghali, Boutros, 1999, *Unvanquished: A US—UN Saga* (New York: Random House).

—— 1995a, *Supplement to An Agenda for Peace* (New York: United Nations).

—— 1995b, *An Agenda for Development* (New York: United Nations).

—— 1992, *An Agenda for Peace* (New York: United Nations).

Boyce, James K., 2002, *Investing in Peace: Aid and Conditionality after Civil Wars* (Oxford: Oxford University Press, Adelphi Paper No. 351).

—— 2000, "Beyond good intentions: External assistance and peacebuilding," in Shepard and Patrick (eds), ch. 9: 367–82.

—— 1995, "External assistance and the peace process in El Salvador," *World Development*, 23/12: 2101–16.

—— and Madalene O'Donnell (eds), 2007, *Peace and the Public Purse: Economic Policies for Postwar State-Building* (Boulder and London: Lynne Rienner Publishers).

Braude, Joseph, 2003, *The New Iraq: Rebuilding the Country for its People, the Middle East, and the World* (New York: Basic Books, 2003).

Bremer, L. Paul, 2006, *My Year in Iraq: The Struggle to Build a Future of Hope* (New York: Simon & Schuster, with the collaboration of Malcolm McConnell).

Brown, Richard H., 2005, "Reconstructing infrastructure," in Junne and Verkoren (eds), ch. 6: 99–116.

Brynen, Rex, 2005, "Donor assistance: Lessons from Palestine for Afghanistan," in Junne and Verkoren (eds), ch. 13: 223–48.

Bugajski, Janusz, R. Bruce Hitchner, and Paul Williams, 2003, *Achieving a Final Status Settlement for Kosovo* (Washington, D.C.: CSIS Press).

Burnside, Craig, and David Dollar, 2000, "Aid, policies and growth," *American Economic Review*, 90/4, (September).

Call, Charles T., 2002, "Assessing El Salvador's transition from civil war to peace," in Stedman *et al.* (eds), ch. 6: 383–420.

—— and William Stanley, 2002, "Civilian security," in Stedman *et al.* (eds), ch. 11: 303–26.

Caplan, Richard, 2005, *International Governance of War-Torn Territories: Rule and Reconstruction* (New York: Oxford University Press).

Caprio, Gerard, Patrick Honohan, and Joseph E. Stiglitz, 2001, *Financial Liberalization: How Far, How Fast?* (New York: Oxford University Press).

Carstens, Agustin, 2004, "Financial Crises," *Finance & Development* (September).

Chesterman, Simon, 2007, *Secretary or General? The UN Secretary-General in World Politics* (Cambridge: Cambridge University Press).

Clément, Jean A.P. (ed.), 2005, *Post-conflict economies in Sub-Saharan Africa: The lessons of the Democratic Republic of Congo* (Washington, D.C., IMF, February).

Coats, Warren, 1999, "The Central Bank of Bosnia and Herzegovina," in Blejer and Škreb (eds), 1999c, ch. 14: 367–99.

—— 2007, "Currency and sovereignty: Why monetary policy is critical," in Boyce and O'Donnell, ch. 8: 213–44.

Collier, Paul, 2001, "Economic causes of civil conflict and their implications for policy," in Crocker *et al.* (eds), ch. 10: 143–62.

Cordesman, Anthony, 2004, *The War After the War: Strategic Lessons of Iraq and Afghanistan* (Washington, D.C.: Center for Strategic and International Studies).

—— 2003, *The Iraq War: Strategies, Tactics, and Military Lessons* (Washington, D.C.: Center for Strategic and International Studies).

Corker, R., D. Rehm, and K. Kostial, 2001, "Kosovo: Macroeconomic issues and fiscal sustainability" (Washington, D.C.: International Monetary Fund).

Costy, Alexander, 2004, "The dilemma of humanitarianism in the post-Taliban transition," in Donini *et al.*, 143–65.

Cousens, Elizabeth M., and Chetan Kumar (eds), 2001, *Peacebuilding as Politics: Cultivating Peace in Fragile Societies* (Boulder and London: Lynne Rienner Publishers).

Covey, Jock, Michael J. Dziedzic, and Leonard R. Hawley, 2005, *The Quest for Viable Peace: International Intervention and Strategies for Conflict Transformation* (Washington, D.C.: United States Institute of Peace Press).

Crocker, Bathsheba, 2004a, "Reconstructing Iraq's Economy," *Washington Quarterly*, 27/4: 73–93.

——— 2004b, "Iraq: Going it alone, gone wrong," in Orr, ch. 16: 263–85.

——— 2004c, "Learning to leverage 'liberator status'" in Orr, ch. 12: 193–209.

Crocker, Chester A., Fen O. Hampson, and Pamela Aall (eds), 2001, *Turbulent Peace: The Challenges of Managing International Conflict* (Washington, D.C.: United States Institute for Peace Press, first edition in 1996).

——— 1999, *Herding Cats: Multiparty Mediation in a Complex World* (Washington, D.C., United States Institute for Peace Press).

Daalder, Ivo, and Michael E. O'Hanlon, 1999, "Unlearning the lessons of Kosovo," *Foreign Policy* (Fall).

Das, Saya B., 2004, "Sustainable peace: Who pays the price?", in Keating and Knight, ch. 12: 263–80.

De Long, J. Bradford, and Barry Eichengreen, 1993, "The Marshall Plan: History's most successful structural adjustment program," in Dornbusch *et al.*, ch. 8: 189–230.

de Soto, Alvaro, 1999, "Ending violent conflict in El Salvador," in Crocker *et al.* (1999), ch. 14: 345–86.

——— and Graciana del Castillo, 1994, "Obstacles to peacebuilding," *Foreign Policy*, 94 (Spring): 69–83 (translated into Spanish in *Revista Tendencias*, 32 (julio/agosto 1994)).

——— ——— 1995, "Implementation of comprehensive peace agreements: Staying the course in El Salvador," *Global Governance* (Spring): 189–204.

del Castillo, Graciana, 2006a, "Auferstehen aus ruinen: Die besonderen bedingungen des wirtschaftlichen wiederaufbaus nach konflikten," *der Überblick*, (4/2006 Dezember): 42–5.

——— 2006b, "El Clima de Negocios en la República Oriental del Uruguay," in Eduardo Fernández-Arias and Silvia Sagari (eds), *Una Nueva Era de Crecimiento Económico en Uruguay* (Washington, D.C.: Interamerican Development Bank), ch. 7: 239–304.

——— 2006c, "Mexico at the vanguard on debt issues," in L. Randall (ed.), *Changing Structure of Mexico: Political, Social, and Economic Prospects* (N.Y.: M.E. Sharpe Publishers), ch. 11: 176–96.

——— 2004, "Assessing sovereign risk," in Schiffrin and Bisat (eds), ch. 12: 132–44.

——— 2003a, "Afghanistan—The way forward," *Global Governance* (April): 153–7.

——— 2002a, "Determinants of the nominal exchange rate: A survey of the literature," in Khan *et al.* (eds), ch. 10: 257–306.

——— 2002b, "External Sector: Accounting, Analysis, and Projections," in E. Croce, M. Da Costa, and H. Juan-Ramón (eds), *Programming and Financial Policies: Application to the Colombian Case* (Washington, D.C.: IMF), ch. 4: 139–86.

——— 2001a, "Post-conflict reconstruction and the challenge to the international organizations: The case of El Salvador," *World Development* (December): 1967–85.

——— 2001b, "Book review of distributive justice and economic development: The case of Chile and developing countries" by Andres Solimano, Eduardo Aninat, and Nancy Birdsall, *Journal of Economic Literature*, vol. XXXIX, no. 2 (June): 613–14.

——— 2000, "Economic reconstruction in post-conflict transitions," in M. Malan and C. Lord (eds), *Prague to Pretoria: Towards a Global Consensus on the Doctrine of Peace Support Operations* (Prague: Institute of International Relations and Pretoria: Institute for Security Studies): 227–48.

—— 1997, "Arms-for-land deal: Lessons from El Salvador," in M. Doyle *et al.*, 342–61.

—— 1995a, "Post-conflict peacebuilding: The challenge to the UN," *CEPAL Review*, 55 (October): 27–38 (translated into Spanish in *Revista de la CEPAL*, 55 (April 1995)).

—— 1995b, "Privatization in Latin America: From myth to reality," *Series on Public Policy Reform* (Santiago, Chile: CEPAL, 1995).

—— 1992a, "Policy fundamentals, interest rates differentials and expected devaluation in the presence of an active crawling peg system," *Journal of International Money and Finance*, 12/3 (June): 292–303.

—— 1992b, "Foreign direct investment, capital formation and the balance of payments of developing countries," in Lehman, C. and R. Moore (eds), *Multinational Culture: Social Impacts of a Global Economy* (Conn.: Greenwood Press, June 1992), ch. 5: 45–60.

—— 1992c, "Expectations of devaluation, the real rate of interest and the private sector in a dual currency economy," in K. Fischer and G. Papaioannou (eds), *Business Finance in Less-Developed Capital Markets* (N.Y.: Quorum Books, May 1992), ch. 18: 335–51.

—— 1990, "El enfoque fiscal de la balanza de pagos," *Estudios de Economía* (Universidad de Chile), 17/2 (Diciembre de 1990): 389–421.

—— 1989, "The role of transnational corporations in South–South trade: Issues and evidence," in V. Ventura-Dias and A. McIntyre (eds), *South–South Trade: Trends, Issues and Obstacles to its Growth* (New York: Praeger), ch. 9: 249–62.

—— 1988, "La tasa de interés y la incertidumbre cambiaria: El caso de Uruguay," *Revista de Economía* (Banco Central del Uruguay), 3/2 (Diciembre): 59–95.

—— 1987, "The MGRC model: A test of the Gulliver effect," in *7th Latin American Meeting of the Econometric Society: Abstracts and Papers*, vol. 1: 425–52 (Sao Paulo, Brazil, August 4–7).

Demekas, Dimitri G., Johannes Herderschee, and Davina F. Jacobs, 2002a, *Kosovo: Institutions and Policies for Reconstruction and Growth* (Washington, D.C.: International Monetary Fund).

—— Jimmy McHugh, and Dora Kosma, 2002b, "The economics of post-conflict aid," *IMF, Working Paper*, WP/02/198 (Washington, D.C.: November).

Diamond, Larry, 2006, "What went wrong and right in Iraq," in Fukuyama (ed.), ch. 8: 173–89.

—— 2005, "Lessons from Iraq," *Journal of Democracy*, 16: 3–7.

Dobbins, James *et al.*, 2003, *America's Role in Nation Building: From Germany to Iraq* (Washington, D.C.: Rand).

—— 2005, *UN's Role in Nation Building: From the Congo to Iraq* (Washington, D.C.: Rand).

Dodge, Toby, 2003, *Inventing Iraq: The Failure of Nation-Building and a History Denied* (New York: Columbia University Press).

—— 2004, "Principles, politics, and pragmatism in the international response to the Afghan crisis," in Donini *et al.*, 117–42.

Donais, Timothy, 2005, *The Political Economy of Peacebuilding in Post-Dayton Bosnia* (London and New York: Routledge).

Donini, Antonio, Norah Niland, and Karn Wermester (eds), 2004, *Nation-Building Unraveled?* (Bloomfield, CT: Kumarian Press).

Dornbusch, R., W. Nolling, and R. Layard, 1993, *Postwar Economic Reconstruction and Lessons for the East Today* (Cambridge, Mass.: The MIT Press).

Downs, George, and Stephen J. Stedman, 2002, "Evaluation issues in peace implementation," in Stedman *et al.*, ch. 2: 43–70.

Doyle, Michael W., 2002, "Strategy and transitional authority," in Stedman *et al.*, ch. 3: 71–88.

—— 2001, "Peacebuilding in Cambodia: Legitimacy and power," in Cousens and Kumar (eds), 89–112.

—— 2000, "International peacebuilding: A theoretical and quantitative analysis," *American Political Science Review*, 94/4, December.

—— Ian Johnstone, and Robert C. Orr (eds), 1997, *Keeping the Peace: Multidimensional UN Operations in Cambodia and El Salvador* (U.K.: Cambridge University Press).

—— and Nicholas Sambanis, 2006, *Making War and Building Peace* (Princeton and Oxford: Princeton University Press).

Dulles, Allen W., 1993, *The Marshall Plan* (Providence/Oxford: Berg Publishers, original 1948 manuscript is located in the Allen W. Dulles Papers at Princeton University).

Fayolle, Ambroise, 2006, "Out of the trap: How to improve financing for fragile states," *Finance & Development*, 43/4 (December): 37–9.

Feil, Scott, 2004, "Laying the foundations: Enhancing security capabilities," in Orr *et al.*, ch. 3: 39–57.

—— 2002, "Building better foundations: Security in post-conflict reconstruction," *Washington Quarterly* (Autumn), 97–109.

Fisher, David (2007), "Humanitarian intervention," in Reed and Ryall (eds), 101–17.

Fisher, Stanley, 2001, "Exchange rates regime: Is the bipolar view correct?" *Finance & Development*, 38/2 (June).

Flournoy, Michèle, 2004, "Interagency strategy and planning for post-conflict reconstruction," in Orr *et al.*, ch. 7: 105–15.

Forman, Shepard, and Stewart Patrick, 2000, *Good Intentions: Pledges of Aid for Post-Conflict Recovery* (Boulder and London: Lynne Rienner Publishers).

Frenkel, Jacob A., 1999a, "Liberalization and financial reforms: Lessons from the Israeli experience," in Blejer and Škreb (eds), 1999a, ch. 10: 368–82.

—— 1999b, "Central Bank Independence and Monetary Policy," in Blejer and Škreb (eds), 1999c, ch. 2: 11–30.

Frydman, Roman, Andrzej Rapaczynski, and John S. Earle, 1993, *The Privatization Process in Central Europe* (London: Central European University Press).

—— —— —— 1993, *The Privatization Process in Russia, Ukraine and the Baltic States* (London: Central European University Press).

Fukuyama, Francis (ed.), 2006, *Nation-Building: Beyond Afghanistan and Iraq* (Baltimore, MD: The Johns Hopkins University Press).

—— 2004, *State-Building: Governance and World Order in the 21st Century* (Ithaca, N.Y.: Cornell University Press).

Galama, Anneke, and Paul van Tongeren, 2002, *Towards Better Peacebuilding Practice: On Lessons Learned, Evaluation Practices and Aid & Conflict* (Utrecht: European Centre for Conflict Prevention).

Galbraith, Peter W., 2006a, *The End of Iraq: How American Incompetence Created a War Without End* (New York: Simon & Schuster).

Gamboa, Nuria, and Barbara Trentavizi, 2001, *La Guatemala Posible* (Guatemala: Serviprensa Centroamericana).

Ghani, Ashraf, Clare Lockhart, Nargis Nehan, and Baqer Massoud, 2007, "The budget as the linchpin of the State: Lessons from Afghanistan," in Boyce and O'Donnell (eds), ch. 6: 153–84.

Giersch, Herbert, Karl-Heinz Paqué, and Holger Schmieding, 1993, "Openness, wage restraint, and macroeconomic stability: West Germany's road to prosperity 1948–1959," in Dornbusch *et al.*, ch. 1: 1–28.

Goodson, Larry P., 2006, "The lessons of nation-building in Afghanistan," in Fukuyama (ed.), ch. 7: 145–69.

Goulding, Marrack, 2002, *Peacemonger* (Albemarle Street, London: John Murray).

—— 2004, "The UN Secretary-General," in Malone (ed.), ch. 18: 267–80.

Guitián, Manuel, 1997, "Scope of government and limits of economic policy," in Blejer and Ter-Minassian (eds).

Habrylyshyn, Oleh, 2004, "Avoid hubris but acknowledge successes," *Finance & Development* (September).

Hamre, John J., and Gordon R. Sullivan, 2002, "Toward post-conflict reconstruction," *Washington Quarterly,* 25/4: 85–96.

Hanke, Steve H., 2002, "Currency boards," *Annals of the American Academy of Political and Social Sciences,* 579 (January): 87–105.

—— 1999, "Some reflections on currency boards," in Blejer and Škreb (eds), 1999c, ch. 13: 341–66.

Hanlon, Joseph, 2005, "Bringing it all together: A case study of Mozambique," in Junne and Verkoren (eds), ch. 15: 273–88.

Hazlitt, Henry, 1946, *Economics in One Lesson* (New York: Harper & Brothers).

Heinbecker, Paul, 2004, "Kosovo," in Malone (ed.), ch. 34: 537–50.

Herrero, José Luis, 2005, "Building state institutions," in Junne and Verkoren (eds), ch. 3: 43–58.

Hilbers, Paul, Russell Krueger, and Marina Moretti, 2000, "New tools for assessing financial system soundness," *Finance & Development* (September).

Hogan, Michael J., 1987, *The Marshall Plan: America, Britain, and the Reconstruction of Western Europe, 1947–1952* (Cambridge, U.K.: Cambridge University Press).

Hohe, Tanja, 2005, "Developing local governance," in Junne and Verkoren (eds), ch. 4: 59–72.

Holiday, David, and William Stanley, 1993, "Building the peace," *Journal of International Affairs,* 46/2 (Winter): 415–38.

Houseman, Gerard, 2006, "The vulnerable economic mainstream: Joseph Stiglitz and the critique of free market analysis," *Challenge* (March–April).

Humphreys, Macartan, Jeffrey D. Sachs, and Joseph E. Stiglitz (eds), 2007, *Escaping the Resource Curse* (New York: Columbia University Press).

Hurtić, Zlatko, Amela Šapčanin, and Susan Woodward, 2000, "Bosnia and Herzegovina," in Forman and Patrick (eds), ch. 8: 315–66.

Jeong, Ho-Won, 2005, *Peacebuilding in Post-Conflict Societies* (Boulder and London: Lynne Rienner Publishers).

Johnstone, Ian, 1997, "Rights and reconciliation in El Salvador," in Doyle *et al.* (eds), 312–41.

Jonas, Susanne, 2000, *Of Centaurs and Doves* (Boulder, Co.: Westview Press).

Jones, Bruce D., 2004, "Aid, peace, and justice in a reordered world," in Donini *et al.* (eds), 207–26.

—— 2002, "The challenges of strategic coordination," in Stedman *et al.*, ch. 4: 89–116.

Junne, Gerd, and Willemijn Verkoren (eds), 2005, *Post-Conflict Development* (Boulder and London: Lynne Rienner Publishers).

Kaldor, Mary, 1999, *New & Old Wars: Organized Violence in a Global Era* (Stanford: Stanford University Press).

—— Terry Lynn Karl, and Yahia Said, 2007, *Oil Wars* (London and Ann Arbor, MI: Pluto Press).

Karl, Terry Lynn, 1992, "El Salvador's negotiated revolution," *Foreign Affairs*, 71/2 (Winter): 147–64.

—— 1989, "El Salvador: Negotiations or total war, an interview of Salvador Samayoa," *World Policy Journal* (Spring): 321–55.

Keating, Tom, and W. Andy Knight, 2004, *Building Sustainable Peace* (Saskatoon, Canada: Houghton Boston Printers).

Keynes, John M., 1920, *The Economic Consequences of the Peace* (New York: Harcourt, Brace and Howe, Inc.).

—— 1919, *The Economic Consequences of the Peace* (London: Macmillan).

—— 1929a, "The German transfer problem," *Economic Journal*, 39: 1–7.

—— 1929b, "The reparations problem: a discussion. II. A rejoinder," *Economic Journal*, 39: 179–82.

—— 1929c, "Mr. Keynes' views on the transfer problem" and "A reply," *Economic Journal*, 39: 388–99 and 404–8.

Khan, Mohsin S., Saleh M. Nsouli, and Chorng-Huey Wong (eds), 2002, *Macroeconomic Management: Programs and Policies* (Washington, D.C.: IMF Institute).

Klein, Naomi, 2007, *The Shock Doctrine* (New York: Metropolitan Books, Henry Holt and Company).

Kouchner, Bernard, 2004, *Les Guerriers de la Paix* (Paris: Bernard Grasset).

Krasno, Jean (ed.), 2004, *The United Nations: Confronting the Challenges of a Global Society* (New York: Lynne Rienner).

Kreilkamp, Jacob S., 2003, "UN post-conflict reconstruction," *International Law and Politics*, 35/3.

Kreimer, Alcira *et al.*, 1998, "The World Bank's experience with post-conflict reconstruction" (Washington, D.C.: The World Bank, Summary Volume).

Laurenti, Jeffrey, 2004, "Financing United Nations," in Krasno (ed.), 271–309.

Leader, Nicholas, and Mohammed Haneef Atmar, 2004, "Political projects: Reform, aid and the State in Afghanistan," in Donini *et al.* (eds), 166–86.

Le Billon, Philippe, "Drilling in deep water: oil, business and war in Angola," in Kaldor, Karl, and Said (eds), ch. 2: 100–29.

Levine, Mark, 1997, "Peacemaking in El Salvador," in Doyle *et al.*, 227–54.

Liévano de Marques, Mirna, 1996, *El Salvador: Un País en Transición* (San Salvador: Gráficos y Textos, S.A. de C.V.).

Lyons, Terrence, 2002, "The role of postsettlement elections," in Stedman *et al.*, ch. 8: 215–36.

McCormick, David H., 1997, "From peacekeeping to peacebuilding: restructuring military and police institutions in El Salvador," in Doyle *et al.*, 282–311.

McMillan, John, 2004, "Avoid hubris and other lessons for reformers," *Finance & Development* (September).

Malcolm, Noel, 1999, *Kosovo: A Short History* (New York: Harper Collins).

Malone, David M., 2006, *The International Struggle over Iraq: Politics in the UN Security Council 1980–2005* (New York: Oxford University Press).

—— (ed.), 2004, *The UN Security Council: From the Cold War to the 21st Century* (Boulder and London: Lynne Rienner).

Meyer, Jeffrey A., and Mark G. Califano, 2006, *Good Intentions Corrupted: The Oil-for-Food Scandal and the Threat to the UN* (New York: Public Affairs, Based on the Reports of the Independent Inquiry Committee).

Milward, Alan S. (1984), *The Reconstruction of Western Europe: 1945–51* (London: Methuen).

—— (1979), *War, Economy and Society: 1939–1945* (Berkeley: University of California Press).

Mingst, Karen A., and Margaret P. Karns, 2000, *The United Nations in the Post-Cold War Era* (Boulder, CO: Westview Press).

Moalla-Fetini, Rakia, Heikki Hatanpää, Shehadah Hussein, and Natalia Koliadina, 2005, *Kosovo: Gearing Policies Toward Growth and Development* (Washington, D.C.: IMF).

Montgomery, John D., and Dennis A. Rondinelli, 2004, *Beyond Reconstruction in Afghanistan* (New York: Palgrave Macmillan).

Mundell, Robert A., 1968a, *Man and Economics* (New York: McGraw-Hill Book Company).

—— 1968b, *International Economics* (New York: Macmillan).

Murphy, Craig N., 2006, *The United Nations Development Programme: A Better Way?* (Cambridge, U.K.: Cambridge University Press).

Ndikumana, Léonce, and James K. Boyce, 1998, "Congo's odious debt: External borrowing and capital flight in Zaire," *Development and Change*, 29(2): 195–217.

—— and Kisangani F. Emizet, 2005, "The economics of civil war: The case of the Democratic Republic of Congo," in Paul Collier and Nicholas Sambanis (eds), *Understanding Civil War: Africa* (Washington, D.C.: The World Bank, Volume 1).

—— and Justine Nannyonjo, 2007, "From failed State to good performer? The Case of Uganda," in Boyce and O'Donnell (eds), ch. 2: 15–54.

O'Brien, Paul, 2004, "Old woods, new paths, and diverging choices for NGOs," in Donini *et al.*, 187–203.

Ohlin, Bertil, 1929a, "The reparations problem: a discussion; transfer difficulties, real and imagined," *Economic Journal*, 39: 172–83.

—— 1929b, "Mr. Keynes' views on the transfer problem. II. A rejoinder from Professor Ohlin," *The Economic Journal*, 39: 400–4.

Orr, Robert C. (ed.), 2004a, *Winning the Peace: An American Strategy for Post-Conflict Reconstruction* (Washington, D.C.: The CSIS Press, Center for Strategic and International Studies).

—— 2004b, "The United States as nation builder: Facing the challenge of post-conflict reconstruction," in Orr *et al.*, ch. 1: 3–18.

—— 2004c, "Constructing a cohesive strategic international response," in Orr *et al.*, ch. 2: 19–36.

—— 2004d, "East Timor: the United States as junior partner," in Orr *et al.*, ch. 13: 211–23.

—— 2001, "Building peace in El Salvador," in Cousens and Kumar, ch. 6: 153–81.

Overseas Development Council, 1995, *Development Assistance in War to Peace Transitions: Case Studies of El Salvador, Mozambique, Nicaragua and Cambodia* (Washington, D.C.: ODC).

Paris, Roland, 2004, *At War's End: Building Peace After Civil Conflict* (New York: Cambridge University Press).

—— 2002, "The perils of liberal international peacebuilding," *International Security*, 28: 637–56.

—— 2001, "Wilson's ghost: The faulty assumptions of post-conflict peacebuilding," in Crocker *et al.* (eds), ch. 45: 765–84.

Pastor, Manuel, Jr., and Michael E. Conroy, 1995, "Distributional implications of macroeconomic policy: Theory and Applications to El Salvador," *World Development*, 23/12: 2117–31.

Paus, Eva, 1995, "Exports, economic growth and the consolidation of peace in El Salvador," *World Development*, 23/12: 2173–93.

Pérez de Cuéllar, Javier, 1997, *Pilgrimage for Peace* (New York: St. Martin Press).

Phelps, Edmund S., 2007, "The good life and the good economy: The humanist perspective of Aristotle, the Pragmatists and Vitalists; and the economic justice of John Rawls" in Kaushik Basu and Ravi Kanbur (eds), 2008, *Arguments for a Better World: Essays in Honor of Amartya Sen* (Oxford: Oxford University Press, Vol. I, forthcoming).

—— 2003, *Designing Inclusion* (Cambridge, U.K.: Cambridge University Press).

—— 1997, *Rewarding Work* (Cambridge, Mass.: Harvard University Press).

—— 1985, *Political Economy* (New York: W.W. Norton & Company).

Pires, Emilia, and Michael Francino, 2007, "National ownership and international trusteeship: The case of Timor-Leste," in Boyce and O'Donnell (eds), ch. 5: 119–53.

Prendergast, John, and Emily Plumb, 2002, "Building local capacity: From implementation to peacebuilding," in Stedman *et al.* (eds), ch. 12: 327–49.

Pritchard, Sarah, 2001, "United Nations involvement in post-conflict reconstruction efforts: New and continuing challenges in the case of East Timor," *UNSW Law Journal*, 24(1): 183–90.

Pronk, Jan, 1996, "Development for peace: The role for the UN," in K. Sharma (ed.), *Imagining Tomorrow: Rethinking the Global Challenge* (New York: Merrill Corporation), 74–82.

Rambo, A. Terry, Nguyen Mann Hung, and Neil L. Jamieson, 1993, "The challenges of Vietnam's reconstruction," *Asia Pacific Issues*, 5 (April).

Rand, 2005, *Building a Successful Palestinian State* (Santa Monica, CA: Rand Corporation).

Reed, Charles, and David Ryall (eds), 2007, *The Price of Peace: Just War in the Twenty-First Century* (New York: Cambridge University Press).

Rosa, Herman, and Michael Foley, 2000, "El Salvador," in Forman and Patrick (eds), ch. 4: 113–58.

Ross, Michael, 2003, "The natural resource curse: How wealth can make you poor," in Bannon and Collier (eds), ch. 2: 17–42.

Rotberg, Robert I. (ed.), 2007, *Building a New Afghanistan* (Washington, D.C.: Brookings Institution Press and World Peace Foundation.

Rubin, Barnett R., 2007a, "Saving Afghanistan," *Foreign Affairs* (January/February).

—— 2002, *Fragmentation of Afghanistan* (New Haven and London: Yale University Press, second edition).

—— and Andrea Armstrong, 2003, "Regional issues in the reconstruction of Afghanistan," *World Policy Journal* (Spring): 31–40.

Sabot, Richard, and István Székely, 1997, *Development Strategy and Management of the Market Economy* (Oxford: Clarendon Press).

Sahay, Ratna, and Carlos Végh, 1995, "Dollarization in transition economies," *Finance & Development* (March).

Schain, Martin A. (2001), *The Marshall Plan: Fifty Years After* (New York: Palgrave).

Schiffrin, Anya, and Amer Bisat (eds), *Covering Globalization: A Reporter's Handbook* (NY: Columbia University Press, November 2004) (in several languages).

Shawcross, William, 2000, *Deliver Us from Evil: Warlords & Peacekeepers in a World of Endless Conflict* (London, UK: Bloomsbury Publishing plc).

Solimano, Andres (ed.), 2008, *The International Mobility of Talent: Types, Causes and Development Impact* (Oxford: Oxford University Press, forthcoming).

—— (ed.), 1998, *Social Inequality* (Ann Harbor: The University of Michigan Press).

Solomons, Dirk, 2005, "Security: An absolute prerequisite," in Junne and Verkoren (eds), ch. 2: 19–42.

Spear, Joanna, 2002, "Disarmament and demobilization" in Stedman *et al.* (eds), ch. 6: 141–82.

Stanley, William, and David Holiday, 2002, "Broad participation, diffuse responsibility: Peace implementation in Guatemala," in Stedman *et al.* (eds), ch. 15: 421–62.

Stedman, Stephen J., 2002, "Introduction," in Stedman *et al.* (eds), ch. 1: 1–42.

—— Donald Rothchild, and Elizabeth M. Cousens, 2002, *Ending Civil Wars: The Implementation of Peace Agreements* (Boulder, CO.: Lynne Rienner).

Stern, Nicholas, 1997, "Macroeconomic policy and the role of the state in a changing world," in Richard Sabot and Istvan Székely (eds), vol. II, ch. 5: 143–74.

Stiglitz, Joseph, 2006a, *Making Globalization Work* (New York: W.W. Norton and Company).

—— 2002, *Globalization and its Discontents* (New York: W.W. Norton and Company).

—— 1997, "The role of governments in the economies of developing countries," in Richard Sabot and Istvan Székely (eds), vol. I, ch. 3: 61–109.

—— and Linda J. Bilmes, 2008, *The Three Trillion Dollar War: The True Cost of the Iraq Conflict* (New York: W.W. Norton and Company).

Stockton, Nicholas, 2004, "Afghanistan, war, aid, and international order," in Donini *et al.*, ch. 2: 9–38.

Sullivan, Joseph G., 1994, "How peace came to El Salvador," *Orbis* (Winter): 83–98.

Tabb, William K., 1995, *The Postwar Japanese System: Cultural Economy and Economic Transformation* (New York: Oxford University Press).

Tanzi, Vito, 1997a, "The role of the state in post-chaos situations," in Richard Sabot and Istvan Székely (eds), vol. II, ch. 8: 255–66.

—— 1997b, "Economic transformation and the policies for long-term growth," in Blejer and Škreb (eds), ch. 12: 313–26.

Taylor, John, 2007a, *Global Financial Warriors* (New York and London: W.W. Norton & Company).

Thier, J. Alexander, 2004, "The politics of peacebuilding. Year One: From Bonn to Kabul," in Donini *et al.*, 39–60.

Torres-Rivas, Edelberto, 1997, "Insurrection and civil war in El Salvador," in Doyle *et al.*, 209–26.

Traub, James, 2006, *The Best Intentions: Kofi Annan and the UN in the Era of American World Power* (New York: Farrar, Strauss, and Giroux).

Tripp, Charles, 2002, *A History of Iraq* (Cambridge: Cambridge University Press).

Vaishnav, Milan, 2004, "Afghanistan: The chimera of the 'light footprint'," in Orr (ed.), ch. 15: 244–62.

Vaishnav, Milan, and Bathsheba N. Crocker, 2004, "Sierra Leone: Making multilateralism work," in Orr (ed.), ch. 14: 224–43.

Valdivieso, Luis M., Endo Toshihide, Luis V. Mendonça, Shamsuddin Tareq, and Alejandro López-Mejía, 2000, *East Timor: Establishing the Foundations for Sound Macroeconomic Management* (Washington, D.C.: International Monetary Fund).

Weinbaum, Marvin G., 2006, "Rebuilding Afghanistan: Impediments, lessons, and prospects," in Fukuyama (ed.), ch. 6: 125–43.

Weiss, Thomas G., 2004, "The humanitarian impulse," in Malone (ed.), ch. 3: 37–54.

—— David P. Forsythe, and Roger A. Coate, 2001, *The United Nations Changing World Politics* (Boulder, CO: Westview Press).

West, Rebecca, 1941, *Black Lamb and Grey Falcon* (New York: Penguin Books, reprinted in 1994).

Wilkins, Timothy A., 1997, "The El Salvador peace accords: using international and domestic law norms to build peace," in Doyle *et al.*, 255–81.

Wood, E., and A. Segovia, 1995, "Macroeconomic policy and the Salvadoran Peace Accords," *World Development*, 23/12: 2079–99.

Woodward, Susan, 2007a, "Does Kosovo's status matter? On the international management of statehood," *Südosteuropa*, 55/1(Spring): 1–25.

—— 2002, "Economic priorities for successful peace implementation," in Stedman *et al.*, ch. 7: 183–214.

—— 1998, "Avoiding another Cyprus or Israel: A debate about the future of Bosnia," *Brookings Review*, 16/1 (Winter): 45–8.

—— 1995, *Balkan Tragedy* (Washington, D.C.: Brookings).

Yannis, Alexandros, 2003, "Kosovo: The political economy of conflict and peacebuilding," in Ballentine and Sherman (eds), ch. 7.

Other articles, working papers, studies, and reports

Aita, Judy, 2004, "U.N. envoy says Iraq needs 'urgent' political process: Lakhdar Brahimi discusses formation of interim Iraqi administration" (Washington File United Nations Correspondent).

Alvarez-Plata, Patricia, and Tilman Brück, 2006, "External debt in post-conflict countries" (Berlin: German Institute for Economic Research, mimeo).

Bearpark, Andy, 2001, "The challenge of Trepca: Taking a realistic approach" (Pristina: UNMIK Feature Release UNMIK/FR0061/01, August 17).

Berdal, Mats, 1996, "Disarmament and demobilization after civil wars," *Adelphi Paper*, 303 (London: IISS and Oxford University Press).

Berg, Andrew, and Eduardo Borenzstein, 2000b, "Full dollarization: The pros and cons," *IMF Economic Series*, 24 (December).

Boyce, James K., 2004, "The international financial institutions: Post-conflict reconstruction and peacebuilding capacities" (Paper prepared for the Seminar on Strengthening the UN's Capacity on Civilian Crisis Management, Copenhagen, 8–9 June).

—— *et al.* (eds), 1995, *Adjustment Toward Peace: Economic Policy and Post-War Reconstruction in El Salvador* (San Salvador: Study commissioned by UNDP). Published as

Economic Policy for Building Peace: The Lessons from El Salvador (Boulder: Lynne Rienner, 1996).

—— and Manuel Pastor, 1997, "International financial institutions and conflict prevention: Five propositions" (paper presented at the Fourth Annual Conference "Progress and Pitfalls in Preventive Action," New York, Council on Foreign Relations, December 11).

Braga de Macedo, Jorge, 2003, "NEPAD peer review and public–private partnership for development," paper presented at the Annual Bank Conference on Development Economics Workshop (Paris: OECD Development Centre, May 14).

Buiter, Willem H., Ricardo Lago, and Nicholas Stern, 1997, "Promoting an effective market economy in a changing world" (London: London School of Economics and Political Science, March).

Camdessus, Michel, 1993, "Serving a globalized world economy: The decade ahead" (Response to a request of Secretary-General Boutros-Ghali for IMF input into his *An Agenda for Development*, mimeo).

—— 1996, "The G-7 in 1996: What is at stake?" (Washington, D.C.: IMF Managing Director's Address to the G-7).

Collier, Paul, and Anke Hoeffler, 2002, "Aid, policy and growth in post-conflict societies," *World Bank Policy Research Working Paper*, no. 2902.

Conte, Frank, 1997, "Rewarding work: How to restore participation and self-support to free enterprise," *Newslink*, 2/1 (Fall).

Cox, Marcus, 2001, "State building and post-conflict reconstruction: Lessons from Bosnia" (Geneva: Centre for Applied Studies in International Negotiations, January).

Dallas Federal Reserve, 2006, "Henry Hazlitt: Journalist advocate of free enterprise," *Economic Insights*, 6/1.

del Castillo, Graciana, 2003b, "Economic reconstruction in post-conflict transitions: Lessons for the Democratic Republic of Congo" (Paris: OECD Development Centre, *Working Paper* 228, December).

—— 2003c, "Promotion of export-oriented foreign direct investment in Uruguay" (New York: Macroeconomic Advisory Group, Study Prepared for the Inter-American Development Bank, July).

—— 1999, "Kosovo economic reconstruction" (Pristina: UNMIK, mimeo, September).

—— and Charles Frank, 2003, "Innovative mechanisms for infrastructure financing" (New York: Macroeconomic Advisory Group, Study Prepared for the Inter-American Development Bank, August).

Devereux, Michael B., and Gregor W. Smith, 2005, "Transfer problem dynamics: Macroeconomics of the Franco-Prussian indemnity," *QED Working Paper*, no. 1025 (Canada: Queen's Economics Department, August).

Donini, Antonio, 2006, *Humanitarian Agenda 2015: Afghanistan Country Study* (Boston, Mass.: Feinstein International Center, Tufts University, June).

Erikson, D.P., 2002, "Haiti: Challenges in development assistance" (Washington, D.C.: Inter-American Dialogue Conference Report October).

Flounders, Sara, 2000, "Kosovo: NATO troops seize mining complex" (Washington, D.C.: International Action Center).

Foreign Policy, 2006, "What to do in Iraq?," *A Roundtable* (March/April): 38–53.

Gardiner, Nile, and Marc Miles, 2003, "Forgive the Iraqi debt" (Washington, D.C.: The Heritage Foundation, Executive Memorandum 871).

Ghandi, Ved, *et al.*, 1995, "Outlines of the 'architecture' of minimalist fiscal framework for countries in post-chaos/post-conflict situations" (Washington, D.C.: International Monetary Fund, Fiscal Department, mimeo). See also IMF (1995d).

Ghani, Ashraf, Clare Lockhart, and Michael Carnahan, 2005, "State-building in fragile and conflict-affected conditions" (Paper presented at a World Bank–UNDP workshop on "Rebuilding Post-Conflict Societies: Lessons from a Decade of Global Experience" held at the Greentree Foundation, September 18–21, mimeo).

Graham, James, 1999, "The violent breakup of Yugoslavia" (Historyorb web site, part III).

Grandolini, Gloria, 1996, "Meeting the challenge of globalization" (Washington, D.C.: World Bank Country Study, June).

Gupta, Sanjieev, Shamsuddin Tareq, Benedict J. Clements, Alex Segura-Ubiergo, Rina Bhattacharya, and Todd D. Mattina, 2005, "Rebuilding Fiscal Institutions in Post-Conflict Countries," *IMF Occasional Paper No. 247* (December 27).

Hoeffler, Anke, 1999, "Challenges of infrastructure rehabilitation and reconstruction in war-affected economies" (Oxford: University of Oxford, mimeo).

Hoff, Karla, and Joseph E. Stiglitz, 2002, "After the big bang? Obstacles to the emergence of the rule of law in post-communism societies" (World Bank/Columbia University, mimeo).

Honda, Jiro, and Liliana Schumacher, 2006, "Adopting full dollarization in post-conflict economies: Would the gains compensate for the losses in Liberia?" (Washington, D.C.: *IMF Working Paper* WP/06/82, March).

Horowitz, Adam, 2003, "U.S. plans to reshape the Iraqi economy," *Z Magazine online* (September).

Initiative for Policy Dialogue, 2004, "Vietnam country dialogue: Summary report" (New York: Columbia University).

Kinzonzi, Venant P., and Paul Frix, 2002, "Stratégie de re-dynamisation des entreprises du portefeuille et restructuration de la dette extérieur de la République Démocratique du Congo: Proposition de création d'un Fonds International d'Investissements et de Reconstruction au Congo: le FIRC" (Paris: OECD Development Centre, February).

Lipworth, Gabrielle, and Erich Spitäller, 1993, "Vietnam—Reform and stabilization: 1986–92" (Washington, D.C.: *IMF Working Paper*, WP/93/46, May).

Lönnberg, Åke, 2002, "Restoring and transforming payments and banking systems in post-conflict economies" (Washington, D.C.: IMF, Monetary and Exchange Affairs Department, mimeo, May).

Loup, Jacques, 2000, "The UNDP Round Tables and the private sector: An issue paper" (Paris: Développement Institutions & Analyses de Long Terme (DIAL), *Working Paper,* DT/2000/01).

Mammen, K. John, 2005, "Amartya Sen—A contrarian view," *Finance & Development* (Letter to the Editor, March).

Maton, Joseph, and Henri-Bernard Solignac Lecomte, 2001, "Congo 1965–1999: Les espoirs déçu du 'Bresil Africain' " (Paris: OECD Development Centre, *Working Paper* 223, September).

Mundell, Robert A., 1991, "Do exchange rates work? Another View" (Washington, D.C.: *IMF Working Paper*, WP/91/37, April).

Negroponte, Diana V., 2006, "Conflict resolution at the end of the Cold War: The case of El Salvador 1989–1994" (Washington, D.C.: Georgetown University, unpublished doctoral dissertation).

Nsouli, Saleh M., 2002, "Capacity building in Africa: The role of international financial institutions" (Washington, D.C.: IMF Economics Forum, Remarks, September 12).

O'Donnell, Madalene, 2005, "UN peacekeeping and the World Bank: Perceptions of senior managers in the field" (New York: Center on International Cooperation).

Oliker, O., R. Kauzlarich, J. Dobbins, K.W. Basseuner, D.L Sampler, J.G. McGinn, M.J. Dziedzic, A. Grissom, B. Pirnie, N. Bensahel, A.I. Guven, 2003, *Aid During Conflict* (Washington, D.C.: Rand Corporation).

O'Neill, William G., 2002, *Kosovo: An Unfinished Peace* (Boulder and London: Lynne Rienner, IPA *Occasional Paper Series*).

Oxford Analytica, 2003, "The challenge of post-conflict reconstruction in Iraq" (Oxford: April).

Pei, Minxin, and Sara Kasper, 2003, "Lessons from the past: The American record on nation building" (Washington, D.C.: Carnegie Endowment for International Peace, *Policy Brief* 24, May).

Pérez de Cuéllar, Javier, 1991, *Anarchy or Order: Annual Reports, 1982–1991* (New York: United Nations).

Riemer, Matthew, 2003, "Post-war patterns in Afghanistan and Iraq," *Eurasia Insight* (August 20).

Rubén, R., *El problema agrario en El Salvador: Notas sobre una economía polarizada, Cuadernos de Investigación,* no. 7 (San Salvador: Centro de Investigaciones Tecnológicas y Científicas, Año II, Abril de 1991).

Rubin, Barnett R., 2007b, "Institutional framework for flower/fragrance production in Afghanistan: Or, who put the R in DDR?" (New York: Center on International Cooperation).

—— 2006, "Afghanistan's uncertain transition from turmoil to normalcy" (New York: Council on Foreign Relations, *Council Special Report*, 12, April).

—— 2004, "Road to ruin: Afghanistan's booming opium industry" (New York: Center for American Progress and Center on International Cooperation, October).

—— 2003, "Identifying options and entry points for disarmament, demobilization, and reintegration in Afghanistan" (New York: Center on International Cooperation, New York University, March).

—— 1995, *Towards Comprehensive Peace in Southeast Europe* (New York: Report of the South Balkans Working Group of the Council on Foreign Relations Center for Preventive Action, June).

—— Ashraf Ghani, William Maley, Ahmed Rashid, and Olivier Roy, 2001, "Afghanistan: Reconstruction and peacebuilding in a regional framework" (Bern, Switzerland: *KOFF Peacebuilding Reports*, 1/200).

—— Humayun Hamidzada, and Abby Stoddard, 2003, "Through the fog of peace building: Evaluating the reconstruction of Afghanistan" (New York: Center on International Cooperation, June).

—— A. Stoddard, H. Hamidzada, and A. Farhadi, 2004, "Building a new Afghanistan: The value of success, the cost of failure" (New York: Center on International Cooperation in cooperation with CARE, March).

Santos, Nuno, 2003a, "Financing small, medium, and micro-enterprises in a post-conflict situation: Microfinance opportunities in the DRC" (Paris: OECD Development Centre, Paper presented at the Séminaire Partenariat Public–Privé pour le Développement de la République Démocratique du Congo, Kinshasa, April 8).

Santos, Nuno, 2003b, "Note on the Seminar Public-Private Partnership for the Development of the DRC" (Paris: OECD Development Centre, April 25).

Schimmelpfennig, Axel, 2007, "Lebanon navigates difficult waters," *IMF Survey* (April 23rd).

Segovia, Alexander, 1995, "The implementation of the peace accords and economic reform in El Salvador" (Study commissioned by SIDA, mimeo).

Solimano, Andrés, 2006, "Mobilizing talent for global development," *Policy Brief* 7 (United Nations University and UNU–WIDER).

Staines, Nicholas, 2004, "Economic performance over the conflict cycle" (Washington, D.C.: *IMF Working Paper*, WP/04/95, June).

Stanford University, 1997, "Why peace agreements often fail to end civil war" (Conference with diplomats involved in negotiating and implementing peace agreements, Annenberg Auditorium on Veterans Day, November 11).

The Stanley Foundation, 1995, *United Nations–Bretton Woods Collaboration: How Much is Enough?* (Arden House, Harriman, NY: Report of the Twenty-Sixth United Nations Issues Conference, February 24–25).

Stiglitz Joseph, 1998, "More instruments and broader goals: Moving toward the post-Washington Consensus" (Helsinki: WIDER Annual Lectures, January).

Strassma, J., 1989, *Land reform in El Salvador* (University of Minnesota, mimeo).

Stuart, Paul, 2002, "The Trepca mining complex: How Kosovo's spoils were distributed," World Socialist Web Site.

Suhrke, Astri, 2006, "When more is less: Aiding state-building in Afghanistan" (Madrid: *Fride Working Paper*, 26, September).

——— Espen Villanger, and Susan Woodward, 2004, "Economic aid to post-conflict countries: Correcting the empirical and theoretical foundations of policy," (Helsinki: UNU Wider Conference, *Making Peace Work*, June 4–5).

Sundararajan, V., W. Alexander, T. Baliño, W. Coats, R.B. Johnston, C.J. Lindgren, T. Nordman, J. Dalton, and A. Hook, 1995, "The Design of a minimal monetary and exchange structure for countries in post-chaos/post-conflict situations" (Washington, D.C.: International Monetary Fund, Monetary and Exchange Division, mimeo). Listed also as IMF (1995c).

Tanzi, Vito, 2000, "On fiscal federalism: Issues to worry about" (Washington, D.C.: IMF, Fiscal Department, mimeo).

Truman, Edwin M., 2007, "Symptons of a failed relationship," *IMF Survey Magazine: What Readers Say* (March 23).

Williams, Alison, 2002, "Post-conflict microfinance in Cambodia" (Post-Conflict Microfinance Research, the Microfinance Gateway).

——— Uch Vantha, and Ngim Soeng, 2001, "Post-conflict microfinance in Cambodia: Report based on quantitative research" (Post-Conflict Microfinance Project, The Microfinance Gateway).

Wilton Park, 2002, "Post-conflict reconstruction: Lessons learnt and best practice" (UK: Wilton Park Conference, WP691, September 30).

Woodward, Susan, 2007b, "The Kosovo Quandary: on the International Management of State-hood," *FRIDE E-Newsletter* #22 (March/April).

——— 2001, "On war and peacebuilding: Unfinished legacy of the 1990s" (New York: Social Science Research Council).

—— 1999, "Kosovo and the region: Consequences of the waiting game" (Rome: Paper presented at the Conference on "Options for Kosovo Final Status", organized by the UN Association of the United States of America (UNA-USA) and Istituto Affari Internazionali, December 12–14).

Zhang, Li-Wen, 2006, "The UN: Beyond repair?" *Columbia* (Summer).

Press articles

Akram, Munir, 2007, "A united front against the Taliban," *New York Times* (April 7).

Al Rahim, Rend, 2007, "A Dayton-like process for Iraq," *Los Angeles Times–Washington Post* (May 13).

Alawi, Iyad, 2003, "America must let Iraq rebuild itself," *New York Times* (October 19).

Alterman, Jon, 2005, "Free market principles could help promote Arab reform," *Financial Times* (October 26).

Barber, Tony, 2007, "Mission agreed to stabilize independent Kosovo," *Financial Times* (December 15).

Bildt, Carl, 2004a, "We should build states not nations," *Financial Times* (January 16).

—— 2004b, "Why Kosovo must not submit to violence," *Financial Times* (March 22).

Bilefsky, Dan, 2008a, "Kosovo builds economy from the ground up," *New York Times* (March 5).

—— 2008b, "In a showdown, Kosovo declares its independence," *New York Times* (February 18).

—— 2007, "After 8 years in limbo, frustrated Kosovo awaits its future," *New York Times* (December 11).

Blas, Javier, 2007, "Iraq to pump first new oil since Saddam's fall," *Financial Times* (May 16).

Blejer, Mario I., and Graciana del Castillo, 2000a, "Today's monetary choices," *Project Syndicate* (July).

—— —— 2000b, "Globalización, estabilidad de precios y la independencia del Banco Central," *El País* (28 de febrero).

Blitz, James, 2007, "Kosovo moves step nearer to secession," *Financial Times* (December 11).

—— 2007, "Economic stability vital for the Middle East," *Financial Times* (September 8).

—— 2007, "Quest for Kosovo compromise," *Financial Times* (October 26).

Bozinovich, Mickey, 2005, "Kosovo's war on property rights," *Serbianna* (December 18).

Bream, Rebecca, 2007, "Stability tempts mining companies back to Congo," *Financial Times* (February 21).

Bremer, L. Paul, 2007, "How I didn't dismantle Iraq's army," *New York Times* (September 6).

Brinkley, Joel, 2006, "Give rebuilding lower priority in future wars," *New York Times* (April 8).

Burns, John F., and Kirk Semple, 2006, "Iraqi insurgency has funds to sustain itself, U.S. finds," *New York Times* (November 26).

Catan, Thomas, Stephen Fidler, and Demetri Sevastopulo, 2004, "Big spender: was the US-led coalition a careless steward of $20bn of Iraqi funds?" *Financial Times* (December 10).

Cave, Damien, 2006, "Former electricity chief of Iraq is charged in graft inquiry," *New York Times* (August 13).

Chung, Joanna, and Stephen Fidler, 2006, "Restructuring under fire: why Iraqi debt is no longer a write-off," *Financial Times* (July 17).

Clark, Neil, 2004, "The spoils of another war: Five years after Nato's attack on Yugoslavia, its administration in Kosovo is pushing through mass privatization," *The Guardian* (September 21).

Cooper, Christopher, and Greg Jaffe, 2004, "Audit splits U.S. and U.N.—inquiry centers on a $20 billion account for projects in Iraq," *Wall Street Journal* (September 17).

Cordesman, Anthony, 2006, "There can be no real exit from Iraq," *Financial Times* (May 3).

Crane, Keith, 2007, "Iraq's jobs-for-peace mirage," *Project Syndicate* (February).

Crooks, Ed, 2007, "Iraq may hold twice as much oil," *Financial Times* (April 18).

—— and Sheila McNulty, 2007, "Big oil plays waiting game over Iraq's reserves," *Financial Times* (September 19).

del Castillo, Graciana, 2007, "Losing the foreign direct investment race," *Project Syndicate* (September).

—— 2006, "The rules of post-conflict reconstruction," *Project Syndicate* (August).

—— and Nicasio del Castillo, 1992, "Si no la Suiza por lo menos la Irlanda de América," *Estrategia* (January).

—— and Daniel García, 2006, "Desmistificando las zonas francas," *El País* (April 17).

—— and Edmund S. Phelps, 2007, "The road to post-war recovery," *Project Syndicate* (July).

—— and Onno Wijnholds, 2003c, "A Dutch treat for Brazil?" *Project* Syndicate (May).

del Castillo, Nicasio, Jorge Gross, Ramón Mullerat, and Manuel Solano, 2000, "Shared-service centers in Latin America," *Euromoney* (agosto/setiembre).

Dempsey, Judy, and Eric Jansson, 2004, "Europe warned of renewed ethnic violence in Balkans," *Financial Times* (March 27/28).

Dinmore, Guy, 2006, "Bush launches drive to back Iraq government," *Financial Times* (June 13).

Dizard, John, 2007, "Iraq's harsh realities disguise its lucrative opportunities," *Financial Times* (May 15).

Dombey, Daniel, Stephen Fidler, and Rachel Morarjee, 2006, "Mission impossible? Why stabilizing Afghanistan will be a stiff test for NATO," *Financial Times* (July 31).

Dominick, Brian, 2004, "U.S. forgives Iraq debt to clear way for IMF reforms," *New Standard* (December 19).

Dugger, Celia W., 2007a, "US Agency's slow pace endangers foreign aid," *New York Times* (December 7).

—— 2007b, "Ending famine, simply by ignoring the experts," *New York Times* (December 2).

England, Andrew, 2006a, "The task of rebuilding a nation," *Financial Times* (December 5, *Special Report on Rwanda*).

—— 2006b, "Lebanese industry counts cost of reconstruction," *Financial Times* (September 26).

—— 2006c, "Concessions to history: When miners in Congo must look beyond the bottom line," *Financial Times* (August 21).

—— 2006d, "Congo's rebel leader watches and waits," *Financial Times* (August 8).

—— 2006e, "Congo mining chief puts private sector contracts under spotlight," *Financial Times* (July 7).

Fallows, James, 2004, "Blind into Baghdad," *Atlantic Monthly* (January/February).

Feinstein, Lee, and Anne-Marie Slaughter, 2004, "Iraq needs more backers on board," *Financial Times* (June 29).

Fidler, Stephen, 2006, "Iraq loses its allure for security companies," *Financial Times* (July 31).

Filkins, Dexter, 2005, "Mystery in Iraq as $300 million is taken abroad," *New York Times* (January 22).

Fisher, Stanley, 2001, "Exchange rates regime: Is the bipolar view correct?" *Finance & Development*, 38/2 (June).

Frankel, Jeffrey, 2003, "A crude peg for the Iraqi dinar," *Financial Times* (June 13).

Fukuyama, Francis, 2004, "America's next president will need to rethink Iraq," *Financial Times* (September 14).

Galbraith, Peter W., 2006b, "Our corner of Iraq," *New York Times* (July 25).

Gall, Carlota, 2005, "Afghan officials urge donors to shift focus," *New York Times* (April 5).

Gelling, Peter, 2006, "As tsunami death toll nears 400, Indonesians flee to hills in fear of another giant wave," *New York Times* (July 20).

Gettleman, Jeffrey, 2006, "Congo votes in its first multiparty election in 46 years," *New York Times* (July 31).

——— and Anjan Dundaram, 2006, "Kabila faces runoff in Congo: Violence delays ceremony," *New York Times* (August 21).

Ghosh, Aparisim, 2005, "Can Iraq rule itself?" *Time Magazine* (January 31).

Glanz, James, 2007, "Iraq compromise on oil law seems to be collapsing," *New York Times* (September 13).

——— 2006a, "An audit sharply criticizes Iraq's bookkeeping," *New York Times* (August 12).

——— 2006b, "Study urges reserve rebuilding force for cases like Iraq," *New York Times* (August 2).

——— 2006c, "Audit finds U.S. hid actual cost of Iraq projects," *New York Times* (July 30).

——— 2006d, "Violence in Iraq: Creating chaos in bank system," *New York Times* (July 29).

——— 2006e, "Series of woes mar Iraq project hailed as model," *New York Times* (July 28).

——— 2006f, "U.S. officer reported ready to plead guilty in bribery case involving Iraq building contracts," *New York Times* (July 8).

——— 2006g, "Rebuilding of Iraqi oil pipeline as disaster waiting to happen," *New York Times* (April 25).

——— 2006h, "U.S. rebuilding in Iraq found to fall short," *New York Times* (January 27).

Hanke, Steve H., 2003a, "An Iraq currency game plan," *International Economy* (Summer).

——— 2003b, "Dinar plans," *Wall Street Journal* (July 21).

Hedges, Christopher, 1998, "Kosovo war's glittering prize rests underground," *New York Times* (July 8).

Higgins, Andrew, 2004, "US ousted tyrant there, too: Now world body struggles with a privatization drive," *Wall Street Journal* (August 2).

Hill, Andrew, 2006, "A theory of evolution for outsourcers," *Financial Times* (June 26).

Hoge, Warren, 2007, "International support is sought at U.N. for Iraq rebuilding plan," *New York Times* (March 17).

——— 2006, "Peacekeepers and diplomats, seeking to end Darfur's violence, hit roadblock," *New York Times* (March 1).

Hoyos, Carola, and Roula Khalaf, 2006, "Will the tap open? Why oil groups dream of the day they can enter Iraq," *Financial Times* (December 8).

Husarska, Anna, 2007a, "A nation kidnapped," *Project Syndicate* (July).

—— 2007b, "Iraq's refugee crisis," *Project Syndicate* (April).

Ibison, David, 2006, "Norwegian oil find to test Iraq government's revenue," *Financial Times* (June 13).

Ignatieff, Michael, 2004, "The year of living dangerously," *New York Times Magazine* (March 14).

—— 2003, "The burden," *New York Times Magazine* (January 5).

—— 2002, "Nation-building lite," *New York Times Magazine* (July 28).

Janney, Asa, 2003, "A Marshall Plan for Iraq?," *Quaker Economist, 86* (October 22).

Jansson, Eric, 2005, "Annan set to call for Kosovo independence talks," *Financial Times* (October 6).

—— 2005, "Kosovo drive to privatize opens up a can of worms," *Financial Times* (August 11).

—— and Neil MacDonald, 2006, "Understated envoy offers hope for deal on Kosovo's future," *Financial Times* (August 28).

Jenkins, Rob, 2006, "Collateral benefit," *Dissent* (Spring 2006).

Karadjis, Michael, 2004, "Kosova: Occupation regime begins privatization," *Green Left Weekly* (November 24).

Khalilzad, Zalmay, 2007, "A shared stake in Iraq's future: How the oil agreement points the way forward," *Washington Post* (March 3).

Kirchgaessner, Stephanie, 2007, "Billions given away in Baghdad free-for-all," *Financial Times* (February 7).

—— 2006a, "Appeal to donors on aid for rebuilding," *Financial Times* (December 8).

—— 2006b, "Iraq rebuilding hit by bad planning," *Financial Times* (August 3).

Krane, Jim, 2006, "Iraq officials calls for oil partnerships," *Associated Press* (September 11).

Kristof, Nicholas D., 2006, "What we need in Iraq: an exit date," *Financial Times* (February 14).

Kulish, Nicholas, 2007, "NATO says it's prepared to keep the peace in Kosovo," *New York Times* (December 9).

LaFraniere, Sharon, 2007, "As Angola rebuilds, most find their poverty persists," *New York Times* (October 14).

Luce, Edward, and Caroline Daniel, 2006, "US reversal on Iraq troop levels," *Financial Times* (July 30).

—— and Demetri Sevastopulo, 2007, "Pentagon insider named Iraq war tsar," *Financial Times* (May 16).

Lynch, Colum, 2005, "Repairing ties with US is key, UN officials says," *Washington Post* (February 26).

MacDonald, Neil, and James Blitz, 2007, "Balkan future: Kosovo's Albanians ready to hold off on settlement," *Financial Times* (December 10).

Mahtani, Dino, 2007, "Angola faces curbs on production," *Financial Times* (December 6).

—— 2006a, "World Bank faces tough questions over role in Congo mining contracts," *Financial Times* (November 17).

—— 2006b, "Gunfire as Congo presidential race enters run-off," *Financial Times* (August 21).

—— 2005, "World Bank concern over Chad for oil revenues," *Financial Times* (October 27).

Marquis, Christopher, 2004, "Clear and uncertain powers await U.S. embassy in Iraq," *New York Times* (May 16).

Moody-Stuart, Mark, 2004, "A warning for the World Bank," *Financial Times* (May 4).

Mulford, David, and Michael Monderer, 2003, "Iraqi debt, like war, divides the west," *Financial Times* (June 22).

Naim, Moisés, 2007, "American's learning disability in Iraq," *PostGlobal* (April 6).

Negus, Steve, 2008, "Iraq surge brings a lull in violence but no reconciliation," *Financial Times* (January 6).

—— 2006a, "Corruption 'is fuelling Iraqi conflicts'," *Financial Times* (November 16).

—— 2006b, "Baghdad queries validity of Kurds' oil deals," *Financial Times* (September 25).

—— 2006c, "Oil output up as price rise curbs smuggling," *Financial Times* (July 27).

Packer, George, 2006, "Nation-building in the Republican palace bubble," *World View Magazine*, 19/1 (Spring).

Pascual, Carlos, and Martin Indyk, 2006, "In Lebanon, even peace is a battle," *New York Times* (August 22).

Pei, Minxin, Samia Amin, and Seth Garz, 2004, "Why nation-building fails in mid-course after US intervention," *International Herald Tribune* (March 17).

Pelhalm, Nicolas, Joshua Chaffin, and James Drummond, 2004, "In the line of fire: the reconstruction of Iraq falters as foreign contractors fall victim to kidnapping and murder," *Financial Times* (May 6).

Perlez, Jane, 2005, "Indonesia sets up agency to oversea Aceh reconstruction," *New York Times* (April 20).

—— 2006, "Aid groups are criticized over tsunami reconstruction," *New York Times* (July 27).

Phelps, Edmund S., 2006, "Subsidies that save," *Project Syndicate* (May).

—— and Graciana del Castillo, 2008, "A strategy to help Afghanistan kick its habit," *Financial Times* (January 4).

Polgreen Lydia, 2007, "Diamonds move from blood to sweat and tears," *New York Times* (March 25).

—— 2006, "War's chaos steals Congo's young by the millions," *New York Times* (July 30).

—— and Celia W. Dugger, 2006, "Chad's oil riches, meant for poor, are diverted," *New York Times* (February 18).

Reed, John, 2006, "Congo set to power ahead with hydroelectric plants," *Financial Times* (October 9).

—— 2005, "Angola plans to join fight against corruption," *Financial Times* (October 27).

Regan, Tom, 2005, "US Inspector General for Iraq paints 'grim' picture of reconstruction effort," *Christian Science Monitor* (November 20).

Rieff, David, 2003, "Blueprint for a mess," *New York Times Magazine* (November 2).

Robinson, Matthew, 2005, "EIB breaks new ground, agrees to lend to Kosovo," *Reuters/News Edge* (May 3).

Rohde, David, 2006, "Afghan symbol for change becomes symbol of failure," *New York Times* (September 5).

Rosen, Nir, 2007, "The flight from Iraq," *New York Times* (May 13).

Rotberg, Robert, 2002, "A yardstick for the best and worst of Africa," *Financial Times* (November 25).

Rubin, Alissa J., 2007, "New UN envoy in Iraq sets out strategy to revive hopes crushed in 2003 attack," *New York Times* (December 3).

Rubin, Elizabeth, 2006, "In the land of the Taliban," *New York Times Magazine* (October 22).

Samuelson, Robert J., 2007, "A 2$ trillion footnote?" *Washington Post* (February 28).

Sanger, David E., "Rebuke for Bush—Situation is 'grave'," *New York Times* (December 7).

Semple, Kirk, 2006 "Shiite leader criticizes plan for stronger U.S. role in Iraq's security," *New York Times* (July 29).

Senanayake, Sumetha, 2006, "Iraq: Kurds warn about delaying Kirkuk referendum," *Radio Free Europe* (December 14).

Sengupta, Somini, 2003, "In Africa, pricking the West's conscience," *New York Times* (June 1).

Sevastopulo, Demetri, and Jon Boone, 2007, "Gates presses NATO to support Kabul," *Financial Times* (December 5).

—— Caroline Daniel, and Edward Luce, 2006, "Baker points finger at Iraq failure," *Financial Times* (December 7).

Shenon, Philip, 2007, "Army says it will withhold $19.6 million from Halliburton, citing potential contract breach," *New York Times* (Februaury 8).

Shumway, Chris, 2005, "U.S. blames own contracting rules for Iraq reconstruction failures," *New Standard* (April 15).

Slaughter, Anne-Marie, 2004, "The clear, cruel lessons of Iraq," *Financial Times* (April 8).

Smith, Craig S., 2007, "On road to Kosovo independence, a warning: Go slow," *New York Times* (February 4).

Smith, Stephen, 2002, "Poker menteur en Afrique centrale," *Le Monde* (August 7).

Stearns, Jason, and Michela Wrong, 2006, "The struggle for a functioning Congo," *Financial Times* (August 4).

Steiner, Michael, 2002, "Step by step in Kosovo," *International Herald Tribune* (July 24).

Stiglitz, Joseph, 2006b, "The Phelps factor," *Project Syndicate* (December).

—— 2006c, "The true cost of the Iraq war," *Project Syndicate* (February).

—— 2005a, "Is central bank independence all it's cracked up to be?" *Project Syndicate* (November).

—— 2005b, "The indispensable UN," *Project Syndicate* (October).

—— 2004a, "The resource curse revisited," *Project Syndicate* (October).

—— 2004b, "Iraq's next shock will be shock therapy," *Project Syndicate* (October).

—— 2003a, "Big lies about central banking," *Project Syndicate* (June).

—— 2003b, "Rumors of war," *Project Syndicate* (January).

—— 2001, "Serbia's advantages in coming late," *Project Syndicate* (June).

Stolberg, Sheryl Gay, 2006, "Will it work in the White House?" *New York Times* (December 7).

Taylor, John B., 2007, "Billions over Baghdad," *New York Times* (February 27).

Thomson, Adam, 2006, "Murderous gangs turn El Salvador into battlefield," *Financial Times* (June 2).

Traub, James, 2004, "Making sense of the mission," *New York Times Magazine* (April 11).

Turner, Mark, 2006, "The 'secular pope' who fell from grace: Annan's difficult decade nears its end," *Financial Times* (October 11).

—— 2006b, "UN review finds procurement abuse," *Financial Times* (January 21).

Wagstyl, Stefan, 2007, "Statehood or stasis: Crunch time nears for Kosovo," *Financial Times* (September 6).

—— 2006, "Struggling towards stability: Why Kosovo may hold the key to the Balkans' future," *Financial Times* (February 20).

—— and Neil MacDonald, 2008, "Born under a bad sign: In the shadow of the great powers, Kosovo claims its statehood," *Financial Times* (February 15).

—— and Frederick Studemann, 2007, "EU set to take the lead on Kosovo amid fears UN talks will fail," *Financial Times* (November 16).

Wallis, William, 2003a, "Africa's conflict diamonds: is the UN-backed certification scheme failing to bring transparency to the trade?" *Financial Times* (October 29).

—— 2003b, "Putting Congo back together again: while conflict rages in the east, hope remains for a peaceful solution," *Financial Times* (May 22).

—— 2002, "Prospect of peace in central Africa hangs in the balance," *Financial Times* (October 23).

White, David, 2006a, "Hopes pinned on regional integration to end aid dependence," *Financial Times* (December 5, *Special Report on Rwanda*).

—— 2006b, "The 'resource curse' anew: why a grand World Bank oil project has fast run into the sand," *Financial Times* (January 23).

Whitelaw, Kevin, 2007, "Rwanda reborn," *US News & World Report* (April 23).

Wolf, Martin, 2007, "Biofuels: an everyday story of special interests and subsidies," *Financial Times* (October 31).

—— 2007, "The need for a new imperialism," *Financial Times* (October 10).

Wood, Nicholas, 2007, "UN officials fear Serbs will disrupt a free Kosovo," *New York Times* (December 10).

—— 2006a, "Serbs criticize UN mediator, further bogging down Kosovo talks," *New York Times* (September 2).

—— 2006b, "Kosovo leaders confer in Vienna, but little progress is seen," *New York Times* (July 25).

—— 2006c, "For Albanians in Kosovo, hope for independence from Serbia," *New York Times* (June 13).

—— 2005, "Ambitious experiment leads Kosovo to a crossroads," *New York Times* (October 3).

—— "Killing of two Serbs raises fear of ethnic unrest in Kosovo," *New York Times* (August 29).

Woodward, Susan, 1998, "Proceed with caution in Kosovo," *Newsday* (June 14).

Worth, Robert F., 2006, "Blast at Shiite shrine sets off sectarian fury in Iraq," *New York Times* (February 23).

Yeager, Holly, 2006, "Murtha's stock continues to grow as domestic backing for Iraq conflict slips," *Financial Times* (July 27).

—— 2006a, "Halliburton's Iraq army contract to end," *Financial Times* (July 13).

Zielbauer, Paul von, 2007, "US urges Iraq to take advantage of lull," *New York Times* (December 3).

—— 2006, "Iraqi officials ask for aid for global war on terror," *New York Times* (July 31).

Editorials

Financial Times, 2007a, "The west must not split over Kosovo" (August 13).

—— 2007b, "Iraq's refugees must be saved from disaster" (April 19).

Financial Times, 2007c, "Kosovo should be granted independence" (March 28).

—— 2006a, "Baker report's whiff of realism on Iraq" (December 7).

—— 2006b, "Iraq Study Group: Hamilton and Baker set out solutions to strife in Iraq" (December 7).

—— 2006c, "Congo's fragile peace" (August 23).

—— 2004, "Kosovo killings" (March 22).

—— 2003, "Iraq as laboratory: Privatisation talk lacks a sense of reality" (September 24).

New York Times, 2007a, "Plenty to blame for Afghanistan" (December 16).

—— 2007b, "Another $200 billion" (October 25).

—— 2006, "Sharing the riches of war in Iraq" (July 24).

—— 2004, "The Balkans flare up" (March 31).

Wall Street Journal Online, 2003, "Iraq's odious debts don't stick Saddam's victims with the bill for his rule" (April 30).

Press releases

Press Release, 2003, "Conclusions du séminaire Partenariat Public–Privé pour le Développement de la République Démocratique du Congo" (Kinshasa, April 7).

Secretary-General Annan Press Conference at the National Press Club (Tokyo, Japan, May 18).

Secretary-General Boutros-Ghali Press Conference at ESCAP (Bangkok, Thailand, April 2003).

Institutional reports

Asian Development Bank, 2006, *Asian Development Outlook* (Manila: ADB).

Center for Strategic and International Studies (CSIS), 2005, *Making Peacebuilding Work: Reforming UN Peacekeeping Operations* (Washington, D.C.: June 6).

International Development Association (IDA) and International Monetary Fund (IMF), 2002, *The Democratic Republic of the Congo: Enhanced Heavily Indebted Poor Countries (HIPC) Initiative* (Washington, D.C.: May 24).

—— —— 2002, *The Democratic Republic of the Congo: Interim Poverty Reduction Strategy Paper, Joint Staff Assessment* (Washington, D.C.: May 24).

International Institute for Democracy and Electoral Assistance (IDEA), 2004, *Reconciliation Lessons Learned from UN Peacekeeping Missions. Case Studies: Sierra Leone and Timor Leste* (Report prepared for the Office of the High Commissioner for Human Rights (OHCHR), November).

International Monetary Fund (IMF), 2006a, *Annual Report* (Washington, D.C.).

—— 2005a, "IMF in focus" (Washington, D.C.: *A Supplement of the IMF Survey*, 34, September. Special Feature: Rebuilding Economies after Conflict).

—— 2005b, "IMF emergency assistance: Supporting recovery from natural disasters and armed conflicts" (Washington, D.C.: IMF web site).

—— 2005c, *Democratic Republic of Timor-Leste: 2005 Article IV Consultation—Staff Report* (Washington, D.C.: July).

—— 2004a, *MFD Technical Assistance to Recent Post-Conflict Countries* (Washington, D.C.: December 13).

—— 2004b, *Background Paper for MFD Technical Assistance to Recent Post-Conflict Countries* (Washington, D.C.: Prepared by the Monetary and Financial Department, December 13).

—— 2004c, *Rebuilding Fiscal Institutions in Post-Conflict Countries* (Washington, D.C.: Prepared by the Fiscal Affairs Department, December 10).

—— 2004d, *Background Paper for Rebuilding Fiscal Institutions in Post-Conflict Countries* (Washington, D.C.: December 10).

—— 2004e, "Reform: What pace works; Counterpoint," *Finance & Development* (September).

—— 2003a, *Update on the Financing of PRGF and HIPC Operations and the Subsidization of Post-Conflict Emergency Assistance* (Washington, D.C.: August 18 and March 20).

—— 2003b, *Democratic Republic of Timor-Leste: 2003 Article IV Consultation—Staff Report* (Washington, D.C.: July 2003).

—— 2002a, "Guidelines on conditionality" (Washington, D.C.: IMF web site).

—— 2002b, "Improving Africa's investment climate," *IMF Survey* (September).

—— 2001a, *The Democratic Republic of the Congo: Selected Issues and Statistical Appendix* (Washington, D.C.: July 3).

—— 2001b, *Assistance to Post-Conflict Countries and the HIPC Framework* (Washington, D.C.: BUFF/01/57, April 19).

—— 2001c, *Assistance to Post-Conflict Countries and the HIPC Framework* (Washington, D.C.: Development Committee, IMFC/Doc/3/01/7 of April 20. See also BUFF/01/57 of April 19).

—— 1999a, "Code of Good Practices on Transparency in Monetary and Financial Policies: Declaration of Principles" (Washington, D.C.:IMF web site).

—— 1999b, *Assistance to Post-Conflict Countries: Progress Report* (Washington, D.C.: Development Committee, April).

—— 1999c, *Annual Report* (Washington, D.C.).

—— 1996, *Annual Report* (Washington, D.C.).

—— 1995a, *Fund Involvement in Post-Conflict Countries* (Washington, D.C.: BUFF/95/98, September 19).

—— 1995b, *Fund involvement in post-conflict countries* (Washington, D.C.: EBS/95/141, August 16).

—— 1995c, "The design of a minimal monetary and exchange rate structure for countries in post-chaos/post-conflict situations," *Background Paper No. 8* (Helsinki, Finland: High Level Group on Development Strategy and Management of the Market Economy, Third Meeting, 8–10 July). Also listed as Sundararajan *et al.*

—— 1995d, 'Outlines of the 'architecture' of a minimalist fiscal framework for countries in post-chaos/post-conflict situations', *Background Paper No. 4* (Helsinki, Finland: High Level Group on Development Strategy and Management of the Market Economy, Third Meeting, 8–10 July). Also listed as Ghandi *et al.*

—— 1995e, "Bilateral and multilateral aid flows and Fund-Supported Programs: Summing up by the Chairman" (Washington, D.C.: BUFF/95/48, June 6).

—— 1995f, *Bilateral and multilateral aid flows and Fund-Supported Programs* (Washington, D.C.: SM/95/73, April 11 and Supplement 1, April 25).

—— and World Bank, 2007, *External Review Committee on Bank-Fund Collaboration* (Washington, D.C.: Final Report, February).

—— —— 1998, *Issues Note on Providing Additional Assistance to Post-Conflict Countries* (Washington, D.C.: EBS/98/155, September 1).

—— —— *Finance & Development* (several issues).

—— —— *IMF Survey* (several issues).

International Peace Academy (2005), *A Fork in the Road? Conversations on the Work of the High Level Panel on Threats, Challenges and Change* (New York: IPA Report).

—— 2004a, *Program on Economic Agendas in Civil Wars: Principal Research Findings and Policy Recommendations* (New York: IPA Report prepared by Karen Ballentine, April).

—— 2004b, *The Iraq Crisis and World Order: Structural and Normative Challenges* (New York: Rapporteur: James Cockayne, with Cyrus Samii, December).

—— 2004c, *Post-Conflict Peacebuilding Revisited: Achievements, Limitations, Challenges* (New York: Prepared by Neclâ Tschirgi for the WSP International/IPA Peacebuilding Forum Conference, October).

—— 2004d, *Making States Work: From State Failure to State-Building* (New York: Report prepared by Simon Chesterman, Michael Ignatieff, and Ramesh Thakur, July).

—— 2004e, *Program on Economic Agendas in Civil Wars: Principal Research Findings and Policy Recommendations* (New York: IPA final report by Karen Ballentine, April).

—— 2003a, *You, the People: the United Nations, Transitional Administrations, and State-Building* (New York: Project on Transitional Administrations, Final Report by Simon Chesterman, November).

—— 2003b, *The Future UN State-Building: Strategic and Operational Challenges and the Legacy of Iraq* (New York: Policy Report, Pocantico Conference Center for the Rockefeller Brothers Fund, November 14–16).

—— 2003c, *Beyond Greed and Grievance: Policy Lessons from Studies in the Political Economy of Armed Conflict* (New York: IPA Policy Report by Karen Ballentine and Heiko Nitzschke, October).

—— 2002a, *Economic Priorities for Peace Implementation* (New York: IPA Policy Paper by Susan L. Woodward).

—— 2002b, *Tiptoeing through Afghanistan: The Future of UN State-Building* (New York: IPA report by Simon Chesterman, September).

—— 2002c, *Justice under International Administration: Kosovo, East Timor and Afghanistan* (New York: IPA report by Simon Chesterman, September).

—— 2002d, *The Political Economy of War and Peace* (New York: Report of the Annual Seminar, May 6–10).

—— 2002e, *Policies and Practices for Regulating Resource Flows to Armed Conflict* (Bellagio, Italy: Conference Report, Rockefeller Foundation Bellagio Study and Conference Center, May 21–23).

—— 2002f, *Options for Promoting Corporate Responsibility in Conflict Zones: Perspectives from the Private Sector* (New York, April 5).

United Nations, 2007a, "United Nations peacebuilding architecture now fully in place" (New York: Security Council debates Peacebuilding Commmission's first year, SC/9144, October 17).

—— 2007b, "General Assembly debates reform on Peacebuilding Commmission's first year" (New York: General Assembly, GA/10634, October 10).

—— 2006a, *Progress report on the prevention of armed conflict* (New York: Report of the Secretary-General to the General Assembly, A/60/891, July 18).

—— 2005a, *2005 World Summit Outcome* (New York: A/RES/60/1, October 24).

—— 2005b, "The Secretary-General's Statement to the General Assembly," (New York: March 21).

——2005c, *In Larger Freedom: Towards Development, Security and Human Rights for All* (New York: Report of the Secretary-General to the General Assembly, A/59/2005, March 21).

——2004a, *A More Secure World: Our Shared Responsibility* (New York: Report of the Secretary-General's High Level Panel on Threats, Challenges and Change, A/59/565, December 2).

——2004b, "Background Note for Expert Group Meeting on Conflict Prevention, Peacebuilding and Development" (New York: November 15).

——2003, *Thirteenth Report of the Secretary-General on the United Nations Organization Mission in the Democratic Republic of Congo* (New York: S/2003/211).

——2002, *Final Report of the Panel of Experts on the Illegal Exploitation of Natural Resources and Other Forms of Wealth of the Democratic Republic of Congo* (New York: S/2002/1146).

——2001, *No exit without strategy: Security Council and the closure or transition of United Nations peacekeeping operations. Report of the Secretary General* (New York: S/2001/394, April 20).

——2000a, *We the Peoples: The Role of the United Nations in the 21st Century* (New York).

——2000b, "United Nations Millennium Declaration" (New York: Resolution adopted September 18, A/55/2).

——2000c, *Report of the Panel on United Nations Peace Operations* (New York: A/55/305, S/2000/809, August). Known as the Brahimi Report.

——2000d, *Imagining Tomorrow: Rethinking the Global Challenge* (New York: Collected and Compiled on the Occasion of the UN Millennium Assembly).

——1996a, *An Inventory of Post-Conflict Peacebuilding Activities* (New York: Report of an Inter-departmental Task Force established by the Secretary-General).

——1996b, *Report of the Secretary-General on the activities of the Office of Internal Oversight Services* (New York: General Assembly, A/51/432).

——1995a, *International Colloquium on Post-Conflict Reconstruction Strategies: The Chairman's Synopsis and Conclusions* (Stadtschlaining, Austria: Austrian Study Centre for Peace and Conflict Resolution, Colloquium chaired by Margaret Joan Anstee, June 23–24).

——1995b, *International Colloquium on Post-Conflict Reconstruction Strategies: Collection of Papers* (Stadtschlaining, Austria: Austrian Study Centre for Peace and Conflict Resolution, June 23–24).

——ECOSOC, 2002, "Tenth Anniversary of Mozambique Peace Agreement Marked at High-Level Meeting of Economic and Social Council" (New York: Press Release, ECOSOC/6030, October 4).

United Nations Development Programme (UNDP), several years, *Human Development Report* (Oxford: Oxford University Press).

——2008, *Fostering Post-Conflict Economic Recovery* (New York: Bureau for Crisis Prevention and Recovery, forthcoming).

——2006, *Practice Note on Disarmament, Demobilization and Reintegration of Ex-Combatants* (at UNDP's web site).

——2003, "UNDP's work in Iraq" (at UNDP's web site, October).

——2001, "Update on the role of UNDP in crisis and post-conflict situations: organizational changes" (New York: 18 December, DP/2002/CRP.3).

——2000, *Sharing New Ground in Post-Conflict Situations: The Role of UNDP in Support of Reintegration Programmes* (New York: Evaluation Office, DP/2000/14, January).

United Nations High Commissioner for Refugees (UNHCR), 1996, *Healing the Wounds: Refugees, Reconstruction and Reconciliation* (Princeton University: Report of the Second Conference, June 30–July 1. Sponsored jointly by United Nations High Commissioner for Refugees and International Peace Academy).

United Nations Verification Mission in Guatemala (MINUGUA), 1997, *Acuerdos de Paz: Guatemala* (Guatemala: Universidad Rafael Landívar, Instituto de Investigaciones Económicas y Sociales).

World Bank, various years, *Social Indicators of Development* (Baltimore: The Johns Hopkins University Press).

—— 2007, "Liberia Partners' Forum" (Washington, D.C.: Speech of Paul Wolfowitz, February 13 (Washington, D.C.: The World Bank).

—— 2005a, *Reshaping the Future: Education and Post-Conflict Reconstruction* (Washington, D.C.: The World Bank).

—— 2005b, *Creating the Conditions for Sustainable Growth and Poverty Reduction: East Timor* (Washington, D.C.: Country Assistance Strategy, Report No. 32700-TP, August 8).

—— 2003a, *The Role of the World Bank in Conflict and Development: An Evolving Agenda* (Washington, D.C.: Conflict Prevention and Reconstruction Unit).

—— 2003b, *Breaking the Conflict Trap: Civil War and Development Policy* (Washington, D.C.: The World Bank and Oxford University Press, prepared by Paul Collier, V.L. Elliot, Håvard Hegre, Anke Hoeffler, Marta Reynal-Querol, Nicholas Sambanis).

—— 2002, *The Structure of Rebel Organizations: Implications for Post-Conflict Reconstruction* (Washington, D.C.: Post-Conflict Reconstruction Unit, June).

—— 2001, *Development Cooperation and Conflict: A New Operational Policy for the Bank* (Washington, D.C.: Post-Conflict Reconstruction Unit, Operation Policy OP/BO 2.30, February).

—— 1998a, *Post-Conflict Reconstruction: The Role of the World Bank* (Washington, D.C.: April).

—— 1998b, *The World Bank's Experience with Post-Conflict Reconstruction* (Washington, D.C.: Operations Evaluation Department (OED), Report prepared by Alcira Kreimer, John Eriksson, Robert Muscat, Margaret Arnold, Colin Scott).

—— and UNDP, 2005, *Workshop Report: Rebuilding Post-Conflict Societies: Lessons from a Decade of Global Experience* (Workshop held at the Greentree Foundation, September 18–21, mimeo).

Country reports: El Salvador

FMLN–Government of El Salvador, 1995, *Agreements on Financial Needs to Conclude the Peace Agreements* (Paris, France: Report of the Consultative Group, June 22).

Gunnarson, Agneta, *et al.*, 2004, *La Cooperación sueca con El Salvador: 1979–2001* (Stockholm: SIDA Evaluation, 04/20, July).

Interamerican Development Bank (IADB), Office of Evaluation and Oversight (OVE), 2005, *Country Program Evaluation: El Salvador, 1992–2004* (Washington, D.C., RE-307, May).

International Monetary Fund (IMF), several years, *El Salvador: Recent Economic Developments* (Washington, D.C.).

—— several years, *El Salvador: Staff Report* (Washington, D.C.).

—— several years, *International Financial Statistics* (Washington, D.C.).

—— 2005d, *El Salvador: 2004 Article IV Consultation—Staff Report* (Washington, D.C.: IMF Country Report No. 05/271, August).

—— 1995g, *El Salvador, Staff Report* (Washington, D.C.: EBS/95/141, August 16).

—— 1994, *El Salvador: Recent Economic Developments* (Washington, D.C.: 94/10, November 1994).

—— 1993, *El Salvador: Staff Report* (Washington, D.C.).

Republic of El Salvador, 1995, *El Salvador: Necesidades financieras para concluir los acuerdos de paz* (Paris, France: Informe para la Reunión del Grupo Consultivo, June 22).

Swedish International Development Cooperation Agency (SIDA), 2003, *SIDA Country Report: El Salvador* (The Embassy of Sweden, Guatemala, May).

United Nations, several years, *Report of the Secretary-General on the United Nations Observer Mission in El Salvador* (Reports to the Security Council of November 23, 1992 (S/24833), May 21, 1993 (S/25812), May 25, 1993 (S/25812/Add.2 containing text of October 13, 1992 Land Agreement); June 29, 1993 (S/26005), November 23, 1993 (S/26790), May 11, 1994 (S/1994/561), August 26, 1994 (S/1994/1000), October 31, 1994 (S/1994/1212), March 24, 1995 (S/1995/220) and April 18, 1995 (S/1995/281 or A/49/888)).

—— several years, *The Situation in Central America: Report of the Secretary General* (New York: October 18, 2000 (A/55/465); April 23, 1996 (A/50/935); October 6, 1995 (A/50/517 or S/1995/407)).

—— 1995c, *The United Nations and El Salvador: 1990–1995* (New York: Volume IV, DPI/1475).

—— 1995d, *Status of 19 May 1994 Timetable for the Implementation of Most Important Outstanding Agreements: Situation as of 24 February 1995* (New York: March 7).

—— 1992a, *El Salvador Agreement: The Path to Peace* (New York: United Nations, DPI/1208-92614, May).

—— 1992b, "The long night of El Salvador is drawing to an end" (Statement by the Secretary-General, delivered at the signing ceremony of the El Salvador Peace Agreement in Mexico City, January 16).

United Nations Development Programme (UNDP), several years, *Human Development Report* (Oxford: Oxford University Press).

—— 2005, *A Glance at the "New Us": The Impact of Migration* (San Salvador: Fourth National Human Development Report on El Salvador).

—— *Launching New Protagonists in Salvadorian Agriculture: The Agricultural Training Programme for Ex-Combatants of the FMLN* (San Salvador, 1993).

United Nations Economic Commission for Latin America (ECLAC/CEPAL), 1993, *Economic Consequences of Peace in El Salvador* (Chile: August 30).

World Bank, 2004a, *El Salvador: Public Expenditure Review* (Washington, D.C.: Report No. 32856-SV, December).

—— 2000, *El Salvador: Post-Conflict Reconstruction* (Washington D.C., Country Case Studies Series, Study prepared by the Operations Evaluations Department (OED) under the direction of Alcira Kreimer).

—— 1998c, *The World Bank's Experience with Post-Conflict Reconstruction. Volume III: El Salvador Case Study* (Washington, D.C., Operations Evaluation Department (OED). Report prepared by Alcira Kreimer *et al.*, May). See also World Bank (1998b).

Country reports: Kosovo

European Commission and The World Bank, 2005, *Information about Kosovo* (Kosovo: Economic Reconstruction and Development in South East Europe).

Economic Cooperation Foundation (ECF), 2002, *The International Protectorate "Toolbox": Lessons from Kosovo* (Israel: Herzliya Conference on Economics and Security, December 2–4, 2002).

Economic Strategy and Project Identification Group (ESPIG), 2004, "Towards a Kosovo Development Plan: The state of the Kosovo economy and possible ways forward," *ESPIG Policy Paper No. 1*, prepared by John Bradley and Gerald Knaus (August).

International Committee of the Red Cross (ICRC), 2000, *Cluster Bombs and Landmines in Kosovo: Explosive Remnants of War* (Geneva: June 2001).

International Crisis Group (ICG), 1999, "Trepca: Making sense of a labyrinth" (mimeo, November 26).

International Monetary Fund (IMF), several years, *Aide-Memoire of the IMF Staff Mission to Kosovo* (Washington, D.C.).

——— 2004f, *Kosovo—Gearing Policies Toward Growth and Development* (Washington, D.C.: November 18).

——— 2003c, *Staff Visit to Kosovo: Concluding Statement* (Washington, D.C.).

——— 2001d, *Progress in Institution-Building and the Economic Policy Challenges Ahead* (Washington, D.C.: December 6).

——— 2001e, "Kosovo: economic, political, and social uncertainties pose challenges to fiscal sustainability," *IMF Survey* (March 19).

——— 2000, *Macroeconomic Issues and Fiscal Sustainability* (Washington, D.C.: November 8).

——— 1999d, *The Economic Consequences of the Kosovo Crisis: An Updated Assessment* (Washington, D.C.: May 25).

——— and World Bank, 1999, *The Economic Consequences of the Kosovo Crisis: A Preliminary Assessment of External Financing Needs and the Role of the Fund and the World Bank in the International Response* (Washington, D.C.: April 16).

Ministry of Trade and Industry (MTI) and UNMIK EU Pillar, 2004, *Trade Policy for Kosovo* (Pristina).

RIINVEST, 2001, *Socially-owned enterprises and their transformation/privatization* (Pristina: March 8, Draft Research Report).

United Nations, various years, *Reports of the Secretary-General on the UN Interim Administration Mission in Kosovo*.

——— 2006b, *UNMIK's Impact on the Kosovo Economy: Spending Effects 1999–2006 and Potential Consequences of Downsizing* (UNMIK: July).

——— 2006c, *The Economic Foundations of Status: Kosovo Economic Outlook 2006* (UNMIK, March).

——— 2005d, *Fuelling Kosovo's Growth Engines* (UNMIK EU Pillar, Economic Policy Office, July).

——— 2004c, *Kosovo Outlook, 2004* (Pristina, UNMIK European Union Pillar, May).

——— 2000e, *UNMIK at Nine Months* (UN web site).

——— 2000f, *Report of the Secretary-General on the Interim Administration Mission in Kosovo*, S/2000/538 of June 6).

United States, Congressional Research Service, The Library of Congress, 2003, *Kosovo and US Policy* (Washington, D.C.: Report for Congress, January 3).

UNMIK, various dates, "UNMIK Press Releases" (UNMIK web site).

World Bank, 2005c, *Kosovo brief 2005* (World Bank web site).

—— 2004b, *Kosovo: Economic Memorandum"* (Washington, D.C.: Report No. 28023-KOS, May).

—— and European Commission, 2002, *Report on Progress Made in Committing, Contracting and Spending Donor Pledges to Kosovo* (Washington, D.C.: May).

Country reports: Afghanistan

Afghanistan, Islamic State of, 2002, *National Development Framework* (at Government's web site).

—— 2002, *Rebuilding Our Nation, Afghanistan's National Programme for Reconstruction* (at Government's web site).

—— 2004, *Securing Afghanistan's Future* (at Government's web site).

—— 2005, *Afghanistan National Development Strategy: An Interim Strategy for Security, Governance, Economic Growth and Poverty Alleviation* (at Government's web site).

Asian Development Bank, 2002a, *Initial Country Strategy and Program (2002–2004): Afghanistan* (Manila, May).

—— 2002b, *Annual Report. Rehabilitation and Reconstruction: ADB's Role in Afghanistan and the Region* (Manila).

—— UNDP, World Bank, 2002, *Afghanistan Preliminary Needs Assessment for Recovery and Reconstruction* (Manila: January).

Care and Center on International Cooperation (CIC), 2004, *Afghanistan Policy Brief* (March–April).

—— —— 2003, "Good intentions will not pave the road to peace," *Afghanistan Policy Brief* (September 15).

—— —— 2003, *Afghanistan Policy Brief* (September 15).

Center on International Cooperation, 2002, *Conference Summary: Regional Approaches to the Reconstructionn of Afghanistan* (Istanbul, Turkey, June 3–5).

International Monetary Fund, 2008a, *Islamic Republic of Afghanistan—Poverty Reduction Strategy Paper: Progress Report* (Washington, D.C.: IMF Country Report No. 08/73, February).

—— 2007a, *Islamic Republic of Afghanistan—Statement by the IMF Mission at the Conclusion of the Discussions for the 2007 Article IV Consultation and Third Review under the Poverty Reduction and Growth Facility Arrangement* (Kabul, November 15).

—— 2007b, *Islamic Republic of Afghanistan: Second Review Under the Three-Year Arrangement Under the Poverty Reduction and Growth Facility—Staff Report; Press Release on the Executive Board Discussion; and Statement by the Executive Director for the Islamic Republic of Afghanistan* (Washington, D.C., IMF Country Report No. 07/252, July).

—— 2007c, *Islamic Republic of Afghanistan—Statement by the IMF Mission at the Conclusion of the Staff Visit* (Kabul, July 24 and February 1).

—— 2006b, "Islamic State of Afghanistan: Statement of the IMF Staff Visit to Discuss Developments Under the Poverty Reduction and Growth Facility-Supported Program" (August 16).

International Monetary Fund, 2006c, *Islamic State of Afghanistan: Seventh Review Under the Staff-Monitored Program and Request for a Three-Year Arrangement Under the Poverty Reduction and Growth Facility—Staff Supplement; Staff Statement* (Washington, D.C.: IMF Country Report No. 06/251, July).

—— 2006d, *Islamic State of Afghanistan: Interim Poverty Reduction Strategy Paper—Joint Staff Advisory Note* (Washington, D.C.: IMF Country Report No. 06/252, July).

—— 2006e, *Islamic State of Afghanistan: Statement of the IMF Staff at the Conclusion of the First Review Under the Poverty Reduction and Growth Facility* (November 26).

—— 2005e, *Islamic State of Afghanistan—Staff Monitored Program: Letter of Intent, Memorandum of Economic and Financial Policies, and Technical Memorandum of Understanding* (Washington, D.C.: IMF, September).

—— 2005f, *Islamic State of Afghanistan: Selected Issues and Statistical Appendix* (Washington, D.C.: IMF Country Report No. 05/34, February).

—— 2005g, *Islamic State of Afghanistan: 2004 Article IV Consultation and Second Review Under the Staff-Monitored Program—Staff Report; Staff Statement* (Washington, D.C.: IMF Country Report No. 05/33, February).

—— 2003d, *Islamic State of Afghanistan: 2003 Article IV Consultations—Staff Report* (Washington, D.C.: IMF Country Report No. 03/391, December).

—— 2003e, *Islamic State of Afghanistan: Rebuilding a Macroeconomic Framework for Reconstruction and Growth* (Washington, D.C.: IMF Country Report No. 03/299, September 21).

—— 2002c, *Islamic State of Afghanistan: Report on Recent Economic Development and Prospects and the Role of the Fund in the Reconstruction process* (Washington, D.C.: IMF Country Report No. 02/219, October).

—— 2002d, "Security issues critical as Afghanistan moves to rebuild its economy: Interview with Paul Chabrier," *IMF Survey*, 31/3 (February 11).

Novib-Oxfam Netherlands, 2004, "On 'securing Afghanistan future': The case for more and not less Government" (Discussion paper, March 31).

United Nations Office on Drugs and Crime (UNODC) and Government of Afghanistan, 2007a, *Afghanistan Opium Survey* (Executive Summary, August).

—— 2007b, *Afghanistan: Opium Winter Rapid Assessment Survey* (Kabul, February).

United States, Commercial Service, 2006, *Doing Business in Afghanistan: A Country Commercial Guide for U.S. Companies* (Washington, D.C., February).

Country reports: Iraq

Center for Strategic and International Studies (CSIS), 2004a, *Progress or Peril? Measuring Iraq's Reconstruction* (Washington DC.: December).

—— 2004b, *Progress or Peril? Measuring Iraq's Reconstruction* (Washington D.C.: September).

—— 2004c, *Progress or Peril? Measuring Iraq's Reconstruction* (Washington D.C.: August–October).

Congressional Research Service (CRS), 2006, *Iraq: Paris Club Debt Relief* (Washington, D.C.: Report for Congress by Martin A. Weiss, January 19).

—— 2005, *Iraq Oil: Reserves, Production, and Potential Revenues* (Washington, D.C.: Report for Congress by Lawrence Kumins, April 13).

Energy Information Administration (EIA), 2006, *International Energy Outlook* (Washington, D.C.: Report No. DOE/EIA-0484, June).

INSEAD, 2005, *Fuel: A Humanitarian Necessity in 2003 Post-Conflict Iraq* (Switzerland).

International Crisis Group, 2003, *Baghdad: A race against the clock* (Washington D.C.: June 11).

International Monetary Fund, 2008b, *Iraq: Request for Stand-By-Arrangement and Cancellation of Current Arrangement—Staff Reports; Staff Supplement; Press Release on the Executive Board Discussion; and Statement by the Executive Director for Iraq* (Washington, D.C.: IMF Country Report No. 08/17, January).

—— 2007d, *Iraq: 2007 Article IV Consultation, Fifth Review Under the Stand-By Arrangement, Financing Assurances Review, and Requests for Extension of the Arrangement, Waiver of Applicability, and Waivers for Nonobservance of Performance Criteria—Staff Report; Public Information Notice and Press Release on the Executive Board Discussion; and Statement by the Executive Director for Iraq* (Washington, D.C.: IMF Country Report No. 07/301, August).

—— 2007e, *Iraq: Third and Fourth Reviews Under the Stand-By Arrangement, Financing Assurances Review, and Requests for Extension of the Arrangement and for Waiver of Nonobservance of a Performance Criterion—Staff Report; Staff Supplement; Press Release on the Executive Board Discussion; and Statement by the Executive Director for Iraq* (Washington, D.C.: IMF Country Report No. 07/115, March).

—— 2007f, *Iraq: Letter of Intent, Memorandum of Economic and Financial Policies, and Technical Memorandum of Understanding* (Baghdad: February 23).

—— 2006f, *Iraq: First and Second Reviews Under the Stand-By Arrangement, Financing Assurances Review, and Request for Waiver of Nonobservance and Applicability of Performance Criteria—Staff Report; Staff Supplement; Press Release on the Executive Board Discussion; and Statement by the Executive Director for Iraq* (Washington, D.C.: IMF Country Report No. 06/301, August).

—— 2006g, *Iraq: Request for Stand-By Arrangement—Staff Report; Staff Supplement; Press Release on the Executive Board Discussion; and Statement by the Executive Director for Iraq* (Washington, D.C.: IMF Country Report No. 06/15, January).

—— 2005h, *Iraq: 2005 Article IV Consultation—Staff Report; Staff Supplement; Public Information Notice on the Executive Board Discussion; and Statement by the Executive Director for Iraq* (Washington, D.C., IMF Country Report No. 05/294, August 16).

—— 2005i, *First and Second Reviews Under the Stand-By Arrangement* (Washington, D.C.: July 17).

—— 2005j, *Iraq: Considerations on Intergovernmental Fiscal Relations for the Constituent Assembly* (Washington D.C.: April 2005, WP/05/69).

—— 2004g, *Iraq: Use of Fund Resources—Request for Emergency Post-Conflict Assistance—Staff Report* (Washington, D.C.: September, Country Report No. 04/325).

—— 2004h, *Iraq—Letter of Intent, Memorandum of Economic and Financial Policies, and Technical Memorandum of Understanding* (Baghdad, September 24).

—— 2003g, *Iraq: Macroeconomic Assessment* (Washington, D.C.: October 21).

International Peace Academy, 2004, *The Iraq Crisis and World Order: Structural and Normative Challenges* (New York: December).

UN Development Group (UNDG) and World Bank, 2003, *United Nations/World Bank Joint Iraq Assessment* (Washington, D.C.: October).

UN Office for the Coordination of Humanitarian Affairs (UNOCHA), 2004, *IRINnews.org* (December 16).

US Government Accountability Office (GAO), 2006, *Report to Congressional Committees* (Washington, D.C.: July).

World Bank, 2007, *International Reconstruction Fund Facility for Iraq. World Bank Trust Fund: Report to Donors* (Washington, D.C.: Progress Report Update—March 1).

—— 2006, *International Reconstruction Fund Facility for Iraq. World Bank Trust Fund: Report to Donors* (Washington, D.C.: Status Report as of December 31).

—— 2005c, *Second Interim Strategy Note for the Republic of Iraq for the Period FY06–07* (Washington, D.C.: Report No. 32115-IQ, August 23).

☐ INDEX